writers UNDER SIEGE

writers UNDER SIEGE

CZECH LITERATURE SINCE 1945

JIŘÍ HOLÝ

sussex
ACADEMIC
PRESS
Brighton • Portland • Toronto

2 4 6 8 10 9 7 5 3

First published in hardcover 2008, reprinted in paperback 2010, in Great Britain by
SUSSEX ACADEMIC PRESS
PO Box 139
Eastbourne BN24 9BP

Distributed in North America by
SUSSEX ACADEMIC PRESS
ISBS Publisher Services
920 NE 58th Ave #300, Portland, OR 97213, USA

British Library Cataloguing in Publication Data
A CIP catalogue record for this book is available from the British Library.

Library of Congress Cataloging-in-Publication Data
Holý, Jiří.
Writers under siege : Czech literature since 1945 / Jiří Holý.
p. cm.
Includes bibliographical references and index.
Originally published as part of: Česká literatura od počátků k dnešku.
English version has been extensively revised and is considered a new work.
Includes bibliographical references and index.
ISBN 978-1-84519-190-0 (h/c : alk. paper)
ISBN 978-1-84519-440-6 (pbk. : alk. paper)
1. Czech literature—20th century—History and criticism. 2. Czech literature—20th century—Translations into English—History and criticism. I. Title.
PG5007.H554 2007
891.8′609005—dc22

2007004313

This publication was supported by Czech Ministry of Education research project 0021620824 / Tato publikace vznikla v rámci grantu MŠM 0021620824 Základy moderního světa v zrcadle literatury a filosofie.

Typeset and designed by Sussex Academic Press, Brighton & Eastbourne.

This book is printed on acid-free paper.

Contents

Preface and Acknowledgments

Writers under Siege: Czech Literature since 1945 is intended for readers interested in the literatures and cultures of Central Europe, and it should be particularly useful to students of Czech and Slavonic Studies. Arne Novák's history of Czech literature up to the Second World War, was published in an English translation (*Czech Literature*, ed. by W. E. Harkins, Ann Arbor, 1976), but until now there has been no English-language publication containing systematic information about Czech literature from 1945 until 2000.

This history of postwar Czech literature first came out in Czech as part of a larger project by Jan Lehár, Alexandr Stich, Jaroslava Janáčková and Jiří Holý (*Česká literatura od počátků k dnešku* [Czech Literature from Its Beginnings to the Present Day], Prague, 1998, expanded edition 2002). An updated version of this history was published in German as *Geschichte der tschechischen Literatur des 20. Jahrhunderts* (Vienna, 2003).

Just like the German version, this English version is a thorough re-working of the Czech original to the extent that it is a completely new work. Certain sections of the Czech original have been cut, while other sections, taking into consideration the requirements of the English-speaking reader, have been re-written and considerably expanded. Many sections of the original Czech text would have been incomprehensible without a thorough explanation of the cultural and historical context. This English history of Czech literature contains information about English-language translations from Czech literature and many quotations from original Czech works. A large number of the quotations, especially from poetry, are given both in the Czech original and in an English translation. The work contains a new section, "Profiles of the Most Important Czech Writers since 1945" (pp. 222–287), which provides biographical and bibliographical details about the most important postwar Czech writers, including information about English translations of their work and about secondary literature in English. The volume also includes a bibliographical list of the most important works in English on Czech history, literary history and politics, as well as a list of anthologies of Czech post-war literature in English.

Projects such as this one could never be realized without the help and cooperation of other people. I would like to thank Mrs Elizabeth Morrison, who spent several years translating my text without knowing whether it would ever be published, Mr Laurence Benjamin for proof-reading the final version and especially to Dr Jan Čulík of the University of Glasgow, who has read the English text several times and made many useful comments. I would also like to thank the publisher, Anita Grahame, at Sussex Academic Press, for her assistance in publishing this work, and the Czech Ministry of Education for supporting the project financially.

Jiří Holý (b. 1953) graduated in Czech and German at Charles University, Prague. He worked as an editor in a publishing house, as a researcher in the Czech Academy of Sciences and taught at the universities of Saarbrücken, Vienna, Regensburg and Berlin. Since 2002, he has been Professor of Czech Literature at the Department of Czech and Comparative Literature, Faculty of Arts, Charles University, Prague. He has published, amongst other things, literary theoretical and critical studies: *Práce a básnivost* (Creativity and Literary Work, 1990), on the Czech prose writer Vladislav Vančura; *Možnosti interpretace* (Interpreting Literature, 2002), an analysis of Czech, Polish and Slovak literary works.

Mrs Elizabeth Morrison (b. 1924) taught German and French at Hutchesons' Grammar School, Glasgow. When she retired she studied Czech at the University of Glasgow. She has done a number of translations of Czech literary critical works (*Dictionary of Literary Biography,* see vols. 215 and 232) as well as of Czech fiction. She has also worked as a consultant on the Czech–English and English–Czech dictionaries by Josef Fronek.

Jan Čulík (b. 1952) studied Czech and English at Charles University, Prague. In the early 1980s, he taught at the Universities of Glasgow and Lancaster. In the 1980s and 1990s, he worked for British television and as a journalist for Radio Free Europe. Currently he is Senior Lecturer in Czech Studies at the University of Glasgow and also teaches at Charles University in Prague, Ostrava University and Masaryk University, Brno. He also edits *Britské listy,* a widely read Czech language cultural and political daily. He is the author of *Knihy za ohradou: Česká literatura v exilových nakladatelstvích 1971–1989* (Books beyond the Fence: Czech Literature in Emigré Publishing Houses 1971–1989, 1991).

The Development of Czech Literature

There have been several distinct watersheds in the development of Czech literature and changes in the whole of Czech culture. One of these occurred at the end of the thirties. On 15 March 1939 Czechoslovakia, which had been a democratic republic in 1918–1938, was occupied by Nazi Germany. This marked the beginning of a time of comprehensive interference in the arts on a great scale. With small exceptions, the time of oppression lasted for fifty years, until 1989. During this time, Czech literature split into "banned" and "approved". Works written both at home and abroad could be banned. The criteria for assigning works to either category changed in the period between the forties and the eighties. A government with a rigid dogma generally alternated with a "time of Thaw".

The longest *détente* took place between 1963 and 1969, and for Czech culture this was an exceptionally fruitful period. However, the principle of state-controlled literature survived and except for a short interlude between 1945 and 1948 the division of literature into banned and approved remained.

It should be added that "banned"does not automatically mean a work is better and "approved" that it is worse. Literary quality cannot be identified with this division. In assessing literary quality, it is not enough just to use the political ideology of an author, however much we sympathize with his beliefs – and this was of particular importance for Czech artists in the second half of the 20th century.

This division in literature gradually led to three literary trends, three branches, or, to be more precise, three communicative spheres of artistic and literary activity. The first is represented by works written at home and published under censorship, i.e. official literature; the second is represented by underground works written at home, i.e. works in manuscript or samizdat; the third includes writing abroad in Czech, i.e. works written and distributed in exile. All three created their own aesthetic and ethical parameters, their own genres and their own readership. Each one began to appeal to a particular section of the public, and they all had their chosen independent genres and forms of communication, etc. At the same time, even the authors abroad, insofar as they continued to write in Czech, wrote in reaction to the situation at home, so in one way or another their position is of interest. What unites all three trends and various other works is the fact that literature was not just "pure literature", but that in general it was a substitute for freedom.

The year 1989 was another significant watershed. The distinction between approved and banned literature, like the barricades at the frontiers, was swept aside. The democratic breakthrough restored freedom and diversity in the arts. Literature ceased to carry out the political, publicizing and moral functions it had done willy-nilly in the preceding decades in a totalitarian society. But what was the effect of this new freedom? Did it not also undermine the influence of literature? People who can now engage in business or in public life at will, who can express their views freely and travel about the world, cease to look to books or the theatre for ideas suppressed by a political regime. They do not need to use them to escape from a life constricted by nonsensical officialdom; they do not scour texts for hidden allegories. Books become part of the market. What is colourfully presented as culture, and is often completely lacking in culture, reduces the influence of traditional forms of literature, as it has done in the West. Authors take on a different role. Nevertheless, literature continues to have a special place and function. Even today it is a counterbalance to the materialism of life in an industrial age and the limitations of a pragmatism that is also a threat to a democratic society. For even in today's society there is still conflict between the demands of public order and prosperity, "the art of the possible" that puts self-satisfaction and easy solutions first, and great works of literature that are always "the art of the impossible", looking beneath the surface of life, anticipating moments of crisis and drawing attention to problems. These works are troubling and unsettling but they bring catharsis through shared experiences. By asking questions about things that are apparently self-evident they reveal a new form of truth about the world. In these great works man constantly seeks a picture of himself, his present and his eternal problems. Literature is still the traditional basis of education even in an age where visual media, film, television, video and computers, reign supreme.

However, to return to the development of Czech literature in the past sixty years, early in 1939, the arts, especially literature, were beginning to suffer unprecedented censorship. After the arrival of the German "Reichsprotektor", Reinhard Heydrich, in the autumn of 1941 censorship became more stringent and was intensified further in that most difficult period of the occupation from 1942 onwards. Many Czech writers were arrested on the basis of racial law or as political activists, and deported to concentration camps, where some of them died (Karel Poláček, Josef Čapek) or were executed (Vladislav Vančura, Julius Fučík). Three years after the war, following the Communist *coup d'état* in February 1948, a similar situation arose and literature was yet more strictly controlled. Even during the German occupation it had been possible occasionally for men such as Vladislav Vančura, František Halas and Josef Palivec to publish works that indirectly but clearly expressed opposition to the regime, but after the February coup this was impossible. Now the ban on publishing affected not only conservatives, Catholics and liberal democrats but also authors like Karel Teige, Jiří Weil (→ PROFILES) and Jiří Kolář (→ PROFILES), who were revolutionary socialists, although they did not totally identify with Stalinism and the rigid norms of "Socialist Realism". Besides silencing public bodies the regime went on to get rid of individuals. Jan Zahradníček (→ PROFILES), František Křelina, Václav Renč, Josef Palivec and others spent ten years in prison and Záviš Kalandra was executed. After a period of *détente* in the sixties when the literary world returned to normal and literature flourished, another wave of repression, called normalization but which was really Neo-Stalinism, followed in the seventies and eighties after the Soviet invasion of Czechoslovakia in August 1968. Once again there were lengthy lists of banned authors, libraries were "purged", journals and reviews were closed down and books that had already been published were destroyed. Once again official history was rewritten according to the needs of the party in power.

As has been said, the fact of being banned does not guarantee a work's literary quality. Writers whose work was not of the top rank were banned and followed everywhere. It is also true to say that the majority of the foremost writers were to a greater or lesser extent affected by the recurrence of the purges. Some were black-listed twice, even three times – during the German occupation, in the fifties and during the period of Neo-Stalinism. The outstanding critics, Václav Černý (→ PROFILES), Bedřich Fučík and Jan Grossman, for example, enjoyed only a short spell of freedom to publish. Many other writers, such as Ludvík Vaculík, Karel Šiktanc and Pavel Kohout (all → PROFILES), who were enthusiastic supporters of socialism after the Second World War, later gradually expressed their doubts, disappointment and disillusionment. After the reform movement was overthrown at the end of the sixties, they found themselves castigated as "old-fashioned rubbish". Those who chose to go to the West, whether after the February 1948 coup or after August 1968, were freer and had an easier life. On the other hand they had to put up with the loss of their natural cultural environment. As a result Ivan Blatný (→ PROFILES) in Britain, for example, suffered severe trauma, Jan Čep in West Germany and France stopped writing and Milan Kundera (→ PROFILES) in France became assimilated into French culture. What about authors unaffected by bans and purges, who were able to devote themselves to writing and publish their books officially? They too clearly had a price to pay for the restrictions in the cultural environment. Their works had to squeeze in between "commitment to the party", "Socialist Realism" and "popular appeal" and almost always paid for this by a steady decline in artistic quality. This was the case with Marie Pujmanová, Václav Řezáč, Jan Drda, Josef Kainar (for Drda and Kainar → PROFILES) after the February coup and with Miroslav Florian, Vladimír Páral, Ladislav Fuks (for Páral and Fuks → PROFILES) and others in the seventies.

It should perhaps be added that literature published with state approval in the seventies and eighties presented a more colourful picture than after the February 1948 coup. Besides the richly rewarded and protected authors approved by the regime, like Jan Kozák, Ivan Skála and Miroslav Florian, there were also many authors, like Bohumil Hrabal and Jaroslav Seifert (both → PROFILES), whose works attained a reasonable level of craftmanship hovering on the border of a fluctuating zone between "permitted" and "banned".

In any case compared with the interwar period the progress of postwar literature was by no means smooth. There was constant interference from outside agencies and literature was forced to follow state-controlled lines. Again and again there were long delays before books were published. The impressive novel *Neznámý člověk* (The Unknown Man) by Milada Součková (→ PROFILES), written during the war, was published in 1962 by a small exile publishing house in the USA, but the author lived to see only one review of it. It did not come out in Prague till 1995, 12 years after the author's death. Josef Škvorecký's (→ PROFILES) famous novel *Zbabělci* (English *The Cowards*, 1970) was completed in 1949 and published in 1958. Vladimír Holan's (→ PROFILES) reflective poetry from the forties and fifties could not be published till 1963. Jaroslav Durych's *Boží duha* (God's Rainbow) was written in 1955 and published in 1969, seven years after the author's death. Jan Zahradníček's (→ PROFILES) *Znamení moci* (The Sign of Power), written in 1951, was published abroad in the sixties, also after his death. It had appeared in the journal *Student* (The Student) in 1968 but the 1970 edition of this book was destroyed and it had to wait till 1990 to be properly published at home. Bohumil Hrabal's (→ PROFILES) main prose work *Jarmilka* (Jarmilka) had an extraordinary, almost unbelievable, fate. It was written in the spring of 1952 and was first of all removed from the author's first work *Hovory lidí* (People's Conversations, 1956); then the whole printed edition of the book under the title *Skřivánek na niti* (Lark on a String, 1959) was destroyed. The story did see the light of day in *Pábitelé* (Palaverers, 1964) but in 1970 the original version was once again destroyed with Hrabal's whole collection *Poupata* (Buds). In 1992, exactly forty years after it was originally written, it was published in its original form. The same thing happened to Jiří Kolář (→ PROFILES). The typesetting of *Roky v dnech* (Years in Days), written between 1946 and 1947, was broken up. A second edition in 1970 suffered the same fate. The collection then appeared in a few dozen samizdat copies but the author had to wait till 1992 for the first edition in book form.

These are not random isolated cases. Outstanding, original, unconventional works had to wait for years, even decades, to be published. Entire literary groups and artistic trends, surrealism, existentialism and Catholic works, were wiped out. In this way banned texts gained notoriety and added interest but of course were voices from the past by the time they were published. The same thing would have happened to the works of, say, Dylan Thomas or Harold Pinter if it had taken twenty or even forty years for them to be published. This is what many Czech authors were condemned to suffer in the postwar years. The true development of Czech literature took place as it were under the surface and only now and then did it emerge and become visible to a wider public.

State interference in literature brought about another problem: the disparity between "official" and "unofficial" values. State institutions and their spokesmen took as their norm not aesthetic values but "political alignment", following the political and ideological line, so that authors of different types and levels of competence came to be lumped together incongruously in official estimation. For example in the seventies Josef Rybák, a minor figure in Czech poetry, was hailed the equal of Vilém Závada, and in prose the third-rate Bohumil Říha was considered the equal of Ladislav Fuks (→ PROFILES). There even evolved a kind of theory of a "main stream" in Czech literature. Suitable authors, past and present, could be taken as belonging to it but the emigrant writers, Ferdinand Peroutka and Milan Kundera, and the dissidents Ludvík Vaculík and Václav Havel (all → PROFILES) could not.

"Unofficial" criticism, introduced clandestinely among friends and later circulated in manuscript or samizdat or printed abroad, was not dependent on the goodwill or arbitrary decision of the regime. It could express its judgements freely and apply artistic standards no longer recognized. But the abnormal state of literature – the great number of writers banned and the lack of straightforward development – affected even "unofficial" criticism. Literature became first and foremost a political and social concern, the writer was judged by his position on civil rights rather than his literary quality. This was more often the case with authors in exile than at home.

Yet it was semi-official or banned authors, always to the fore whenever there was any relaxation of control or greater democracy, who contributed most of the best works to postwar Czech literature. As proof it should be sufficient to mention the names of the poets Vladimír Holan, Jiří Kolář, Jaroslav Seifert, František Hrubín, Jan Zahradníček, Jan Skácel, Karel Šiktanc and Ivan Wernisch (all → PROFILES), the prose writers Bohumil Hrabal, Věra Linhartová, Milan Kundera, Josef Škvorecký, Ludvík Vaculík (all → PROFILES) and the critics Václav Černý (→ PROFILES), Jan Grossman, Jiří Opelík and Jan Lopatka. In the theatre there were Václav Havel (→ PROFILES) and Josef Topol and those who created the "little" theatres from the end of the fifties to the present day. These people all belonged to different generations with different ideas about the craft of writing and with different artistic aims. Only one thing, apart from the quality of their work, unites them. They were all banned, sometimes many times, from practising their art.

Political and ideological pressure severely distorted literature but for that very reason a noteworthy phenomenon ensued. The written word, plain or coded, became more than ever the centre of attention. Literature therefore gained something, although conditions for writers were difficult and their lives at times were severely restricted. Closely followed, threatened, they nevertheless occupied a position of privilege.

The development of Czech literature after the Second World War cannot be separated from politics. More often than at other times the activities of writers became a matter of public interest. In this way literature was both created and distorted. It arose out of external conditions and in turn affected them. It rebelled against the social regime and moulded it. As this is intended to be a historical account of literature, considerable attention will therefore be devoted to the sociocultural background of the times.

The Forties and Fifties

"The real tragedy of contemporary Czech literature does not lie in the fact that voices shouting out what after all everyone knew were silenced, but that for years afterwards the conditions do not exist for all aspects of our national culture to appear as a rich and varied whole."

(Josef Jedlička)[1]

From May to February

1. Reverberations of War

In May 1945 the most terrible war of all time came to an end in Europe. Besides soldiers who had served with foreign armies and political exiles, writers also gradually began returning home. Ivan Jelínek, František Langer, Viktor Fischl and Jiří Mucha came back from Britain; Egon Hostovský, Jan Werich and, somewhat later, Jiří Voskovec came back from the United States. Zdeněk Nejedlý returned from the Soviet Union. The poet Josef Palivec, the journalist and critic Ferdinand Peroutka, the man of the theatre Emil František Burian and the critic Václav Černý, who had been in the resistance movement, returned from a Nazi prison. Their fellow resistance workers Vladislav Vančura, Julius Fučík, Bedřich Václavek, Milena Jesenská, Jaroslav Jan Paulík and Jaroslav Kratochvíl did not come back. They were either executed or died in prison. Among the eighty thousand persecuted because of their race were the prose writer Karel Poláček, the young poet Hanuš Bonn and most notably Bonn's friend Jiří Orten, who was fatally injured by a car in the summer of 1941 before Jews began to be removed to concentration camps. Josef Čapek, imprisoned as early as 1939, died in the Bergen-Belsen concentration camp in April 1945.

People were slow to recover from the suffering, humiliation and deprivation of wartime. In the first months and years after the occupation books of "prison literature" were published. These were written not only by well-known authors but also by completely unknown writers like the anonymous woman imprisoned in Auschwitz in 1944 who wrote:

Ale až bouře přežene se,
kdo pochopí, kdo pochopí,
že tady v cizím hrobě hnije,
kdo řekne, pro čí utopie,
zrazené mládí Evropy![2]

But until the storm is past
who will understand, who will understand,
that here in a foreign grave moulders
someone who could tell for whose Utopia
the youth of Europe are destroyed![3]

JULIUS FUČÍK's *Reportáž, psaná na oprátce* (1945; published in English as *Notes from the Gallows*, 1948)[4] was written while he was in Pankrác prison and became the best known of these works. It even achieved world renown. It gives a dramatic and emotional record of the fight against the Nazis, the interrogations, his fellow prisoners and warders. The book fluctuates between an eyewitness report and the author's account of himself as a resistance hero. In spite of his grim personal situation the author never doubts that Nazism will be defeated. He believes in Communism as the only way forward for humanity. This over-simplified vision of the future detracts from the artistic merit of the work. However, for that very reason Julius Fučík and his work were in harmony with, and became a symbol of, postwar Stalinist Communism. A complete critical edition of this book, edited by a group of reputable historians, including the (originally suppressed) sections in which the author admits that he "talked" during interrogations and so he was not an insuperable hero, was not published until after 1989.[5]

The poetry of JOSEF ČAPEK (brother of the well-known writer Karel Čapek), published with the title *Básně z koncentračního tábora* (Poems from a Concentration Camp, 1946), is far from passionate, optimistic rhetoric. Inspired by personal experience and his memories of prison, it makes an existentialist response to the fate of mankind succumbing to the rule of evil.

A number of literary works written at the end of, or just after, the war were eyewitness accounts dealing with the same themes of cruelty, cowardice and heroism during the occupation. They were predominantly factual in nature, passionate in emotion and characterized by sharp contrasts of light and shade. Most popular were short poems and pieces of prose. Jaroslav Seifert's (→ PROFILES) poems from the closing section of *Přilba hlíny* (A Helmetful of Earth, 1945), František Halas's poem *Barikáda* (The Barricade, 1945), Jiří Kolář's (→ PROFILES) slim volume *Sedm kantát* (Seven Cantatas, 1945) and others were of this type. JAN DRDA's (→ PROFILES) successful collection of short stories *Němá barikáda* (The Silent Barricade, 1946)[6] was written from the same point of view. It portrays the quiet bravery of the Czech people during the occupation and the uprising.[7] His earlier novels, searching man's innermost being, were of epic proportions. They were based on traditional fairy-tales and folklore, as was his stage play *Hrátky s čertem* (Chatting with the Devil, 1945, filmed by Josef Mach, 1956). The play, written during the war on the lines of a fairy-tale, became an allegory of the struggle with evil – in other words the struggle with the occupying forces. Jan Drda's postwar work was very different – concise, almost documentary. It also indicates the changes in people's taste in literature, using colloquial language and nothing but salient details, yet more and more stressing the black and white values of *Němá barikáda*: treacherous Germans – brave Czechs. The tendency towards documentary style is also evident in JIŘÍ MUCHA's short stories *Problémy nadporučíka Knapa* (in English *The Problems of Lieutenant Knap*, 1945) which was not published till 1946 although it had already appeared in English in 1945, and the reports *Oheň proti ohni* (Fighting Fire with Fire, 1947). Both works are the fruits of the author's experiences as a soldier in France and Britain.[8]

2. The Testimony of Poetry

The middle generation poets František Hrubín, Jan Zahradníček and Vladimír Holan published outstanding poetry with topical themes as did the somewhat older František Halas and the younger poet Vladimír Vokolek.

In 1942, while the Battle of Stalingrad was going on, FRANTIŠEK HRUBÍN (→ PROFILES), in great distress at what was happening in the war, wrote the poem *Stalingrad* (Stalingrad). He interpreted the battle on the eastern front as the clash between the powers of good and evil, and in repetitive prayer-like stanzas ("Chraň, Pane, město Stalingrad" – Lord, save Stalingrad) expressed his hope that salvation would come from the Russian people. In the poem *Jobova noc* (The Night of Job, 1945) Hrubín further developed this theme, depicting war as the struggle between an "old" and a "new" country and transforming these biblical symbols into political entities. The new land was the Soviet Union, a model for the just society. At the same time he worked in a picture of Bohemia as a sorely tried but victorious country.

In his later work František Hrubín brought back an existentialist dimension into his poetry particularly in the poem *Hirošima* (Hiroshima, 1948). Using a series of illustrations taken from contemporary Prague, such as a sick child, a pair of lovers, he shows that the tragedy of Hiroshima is ever present in modern life. Everything takes place in an indivisible cosmos, where epoch-making events become part and parcel of the everyday life of the world and things that seem no way out of the ordinary take on the quality of myth.

Hrubín's poetry was now deliberately less formally perfect, more down to earth, than his wartime poetry. The same trend was also evident in the work of FRANTIŠEK HALAS. Halas, who had been active in the resistance movement during the war, put himself at the service of the new state as a poet and a citizen. He held high public office for two years and even wrote texts for socialist songs and propaganda rhymes for banners. By 1946 however he had begun to produce texts of a totally different nature, full of scepticism and anxiety. Before his death in 1949 František Halas arranged them in a collection entitled *A co?* (What Now?), which was denied publication till 1957, eight years later. The poetry here is "rugged" and far from poetically melodious. As he became aware of the first signs of totalitarianism at home, he was horrified; seeing humanity threatened by further catastrophes, he sought a new "non-poetic" meaning for poetry and a purpose for human existence.

VLADIMÍR HOLAN'S (→ PROFILES) work also went through a succession of changes. He too was devastated by the events of the coup. In his *Panychida* (Panychida, 1945; panychida is an ancient Slavonic ritual for the dead), as in František Hrubín's *Jobova noc* (The Night of Job), we find biblical symbolism (demons and the Last Judgement) given topical significance. A positive contrast to the heart-rending cruelty of the poems in *Panychida* is the book of poetry *Rudoarmějci* (Red Army Soldiers, 1947), a series of portraits of ordinary Soviet soldiers whose unaffected naturalness and cheerful naïvety touched the poet. Holan's poetry is distinctively "unpoetic" – verging on prose – a style aimed at by the young poets of *Skupina 42* (Group 42, see pp. 15–16).

JAN ZAHRADNÍČEK (→ PROFILES), a friend of František Hrubín and František Halas before and during the war, also wrote poetry as a direct reaction to the occupation. He also described the suffering of the Czech Lands in psalms and litanies. In the poem *Stará země* (The Old Country), written in 1944 and published in a collection of the same name in 1946, the homeland is described as "the mother of the poor", just as it is in Hrubín's poems. However here the poor do not become fighters for a better future, and the poet does not place any hope in the Soviet Union. Jan Zahradníček eschewed the general euphoria of the liberation. For him war was a punishment from God; like for other Catholic writers, his hope for the future lay in moral regeneration in the spirit of Christianity. This is the idea expressed in *Rouška Veroničina* (Veronica's Robe) that appeared in a small edition in 1949, and particularly in the long poem *La Saletta* (La Salette, 1947). La Salette is a place in the French Alps where according to tradition the Virgin Mary announced the second coming of Christ. The author sees this as a warning to the modern world – a world from which love and thoughts of eternity are slipping away, a world of foolish pride, empty slogans and obsession with material possessions.

nechce se mi halekat ano a halekat ne
podle toho jen, odkud fouká
děsím se mravenišť okusujících krabičku od zápalek
děsím se stád
prežvykujících od rána do večera
jediný žvást –

jsem tu, můj Bože
na planetě naší rychle se otáčející
návštěvou u krásy
bytem v hrůze
a mezi hrůzou a krásou se potáceje
tak sotva stačím si rozvážiti
co všechno ztraceno, co všechno
ztratit lze ještě[9]

I have no desire to call out yes or no
according to the way the wind blows
I dread the heap of ants gnawing matchboxes
I dread the herds
chewing from morning to night
nothing but rubbish –

I am here, my God,
on our fast spinning planet
visiting beauty
living in horror
and reeling between horror and beauty
so that I can barely think about
all that is lost, all that
is yet to be lost

The aggression in some passages in the poem make it read like a pamphlet, but in construction – time merges with place – and in deep anxiety about new threats to humanity, it is the equal of Hrubín's *Hirošima* and Halas's later poetry.

La Saletta and *Hirošima* are very close in spirit to the poem *Atlantis* (Atlantis, 1947) by another Catholic, VLADIMÍR VOKOLEK. This poem was not published till 1967 when it was included in his book *Mezi rybou a ptákem* (Between Fish and Fowl). The reference to the fable of Atlantis is an obvious allusion to the catastrophes threatening the world. "The birds stay in the air a little longer / than the last aeroplane and perish in the sea / [. . .] / A man leaps from a burning plane and dies / if an angel does not spread his wings at the last minute."[10] Vokolek's *Atlantis* sounds the same warning note as Vítězslav Nezval's later drama *Dnes ještě zapadá slunce nad Atlantidou* (The Sun Is Still Setting Today over Atlantis, 1956). Unlike Nezval however Vokolek sees hope for the salvation of humanity but only through a return to eternal spiritual values.

3. The Politico-Cultural Debate

Social development however followed a different path. The Czech president, Edvard Beneš himself, the recognized successor to T. G. Masaryk and the highest public authority, inclined towards contact with the Soviet Union. He believed in its gradual democratization. He thought that continuity with the interwar democratic Czechoslovak Republic should be maintained, but that at the same time a "new postwar democracy – democracy as understood by the socialists" should be built. The idea of uniting democracy and socialist reform was welcomed by most of the nation. The Munich agreement was still vividly remembered for the part it played in the events leading to the occupation and war. The struggle with Hitler's Germany not only decided the fate of Europe, but also the continued existence or extinction of the Czech nation. From 1940 it became obvious what the Germans planned for the Czechs. "The Czech element", that is the Czech nation, was to be destroyed; the population was to be deported and there was to be partial assimilation of the Czechs after a German victory. At the same time the question being asked in the Czech resistance was would it be possible to live with the Germans again after the defeat of Nazism? Official Nazi anti-Soviet wartime propaganda simply increased sympathy for the Soviet Union on the part of the Czechs and other occupied countries. This sentiment was very much stronger after the liberation, and people put their hope in Communism as the fairest system of world organization. In the parliamentary elections of 1946 the Communists were outstandingly successful. They made skilful use of the radicalism that followed the war, like the revolutions after the First World War, and set about steadily and ruthlessly acquiring a monopoly of power. The political situation abroad played into their hands. The Soviet Union was now dominant in Central Europe and not France as in the twenties. The initial cooperation of the parties in the National Front, with the exception of the right, now inevitably became fraught with infighting, culminating in 1948 in the defeat of the democratic parties and the resignation of Beneš.

The political situation was directly reflected in the arts. With the expulsion of the Germans – and estimates of the number of German victims of this policy vary between thirty and forty thousand – Bohemian culture lost that special quality that had been a feature in its creation since the Middle Ages. It was not only Nazis who were affected but also committed anti-fascist writers like the social liberal Josef Mühlberger, an advocate of Czech–German cooperation, who was sent to a forced labour camp in 1945 and finally chose to be deported with his fellow countrymen.

Between May 1945 and February 1948 signs of pluralism and democracy were still evident in literature. Disagreements centred on the issue of cultural orientation. The burning question was Should we be part of the East or the West? It was generally agreed that there should be as close an understanding as possible in matters of culture with other Slavonic nations, especially with the Soviet Union. Even the naïve idea of Pan-Slavism was resurrected. Meanwhile the Communists were proclaiming the exclusion of the West and what they called its old outworn culture. They favoured "a new developing great eastern civilization" as Ladislav Štoll wrote in the Communist newspaper *Rudé Právo* (Red Rights) in 1945. Václav Černý (→ PROFILES) saw things differently. In 1946 he wrote in *Kritický měsíčník* (Criticism Monthly), "East *and* West [. . .] freedom to consider all political parties in the world [. . .] is an absolute necessity if our culture is to remain Czech and be truly *the people's culture*!"[11]

News from the Soviet Union of postwar cultural purges brought about further debate. The writers Mikhail Zoshchenko and Anna Akhmatova, the composer Dmitry Shostakovich, the film-maker Sergei Eisenstein and others were persecuted as "malicious poisoners". This heralded a change in the cultural and political climate, a return to the most rigid Stalinism. Communist ideologists dutifully supported these purges but many honest socialists like František Halas and Jindřich Chalupecký were embarrassed and defended artistic freedom. Only a few individuals, such as the historian Jan Slavík, the prose writer Edvard Valenta and the essayist František Kovárna, criticized Soviet methods clearly and unambiguously:[12]

> "What concerns us, and what must be our sole concern, is the relationship of the arts to politics as it is now and as it ought to be. [. . .] Will the artist and the politician be bound by the law that applies to them both? Or are our politicians going to have the freedom to interfere in the arts?"[13]

It was the conservative authors, especially the Catholics, who first felt the growing impact of the extreme left during the years 1945–1948. Soon after the May revolution the Catholic writers Jakub Deml, Jaroslav Durych, Jan Čep and Jan Zahradníček (→ PROFILES) were pilloried in the Communist press as collaborators with Nazi regimes. For example a writ (*malý dekret*) was issued against Jakub Deml accusing him of collaboration, and again in the summer of 1948 he was accused of high treason. Only thanks to the courageous intervention of Vítězslav Nezval did the judge acquit him. Similarly Jaroslav Durych was accused of being a "reactionary" for a statement he had made after Munich. When he was then asked if he was for the Nazis or the Communists he answered, "Take your pick. Either lot will destroy us!" At the Congress in the summer of 1946 where the Syndicate of Czech Writers was set up there were practically no Catholic representatives. One of the main points for discussion at the Congress was the relationship of politics to literature. This issue was addressed in the opening speech itself. President Edvard Beneš gave the speech but it was Václav Černý who wrote it. According to him the purpose of literature was not to provide propaganda for any one party. To describe its function he used T. G. Masaryk's designation "non-political politics". "No party, class or other non-literary influences should encroach on the freedom of expression of literature and the arts. There should be no direct political influence and of course no state interference."[14] Writers who believed in democracy, and tolerant Communists like František Halas, were in agreement with such views but they remained in the minority. The final resolution of the Congress no longer spoke of the independence of literature but of the need for writers to stand by the nation – commendable certainly – but as it turned out easily abused. By the beginning of 1946 the critic Miloš Dvořák was writing in the Catholic review *Akord* (The Chord) about the danger of turning away from the source of traditional European spirituality: "True freedom can develop only from moral perfection in man and the nation." And before February 1948 he added a warning note: "Today the spirit of freedom is blatantly suppressed, humiliated, cast out. In its place there is control of the intellect."[15]

4. The War Generation

Alongside the older and middle generations of writers, whose work has already been discussed, some younger writers were forming themselves into groups. One of them, Jiří Šotola, later wrote "we were fifteen when war broke out and it will remain in our blood like broken glass". The oppressive atmosphere of the occupation led the majority of the younger writers to take a pessimistic view of life. Many were impressed by existentialism in French literature and for them Václav Černý (→ PROFILES) was its chief exponent. Interest in existentialism led to a surge of interest in the works of Franz Kafka. The typical themes of this generation were anxiety, seeking and listening, and "intelligent unease" as Zdeněk Urbánek called it. The watchword was no longer joyful discovery of the beauties of the world as in poetism after the First World War. There was much greater emphasis on man as an individual in isolation. The poet of anxiety Richard Weiner and Vladimír Holan's (→ PROFILES) complex poetry with deeply hidden meanings became to a certain extent models for this generation of poets, but František Halas and his poetry of lonely human existence was their chief model. Of all the foreign poets it was the native of Prague Rainer Maria Rilke who continued to have the greatest influence on them.

Of course "the war generation" did not all share the same ideas, and it was much harder for them to have a literary career than it was for the past generation, in Nezval's and Seifert's time. Some poets like Ivan Blatný, Josef Hiršal, Josef Kainar and Jiří Kolář had begun publishing during the war, and some like Ladislav Fikar, Ludvík Kundera, Ivan Slavík and Ivan Diviš were publishing immediately after it. Then most were forced to stop writing, and this disruption continued till the sixties. Prose writers like Bohumil Hrabal and Josef Škvorecký usually had great difficulty in getting published and, like Ladislav Fuks and Ludvík Vaculík, did not achieve their full potential till the sixties.

Only some of the young poets like the surrealist group *Ra* persisted with avant-garde poetics. This group included Ludvík Kundera, Zdeněk Lorenc, the painters Josef Istler and Václav Tikal and a related group were the Spořilov surrealists (Spořilov was then a suburban district in Prague) with Zbyněk Havlíček as the leading spirit. Other poets made known their sympathy for socialism thus forming the embryo of official poetry after the February 1948 coup. The specifically Catholic poets formed a group of their own. Some like IVAN SLAVÍK, in his remarkable collection *Snímání* (Taking Down from the Cross, 1947), were close in spirit to Durych. The poetry of Jiří Orten, who died in 1941 when he was twenty-one, won great acclaim but his later books of poetry could not be published till after the war. LADISLAV FIKAR, in his collection *Samotín* (Samotín, 1945), comes closest to Orten in his sophisticated use of words, subtle changes of mood and his insistence on purity and morality.

Chtěl bych být malířem.
Barvu jak dívku brát.
Mít, laskat její zem:
kotník a vlas a nárt.

Malovat déšť a sen
a ženy. Nahé tak –
Vracet se oblouzen
jak k stáru slepý pták.[16]

I should like to be a painter
and use colour like a girl.
Have, caress her body;
ankle and hair and instep.

Paint the rain and dreams
and women. Naked –
Return dazzled
as a bird, blinded by old age.

Samotín, named after the poet's birthplace in the Czech–Moravian Highlands (Vysočina) was the only collection Ladislav Fikar published during his lifetime. After its publication he devoted himself to translation and administration of the arts. The unfinished second book he had been writing in the early seventies was not published till after his death.

A group that moved in the opposite direction – portraying contemporary urban life using harsh discordances – was *Skupina 42* (Group 42). The group was formed during the war and like the surrealists included the painters and graphic artists František Gross, František Hudeček and Kamil Lhoták as well as poets. The writers in *Group 42* deliberately aimed at being "unpoetical", rejecting sentimentality and excessive lyricism. Their verses are "crude" and disjointed. They sketch lively chaos, the coming into being of things and events rather than their established state. JINDŘICH CHALUPECKÝ, the organizer and theoretician of *Group 42*, wrote an article *Generace* (Generation) outlining the policy of the group: " . . . the progress of the arts at the present day does not depend on the – much-vaunted! – practice of attributing personal significance to hundreds of subtleties of meaning [. . .]. On the contrary it can reach fulfilment only through increasing intensity, vehemence and harshness – by which we mean absolutely strict *accuracy* . . . " (1942).[17]

Unlike the prewar modernists and the Francophile avant-garde poets between the wars, *Group 42* looked to modern Anglo-American culture for inspiration. In the poems of Carl Sandburg and Edgar Lee Masters, and Walt Whitman before them, the voice of contemporary urban civilization alternated with the elemental forces of nature. The poetry of the Anglo-American T. S. Eliot, and especially the work of the Anglo-Irishman James Joyce, embodied the modern idea that the commonplace activities of everyday life were at the same time both trivial and of immense significance.

The poets of *Group 42* held similar views. Their poetry was fragmented, prosaic and tended to be narrative. These, its most distinctive qualities, were fully implemented by JIŘÍ KOLÁŘ (→ PROFILES) in the collection *Dny v roce* (Days in a Year, 1948), the diary of a poet with entries where everyday occurrences in places expand into cosmic phenomena. Another extraordinary collection was *Nové mýty* (New Myths, 1946) by JOSEF KAINAR (→ PROFILES) with the famous poem *Stříhali dohola malého chlapečka* (They Cut Off All the Little Boy's Hair). In it the picture of a man bound to the iron chair of his fate grows out of the banal facts of daily life – such as cutting hair. JAN HANČ went to the extremes of unpoetic writing in

Události (Incidents, 1948), his slim volume of poems and short prose works. Hanč's following works, diaries from the fifties and early sixties were not published till long after the author's death. Besides Kolář and Kainar the foremost writer of *Group 42* was the exceptionally gifted poet IVAN BLATNÝ (→ PROFILES). The most outstanding work after the first period of his writing, when he wrote Seifert-like melancholy lyrical poetry, was the book of poetry *Tento večer* (This Evening, 1945). In it we find actual facts, snatches of ordinary conversations and fragments of dreams, everything deliberately crudely mixed together.

Říkám že každý okamžik je hoden básně!
Zkouším ji na ulici kde je holomráz!
Ve ztvrdlém vyhlazeném mozku z kterého nevyvěrá hudba
V hnízdě kde není líheň metafor
S nápisem: Kupujeme hadry kosti
V lešení na kterém bliká umrlčí lucernička
U šedých nemocničních průjezdů[18]

I say that every moment is worthy of a poem!
I try one out in the street when there is black frost!
In the hardened smooth brain from which music does not spring
In the nest where there is no brood of metaphors
With the title: Let's buy rags and bones
On the scaffolding where dead man's lantern flashes
At the grey façades of hospitals

Ivan Blatný's best poem is easily the excellent *Terrestris* (Terrestris) from his next book *Hledání přítomného času* (The Search for the Present Time, 1947). The eponymous character, an inaccessible beautiful woman and ugly witch in one, embodies the vulgarity, cruelty and sublimity of life.

Even though the members of *Group 42* were mostly left-wing sympathizers, they were not allowed to continue to work after February 1948. Blatný chose to go into exile. Jiří Kolář (→ PROFILES), Jiřina Hauková and Jan Hanč, like Jindřich Chalupecký and the critic Jan Grossman who was very close to *Group 42*, could not publish. Only Josef Kainar (→ PROFILES) changed radically and wrote poetry according to the literary criteria approved by the government. But even during the short time when *Group 42* could publish openly it exerted a powerful influence on contemporary and later literature. It extended its influence not only to the members of the same generation like Ivan Slavík, but also to the somewhat older OLDŘICH MIKULÁŠEK (→ PROFILES) – especially in his collection *Pulsy* (Pulses, 1947). There were also traces of its influence in the middle generation of František Halas, Vladimír Holan and František Hrubín (Holan and Hrubín → PROFILES). Later, under the surface of official post-February culture, the poetry of *Group 42* influenced other authors such as Egon Bondy and Bohumil Hrabal (→ PROFILES).[19]

5. Prose

Compared with poetry, prose writing in the postwar period remained in the background. Czech prose lost three great writers with the untimely deaths of the Čapek brothers and Vladislav Vančura. Jaromír John, one of the older prose writers, came to the fore with his wide-ranging novel *Pampovánek* (Pampovánek), which came out in 1948 and was expanded in 1949. It is the strange story of an outcast from society who claims to be the Messiah. It is characteristic of the author that he bases the novel on a multiplicity of real and fictitious documents and on playful irony. The Catholic writer Jan Čep's short stories *Polní tráva* (The Grass of the Field, 1946) continued on the same lines as his previous work. They concentrated on situations where human beings are pushed to the limit, and above all on death, which opens up horizons of eternity.

In his novel *Makanna, otec divů* (Makanna, Father of Miracles, 1946), set in the Middle Ages, JIŘÍ WEIL (→ PROFILES), a writer of the middle generation, uses the theme of the false Messiah. Unlike John's simpleton, however, Weil's Hekím is from the outset a conscious deceiver who manipulates people and distorts ideas. In his next novel *Život s hvězdou* (published in English as *Life with a Star*, 1988) he came closer to *Group 42*. The book indeed appeared in 1949 but shortly afterwards it was banned and the author was no longer allowed to publish. For this book he chose a subject from the time of the German occupation – the story of a Jewish civil servant, Roubíček, waiting in the suburbs of Prague to be taken to a concentration camp. But it is not an exposition of Nazi brutality or superhuman heroic resistance like the works of Julius Fučík and Jan Drda. Gone is the black-and-white categorization of good and evil. The hero and narrator is a loner concerned with trivial everyday things. He dreams of a cup of coffee or of his former lover Růženka; he describes his past and present experiences dispassionately. The horror and even the absurdity of that time does not come from horrifying scenes but from the "normal" way Nazi totalitarianism works, from the acceptance of the degradation of human relationships as a matter of course – in some respects the story is told in a very Kafka-like manner.

Jiří Weil was able to base his descriptions on his own experience. A Jew, he managed to avoid being taken to a concentration camp and lived in hiding till the liberation. Another eminent prose writer of Jewish origin, EGON HOSTOVSKÝ (→ PROFILES), drew on his own experiences as a refugee and emigrant. His novel *Cizinec hledá byt* (A Foreigner Looks for a Flat, 1947) describes the peregrinations of a Czech doctor, Marek, in the maze of postwar New York.[20] The author's next novel *Nezvěstný* (translated into English as *Missing*, 1952) was published in Danish in 1949 during his second period of exile. It was not published in Prague till 1994. It describes another loner, Erik Brunner, tossed from pillar to post in the fight between hostile forces at the time of the February 1948 coup. Graham Greene persuaded the London publisher Eyre & Spottiswoode to bring out Hostovský's novel *Seven Times the Leading Men* (1945; in Czech *Sedmkrát v hlavní úloze*, New York, 1942), thus initiating his literary career in the West. Greene later wrote about Hostovský:

> "My first meeting with Egon Hostovský had some of the flavour of his own works, a complex flavour of black humour, melodrama and despair. It was in Prague during the week of the Communist Revolution. Hostovský came into my hotel bedroom straight from his last meeting at his Foreign Office with his beloved boss Masaryk [Foreign Secretary Jan Masaryk] – who was to suffer defenestration a few days later. We sat on the bed finishing up my bottle of Scotch whisky, and the streets outside were noisy with processions of trade unionists, shouting away their freedom. [. . .] Perhaps one had to have lived a little in that strange world where a way of life was crumbling like stale cake, to appreciate to the full Mr. Hostovský's art. This is not the art of a refugee. He has carried his country and the atmosphere of his time with him, and there is at least one flavour which no one will find in his work and that is the flavour of bitterness and exile."[21]

Hostovský's prose does not have the dry matter-of-factness of Jiří Weil's or Jiří Kolář's, but here too descriptions of disrupted lives turn into something analogous – an existentialist exposition of a cold inhuman world, alienating man. Jiří Kolář wrote that "everyone thinks about humanity and nobody thinks of human beings", and in Hostovský we read "how many mortals today try to save all humanity and at the same time torture and kill men".

The following year such fears were more than amply confirmed. For a long time Czech literature of the same very high quality as that of the immediate postwar period could be produced only occasionally and in secret. It was generally not possible to write until the sixties.

THE BLEAK YEARS

1. Stalinism

Dnes básník ani neví, proč tu je,
už se tu život veršem nerozsvěcí,
dnes už se jenom stenografuje
úpění rozpadajících se věcí.[22]

Nowadays the poet does not even know why he is here,
life is no longer illuminated by poetry,
nowadays only shorthand
records the pain of things disintegrating.
(František Hrubín, Svit hvězdy umřelé [Light of a Dying Star], 1949)

The social system that came into being soon after the February 1948 coup abolished democracy and civil rights. Only one ideology was allowed, Marxism, which was substituted for freedom of thought and nonconformist ideas. Furthermore, this was distorted by Stalinism.[23]

The principles of Stalinism, which considered itself the highest achievement of history, came from the Soviet Union and were adopted by the leaders of the Communist Party. Ideas that did not conform were taken to be hostile and silenced by force. This applied also to literature. The new regime suppressed the majority of literary journals and reviews – the Catholic *Akord* (The Chord), Václav Černý's (→ PROFILES) the liberal *Kritický měsíčník* (Criticism Monthly), and *Listy* (Pages), which was close to *Group 42*. It also carried out a purge on schools and universities, and suppressed information about the arts abroad – for example Albert Camus and William Faulkner were regularly described as poisonous offshoots of bourgeois culture. At home, literature that did not conform was banned or destroyed. The import and sale of anything published in the West was stopped. Mail was censored and "hostile" broadcasts jammed. Many people went into exile; even more could neither publish nor take public office. The title of JIŘINA HAUKOVÁ'S manuscript collection *Holomrazy* (Black Frost, 1949–1952) was symptomatic of the prevailing atmosphere. Her poetry was concerned with personal crises. She was not one of the group of writers reacting against what was happening in the country; however, she did write:

Stíny blíny stíny blíny
jak se krabatí
stíny puklé domoviny
za drát ostnatý

Jiskernatky břitká slova
cizopasná sněť
z prázdných řečí vyznavačů
plazí se havěť[24]

Shadows henbane shadows henbane
as frown
shadows of a wrinkled homeland
behind barbed wire

razor-sharp words spark-like
parasitic blight
out of the empty words of proselytes
vermin crawl

The first register of books withdrawn from libraries had already been compiled by October 1948. The books were systematically destroyed or suppressed during the dissolution of the monasteries and convents. Another "purge of the libraries" took place in 1953. The total number of books destroyed between 1948 and 1958 amounted to 27 million. JOSEF JEDLIČKA, in his short story *Kde život náš je v půli se svou poutí* (Where We Are Halfway through Life's Pilgrimage), and after him BOHUMIL HRABAL (→ PROFILES), in his *Příliš hlučná samota* (published in English as *Too Loud a Solitude*, 1990, see p. 145), and LADISLAV DVOŘÁK (see p. 75), in his story *Jak hromady pobitých ptáků* (Like Heaps of Slaughtered Birds), bear literary witness to the pulping of books. For instance, here is Dvořák's picture of this destruction:

> "Here the condemned books were lying, torn, trampled underfoot, with spines ripped and covers tattered, pages scattered and crumpled, piled high like heaps of slaughtered birds. Silken bookmarks and capital letters torn from their spines hung on a single thread like ribbons on funeral wreaths."[25]

In April 1948 the Congress of National Culture took place and the party ideologists Václav Kopecký, Zdeněk Nejedlý and Ladislav Štoll were the main speakers.

To comply with the spirit of central bureaucratic control of society, printing works, publishing houses and theatres were nationalized. The newly formed Union of Czechoslovak Writers (Svaz československých spisovatelů) also came under the control of the party and the state. Unlike the previous syndicate that had 1,675 members, this organization was rigorously selective: only 300 writers including Slovaks were accepted (the old syndicate had only Czech members) and a further 120 were put forward. Of course the greatest poets František Halas, Jaroslav Seifert, Jan Zahradníček and Vladimír Holan were not members, nor were the critics Karel Teige, Václav Černý and Bedřich Fučík. At the first Congress in the spring of 1949 Zdeněk Nejedlý set out a narrow political concept of art, completely different from Beneš's speech at the 1946 Congress: " . . . the main question is: who stands on whose side of the barricade? [. . .] Today anyone who stands for so-called 'pure art' [. . .] will find himself on the other side of the barricade, but what does that mean today? It means the greatest service to reaction." In the same vein Jan Drda, the new president of the Union, repudiated "the hypocritical call for absolute freedom and independence" and instead called for "joyful union with the working class".[26]

At the conference on poetry in January 1950 Ladislav Štoll and Jiří Taufer adopted an even more uncompromising position. They condemned not only Catholics and Liberal Democrats but also most distinguished left-wing writers like František Halas, Jiří Kolář, Ivan Blatný and Karel Teige. Works from the avant-garde period of Vítězslav Nezval and Konstantin Biebl, who supported socialism after the February 1948 coup, were considered damaging and were suppressed.

Ladislav Štoll's lecture entitled *Třicet let bojů za českou socialistickou poezii* (Thirty Years of Struggle to Create a Czech Socialist Poetry, an expanded version published in book form, 1950) reflected the views of the higher echelons of government. It was soon published and came to represent the obligatory guidelines. Restrictions were placed on what was acceptable as traditional literature; for example, Baroque literature was suppressed as "the work of reactionary writers". Classical authors of 19th-century descriptive realism like Josef Kajetán Tyl, Vítězslav Hálek and Alois Jirásek were preferred and represented as precursors of revolutionary socialism. Anyone who showed the slightest tendency to disagree with the regime and its discriminatory policy in the arts was viewed with suspicion. Young Communist critics, members of the Czechoslovak Socialist Youth Movement, in the pages of *Tvorba* (Creations) outdid themselves in attacks on "reactionaries". With no chance for anyone to argue his case, campaigns were led against the first Czechoslovak president Tomáš Garrigue Masaryk, the liberal journalists and critics Ferdinand Peroutka, Arne Novák, Václav Černý, the Catholic Jan Zahradníček and the cultured poet Josef Palivec, Karel Čapek's brother-in-law, who was dubbed "devoted servant of the man-eating capitalist class". Jiří Weil, Jiří Orten, existentialism ("one of the poisonous tentacles of dying capitalism") and surrealism were also attacked. Karel Teige clashed with orthodox Stalinism and was denigrated as "an agent of Trotskyism"; structuralism of the Prague School was denounced as "bourgeois pseudo-science". Censorship on the lines of the Soviet institutions affected not only the big publishing houses, daily newspapers and reviews, radio and films, but also local newspapers and placards.

Purges, not allowing people to publish or work, abolishing criticism, and seeking out enemies was, however, only the prelude to harassing individuals and bringing lawsuits against them. Entire groups of writers became victims of new laws making certain things illegal. In compliance with government policy, courts applied the so-called "working class" law in two ways: on the one hand, new laws were passed whereby criticism of the government, gathering and disseminating information (activities which the Czech legal code had since 1857 deemed the right of any citizen) became criminal offences. On the other hand, courts interpreted the law in terms of class. Not only unlawful conduct but any action "against the interests of the working class" was punished. This made it possible to sentence absolutely anybody. Political lawsuits were brought against more than two hundred thousand citizens of the republic.[27] While under arrest the accused were usually bullied and forced into making confessions according to previously prepared scenarios. This resulted in bizarre situations where high-ranking churchmen used Marxist terminology in their answers in the show trials of 1950.

> "We were tortured, plagued with hunger and cold; we had no contact with our families, then we were judged to be guilty of high treason [. . .]. When the people find out all that they did to us in the uranium mines, in the crystal grinding shops, in the stone quarries and the coal pits, when they hear of the starvation and the beatings when they tried to break our backs and when they hear what they did to our families, they will be appalled." (Václav Prokůpek, 1968)[28]

The majority of the writers condemned were Catholics. Jan Zahradníček, Zdeněk Kalista, Václav Renč, Bedřich Fučík, Růžena Vacková, Josef Kostohryz, Zdeněk Rotrekl and others spent ten years or more in prison. The pretext for their imprisonment was a memorandum about the state of the arts in Czechoslovakia after the February 1948 coup, drawn up by the poet Josef Kostohryz and signed by several, mostly Catholic, writers. The accused were of course pronounced guilty and further "proved" to be guilty of many more crimes – spying, conspiracy to bring about a potential coup and so on. A group of prewar ruralists (authors highlighting traditional values and the values of country life), Křelina, Knap and Prokůpek, closely related to the Catholics, also suffered heavily. The poet and translator of Paul Valéry, Josef Palivec, was condemned to twenty years hard labour for sending abroad reports about the situation in prisons in Czechoslovakia, about the rape of women prisoners by warders, about forced labour camps and other offences. Even liberal democratic writers (Jiří Mucha, Edvard Valenta) and unorthodox Communists were imprisoned: Záviš Kalandra, a historian and writer on the arts, who had survived a Nazi concentration camp, was tried and executed in 1950 along with the socialist politician Milada Horáková, who had actively fought against the Communists. The avant-garde critic Karel Teige was saved from prison only by his premature death and Jiří Weil (→ PROFILES) who criticized Stalinism in the interwar novel *Moskva-hranice*

(Moscow-Frontier, 1937) on the basis of his personal experience, saved himself through humiliating self-criticism. In Slovakia the former left-wing avant-gardist Laco Novomeský, who was connected with the revue *Dav* (The Crowd), was convicted. Among the "jailbirds" in the uranium mines at Jáchymov and elsewhere were students and young people about twenty years of age, like Karel Pecka, Petr Kopta and Jiří Stránský, who were able to regain their freedom and devote themselves to literature – but not till many years later. In 1952, while searching Václav Černy's (→ PROFILES) home, the police found Jiří Kolář's (→ PROFILES) "protest" manuscript *Prométheova játra* (Prometheus' Guts). Černý and Kolář were arrested. Both were saved from further imprisonment only by the deaths of Stalin and the Czech Communist leader Gottwald soon afterwards. This brought about changes at the highest level. In Czechoslovakia Klement Gottwald was replaced by Antonín Zápotocký who was himself replaced by Antonín Novotný four years later, leading to a milder form of tyranny.

2. Literature in the Grip of Dogmatism

It would be a mistake, however, to think that the majority of writers whose work was acceptable in the fifties supported the new regime only for gain or out of fear. Some of them believed the Communist slogans out of an honest desire to build a fairer society. They were encouraged by the illusion of the useful artist serving the Ideal with his work.

> "Anyone who thinks that the Communist regimes in Central Europe are exclusively the work of criminals is overlooking a basic truth: the criminal regimes were made not by criminals but by enthusiasts convinced they had discovered the only road to paradise. They defended that road so valiantly that they were forced to execute many people. Later it became clear that there was no paradise, that the enthusiasts were therefore murderers."[29]

But even for writers with real authority the limitations became increasingly restrictive. The purpose of art was assumed to be the furtherance of an *idée fixe* about the social order. Bound up with this was the artistic theory of Socialist Realism. The concept of Socialist Realism came into being in the early thirties in the Soviet Union. Even before the war it was developed in Czechoslovakia by the Marxist theoreticians Bedřich Václavek and Kurt Konrad for whom Socialist Realism was literature representing the world from a revolutionary point of view. It was a combination of the elements of 19th-century realism with some avant-garde ideas. The group *Blok* (Block) that included Marie Majerová, Marie Pujmanová, Jiří Weil (→ PROFILES) and the Czech Peter Jilemnický, who wrote in Slovak, showed similar tendencies in their work. After the February 1948 coup, however, Socialist Realism acquired a different meaning. Anything approaching avant-garde ideas was considered unhealthy modernism and excluded. Konrad's requirement that man was to be "looked at in all his diversity" had disappeared, for man was perceived solely as a product of society and the representative of a social class. The chief characteristics of this "Socialist Realism II", as it was dubbed by Heinrich Kunstmann,[30] were now party discipline, meaning ideological values in the spirit of the contemporary regime, and *lidovost,* that is "popular appeal", general intelligibility. The most demanding literary works were suppressed. Literature was thus reduced to functioning as advertisements for party policy. It was supposed to be instructive to read about the diligent worker reaching the highest level of production, the vigilant functionary or the politically correct member of a cooperative. Literature was supposed to fight against "imperialism", against indigenous reactionary forces, against the hesitancy of the authors themselves. "I will give the hand grenade of my poem for the last battle of the proletariat," said poet Vlastimil Školaudy.[31] "Like a machine gun, let my verse be charged / with the truth and let it hit where it is necessary,"[32] says Josef Kainar (→ PROFILES) in *Veliká láska* (Great Love, 1950). Novels combining popular education and traditional partiality for the history of the 19th century turned enthusiastically to the past, but historical events were adapted to the needs of the time. The mediaeval religious reformer Jan Hus, for example, in MILOŠ VÁCLAV KRATOCHVÍL's novel *Mistr Jan* (Master John, 1951)[33], was portrayed as a social rebel. Just as in the Soviet Union the literary genres most favoured were novels about "building socialism", history in the form of the novel, plays about industrial production and propaganda poetry. Other traditional types of literature, the psychological novel and love poetry were considered undesirable. Sentimental novels for women and detective stories were also denounced as "decadent" and "outdated".

Not only was independent thought suppressed but any suggestion of individual style was also discouraged. Even well-known older writers like the novelists Marie Pujmanová, Václav Řezáč and Jan Drda (→ PROFILES), the poets Vítězslav Nezval (→ PROFILES) and Konstantin Biebl,[34] Emil František Burian, man of the theatre, and the literary scholar Jan Mukařovský descended to this type of trivia. According to VÁCLAV ŘEZÁČ literature should "ask a question clearly and answer it for the reader in such a way that he should be able to see all its complexities and respond directly to it". His own novels *Nástup* (The Line-Up, 1951; filmed by Otakar Vávra, 1952) and *Bitva* (The Battle, 1954)[35] were written in this spirit, keeping within all the postwar restrictions. They were two of the most widely read books in the fifties. In *Nástup* Řezáč borrowed some of his subject matter from Jiří Mucha's novel *Válka pokračuje* (The War Continues, 1949) but unlike it and unlike his own previous works, he dispensed with any psychological analysis. The characters have become like chessmen simply repeating standard moves. The categorical distinction between right and wrong, the insipidity of the narrative and the boring dialogue make *Bitva* in particular a dull, pretentious piece of work.

The work of MARIE PUJMANOVÁ demonstrates the difference between prewar and post February Socialist Realism. Her remarkable novel *Lidé na křižovatce* (People at the Crossroads, 1937) was followed by the two other works of the trilogy: *Hra s ohněm* (Playing with Fire, 1948) and *Život proti smrti* (Life versus Death, 1952; the author was forced to revise the original version of this novel). Gradually the characters turned into ideological symbols and the novel ceased to be a perceptive psychological study. The plot of the novel merely reinforced the official image of the recent past.

3. Exile

Not everyone was enthusiastic about building socialism. Roughly sixty thousand Czechoslovak citizens found refuge in the West. In the course of the fifties and sixties their number rose to 250,000. Among the exiles were well-known literary figures – the novelists Egon Hostovský, Jan Čep, Zdeněk Němeček and Milada Součková, the poets Ivan Blatný and Ivan Jelínek, Jiří Voskovec, the man of the theatre, critic and journalist Ferdinand Peroutka, the essayists František Kovárna and Petr Den. Viktor Fischl was perhaps the only one who travelled in 1949 to Israel with official permission, where he worked for the Israeli diplomatic service. The others lived in more difficult circumstances than the next great wave of emigrants after the invasion of Soviet troops in August 1968. Western Europe, especially West Germany, was still a long way from achieving its subsequent prosperity. Life in the United States and Canada was not idyllic for Czech men of letters either. The diplomat, globetrotter and novelist Zdeněk Němeček wrote from Canada in 1948: "I came to a land of fierce, ruthless liberalism [. . .] where civil liberty is complete, including the freedom to sleep under a bridge. The state intervenes in nothing at all – including the arts. A sculptor is of no use here – unless perhaps as a stonemason. [. . .] At the same time I must warn you, literally, that the people here are decent and pleasant, in general!"[36]

The final incorporation of Czechoslovakia into the Soviet bloc and America's policy of keeping Communism at bay put an "iron curtain" between East and West. This was obviously necessary because of the threat to Western democracy but for the lands east of the Elbe it was fatal. Literature written in exile was printed but was isolated from the homeland. For many years exiles had no news even of their closest relations. Authors abroad had their work published but generally had no hope of becoming known to a wider public, to say nothing of royalties. Some like Ivan Blatný (→ profiles) stopped writing, and some restricted their output. Jan Čep confined himself to essays; another eminent novelist, Milada Součková (→ profiles) wrote only essays on literary subjects and poems.

The relationship between Czech and Slovak emigrants was not without conflict either. A large number of Slovak writers had supported the semi-fascist and nationalist Slovak state during the war, including the outstanding novelist Jozef Cíger Hronský, and the Catholic modernist poets Rudolf Dilong and Karol Strmeň had already emigrated by 1945. They wanted nothing to do with Czechoslovak institutions. The Czech emigrants were also divided. Besides the Council of Free Czechoslovakia, which supported people close to the former Czech president Edvard Beneš, there was also a faction that clearly distanced itself from Beneš's politics both during and after the war.

Exile literature had its beginnings among those who had got out of the country and were living in difficult circumstances. The situation certainly improved with the setting up of Radio Free Europe in 1951 with its regular broadcasts in Czech and Slovak, in which Ferdinand Peroutka and Julius Firt were particularly active. However, Czech literary life in the West was slow to develop and did so only thanks to the hard work of individuals. The *Křesťanská akademie* (Christian Academy) in Rome was very important for Catholic literature. The series of essays *Studium* (Studies) and the series of poetry and short stories *Vigilie* (Vigil) included works by Jan Čep, Jan Zahradníček and others. At the end of the sixties Jaroslav Durych's four-part novel *Služebníci neužiteční* (Wicked Servants) was also published there. ANTONÍN VLACH and his namesake ROBERT VLACH were dedicated organizers of literature in exile. From 1953 Antonín Vlach, in Hamburg, was the manager, and Robert Vlach, who lived in Sweden, the publisher and editor of *Sklizeň* (The Harvest), the best Czech monthly arts journal of the day. In it there was fiction as well as criticism and reflections on the subject of exile and the homeland. One of the contributors to *Sklizeň* was PETR DEN, a pen name for Ladislav Radimský, who went on to analyze problems more profoundly during his time as an exiled journalist:

> "Jan Čep wrote in the cultural review *Rok 1957* (Year 1957) that no modern society could claim to be called civilized unless it was based on the principle of the plurality of cultural ideas. He rightly complained that during the Communist regime at home a large part of the nation was forcibly excluded from cultured dialogue.
> It seems to me that this serious deficiency is not just a deficiency of the Communist regime and that we were suffering from it before – although of course it was in no way as monstrous as today. Had we not already been for several decades a land where there was no true debate or at least a land where there was no discussion on matters of basic importance? We could of course argue and quarrel but only about matters of little import, only about everyday politics and power."[37]

ROBERT VLACH, poet and journalist, lectured on Slavonic Studies in Western universities. He was the driving force behind the very important series *Sklizeň svobodné tvorby* (Harvest of Free Writing) in which about four dozen titles of exiled works appeared.

In the mid-fifties three representative anthologies were published: anthologies of poetry *Neviditelný domov* (Our Invisible Homeland, ed. Peter Demetz, Paris 1954), *Čas stavění* (The Time to Build, ed. Antonín Vlach, Vienna, 1956) and a collection of prose works, *Peníz exulantův* (Coin of the Exiles, Munich, 1956). This was edited by Antonín Kratochvil and dedicated to the authors in prison at home. At that time the exiles gradually lost the belief that they would soon return home, one that most of them had held when they left for the West.

The result was nostalgia. Robert Vlach wrote "sbohem, má Praho, ztracená pod azbukou" (Goodbye my Prague, lost under the Cyrillic alphabet). But at the same time there were practical attempts to establish two-way contact with the homeland. The journal *Skutečnost* (Reality) was an attempt to do this at the end of the forties and the beginning of the fifties. The younger generation of exiles concentrated mainly on politics. After the demise of *Skutečnost*, one of the contributors, PAVEL TIGRID, founded the quarterly *Svědectví* (Testimony). Its first number was brought out on 28 October 1956 in New York to mark the anniversary of the foundation of an independent Czechoslovakia. From the end of the fifties it was edited in Paris where it appeared till the end of the eighties. *Svědectví* was also political but it regularly concerned itself (as did, incidentally, the Polish émigré review *Kultura*) with the arts. Pavel Tigrid, the most important journalist in exile apart from Ferdinand Peroutka (→ PROFILES) and Petr Den, edited it for the entire thirty-five years of its existence. The review set itself the task of being the platform for the various groups of Czech emigrants. Basically it attacked Communist ideology, but at the same time it did not neglect events at home and above all it did not automatically exclude anyone, even the Czech Communists, from "searching together for ways leading to a peaceful future, freedom and justice" (Tigrid in the first issue). For that reason *Svědectví* won the secret collaboration of people in Czechoslovakia.

The main types of literature published in the West in the fifties and sixties were journalism and nostalgic poetry. Novels were rarely published. *Neznámý člověk* (The Unknown Man) by MILADA SOUČKOVÁ (→ PROFILES) appeared in 1962 but it had been written during the war and was not published in Prague till 1995. After the death of Zdeněk Němeček in 1957 the only important novelist still writing was EGON HOSTOVSKÝ (→ PROFILES; see pp. 17–18), who was living in the United States. Hostovský began his literary career before the Second World War by writing psychological short stories and novels. After the war he started using the techniques of the thriller, for instance in his novel *Půlnoční pacient* (translated as *The Midnight Patient*, 1954; in Czech, New York, 1959; filmed by H. G. Clouzot in 1957 as *Les Espions*). His wide-ranging novel *Všeobecné spiknutí* (A General Conspiracy), which had been a long time in preparation, came out in English as *The Plot* in 1961, but was only published in Czech in Prague in 1969. It was, however, not a success in the United States.

The writers in exile, cut off from the domestic arts scene, usually preserved the older literary language and stressed the values of home and the Czech homeland. Some authors like IVAN JELÍNEK (see p. 172), whose best work was done in the seventies and eighties, tended to write in a formal polished style. Occasionally this gave the effect of "foreignness" and existentialist uncertainty as in Egon Hostovský's prose, or else it produced the opposite effect, calm acceptance of the order of the cosmos juxtaposed with the neurotic unease of the present age – as in the poems of JIŘÍ KOVTUN (see p. 173) and the later prose works of VIKTOR FISCHL (see pp. 172–173) and Jiří Kovtun.

4. Underground Literature

It was not state-approved literature that maintained the freedom of literature during the fifties, but the unofficial literature existing beside literature in exile. Sometimes this is spoken of as "samizdat" but it is better to reserve this term for the period after 1970 when samizdat formed a kind of independent group circulating established publications. It was a distribution net having journals and connections with other activities, concerts, happenings, theatre in private houses, video journals, illegal churches, the work of *Charter 77*, and ties with literature in exile. None of this basically applies to the fifties and it would not even have been possible during Stalinism. "Underground literature", the term applied later to these stringent conditions, and literally true, included for example the prison poems *Dům Strach* (House of Fear) of JAN ZAHRADNÍČEK (→ PROFILES) and those of ZDENĚK ROTREKL (*Malachit* [Malachite])[38] which were sometimes circulated orally among his fellow prisoners. Other unofficial texts – that is texts that were unedited and unpublished – were the work of isolated individuals – for example the novels of Jaroslav Durych and the poetry of Vladimír Holan – and were mostly circulated among small groups. The surrealist collections *Znamení zvěrokruhu* (Signs of the Zodiac, 1951) fall into this category. There were editions every month from January to October but only a single copy of each. Only nine of the ten have survived, for the police seized one of them. The theoreticians and writers KAREL TEIGE, VRATISLAV EFFENBERGER and KAREL HYNEK were contributors, together with the graphic artists Josef Istler, Václav Tikal, Mikuláš Medek and others. Each edition contained original drawings and had reproductions pasted in so that they resembled mediaeval manuscripts. Effenberger commented in 1949:

> "If the question of artistic freedom (without which development in art is impossible) was solved by one side simply preventing its discussion, it would not mean that with no opportunity to publish, the kind of literature against which the present stringent administrative measures are aimed, would also perish."

VLADIMÍR HOLAN (→ PROFILES) continued to work in secret. His poetry viewed life from a standpoint of its mystery and tragedy. For Holan the essence of the poetic world was the constant tension between the world of phenomena and the world of the ideal, between reality and appearance. His poetry is based on complicated allusions, symbols and myths but at the same time it includes unambiguous terms, bald facts and harsh invective.

A už mám dost vaší sprostoty,
a nezabil-li jsem se ještě, pak jen proto,
že jsem si nedal život
a že ještě kohosi miluju, protože miluju sebe . . .
Můžete se smát, ale orla napadne jen orlice
a raněného Achilla jen Bríseovna.
Být není lehké . . . Lehká jsou jen hovna . . . [39]
(*Nepřátelům*, 1949, published 1964)

And I have enough of your coarseness,
and if I haven't killed myself it is only
that my life is not my own
and I still love someone because I love myself . . .
You may laugh, but only the she-eagle attacks an eagle

and only Brises's daughter the wounded Achilles.
To be is not easy . . . Shitting is easy . . . [40]
(*To the Enemy*)

The poems in the collection *Příběhy* (Tales) were written in total isolation during the grim years after the February 1948 coup. Some of these poems had appeared individually in the fifties in journals and in special book club editions. The collection itself was not published till 1963.

In these poems Holan's tendency to use prose-like structures and vocabulary is even more marked. Just as in *Rudoarmějci* (Red Army Soldiers, 1947, see p. 10) regular rhyme and rhythm disappeared and free verse and the theme of a life in ruins was introduced. The heroine in *Óda na radost* (Ode to Joy), from the collection *Příběhy*, the divinely beautiful pure Lucia, who "simply radiated joy" and "brought others joy", could be said to personify this theme. The name Lucia is an obvious allusion to the Latin *lux*, meaning light, radiance and salvation. Unlike Friedrich Schiller's *Ode to Joy*, set to music by Beethoven in his Ninth Symphony, Holan's poem of the same name does not end in brotherhood and hope. Through no fault of her own Lucia causes the death of a young man infatuated by her beauty and she has to leave home. One day when she is sweeping the floor she unfortunately overturns a lighted lamp (once again the theme of light) and burns to death in dreadful agony. Her terrible story bears the hallmarks of a tale of martyrdom but it is also evidence of the almost devilish malevolence of fate, as if the author doubts that human life and the world in general has any meaning at all.

At that time Holan was writing contemplative lyrical poems, which were collected in the book *Bolest* (Pain, 1965). He was also composing the greater part of *Noc s Hamletem,* which was published in 1964. In 1980 it was published in English as *A Night with Hamlet* and a new translation came out in 1988. In *Bolest* and *Noc s Hamletem* we find the motifs of walls and precipices suggesting the crushing pressures of life that is pictured as merely scraping a living. But they are shot through with marvellous sparks of "Poetry", moments when man glimpses the hidden meaning of life. Love is animal lust but it is also the promise of grace and selfless maternal devotion. In a nocturnal discussion with Hamlet, his alter ego, the poet wonders whether we are or are not damned. He comes to the conclusion that we must accept our tragic and uncertain lot.

Like Holan on Kampa in Prague by the Vltava river, another loner, BOHUSLAV REYNEK, was continuing his work in secret in Petrkov in the Czech-Moravian Highlands (Vysočina). His poems were also not published till many years later,[41] and in them the poet often poses the question of evil and guilt. However, his poems are more directly accessible than Holan's encoded verses and are based on Christian values. Pictures of simple country life, a winter landscape, a cottage and cowshed, cats, swallows and thistles are transformed into heralds of eternity, into horror and hope of redemption.

Before being imprisoned in the summer of 1951, JAN ZAHRADNÍČEK (→ PROFILES) was able to finish his poetic account of the chill dark days entitled

Znamení moci (in English *Sign of Power,* in *Kosmas*, 19 [2005], no. 1), which was published in Rome in book form and in a journal in Prague in 1968. The form of the work and its vision of the world are in full harmony with his earlier work *La Saletta* (La Salette, see pp. 10–11).

In *Znamení moci* there are signs of the approaching end, that is of the Last Judgement. Zahradníček expressed this even more vividly as "darkness was falling","before the eyes was emptiness and behind the eyes emptiness","it was getting late". Man in his pride had violated the laws of nature and of the Creator. Yet according to the writer the real power over the world remained in the hand of God, and the only hope lay in a return to Christ and the patron saint of Bohemia and the traditional symbol of Czech national feeling, St Wenceslas.

In these two long poems Zahradníček's poetic techniques differ from those he had used in the past. Perfection of form and melody are absent and there is no regular rhyme. In places his language is almost satirical – as in "přízrak štěničných měst" (the spectre of bug-infested towns), "pan Kráva" (Mr Cow). Other poems are more like prayers or odes. Alternating times and motifs allow his work to express a host of different meanings.

Two other spiritually orientated poets who should be mentioned are IVAN SLAVÍK and JAN KAMENÍK. Both came to literature later, at the end of the war and after it. Ivan Slavík was also a translator and essayist. Jan Kameník (own name Ludmila Macešková) was about the same age as Seifert but she did not begin writing poetry till she was older and her work was original, verging on the mystical. They were both able to publish their work for a short time in the sixties but only in the nineties could their poems be read in their entirety.

In the fifties, apart from literature with spiritual leanings, there was another significant trend in unpublished literature – the realistic portrayal of everyday life. If the Christian writers like Zahradníček, Durych and Reynek stressed the transcendental values that Marxist ideology officially "abolished", this school of writers took a provocative realistic look behind the scenes, a view completely incompatible with the official picture. These authors, Jiří Kolář, Jan Hanč and Jiřina Hauková, often used the poetics of *Group 42* (see pp. 15–16) – or were inspired by it, like Bohumil Hrabal and Josef Hiršal. Josef Škvorecký, Egon Bondy and Jan Zábrana were close to it and to a certain extent were also inspired by the surrealists.

A key figure among the unpublished writers was JIŘÍ KOLÁŘ (→ PROFILES). Although it was impossible for him to publish, he persisted in writing, basing his work on an authentic picture of everyday life that embodied the myth of modern civilization. Only a few of Kolář's close friends knew of his post-February coup poems in his poetic diary *Očitý svědek* (Eyewitness, 1949) and *Prométheova játra* (Prometheus' Guts, 1950). Nevertheless they made a deep impression – both by the originality of their form and the author's unwavering moral stance.

> Nemám už opravdu žádnou naději
> Nevím kde bych ji vzal
> A také mi ji nemá kdo dát

A přeci bych chtěl pracovat
Ještě víc než to činím
Psát
A dokonce
Odvažím-li se něco z toho co mi dala noc
Přečíst těm pěti nebo šesti přátelům
[. . .]
Neboť dnes večer nebo zítra
Nevím
Může přijít pán s odznakem nebo v kožáku
A učiní všemu konec[42]

I really have no more hope
And I wouldn't know where to get any
And I don't have anyone to give me any
And yet I should like to work
Even more than I am doing
To write
And even
If I dare, read to my five or six friends
What came to me in the night
[. . .]
For tonight or tomorrow
I don't know
A man with a badge or in a leather coat
Might come and put an end to it all

(*Prométheova játra* [Prometheus' Guts, 1950])

Some wide-ranging poems were also included in *Prométheova játra* which appeared for the first time in samizdat in 1979 and was published in Prague in 1990. In the introductory section the author linked together two texts, his own transcription of a single motif from Ladislav Klíma's terrible story and the short story by the Polish author Zofia Nałkowska about a woman who was shot dead escaping while being transported by the Nazis. The two texts are first transposed into verse and then combined. This part of the book is subtitled *Rod Genorův* (The Genor Dynasty). The closing section brings back the theme of the subtitle – this is a generation of tortured, tyrannized people.

Kolář turned to writing reflections on the nature of art and made various types of collages (→ PROFILES). By the fifties Jiří Kolář had surrounded himself with a group of friends who met at the famous "Kolář's table" in the Prague *Slavia* coffee house. Among them were the painter Kamil Lhoták, the musician Jan Rychlík and the poet and translator Josef Hiršal, whose work created a kind of rural interlude in the midst of the city-orientated poetry of *Group 42*, the poet, translator and essayist Emanuel Frynta, and the prose writer and translator Zdeněk Urbánek. Another group of younger writers, whose artistic outlook was very similar consisted of the prose writers Josef Jedlička, Josef Škvorecký and the all-round man of letters Jan Zábrana, who for a long time like many others was allowed to work only as a translator. The bulk of his own writing was not published till the nineties, after his death. JOSEF JEDLIČKA's short story *Kde život náš je v půli se svou poutí* (Where We Are Halfway through Life's Pilgrimage) was written in the mid-fifties but not published till 1966. JOSEF ŠKVORECKÝ'S (→ PROFILES) *Zbabělci* (published in English as *The Cowards*, 1970) was written between 1948 and 1949 (see pp. 51–52).

These authors tended to write, like Kolář, about the everyday experiences of the "ordinary" man. They looked at life from below like a hidden camera, producing pictures that were in sharp contrast to those in official literature, which presented a tidy view of life based on preconceived values. In contrast to the omniscient narrator, obligatory for officially published literature, these authors used a highly personalized subjective point of view. Other topics in opposition to the view of man as a purely social being and a product of his class began to emerge, especially those with erotic or existentialist elements. No longer trite and hackneyed, the language was highly individual, whether it was poetic as in Jedlička or the lively common Czech with vulgarisms to be found in Škvorecký, Zábrana and Jedlička too. JOSEF JEDLIČKA'S *Kde život náš je v půli se svou poutí* (Where We Are Halfway through Life's Pilgrimage – the title is a quotation from Dante's *Divine Comedy*) is set in the industrial zone of North Bohemia. On the basis of the author's own experience it describes postwar revolutionary enthusiasm and cruel disillusionment. It departs from the construction and linear development of the traditional novel. The author deliberately interrupts the flow of the narrative by inverting the order of events, adding sub-plots and flashbacks, including reflective passages, official documents, quotations and visions. The prose proceeds on "random" time and place levels. This image of the world sweeps away the illusion of ordered "objectivity", an essential characteristic of novels published officially and linked to clearly defined values.

In his texts VLADIMÍR VOKOLEK also made use of actual facts and events. A middle generation writer and friend of Jan Zahradníček, he had previously written poems with traditional spiritual tendencies but from the end of the forties Vokolek's literary principles changed. His novel *Tak pravil Švejk* (Thus Spoke Švejk, 1958–1959; published in 1995) exploits in an ironic fashion modern expressions and absurd contemporary situations. They are like the latterday mediaeval "praise of folly". Hašek's famous hero good soldier Švejk finds himself in the corridors of power of post-February socialism:

> "A Great Age is calling me from all quarters: Comrade Švejk! And am I supposed to act as if I did not hear the voice of the Great Age? Have I to go on putting up with this dull and dreary life? Here I am! I beg to report and stand to attention. Comrade Švejk, the voice of a Great Age is calling. Have you reported your percentages? What's to be done, friends? I don't deny it, I confess I haven't reported it, but I will."[43]

EGON BONDY, the pen name of Zbyněk Fišer chosen as a protest against Stalinist anti-Semitic propaganda, took nonconformism to the extreme in his poems. "Total Realism" for him meant the unvarnished account of an individual on the fringe of society, the use of quotations from contemporary sources, parodies, completely negating the regime's culture.[44] "Total Realism" became one of Bohumil Hrabal's poetic sources. Bondy and Hrabal were part of the group around the manuscript issues of *Půlnoc* (Midnight).[45] BOHUMIL HRABAL'S (→ PROFILES) pivotal works, the short poem *Krásná Poldi* (Beautiful Poldi, 1950) and his short story (Jarmilka, 1952) remained long unpublished or appeared in "innocuous" form, with anything controversial removed.

> "I hurried towards her and when I gazed at her she dropped her eyes. She was six months pregnant, she opened her mouth and again I realised half of her teeth were missing. But her very simplicity made her the loveliest of the lovely. I walked beside her and whispered: Jarmilka when are we going to get married? And she answered: When the shit hits the fan! I pretended to be outraged: So that's it, you don't love me any more? And without hesitating she said: No . . . because you are always rushing about as if your arse was on fire!" (Manuscript, spring 1952)[46]

> "I hurried towards her and looked her straight in the face till she dropped her eyes. She was six months pregnant and when she opened her mouth I noticed again that half her teeth were missing. But she was unaffected and that made her the loveliest of the lovely.
>
> I walked beside her and whispered: 'Well Jarmilka, when are we going to get married?'
>
> And she answered: 'When cow-pats grow flowers!'
>
> I said: 'You don't love me any more then?'
>
> She said firmly: 'No, because you are always running around Poldovka as if you had ants in your pants.'"[47]

Hrabal's poetic vision of the commonplace, the intermingling of reportage, poetry, coarseness and gruff tenderness, was formed at the very beginning of the "bleak" years. With Kolář's poetic diaries and Hrabal's writing the trend of "realism" reached its peak. In the mid-fifties there were some attempts to bring unofficial literature to the notice of the public. In the spring of 1955 for example the eighteen-year-old Václav Havel organized a gathering of young unpublished authors in the Arts Centre in Brno, entitled *Život je všude* (Life Is Everywhere). A year later Josef Hiršal and Jiří Kolář made an manuscript anthology of the same name to which the contributors were also Bohumil Hrabal, Josef Škvorecký using the pen name Pepýt, Milan Hendrych, Emil Juliš, Jan Zábrana, Václav Havel and Jiří Kuběna (it was finally published in 2005).[48]

After the February 1948 coup Czech surrealism, like the literature of the commonplace, was also driven underground.[49] This was the case of the prematurely deceased KAREL HYNEK. His writings, full of playful mysticism and black humour,[50] as were the works by the second-generation surrealist poet ZBYNĚK HAVLÍČEK, whose economical precise poetic language in *Stalinská epocha* (Stalin's Times) and *Kabinet doktora Caligariho* (The Cabinet of Dr Caligari) differs from the vibrant, associative flow of words in Vítězslav Nezval's (→ PROFILES) surrealist poems of the thirties. Although written in 1951 these poems first appeared in book form in a collection of his poems in 1994.[51] Havlíček draws on the erotic, and on contemporary science and technology for his metaphors. In order to express the strange kind of terror prevailing at the time he combines the purely abstract with the concrete, for example, "a pint of Marxism".

After the death of Karel Teige in 1951 VRATISLAV EFFENBERGER became the organizer and theoretician of the surrealist movement.[52] Surrealism was no longer perceived as sympathetic to the Communist revolution as it had been before the war. However, surrealist poetry, "concrete irrationality", could still stand as a rebellious, liberating force against the stark rationalism of industrial civilization.

Understandably the response to these unpublished works was very limited. Of course their authors, in a few pivotal works along with literature in exile and isolated works of official literature, kept alive the culture that the Stalinist regime was brutally suppressing. They also kept alive, albeit within a limited circle, an awareness of moral values. From the end of the fifties they found their way into journals and publishing houses and changed the face of literature.

5. Signs of the Thaw

Even official literature published at home was conservative in character but in a totally different sense from the conservatism of literature in exile. Criticism degenerated into a variety of empty phrases about "the new man" and "a new life". In practice, however, the old descriptive type of writing, abounding in moralizing platitudes intended to illustrate conventional modes of behaviour, was strongly encouraged. Ideology found its way into every sphere of life, the most personal not excepted, so that after a few years even some appeals to the public, intended to be taken seriously, merely sounded ridiculous.

Já nemohu zpívat skromně,
radostí jsem bez sebe,
představte si, že se do mě
zamiloval SNB.[53]

I cannot be modest,
I am beside myself with joy,
just think
a policeman has fallen in love with me.

(Pavel Kohout, *Čas lásky a boje* [A Time of Love and Struggle], 1954)

A more significant critical debate about the poems of PAVEL KOHOUT (→ PROFILES), indicative of the decline of dogmatism, was already taking place during 1954 and 1955 in the newly founded Brno review *Host do domu* (A Guest in the House). Kohout's poems were still highly regarded when the young critic, later novelist, JAN TREFULKA openly criticized their deficiences – shallow optimism, platitudes, rich but empty language. He claimed that "neither political correctness nor enthusiasm are in themselves virtues in poetry". He even pointed out that modern Czech poets like Antonín Sova, František Halas, Jaroslav Seifert and František Hrubín were excluded from the secondary school syllabus.

Trefulka was supported in the debate by other literary figures, most notably by JAN SKÁCEL (→ PROFILES and see pp. 44–45), who became a well-known poet in the sixties (see p. 73). Skácel wrote that Trefulka "had saved Czech criticism from the suspicion that under certain circumstances it was deaf and dumb". Others bitterly opposed Trefulka and Skácel and accused them of lacking ideology and party loyalty.[54] As a result measures were taken to penalize the authors writing for *Host do domu*. One of the editors, Ludvík Kundera, and a member of the editorial board, Oldřich Mikulášek, (→ PROFILES) resigned, but the debate itself was an early indication of the "Thaw".

A few years previously JAROSLAV SEIFERT (→ PROFILES) and his lyric poem *Píseň o Viktorce* (The Story of Viktorka, 1950) had been the target of criticism that bordered on open condemnation. In this work the poet developed his perennial theme of love and nostalgia. Viktorka is a tragic, romantic, proto-feminist figure in the 1853 classic Czech novel *Babička* by Božena Němcová (translated as *The Grandmother*, 1891). In *Píseň o Viktorce*, Viktorka's predicament merges with that of Němcová. Yet this tender lyrical poetry was taken to be hostile to socialism. It was probably only through the intervention of his old friend Vítězslav Nezval that Seifert was saved from severe repercussions. In those years VÍTĚZSLAV NEZVAL'S (→ PROFILES) behaviour was inconsistent. On the one hand he praised Stalin, Gottwald and Štoll, on the other he energetically supported Jaroslav Seifert, Jakub Deml, František Langer and Jiří Kolář. The standard of Nezval's poetry deteriorated appreciably, yet a poem like *Moře* (The Sea) in the book of poetry *Chrpy a města* (Cornflowers and Cities, 1955) retained traces of the avant-garde poetics to which young poets like Milan Kundera, Miroslav Florian and Jiří Šotola could relate. VILÉM ZÁVADA was never a Communist believer, but accepted the ideology for opportunist reasons. Nevertheless he displayed great personal courage in helping writers and their families who were being persecuted, as for example when he testified for the imprisoned Bedřich Fučík. Some of the poems in the collection *Polní kvítí* (Field Flowers, 1955), in which Závada used the four-lined stanzas like Jan Neruda's classic 19th-century work *Prosté motivy* (Simple Themes), were similar in mood to the poetry of the group of the younger poets, *Květen* (see pp. 45–47).

In the early part of the fifties only a few of the works published managed to overcome the restrictions in force. Among them were the novels of ADOLF BRANALD. His two-part novel *Severní nádraží* (The North Station, 1949) and *Lazaretní vlak* (Hospital Train, 1950) are about the German occupation, the resistance and the May uprising in the main station in Prague, the model for which was Masaryk Station where the author worked. Branald succeeded in conveying the prevailing mood of the railway workers through many interesting, true-to-life, dramatic details reminiscent of Karel Čapek. The same skills were also evident in his novel *Chléb a písně* (Bread and Songs, 1952), set in the second half of the 19th century. Another remarkable historical novel was VLADIMÍR NEFF'S *Srpnovští páni* (The Lords of Srpnov, 1953) which by its irony and humour departed from the current vogue. That same year in the theatre VÁCLAV JELÍNEK attempted to satirize the new bureaucracy. His play *Skandál v obrazárně* (Scandal in the Picture Gallery) was the most frequently staged one that entire season but it was removed from the repertoire. Both LADISLAV FIKAR, in his inventive translation of Stepan Shchipachev's poems (1952), and Václav Krška in his film adaptations of the anarchist early 20th-century poet Fráňa Šrámek's works,[55] retained at least in part the natural and erotic lyricism that had been squeezed out of poetry.

Halfway between dogmatism and real literature were KAREL PTÁČNÍK's novel *Ročník jedenadvacet* (1954, filmed by Václav Gajer, 1957; published in English as *Born 1921*, 1965), which described, without the regulation heroism, the lives of young Czechs forced to work in German industry during the war, and JAN OTČENÁŠEK's *Občan Brych* (Citizen Brych, 1955), which presented a more complicated psychological picture of a "vacillating" intellectual. NORBERT FRÝD went further in his novel *Krabice živých* (1956, published in English as *A Box of Lives,* 1962). Drawing on his own experience he portrayed life in a German concentration camp unemotionally and with detachment, telling the story from different points of view. Of course his hero, following in the footsteps of Ptáčník's Karel and Otčenášek's Brych, had definite political aspirations. PAVEL KOHOUT'S (→ PROFILES) play about the army, *Zářijové noci* (September Nights), had its first performance in 1955 when it aroused great interest. It was filmed by Vojtěch Jasný in 1957. Audiences saw it as a daring criticism of the current situation. Nevertheless, the conflict was finally resolved in a clichéd fashion, that is, by the arrival of a wise superior. Understandably, with time works of this kind had less impact, but in their day they were a significant development, breaking through the rigid standards prevailing at the beginning of the fifties.

In 1955 Vítězslav Nezval caused a sensation with his spirited defence of Guillaume Apollinaire in the *Literární noviny* (Literary News) and immediately afterwards, inspired by Nezval, MILAN KUNDERA (→ PROFILES) wrote a highly significant defence of modern art. He spoke not only of Nezval's avant-gardism but also of Paul Valéry, Boris Pasternak and Vladimír Holan. Like all contemporary debate, Kundera's thinking was circumscribed by the concept of "socialist art". However, he included far more in his concept of "socialist art" than Ladislav Štoll in his speech.

At that time some writers who had been totally or occasionally banned like Vladimír Holan, Jaroslav Durych, Jakub Deml, Jaroslav Seifert, František Hrubín and František Langer, started to come to the notice of the public. In the late fifties they were followed by Edvard Valenta, Jiří Weil and by Jiří Kolář with a single book. František Halas's last book *A co?* (What Now?; see p. 9) and a large selection from Jiří Orten's *Deníky* (Diaries, 1958) also caused a commotion. When a new edition of Voskovec's and Werich's plays was published, JAN WERICH attempted to re-establish links with the prewar *Osvobozené divadlo* (Liberated Theatre) and to renew, at least in part, his intellectual buffoonery and satire.

Once severed, these links were slow to be re-established and were not fully restored till the end of the sixties.

1 Vítězslav Nezval (1900–1958) by Adolf Hoffmeister (1930)

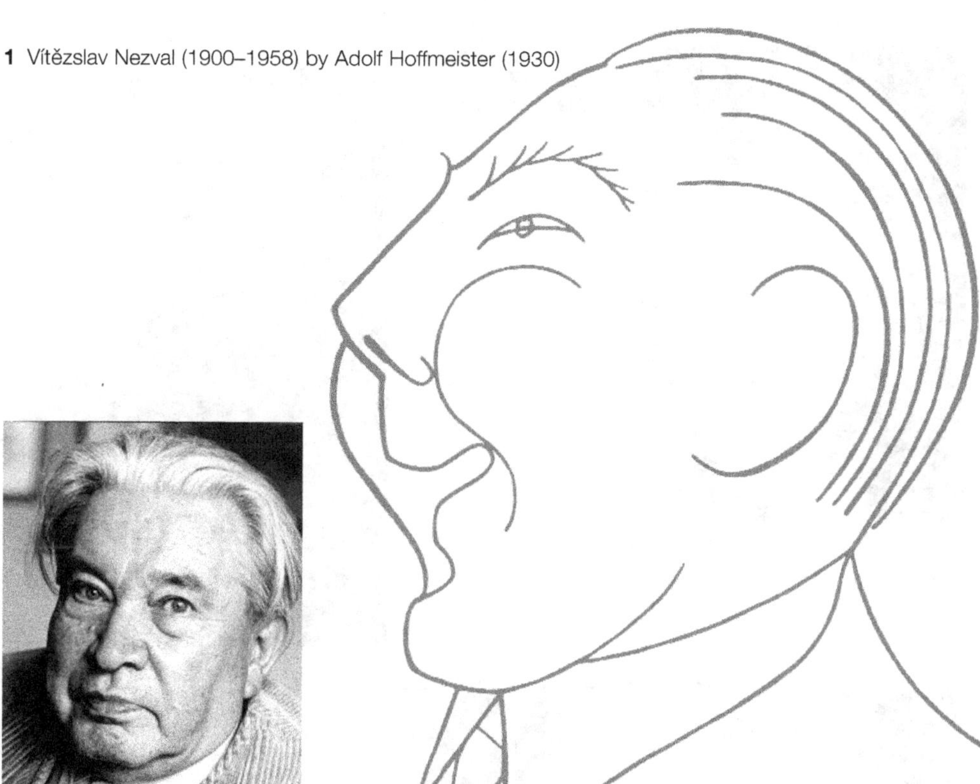

2 Jaroslav Seifert (1901–1986) in the 1970s (Milan Jankovič)

3 František Halas (1901–1949), his wife and his sons (1949, Dagmar Hochová)

4 František Hrubín (1910–1971) in 1960 (Dagmar Hochová)

5 Vladimír Holan (1905–1980) in the early 1970s (Milan Jankovič)

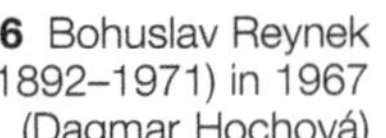

6 Bohuslav Reynek (1892–1971) in 1967 (Dagmar Hochová)

7 Oldřich Mikulášek (1910–1985) in 1977 (Milan Jankovič)

8 Jan Skácel (1922–1989) in 1967 (Dagmar Hochová)

10 Miroslav Holub by Had'ák (Miroslav Lid'ák, 1964)

11 Arnošt Lustig (1926) in 1990 (Viktor Stoilov)

9 Miroslav Holub (1923–1998) in the 1960s (Dagmar Hochová)

12 A poster for *Démanty noci* (Diamonds in the Night), a film by Jan Němec (1964) inspired by Lustig's story *Tma nemá stín* (Darkness Casts No Shadow) (Jiří Svoboda)

13 Josef Škvorecký (1924) and his wife Zdena Salivarová (1933) in 1997 (Dagmar Hochová)

14 Bohumil Hrabal (1914–1997) in the early 1970s (Milan Jankovič)

The Thaw

1. The Decline of Stalinism

The second half of the fifties is often called the "Thaw", an idea coming from the Russian novel of the same name by Ilya Ehrenburg. Although it is not exactly the best of that author's work, it is associated with the decline of Stalinism. The 20th Congress of the Soviet Communist Party at the beginning of 1956 became a sensation world-wide when Nikita Khrushchev for the first time openly condemned the huge-scale illegal persecutions during the Stalin era. Of course he explained away Stalinism as a "deformation" and "the cult of personality", a wrong turning on the right road to Communism. This more moderate outlook brought about great changes in all the socialist states in Europe. The most uncompromising stage of the cold war came to an end and introduced a time of "peaceful rivalry" between East and West resulting in the first rehabilitation of victims, including artists. In the course of 1956 roughly half of the 10 million prisoners in Soviet Gulags were released.

In Czechoslovakia it was the writers who spoke out loudest. At the 2nd Congress of the Czechoslovak Writers' Union in the spring of 1956, not long after Khrushchev's speech in Moscow, two poets in particular, František Hrubín and Jaroslav Seifert, openly criticized the politics of culture. FRANTIŠEK HRUBÍN (→ PROFILES) compared the plight of Czech poetry to an icebound swan saying, "Let us live and work in such a way that people do not turn away from us [. . .], so that they think of us as true creative artists who cannot be corrupted by anyone or anything."[56] JAROSLAV SEIFERT (→ PROFILES) spoke of the fate of writers who were in prison and those who were being persecuted. He called for the righting of wrongs and demanded that literature should once again become the conscience of the nation.[57] The students soon followed the writers. In Slovak Bratislava and later in Prague the university students came out on to the streets on traditional rag days demanding the freedom of the press and democracy in political life.

That same year 1956 the "absurd" satire by the Slovak DOMINIK TATARKA, *Démon súhlasu* (The Demon of Conformism), caused a sensation when it was published in journal form (it was 1963 before it was expanded and published as a book). It analyzed the decline of moral awareness in people that the post-February regime had been encouraging: "A poet from any age, even one from our own time, cannot do otherwise: he must defend people against the abuse of power. Against divine power he must uphold the inalienable right of personality."[58]

A number of writers and theoreticians attempted to come to terms with literary dogmatism. Most however remained enthralled by the ideological conception of art. One of the few who consistently talked of a "crisis in literature" was JAN GROSSMAN. He wrote about the suppression of individuality and originality and the prevailing categorization of things as black or white in terms that were nothing but empty phrases, so that, for example, for many students three individuals, the Slovak Robin Hood Juraj Jánošík, the Czech farmer and leader of the peasant uprising by the West Bohemia tribe of "Chod" people Jan Kozina, and the early 20th-century poet-rebel Petr Bezruč merged into a single entity. In other words they learned the same thing about all three – "they fought against their masters".

> "Basically this demonstrated the attempt, already mentioned, to prevent any experiments in the relationship of literature to its subject matter, any investigation where the results are not known in advance and which might be on a collision course with dogma. [. . .] Literary works as works of art are surely more than just means of gaining knowledge about the world. But in this period, literature ceased to be regarded as art. A literary work became in effect the authority and the documentation for a study of the class war." (Jan Grossman, O krizi v literatuře [The Crisis in Literature], *Nový život* [A New Life], 1956)[59]

So consistent criticism of dogmatism developed into criticism of the politics of class as the main standard by which the arts and sciences were judged. This was also the view of the philosophical discussions in *Literární noviny* (Literary News) in 1956. IVAN SVITÁK demanded forcefully that "theory should be free of propaganda". He went on to write that "it is no longer possible to set facts at naught, the discrepancy between ideological and scientific thinking will certainly come to light in the end".[60] KAREL KOSÍK and JOSEF ZUMR advocated a return to Hegelian dialectics and rejected "the domination of ideology in Marxism".[61] In the review *Květen* (May) JOSEF VOHRYZEK went as far as to repudiate ideology in state publications.

It was not long before the dogmatists counter-attacked. They were encouraged by the bloody suppression of the anti-Communist uprising in Budapest, the retreat of the Polish reformers, the Suez Crisis and the tougher line taken subsequently by the Soviets. The Conference of the Union of Czechoslovak Writers in 1959 was again under the direction of LADISLAV ŠTOLL.[62] A new wave of vetting followed. In particular the purge affected literature in the most important Prague publishing house *Československý spisovatel* (Czechoslovak Writers' Publishing

House) which the director Ladislav Fikar, deputy director Vítězslav Kocourek and the editors Jan Grossman, Josef Hiršal and Kamil Bednář were forced to leave. Texts by Bohumil Hrabal that were ready for publication were banned. Alfréd Radok's second programme for the *Laterna magika* (Magic Lantern), an imaginative combination of theatre, film and dance,[63] was also banned. The poems of František Halas and Jiří Orten with Grossman's essays had already been subjected to severe criticism on ideological grounds. A fierce campaign was also launched against Josef Škvorecký's *Zbabělci* (The Cowards, see 51–52).

Of course the methods of repression used at the end of the fifties were not as cruel as after the February 1948 coup. Most of the people affected were allowed to go on working in other branches of the arts. LADISLAV FIKAR became chief literary adviser to the state film industry and helped to create the "New Wave" in Czech cinematography in the sixties. ALFRÉD RADOK produced several outstanding performances in the *Městská divadla pražská* (Municipal Theatres in Prague). JAN GROSSMAN became artistic director of the *Divadlo Na zábradlí* (Theatre on the Balustrade) and contributed substantially to its fame throughout Europe. And after 1962 a new, more widespread spirit of relaxation came into being.

From the mid-fifties contacts were gradually renewed, albeit with considerable difficulty, with world culture. Theatres put on plays by Bertolt Brecht although their poetic theory clashed with the illusion of realism that had been obligatory till then. The Russian writers Sergei Esenin and Isaac Babel, even the emigrant Ivan Bunin were again published. So Western literature was no longer limited to what was seen in Czechoslovakia as "Socialist Realist" authors. Other "progressive writers", in the terminology of the day, like the German Heinrich Böll, the Italian Alberto Moravia, the British Graham Greene and the Americans Ernest Hemingway, William Faulkner and Robinson Jeffers were published. The Prague publishing house *SNKLHU* (The State Publishing House for Literature, Music and Art) – the name was later changed to *Odeon* – and the review *Světová literatura* (World Literature) were chiefly responsible. In 1958 Josef Hiršal's translation of Christian Morgenstern and Franz Kafka's *Trial* in the translation by Pavel Eisner came out. At the same time Zdeněk Urbánek's translations of William Faulkner and James Joyce were published. These works allowed a little light to appear on the cultural horizon after years of darkness. They acted as an inspiration and a challenge to the arts at home.

2. Poetry

Of all the poets who returned to literature FRANTIŠEK HRUBÍN (→ PROFILES) became the most acclaimed at the time. In the years following the bitter criticism of *Hirošima* (see p. 9), he was allowed to publish nothing but poems for children – which were better than anyone else had produced in this genre[64] – and translations. In 1956 *Můj zpěv* (My Song) was published; it was a book that, after a gloomy, depressing beginning, leads on to harmony with man, the works of man and nature. Hrubín's poem *Proměna* (Metamorphosis) had been written earlier than *Můj zpěv*, but was not published until 1957, in a limited edition, and then again in a regular edition in 1958. *Proměna* relates to *Hirošima*, pointing out the precariousness of life and the threat to human existence. One ordinary summer Sunday afternoon news of new atomic bomb tests filters through to Prague on the Vltava river. This situation is interwoven into the ancient tale of the flight of Daedalus and Icarus which ended with the fall and death of Icarus.

Proměna was originally written in prose. In fact it was to prose that Hrubín often turned in his last creative phase from the end of the fifties until the end of his life. In 1958 his prose poem *U stolu* (At Table) appeared. This is a book of memoirs that in a single afternoon manages to portray the whole world of childhood and the countryside.

Very different in every way was OLDŘICH MIKULÁŠEK (→ PROFILES), a poet of the middle generation. He brought to poetry an intensity stemming from personal experience, an unsophisticated dramatic quality, the ambience of South Moravia and Brno as a counterpart to Prague, the Sázava basin and the South Bohemian ponds of František Hrubín. The collection *Ortely a milosti* (Judgment and Mercy, 1958) that he had begun in the forties is based on the tension of opposing concepts – death, emptiness, tormenting sensuality, the greyness of conventiality as opposed to the "red glow" of passion, the intoxication of love, wine, the beauty of a woman's body, the pulsating rhythm of the blood, the giddiness of the dance. *Ortely a milosti* includes the poem *Vyvolavač* (The Town Crier) that was strongly criticized at the time for its so-called "hopeless sensuality". The town crier of the title, like a demon tempter, seeks his victims among the poorest of the poor and offers them death; but even they spurn death and prefer what could be a life of despair.[65]

Whilst the poetry in Hrubín's *Můj zpěv* flowed smoothly, in *Ortely a milosti* the versification is irregular and in the key section *Judgment* it is particularly rugged. The numerous repetitions and variations do not result in a harmonious whole as they do in, for instance, Hrubín's poem *Zpěv lásky a života* (A Song of Life and Love). The diversity of Mikulášek's style, ranging from a characteristic poetic language to neologisms and colloquialisms, common Czech, dialect and snatches of folk songs, matches perfectly his vision of the world as full of contradictions at odds with each other.

The source of inspiration for the poetry of Mikulášek's younger friend JAN SKÁCEL (→ PROFILES) was also Moravia, Moravian Slovakia and the Highlands (Vysočina). His poetry is milder in tone, its drama is more implicit and the love element only suggested. His very first book of poetry, *Kolik příležitostí má růže* (The Many Occasions of a Rose, 1957) portrays a world founded on the traditional values of home and a childhood spent in the country. Man is present throughout the whole world of nature and the countryside itself is part of man.

> Dnes hosty mám,
> mám hosty.
> Dnes na návštěvu přišla ke mně růže.

Dej, bože, ať jsem nehledaný, prostý
jak drahý šperk,
jak v bitce nahý nůž,
a v srdci čisto je jak ve skleničce.[66]

Today I've visitors,
I've visitors!
Today I had a visit from a rose.
Lord, let me be unlooked-for, simple
like a precious jewel,
like a bare knife in a brawl,
and pure in heart as a sparkling glass.[67]

Skácel does not use rhyme nor does he overwhelm the reader with images. Instead he looks for deeper meanings and forces the reader to think.

Léty jsem zmoudřel.
Co je moudrost – nevím.[68]

With the years I acquired wisdom.
But what wisdom is – I do not know.
(*Co zbylo z anděla* [What Has Remained of the Angel], 1960)

Mikulášek and Skácel further developed František Halas's conception of Czech lyricism, which prefers "the greatness of doubt" to "the triviality of certainty" and which the politics of culture anathematized after the February 1948 coup as "the poetry of an epoch of corruption, disease and destruction". Thanks to Ludvík Kundera, Halas's last collection *A co?* (What Now?) was published in 1957 eight years after the poet's death. That same year Halas's complete works were also published.[69]

During the "Thaw" a group of writers with their own aesthetic programme became known to the public for the first time since 1948. These were the authors who came together in connection with the review *Květen* (May) published between 1955 and 1959. They could be considered the younger war generation, for Jiří Šotola and Miroslav Holub, for instance, had published their first poems during the war and immediately afterwards; or they might be thought of as a transitional generation belonging to the period between the war and the sixties.The most important members of the group were Jiří Šotola, Miroslav Holub, Miroslav Florian, Karel Šiktanc and Josef Brukner. The prose writers had a less distinctive style; nevertheless Karel Ptáčník, Ivan Klíma, Arnošt Lustig, Josef Nesvadba and others, including even Ludvík Vaculík and Ladislav Fuks, also published in *Květen*. Their ideas were given wider publicity by the critics Jaroslav Boček, Josef Vohryzek, Miroslav Červenka.

Like the Soviet "New Wave" authors Yevgeny Evtushenko and Andrei Voznesensky and the young Polish writers Tadeusz Różewicz and Slawomir Mrożek, those associated with *Květen* rejected the superficial rhetoric of post-

February literature. Miroslav Holub proclaimed instead the truth of the "everyday" and Jiří Šotola talked of the experience of "simple, everyday life". These ideas were much closer to the neo-realism of contemporary Italian film. They stressed the importance of depicting reality in detailed, concrete terms and not in generalities. They changed the norms of poetic expression. Unlike the melodious regular versification that had been the norm, they deliberately used less rigid forms, often going so far as to use free verse.[70]

The very titles of MIROSLAV HOLUB'S (→ PROFILES) first books, *Denní služba* (Daily Duty, 1958) and *Achilles a želva* (Achilles and the Tortoise, 1960), are pregnant with meaning. *Večer v laboratoři* (Evening in the Laboratory), published in the first year of the review *Květen*, *Budík* (The Alarm Clock) and *Uzávěrka* (Deadline) appear generally "unpoetic". The poems have neither rhyme nor rhythm; they rely on nouns and verbs and dispense completely with decorative attributes. Describing laboratories and operating theatres was an innovation in Czech poetry. Here Miroslav Holub was basing his work on his professional background. Unlike the majority of literary figures, Holub had studied medicine and for many years worked as a biologist. The unassuming creativity of the author's heroes makes the world around them a more humane place and becomes accepted as a virtue.

V mikroskopu

I tady jsou krajiny snící,
měsíční, opuštěné.
I tady jsou zástupy
polem pracující.
A buňky, bojovníci,
pro všechno na světě
životy kladou.

I tady jsou hřbitovy,
sláva a sníh.
A slyším hukot
bouření stavů nesmírných.[71]

In the Microscope

Here too are dreaming landscapes,
lunar, derelict.
Here too are the masses
tillers of the soil.
And cells, fighters
who lay down their lives
for a song.

Here too are cemeteries,
fame and snow.
And I hear murmuring,

the revolt of immense estates.[72]
(translated by Ian Milner)

The "town" poet Holub is very like the "country" poet Skácel in his economy of expression and his insistence on moral responsibility. Other contributors to *Květen* continued to write more in the style of Vítězslav Nezval and in the tradition of poetism and Czech avant-garde poetry. This is true of MIROSLAV FLORIAN and particularly of JIŘÍ ŠOTOLA. Compared to Holub, Šotola is more personal and romantic. He aspires to write "the great poem", to understand the multifarious trends in the contemporary world, to be a witness for his generation.

Co že jsme chtěli? – jít, kde není stop.
Nedožít konce. Nikde nemít hrob.
Navrtat mraky. Padat dolů.
Za rudým květem běžet k pólu.
A urvat aspoň metr, aspoň hrst
země, jiež dosud nedotkl se lidský prst.
Zadarmo. Mlčky. Tak jak roste strom a jako vlna pluje.
A nečekat,
až někdo poděkuje.[73]

What did we desire? – To tread where no foot has trod.
To reach no end. To have no grave.
To drill through the clouds. To fall down.
To hasten beyond the red glow to the pole.
To grab at least a metre, a handful
of earth, untouched as yet by human hand.
Free of charge. Silently. As the tree grows and the wave flows.
And not to wait
for thanks from anyone.
(Jiří Šotola, *Svět náš vezdejší* [Our Everyday World], 1957)

MILAN KUNDERA (→ PROFILES) was not a professed supporter of the *Květen* writers. However, his collection, *Monology* (Monologues, 1957) subtitled "Kniha o lásce" (A Book about Love), which he revised in 1964 and again in 1965, had much in common with them, rejecting previously accepted certainties and positive values and portraying a complex inner world. Here sexual love is no longer conventionally treated as an idyll. As in Šotola, the bitterness and rapture spring from personal experience. EDUARD PETIŠKA was another contemporary of Šotola and Holub, whose work was on similar lines. The poems in his book *Okamžiky* (Moments, 1957), austere tales set in a hospital, try to present morality without sentimentality. This ethical dimension is also evident in Petiška's other works, psychological novels with a lyrical sub-text, adaptations of Bible stories, Greek legends and books for children. Even JOSEF KAINAR'S (→ PROFILES) poetry was similar to the poetry of the everyday – but at the end of the decade he gradually returned to his own down-to-earth, plebeian viewpoint: *Člověka hořce mám rád* (I Love Man – Bitterly, 1959).

The poetic naïvety of MILOŠ MACOUREK, modelled on Jacques Prévert's, *Člověk by nevěřil svým očím* (You Couldn't Believe Your Eyes, 1958), brought him close to *Květen*. The *Květen* group was however moved by different influences. The lyrics for the songs of Jiří Suchý, Jaroslav Jakoubek and Pavel Kopta were associated with the revival of jazz and the start of "the fringe theatres".

In their day all these works seemed provocatively different from post-February 1948 literature and for that reason alone were open to criticism. Kundera's *Monology* was accused of "cynicism"; a party official called Holub's poetry "a weed among the flowers of Czech poetry". The review *Květen* was shut down in 1959. In retrospect, especially if we compare *Group 42* (see pp. 15–16) and the unpublished texts of the fifties, it is easy to see the connection with the official, "constructive" phase in poetry, from which the writers in *Květen* had controversially dissociated themselves. Turning to everyday life for inspiration mostly did not mean giving up optimism and encouragement or the basic assumption that man is above all a social being and must act in harmony with history. Gradually individual contributors to *Květen* and others sympathetic to them, such as Milan Kundera, Ivan Klíma and Ludvík Vaculík, abandoned these notions. As early as 1957 the most perceptive critic of the *Květen* circle, Josef Vohryzek, had written:

> " . . . there are two ways of persisting with dogmatism: by repeating dogmas and their 'contradictions'. [. . .] Asking new questions without analysing existing dogma simply means creating new dogma. At the same time, analysis without asking new questions is nothing but the analysis of dogma [. . .], which is pointless, just as it is pointless to criticize dogma on the grounds of dogmatism."[74]

3. Drama and the Theatre

There was also a revival in drama and the theatre. No longer in vogue were the naïve political "factory plays" where the climax was reached with the exposure of sabotage by some elaborate strategy and the hero joining the party. Characters in plays were now more complicated and plots less simplistic. One example of this trend was *Inteligenti* (The Intellectuals) by MILAN JARIŠ, which was first produced in 1955 and reworked in 1957. Even more important was PAVEL KOHOUT'S (→ PROFILES) *Taková láska* (Such Great Love),[75] which had its first performance in 1957 and was the first postwar Czech drama to win international recognition in the West. The subject did not receive conventional treatment; it is a play about love, disappointment, unattributed guilt and about judgment not based on accepted norms. The action goes round in a circle starting with the tragic unexplained death of a young woman. The author uses several anti-illusory devices – a play within a play, the repetition of key scenes with the same dialogue but in a new semantic situation – to show that reality can be understood on various levels and that relations between people are not necessarily what they seem. *Taková láska* continues the tradition of the problem drama current between the wars. In particular it is in the tradition of František Langer, a new edition of whose plays was published at the time.[76]

Another movement in the theatre was the restoration of satire. After the war the *Divadlo satiry* (Satirical Theatre) in Prague had cultivated a number of young talented writers – authors such as Josef Kainar, Vratislav Blažek and others, but after the February 1948 coup and the staging of Blažek's play *Kde je Kuťák?* (Where Is Kuťák?, 1948), the theatre was closed. In practical terms this meant that satire itself was abolished. Certainly criticism called for satire and was welcome as long as it meant attacks on the past and on the West. Satire of the current day had to be "constructive" and "positive".[77]

At the end of the fifties VRATISLAV BLAŽEK again used satire in the true sense of the word. The play that initiated the revival of satire was his *Třetí přání* (Three Wishes) that was given its first performance in 1958. It was originally written for a film directed by Ján Kadár and Elmar Klos but the film did not pass the censor and was not shown till 1963. It was based on the well-known subject of fairy-tales, the granting and fulfilling of wishes, but the action takes place in the present day within an ordinary Czech family. An old man with magic powers grants the hero three wishes. Young Peter, in somewhat unfairy-tale style, wishes for a flat, a car and promotion in his job. The fulfilment of the three wishes, however, creates problems. The message of the work is that one must actively fight for one's individual rights, not relying on help from a fairy-tale old man or anyone else. The same device, the surprise entry of a supernatural being into normal present-day life, was later used by Karel Michal in his satirical stories *Bubáci pro všední den* (Weekday Ghosts, 1961, see p. 103). It may well have been first used by Karel Čapek in his fairy-tales. Another of Blažek's plays, *Příliš štědrý večer* (Too Much Christmas Eve, 1960), graphically highlights the contradiction between the ideals people profess and what they actually do. One of the characters who had personally suffered from the injustice of the regime says, "Not even a thousand honest people by merely taking delight in being honest can stand up against a single hypocrite who takes action."[78]

Eventually good plays with true dramatic content began to be staged. Plays about industrial production, plays of village life and historical plays had been based exclusively on ideology, and even this was reduced to its simplest form. From the end of the fifties and in the sixties symbolism, metaphor and hyperbole came to be used more and more. Drama dropped its patronizing, moralizing tone. Traditional methods of construction and oversimplification were abandoned. Like the avant-gardists before the war, dramatists made full use of epic and lyric sources. FRANTIŠEK HRUBÍN'S (→ PROFILES) *Srpnová neděle* (A Sunday in August, filmed by Otakar Vávra, 1960) in Otomar Krejča's 1958 production in the *National Theatre*, Milan Kundera's *Majitelé klíčů* (The Owners of the Keys, 1962) and JOSEF TOPOL'S stylized poetic plays (see pp. 101–102) were clear indications of the direction drama was taking. It was beginning to have more in common with cinematography, cabaret, jazz and musicals. By 1957, in the *Reduta* (Reduta Theatre) in Prague, IVAN VYSKOČIL and JIŘÍ SUCHÝ were organizing "text-appeals"– a word that Vyskočil created jokingly from sex-appeal. These were variety shows with poetry, practical jokes, sketches, short stories and songs. A year later *Divadlo Na zábradlí* (The Theatre on the Balustrade) came into being and the next year the theatre *Semafor* opened, also in Prague. These were the first of the famous little or fringe theatres.

The theatre and the views of actors and directors now had much greater influence than in the past. Typical of the day was the director ALFRÉD RADOK, who was the driving force behind the creation of the *Laterna magika* (Magic Lantern), an imaginative combination of theatre and film, which had enjoyed great success at the World Exhibition in Brussels in 1958.[79] Radok surrounded himself with talented collaborators, among them Vladimír Svitáček, Ján Roháč, Miloš Forman, who later became an internationally respected film director, and Václav Havel. The Magic Lantern's second programme was inspired partly by the cantata *Otvírání studánek* (Opening of the Wells) by Miloslav Bureš and Bohuslav Martinů. It was however banned by the Cultural Council of the Central Committee of the Communist Party of Czechoslovakia. Josef Hiršal, who was working at the time with the Magic Lantern, gave an account of what happened:

> "Václav Kopecký was the first to speak. [. . .] 'You've lost, Radok, you've lost. Your programme is a mess, it's dull and it's not our kind of thing. Floating images! You should be showing the great achievements of Communism, our present, our successes and not your *Wells*. What kind of feelings do they inspire? Sadness, hopelessness. That's not our idea of life! [. . .] To let us down like that! And what about that girl going about with that jug to fetch water?' A depressed Radok answered: 'What's in these Springs is a symbol of cleanliness, Comrade deputy. Cleanliness, for nothing can live without it.' 'Away with you, that's just fancy talk! [. . .] Away with you, after all that's what Láďa here has criticized you for. Láďa is our greatest critic. That's right, isn't it Láďa?' He turned to Ladislav Štoll. [. . .] Štoll detached himself from the circle and came up to Radok: 'Comrade Radok,' he said, 'you obviously think we're all stupid, that we don't understand your programme and have nothing to say to you about it. But you're wrong, you know. Every one of these thirty comrades here has his own opinion and has plenty of experience. Your programme is thoroughly unsuitable. As our Comrade deputy so rightly put it: It's not our kind of thing. [. . .] No, no, Comrade Radok, it's not just irresponsible, it's bad and ideologically nothing short of pernicious.'"[80]

4. Prose

At the end of the fifties and the beginning of the sixties, Czech prose still lagged behind poetry and drama. This was understandable for the novel in particular was directly connected with contemporary intellectual and political movements. After the "Thaw" at the end of the fifties and the beginning of the sixties, Stalinism was restored and the arts were continually subjected to strict censorship. In this unsettled atmosphere there was a real but short-lived spurt of activity in essays, short stories and novels.

Two remarkable novels published at that time in Bohemia were Edvard

Valenta's *Jdi za zeleným světlem* (Follow the Green Light, 1956) and Josef Škvorecký's *Zbabělci* (1958; published in English as *The Cowards*, 1970). Both novels had been written during the "freeze" by novelists who either were not allowed, or did not wish to publish after the February 1948 coup. EDVARD VALENTA belonged to the older generation who had worked on the editorial staff of the famous *Lidové noviny* (The People's Paper), a liberal-democratic daily for which Karel and Josef Čapek and other authors wrote in the interwar period. His journalistic training is clearly evident in the clarity of his prose and his interesting plots. After the war Valenta became strongly committed to the defence of democracy in Ferdinand Peroutka's (→ PROFILES) *Dnešek* (Today), and was imprisoned from 1948 to 1949. Josef Škvorecký (→ PROFILES) was one of the younger members of the "war" generation. Throughout the fifties he worked as an editor and translator of American literature. He was one of the authors whose unpublished manuscripts circulated among small groups of people. In the early fifties, besides *Zbabělci* he finished his collection of stories *Konec nylonového věku* (The End of the Nylon Era), which was published in 1967, and the novel *Tankový prapor* (The Tank Battalion; published in English as *The Republic of Whores*, 1993), which was not published in Czech till 1971 in Toronto.

Edvard Valenta's *Jdi za zeleným světlem*, set during the occupation, had already dealt a blow to the stereotyped patterns of previous years. The author concentrated on the psychological analysis of character and used inner monologue to reveal his characters' innermost thoughts, moving skilfully between first person and objective third person narrative. With no omniscient narrator other devices had to be used. It could no longer be assumed that reality could be described in simple unambiguous terms. The main character in Valenta's novel is a writer and an intellectual, at a crisis in his life like Brych, in the officially approved novel by Jan Otčenášek *Občan Brych* (Citizen Brych, 1955, see p. 36).[81] Like Brych, the novel also contains several autobiographical features. Unlike Brych, however, Valenta's Šimon and the novel as a whole are much more convincing.

The most radical character to break away from the rigid conventions in novel writing was Josef Škvorecký's hero and narrator, the twenty-year-old dandy Danny Smiřický. At the end of the novel he remains as ideologically uncommitted as he was at the beginning. In the confusion of the 1945 revolution in Kostelec, a fictitious town in East Bohemia that Švorecký based on his native Náchod, he maintains his scepticism about religion and Communism; in fact he remains sceptical about anything that does not concern him personally. He even makes fun of the virtues of patriotism and humanism. He becomes an involuntary hero when he puts a German tank out of action but immediately makes light of his exploit. For him the only things that seem to make sense in his life are his erotic relationship with Irena, a relationship that is superficial rather than deep, and above all the jazz music that he makes with a group of friends. Jazz obviously influenced the style of *Zbabělci* – the language and rhythm resemble blues and boogie-woogie:

> "Suddenly the people in the square were still. We stood, and like a priest lifting the chalice during mass, we put our horns to our mouths. [. . .] We played it staccato

> and arrogantly, we blared the melody so that the burghers walking near the church turned toward us. [. . .] Our band caught fire, we were roaring and swinging until we finished the number. When we sat down, we immediately burst into Organ Grinder Swing. The crowd around the bandstand started to move and in the next moment the plaza was full of jiving couples."[82]

No wonder a character like this caused a storm of protest among the guardians of ideological purity. Škvorecký's novel was published at the end of 1958. At first it was well received but after a few weeks it was banned from sale and from the libraries. The journal *Tvorba* (Creations) wrote that the book spat in the face of the heroes of the resistance. The Communist daily *Rudé Právo* (Red Rights) called it "worm-infested fruit". The Central Committee of the Czechoslovak Communist Party took up the case and as a result not only was the work in question attacked for "recording the wrong ideas of a certain section of our young people" but its publishers, *Československý spisovatel* (Czechoslovak Writers' Publishing House) and the critics who praised it also found themselves in trouble. The novel became a springboard for a campaign against "liberalism" and "revisionism".[83]

Meanwhile the fuss that surrounded *Zbabělci* overshadowed its literary qualities and affected the development of Czech prose. The use of the first person narrative throughout makes the psychology of the novel convincing as it is based on the narrator's innermost thoughts. The pithy dialogue sounds authentic and not only moves the story on but also holds the key to the sub-text, for the characters often deliberately do not say what they are privately thinking. Later Škvorecký recalled how he learned to write dialogue and that he had been inspired by Ernest Hemingway's novel *A Farewell to Arms*. No less revolutionary was his liberal use of common Czech and slang.

The irreverent description in *Zbabělci* of the 1945 May revolution deprived it of its mystique and was in direct conflict with the obligatory glorified picture presented in Jan Drda's (→ PROFILES) *Němá barikáda* (see pp. 8–9) and elsewhere. It was not till the beginning of the seventies that JIŘÍ KOVTUN elected to give the subject a different treatment in his *Pražská ekloga* (Prague Eclogue, Munich, 1973; Brno 1992).

The historical novel also changed and became more sophisticated. The psychology of the characters was now studied in much greater detail, notably in MIROSLAV HANUŠ's two-part novel, *Osud národa* and *Poutník v Amsterodamu* (The Fate of the Nation, 1957; Pilgrim in Amsterdam, 1960). These two works deal with the life of the great 17th-century Czech theologian and pedagogue Jan Amos Komenský (Comenius). Gradually different ideas about novels with historical subjects began to gain ground. History was no longer depicted as a mere sequence of great events, subsequently embellished in the telling. In a reversal of roles, the characters in their natural surroundings now formed the basis of the historical novel. History was seen to be created by the behaviour of characters and their experience. In 1957 *Sňatky z rozumu* (Marriage of Convenience), part one of VLADIMÍR NEFF's lengthy five-part cycle, was published. This cycle deals with the rise and fall of the Czech bourgeoisie at the end of the 19th and the beginning of the 20th century. Neff manages to be sophisticated, entertaining and gently ironic in his manner of telling the story, especially in the early volumes.[84]

VALJA STÝBLOVÁ used psychological introspection in the short novel *Mne soudila noc* (1957; published in English as *Abortionists*, 1961). The work was written immediately after the war and dealt with the issues of morality and responsibility, using illegal abortions as examples.[85]

Towards the end of the fifties the fashion in prose writing was for shorter pieces, articles, short stories and novellas almost journalistic in style, or lyric poetry. The poetry of the everyday was in fashion and prose works were based on very similar ideas. Actual situations, moments in the lives of "ordinary people", acted as a counterbalance to vague, superficial, meaningless abstractions.

Interest in the works of Karel Čapek revived to a certain extent. But unlike Čapek, most writers at that time shared the same clear ideas. This is evident in the works of the younger authors, LUDVÍK AŠKENAZY'S *Dětské etudy* (Studies of Childhood, 1955), *Psí život* (1959; published in English as *A Dog's Life*, 1963;[86] the short stories and essays of JINDŘIŠKA SMETANOVÁ'S *Koncert pod platanem* (The Concert under the Plane Tree, 1959) and in JOSEF NESVADBA'S *Einsteinův mozek* (Einstein's Brain, 1960).[87] However, the same trend was also evident in the middle generation writer ADOLF BRANALD'S *Ztráty a nálezy* (Lost and Found, 1961). Perhaps inspired by William Saroyan, Aškenazy used childlike naïvety and imagination as a contrast to the humdrum world of adults. Also Jindřiška Smetanová's poeticism transformed the apparently drab lives of the inhabitants of Kampa, the peninsula on the river Vltava in Prague. Josef Nesvadba wrote science fiction in the tradition of 19th-century Czech writer Jakub Arbes. In his reportage, as in all his work, Branald relied on a wealth of accurate documentary evidence. All these works opened up new vistas for Czech literature, still paralyzed by its treatment under Stalin, and made artistic progress possible.

In 1960, the first volumes of the series *Život kolem nás* (Life around Us) were published by *Československý spisovatel* (Czechoslovak Writers' Publishing House). It introduced Jan Procházka, Ivan Klíma, Alexandr Kliment, Jan Trefulka and others, young writers born at the end of the twenties and the beginning of the thirties. Rather than full-length novels, they wrote short novels and stories, and journalistic articles that gave them the chance to take an objective look at facts. ALEXANDR KLIMENT was the most interesting of these new writers. The critics had reservations about his short novel *Marie* (Mary, 1960)[88], but it won great acclaim from the readers.

The book was published at the beginning of 1960. It is the story of the breakdown of a marriage seen through the eyes of a housewife. From ordinary characters and everyday worries the author creates an extraordinary work. It is a record of one individual's most intimate thoughts which call into question accepted ideas and show how complicated human relationships can be:

> "*They are obliged to live together, to be faithful to each other and to help each other.* [. . .] Who did they make this law for? For people who had stopped loving each

other, so that they could both be bored together because it was their duty? [. . .] Or did they make it for people who love each other and don't need it at all? So what's the point of this law and what's it got to do with love? Where's the connection? Love and the law, love and rules? Isn't there something wrong somewhere? With the law? Or us?"[89]

Unlike the works of his contemporaries Kliment's *Marie* constantly asks questions, but it does not offer ready-made answers and the problem is left unresolved at the end.

There was also a change in the focus of interest from people in general to the individual, from public to private affairs and from lengthy novels to smaller works even when the subject was the Second World War. JAN OTČENÁŠEK's *Romeo, Julie a tma* (1958; in English *Romeo and Juliet and the Darkness*, 1960; filmed by Jiří Weiss, 1959) was composed on the lines of Shakespeare's play about families and a love affair that ended in tragedy, but here there was the suggestion that the lovers had another hostile force to contend with, the "darkness" of the Nazi occupation.

At first sight the heroes in ARNOŠT LUSTIG's (→ PROFILES) short story collections *Noc a naděje* (1958; *Night and Hope*, 1962; filmed by Zbyněk Brynych as *Transport z ráje* [A Convoy Leaving Paradise]) and *Démanty noci* (1958; *Diamonds of the Night*, 1962; new translation 1977) seem less impressive. The background for the stories is usually the Jewish ghetto in Theresienstadt, where the Jews from Bohemia and Moravia were transported during the war, or a concentration camp.

Lustig knew the ghetto and the concentration camps from personal experience in the years between 1942 and 1945. After the war he went to university and worked as an editor and a film scriptwriter. Later in conversation he said:

"I remember in September 1944 getting off a train and finding myself on a railway platform at Auschwitz-Birkenau. We felt like animals during an eclipse of the sun or a forest fire or just before an earthquake. In the space of a few minutes everyone – children up to the age of fifteen, women and men over forty, people who were ill, who wore glasses or who had grey hair – found themselves in bathhouses where gas (Zyklon-B) instead of water poured down from the showers."[90]

In March 1945 he managed to escape while being transported to a prison camp. A fictional version of this event, a text entitled *Tma nemá stín*, was included in the book *Démanty noci* (Diamonds of the Night). An expanded version of this story was published separately in the USA as *Darkness Casts No Shadow* (1977). This short story also became the inspiration for a remarkable film by Jan Němec, *Démanty noci* (Diamonds of the Night, 1964).

Lustig's characters are often children or old people, unheroic "ordinary" people who find themselves in extraordinary life or death situations. The author uses third person narrative with a lot of dialogue. He describes the surroundings, appearance and behaviour of the characters without emotion. Yet, like Josef Škvorecký, Alexandr Kliment and Jiří Weil in *Život s hvězdou* (see p. 17), he manages to tell the story from their perspective. Sometimes time, not identifiable with time measured by a clock, but subjective time, internal and measured by experience, takes over. In *Noc a naděje*, Lustig tells the story of the love of Štěpán and Anna in a much more casual, matter of fact way, and with more restraint than Jan Otčenášek in his novella, and as a result with greater dramatic effect.

So prose writing and the whole of Czech literature was moving away from constructionism to writing about life.

THE SIXTIES

"Informal liberalism from Western civilization permeated the whole of the arts in the interwar republic, yet something important was established and matured, something that managed to survive the Nazi Protectorate and the fifties, to reawaken in the sixties generation of artists."

(Jiří Voskovec)[1]

Between Dogmatism and Reformism

1. The Rise of Criticism

The post-February 1948 era was a period of disintegration – many authors, literary movements and topics were now banned. This resulted in the levelling out of published literature and a flood of colourless, mediocre publications from which only a few minor works stood out. In the sixties the reverse process took place; there was a gradual integration of permitted and banned literature. The range of published literature widened with new topics, progressive ideas and new personalities. In fact this was true of all Czech culture and to a certain extent also of society as a whole.[2]

In the sixties the media and the arts reviews played a key role. These reviews, especially the journal *Literární noviny* (Literary News), were very popular with their readers. From 1964 *Literární noviny* was edited by Milan Jungmann, and in the sixties its circulation never fell below 100,000. As contributors to *Literární noviny*, Milan Kundera, Ludvík Vaculík, Karel Kosík, Ivan Klíma and A. J. Liehm enjoyed unprecedented prestige, as did the Moravians Jan Skácel, Jan Trefulka, Ludvík Kundera, Oleg Sus and Milan Uhde, who were of the group attached to *Host do domu* (A Guest in the House), the Brno monthly (fortnightly from the end of the sixties). The Slovaks Dominik Tatarka, Ladislav Mňačko and Laco Novomeský wrote for the Bratislava periodical *Kultúrny život* (Cultural Life). Ladislav Mňačko's *Oneskorené reportáže* (Reports That Come Too Late, 1963), describing how laws were broken and crimes committed in the name of the party. It became a bestseller and sold half a million copies. The periodical *Divadlo* (The Theatre) covered matters beyond the scope of drama and the theatre. Jan Patočka and Jan Groomsman, for example, both wrote for it. From about 1963 these and the reviews *Tvář* (Countenance) and later *Sešity* (Notebooks) of the younger generation played an important role.[3] Young people in fact cared little about the political rhetoric that urged them to devote themselves to the building up of socialism under the leadership of the Communist Party of Czechoslovakia. They were more attracted to the lifestyle of the young people in the West, rock and beat music, carefree hitchhiking and the eye-catching fashions of black sweaters, jeans and miniskirts, everything that was the antithesis of official grey uniformity. They enjoyed the poetry of the American beatniks. As early as 1958 Jan Zábrana published the first translation of Allen Ginsberg in the review *Světová literatura* (World Literature). His selection from Lawrence Ferlinghetti came out in 1964. The songs of the Beatles and the hippie protest movement with its slogan "make love not war" were also popular.

The state defended the bans and suppressions of such "ideological deviations". When in 1965 the unconventional beatnik Allen Ginsberg visited Prague and made unflattering remarks about the political regime in his notebook, which he lost in a pub and was found by the secret police, he was branded a disturbing element and expelled. In the autumn of 1966 the police carried out a raid on a group of young people who had gathered at the National Museum in Prague. Some were imprisoned, some were beaten and some had their hair forcibly cut, while others committed suicide. The ban forbidding long-haired youths to appear in public (meaning in the theatre, in stations, in pubs and on trains), remained in place for a year afterwards. Among those detained was the nineteen-year-old JAROSLAV HUTKA, who later became a well-known song-writer and musician. He wrote at the time:

> I sympathize with people who do not want to work
> and who hang around the museum
> free as the question mark that turns anything it wants into a question
> with those wandering around the streets
> and at dawn stealing rolls from the doorsteps
> in love with the fantastic party of life
> who can give a smart answer back to the curses of the crowd
> who can weep because of them
> who are afraid to come out of the house
> who walk like whipped dogs
> who in a burst of absentmindedness tease a passerby
> who allow themselves a smile for no reason
> who let themselves be shut up with madmen
> who commit suicide and love independence
> free as a question mark[4]

2. Freedom of Expression

Throughout the sixties control of the state remained in the hands of highly placed party officials. Even though the time had passed when the state authorities committed terrorist acts against the population and infringed human rights on a large scale, the authoritative regime remained firmly in power till the end of 1967. From the end of 1962 a new wave of criticism of Stalinism in the Soviet Union, and a serious economic crisis in Czechoslovakia in the early sixties, forced conservative Communists into retreat. Efforts to reach the standard of the West in technology and the economy forced the removal of some barriers, notably regarding the exchange of information and freedom to travel. In 1965 170,000 citizens of Czechoslovakia were able to travel to the West and two years later the number had risen to 300,000. That was the time when Czech readers became familiar with not only classic American authors like William Faulkner and Ernest Hemingway but also with the names of some younger writers like Jerome David Salinger, William Styron and Jack Kerouac. They also had access to the Russian Alexander Solzhenitsyn's novel *One Day in the Life of Ivan Denisovich* and the short story "An Incident at Krechetovka Station", which described conditions in Stalinist Russia.

The changes in culture and society in the sixties did not take place suddenly and violently, as they did after the February coup of 1948. They came about gradually, in everyday disagreements with bureaucratic agencies which had the right to control and censor. However, bureaucracy was being undermined from without by increasing liberalization and demoralized from within by the strength of the reform movement in the Communist Party. In 1963 the Slovak critic Milan Hamada wrote in the journal *Kultúrny život*: "The statements made by politicians have limited validity. What they do not and cannot know, artists, for example, can and must know. It is perhaps necessary to humanize every politician. Let the artist keep out of politics, let him humanize." Understandably this kind of statement annoyed politicians. In the spring of 1964 the praesidium of the Central Committee of the Communist Party of Czechoslovakia passed a resolution called *Poslání a stav kulturních časopisů* (The Message and Status of Cultural Reviews). In it the "leaven of creative thought" was acknowledged, but in keeping with previous resolutions, it of course warned about "kowtowing to the influences of bourgeois culture" and even about "the spreading of opinions that are obviously at variance with the policy of the party".

Two years later the cultural resolution passed at the Communist Party Congress was no longer as stringent. It allowed the open exchange of information, experimentation and confrontation, and even rejected the notion of artistic creativity as purely "the collection of previously defined aesthetic norms and processes". Nevertheless it called for watchfulness: "liberalism" was a threat detracting from Marxist ideology. The conclusion was obvious: "The party and its institutions have the final say in all these matters."[5]

These statements indicate shifts in cultural policy. Gradually restrictions became fewer – but at the same time the determination to remain in control, albeit in an enlightened manner, was still there. The drastic measures of earlier years were replaced by less severe expedients; alternate loosening and tightening of the screw, negotiation, persuasion, occasional threats, economic pressure. There were fewer offensive campaigns and less obvious repression. There was however a campaign against the group attached to the review *Tvář*, which was banned in 1965, and in

1967 Jan Beneš was sentenced to five years' imprisonment for writing under an assumed name for the émigré review *Svědectví* (Testimony), allegedly sending "inflammatory reports" and "libelling" the socialist regime. Complete suppression and deletion of parts of critical articles was the order of the day, to such an extent that some incidents became a bit of a joke. In 1962 the journalist and author Vladimír Škutina was sentenced to several months' imprisonment for insulting the head of state. Škutina himself denied the charge but after judgment was pronounced he spoke up and said that he publicly admitted the truth of what he was charged with, namely, that President Antonín Novotný was an ass. Later the affair concerning the famous *Literární noviny* caricaturist Haďák (pen name of Miroslav Liďák) caused a sensation. He had drawn the state emblem with Švejk in a heroic posture holding a pint of beer in place of the Czech lion. Haďák was pilloried in the highest places for "defaming" his country. He was given a year's suspended sentence but all this did was to increase his popularity.

Children's literature was an area which had escaped censorship since the 1950s. Thus the pioneering modern fairy-tales by Karel and Josef Čapek and the highly inventive yet accessible children's poetry by František Hrubín (see pp. 9, 43–44 and → PROFILES) found a lot of followers. For instance, the animated character of "The Mole" (*Krtek*) created by Zdeněk Miler, became internationally well known. The scripts for the "Mole" films were written by such authors as Eduard Petiška or Ivan Klíma. The character of the "honest highwayman Rumcajs" and other fairy-tales by VÁCLAV ČTVRTEK (*Maková panenka*, 1970; published in English as *Poppy Doll*, 1995) also became also very well known. All these texts used linguistic as well as situational humour. MILOŠ MACOUREK used fantastic motifs in his humoristic, absurd fairy-tales, which were published in an English volume entitled *Curious Tales* in 1980. JIŘÍ TRNKA, an original illustrator, film animator and writer, whose book entitled *Through the Magic Gate* came out in English in 1962, was one of the most important and versatile artistic personalities of the postwar era.[6] In his work, poetic lyricism merged with imaginative treatment and he created such a strong, visual style that it has become extremely difficult for later artists to go beyond it. The artistic puppet films by Jiří Trnka, *Osudy dobrého vojáka Švejka* (The Good Soldier Švejk and His Fortunes, 1954–1955) and *Sen noci svatojánské* (A Midsummer Night's Dream, 1959),[7] are good examples of this style. Hermína Týrlová's and Karel Zeman's animated cartoons and puppet films also gained an international reputation.

From the time of the National Revival at the beginning of the 19th century, translation had been an important part of Czech literature. It took the place of original literature, which had not yet fully developed. This situation was repeated in the postwar era. After the 1948 February coup authors who could not or did not wish to publish their original works turned to translation. Many of Vladimír Holan's and František Hrubín's translations were done for these reasons. In 1962 Oldřich Králík published a large selection of Vladimír Holan's (→ PROFILES) translations in a volume entitled *Cestou* (Along the Road). In 1952 the translation of Dante's *Divine Comedy* by Otto František Babler with the collaboration of Jan Zahradníček was published. A large group of war generation writers followed their example – Zdeněk Urbánek, Josef Hiršal, Jiří Kolář (→ PROFILES), Jiřina Hauková, Ladislav Fikar, Ivan Slavík, Ludvík Kundera, Emanuel Frynta, Jan Vladislav, Rio Preisner – and also some of the somewhat younger authors – Petr Kopta, Petr Pujman, Jan Zábrana, Vladimír Kafka, Jiří Pechar and Antonín Přidal. Most of them gradually saw their own literary works appear in print, greatly extending the range of works published.

New translations of the classics and new names became known as the world opened up. After the translations of Christian Morgenstern by Josef Hiršal and of Robinson Jeffers by Kamil Bednář (see p. 70) came Zdeněk Urbánek's translation of William Shakespeare, a more sophisticated and up-to-date work than the earlier translation by Erich Adolf Saudek. *Hamlet* with Radovan Lukavský in the title role was staged every year from 1959 to 1965 in the National Theatre in Prague. Zdeněk Urbánek translated the familiar quotation "there's something rotten in the state of Denmark" as "páchne to v naší zemi hnilobou" (there is something rotten in our country), relating it unequivocally to the political situation in Czechoslovakia. American writers and Solzhenitsyn were already being talked about. Other translations, works of literature in their own right, should perhaps be mentioned: the translations of the novels by Hermann Broch, Albert Camus and William Golding; the plays by Friedrich Dürrenmatt; the works of the Spanish-American writers Jorge Luis Borges and Gabriel García Márquez; the French "Nouveau Roman", which had a certain influence on the work of Alexandr Kliment, Jiří Fried and Karel Milota; the absurd drama of Eugène Ionesco, Samuel Beckett and Harold Pinter. A parallel development to the theatre of the absurd was taking place independently with Václav Havel and Ladislav Smoček. At the end of the sixties world famous authors like the Pole Czesław Miłosz and the Russian Vladimir Nabokov, "the dangerous emigrants", could get into print at least in review. However, readers had to wait another twenty years before their works came out in book form.

With more freedom there was greater contact with exiles and those who had remained in the West. In the early sixties there were sections in the Central Committee of the Communist Party of Czechoslovakia and the State Police whose mission it was to fight against exiled and "bourgeois" journalism. Annually the police confiscated a number of publications and other printed matter from the West and also from Poland, Yugoslavia and even from China. In 1963 there were two million confiscations, a year later there were two and a half million. The Communist daily *Rudé Právo* (Red Rights) continued to call the exiles "CIA mercenaries" and "perfidious traitors", but gradually opinions changed. In March 1967 there was a television programme condemning emigration to the West, but, unprecedentedly, even voices of people who raised objections to this kind of campaign were included in the programme.

So the barrier between literature in exile and domestic literature began to crumble. Besides Jan Beneš, the novelist Karel Michal, the essayist and graphic artist Karel Trinkewitz and the philosopher Ladislav Hejdánek wrote for *Svědectví* under assumed names. But even among the exiles people's attitudes developed and new ideas were voiced. Apart from *Svědectví* there was a range of other important reviews, especially the Catholic *Studie* in Rome, founded in 1958, and the liberal *Proměny* in New York, founded in 1964. *Studie* (Studies) was one of the *Křesťanská akademie* (Christian Academy) publications. *Proměny* (Metamorphoses) was published by another exile organization *Československá společnost pro vědy a umění* (The Czechoslovak Society of Arts and Sciences), which was established at the end of the fifties. By the late fifties, when hope was fading for the break-up by force of the regime in Czechoslovakia, for it was obvious that the West recognized the continued existence of the Soviet bloc in its present form, the more forward-looking exiled men of letters abandoned hard-line anti-Communism. They relied on gradual internal change in Czech society, so they strove for systematic contact with home and mutual exchange of information:

> " . . . if there is no real internal revival there can be no fundamental change. [. . .] This concept, you may perhaps agree, must somehow be absorbed into the blood of every Czech: it must begin in himself [. . .], he must dig out this free space for himself, no-one else can do it for him."[8]

3. Politico-Cultural Polemics

At the beginning of the sixties the poet Jan Skácel (→ PROFILES) wrote in *Host do domu* (A Guest in the House) that he wished the Czech critics "courage and open windows" for the new decade. For several years his wish was granted to an unexpected degree.

In *Literární noviny* (Literary News) in the summer of 1963, JIŘÍ BRABEC condemned *Třicet let bojů za českou socialistickou poezii* (Thirty Years of Struggle to Create a Czech Socialist Poetry, see p. 21), the official account of new Czech literature. Štoll's writings had first been criticized in the early fifties but Brabec's reasoning was more convincing. It was no longer a question of refuting individual arguments. At stake was the actual system of thinking, making automatic judgments without taking the facts into account. Brabec maintained that Štoll was still ignoring history in the speeches he was making and this approach was a danger to the development of scholarly thinking.[9]

LADISLAV ŠTOLL, recently appointed to the Academy and still very powerful, reacted sharply to the article in *Literární noviny* but he was unable to completely silence Brabec and other critics of his work. Controversy became widespread; journalists and critics began to draw attention to problems and ask questions that had previously been taboo. The years 1962–1963 were a landmark period, the dogmatists suffering many defeats that may be summarized under several headings.

Some important writers began to publish again. The Slovak poet LACO NOVOMESKÝ, imprisoned after the February 1948 coup, was able to attend the 1963 Congress of Writers where he received a resounding ovation.[10] In the course of two years, eight books of VLADIMÍR HOLAN'S (→ PROFILES) poetry were published. Two of these in particular, *Příběhy* (Tales, 1963) and *Noc s Hamletem* (1964; *A Night with Hamlet*, 1980, see pp. 29, 69–70) caused a sensation. The works of JIŘÍ KOLÁŘ (→ PROFILES) began to be published again. With one exception, from 1949 to 1963 he had been able to publish only books for children. The memoirs of FRANTIŠEK LANGER *Byli a bylo* (How They Were and How It Was), aroused great interest. He had been for many years a friend of the Čapek brothers and his memoirs recalled the democratic culture of the early days of the century and the First Czechoslovak Republic 1918–1938.[11] ALEXANDER MATUŠKA, the Slovak essayist, also revived interest in the work of Karel Čapek by his *Člověk proti skaze (Pokus o Karla Čapka)* (1963, published in English as *Karel Čapek. Man against Destruction* in 1964).

It should of course be remembered that in these difficult times some authors, chiefly Catholics, continued to be proscribed. The poets Václav Renč and Zdeněk Rotrekl were released from prison in 1962 and Josef Kostohryz a year later. Růžena Vacková, the writer on aesthetics, was not released till 1967. Life outside prison was difficult and their return to the arts somewhat precarious. Nor could exiled authors be sure of having their books published; for example Egon Hostovský and Jan Čep were not published at home until the end of the sixties. Yet unofficial literature, banned by the authorities, was gradually becoming available to the public.

Another sign of the times was the controversy about avant-gardism. After the February 1948 coup the interwar avant-garde movement, and in particular Karel Teige, the leading avant-garde theoretician, were denounced as literary saboteurs if not enemy agents. As early as the mid-fifties, Vítězslav Nezval and MILAN KUNDERA (both → PROFILES) had attempted to restore the reputation of the avant-gardists (see p. 35). In 1960 Kundera's book on the avant-gardist novelist Vladislav Vančura *Umění románu* (The Art of the Novel)[12] was published. This was followed in 1962 by a book that had long been in preparation, KVĚTOSLAV CHVATÍK'S *Bedřich Václavek a vývoj marxistické estetiky* (Bedřich Václavek and the Development of Marxist Aesthetics) and also by a number of essays by OLEG SUS, a specialist in aesthetics who worked in Brno.[13] These works focused on the aims of the avant-gardists and presented them without emotion, without black or white judgments. They backed up their claims by using many contemporary texts and pictures. Meanwhile, like Brabec, Chvatík used Marxist historicism and in so doing refuted ideological rhetoric. Understandably this view of Marxism infuriated Štoll and his followers, but the critics who advocated reform considered it a positive step and gave it their support. In the ensuing controversy in the journal *Česká literatura* (Czech Literature) in 1963 Chvatík was now free to praise avant-gardism as "antidogmatic, rich in humanity, rebelling against regimentation in all areas of life".[14] The way was now clear for the publication of Karel Teige's works[15] and for bringing the Surrealist Group, till then working underground, to the notice of the public.[16]

An immediate consequence of diversification was that Chvatík and Sus's ideas about the avant-garde were criticized from another quarter. The rising generation of the sixties, above all the writers connected with *Tvář* (Countenance) and *Sešity*

(Notebooks) found avant-garde ideas and fantasies strange and uninspiring. By 1963 Jan Lopatka was criticizing Oleg Sus in *Literární noviny* and later he strongly criticized Milan Kundera's conception of the avant-garde. In 1966 the poet Zbyněk Hejda said that "avant-garde ideology was now history", a remark that was quoted in the collection *Podoby II* (Resemblances II), 1969.[17]

Another event that aroused interest was the 1963 conference in Liblice, organized by the specialist in German literature EDUARD GOLDSTÜCKER, on the works of Franz Kafka. The East German men of letters, who in obedience to the party line considered Kafka morbid and "a vampire", now found themselves on the defensive. The advocates of open Marxism, especially the Frenchman Roger Garaudy, the Austrian Ernst Fischer and some theoreticians, pointed out the relevance of Kafka for the present day.[18] After the conference the exiled Ladislav Radimský wrote, "Kafka is the first exile to return home victorious."[19]

So the most famous Prague writer of all time became known to the literary public, and with him a number of other distinguished German writers from Bohemia and Moravia. In the first year of the review *Tvář* the critic PŘEMYSL BLAŽÍČEK condemned Goldstücker for insisting on looking in Kafka's works for criticism of the bourgeois world and the road to socialism. This approach to literature – and Blažíček finds evidence of it on a greater scale in other "progressive" writers – does not recognize the essence of literature, works of literature remain part of ideology.[20]

Other studies on the subject of Kafka sometimes spilled over into the subject of totalitarianism and the attitudes it engenders.[21] JOSEF JEDLIČKA, novelist and essayist, wrote:

> "Before the eyes of Kafka the insurance agent, blood sprayed out from the representatives of the law beaten by Whipper's birch – and before our eyes the ovens were lit in the gas chambers, the deported soldiers fought at the station at Krechetovka for a handful of flour, children burned to death at Hiroshima [. . .], we have been blasted by lies, half-truths, foolish speeches and blasphemy – and until today we have not asked whether, after all, we might be guilty of all this, if all that should be forced upon us by a system beyond our comprehension [. . .]. And yet there has been a change in our thinking [. . .], we are not going to wait till a bailiff suddenly arrives and announces we are to be taken to court, but aware of the crisis we shall come forward voluntarily and admit our guilt. That will be the breakthrough into freedom [. . .]. Of course in order to be capable of that change of heart we must truly 'be worth something', because that way of winning freedom will bring heavy burdens; it is the freedom to be helpless, lonely, the freedom of endless beginnings, it is the freedom that means responsibility. There are no other kinds of freedom."[22]

This essay of Jedlička's was written even before Jan Patočka's famous reflections on "the solidarity of the shaken"; which had a profound effect on dissent and the samizdat culture of the seventies and eighties.

The tenets of Marxism were no longer unassailable but had become the subject of philosophical discussion and criticism. In 1963 in *Literární noviny* IVAN SVITÁK

number of conventions: certain questions were asked to which the answers had already been decided, as if there were some kind of ideal fixed reality which was then passed off as more real and truer than the empirical reality of daily life. Gradually Czech and Slovak intellectuals also began to think along the same lines.

From the beginning of the sixties a new generation of writers was making an impact on Czech literature. However, debate about the arts and literature did not centre only on squabbles between the generations and new trends in the arts. For example, promoting Concrete Poetry, absurd drama, the "Nouveau Roman", literary experiments in general and existentialism was part of the wider fight against the schematism of previous years. These attempts to widen the horizons of literature, transcending the generations, tended to make public life more democratic. Literature – like other branches of the arts – renewed associations that had been severed in the fifties. Year by year it presented a more varied, more colourful picture; writers achieved freedom to work and at the same time they became spokesmen for social reform.

A Happy Era in Literature

1. Poetry

The sixties could be called the happiest era in postwar Czech literature. There was less oppression and less external pressure. The public became more interested in literature and it gained prestige. The late sixties differed as sharply from the preceding years as from the years that followed. Certainly there was still censorship till the end of 1967 but it was much less strict. And there was a positive aspect to state sponsorship of the arts. Its generous subsidies made it possible to publish a great many reviews and books, to stage theatrical productions and to produce sophisticated films.

The publication of the second edition of Josef Škvorecký's (→ PROFILES) *Zbabělci* (The Cowards, see pp. 51–52) was the signal for *détente*. As late as 1959 Ladislav Štoll pronounced his final judgment in the case of *Zbabělci*, saying: "It is artistically unfair, untrue, and cynical."[25] The book was banned and withdrawn from the libraries. In 1964 a new edition of *Zbabělci* was published but with some minor adaptations. The critics without exception received it favourably. In the spring of that year the poet Vladimír Holan, whose books of poems had begun to be published again after being banned only a few months previously, was awarded the official state prize, which was another change in the atmosphere surrounding the arts.

With the thaw, published literature no longer followed a standard line but diversified in many different directions. In poetry since Milan Kundera's *Monology* (Monologues, see p. 47) erotica and unhappy love had ceased to be unacceptable and love poetry flourished. František Halas and Jiří Orten were the models for poets to follow. The influence of OLDŘICH MIKULÁŠEK (→ PROFILES) became ever stronger, his vision of life in *Ortely a milosti* (Judgment and Mercy, see p. 44) as spells of enthralling joy and bewildering gloom was further developed in the collections of the sixties through images of wine, the natural world and nature in man, and especially of love, dangerous passions, ecstacies of body and soul.

> zatímco chodník jde si po svém dál,
> dějiny přou se v štíhlých nohou ženy
> a mladí muži jak vlajkové lodi
> zastírají povláváním kravat,
> co se děje těsně pod nimi,
> v kajutách hrudí,
> v podpalubí duší,
> když tu se náhle vznesl jeden z nich
> mávaje rukama, jako by se bránil
> a někdo řekl, kdyby aspoň vyndal
> cigaretu z úst[26]

> while the pavement is going about its own business,
> history is squabbling about a woman's slim legs
> and young men like flagships
> conceal with fluttering ties,
> what is going on just under them,
> in the cabins of their hearts,
> in the lower decks of their souls,
> when suddenly one of them steps forth
> waving his arms as if to defend himself
> and someone said, he could at least
> take his cigarette out of his mouth
>
> (*Svlékání hadů* [Sloughing of Snakes], 1963)

The magic of the poet Vladimír Holan (→ Profiles) lay in the integrity and daring use of metaphor.

> "*Kdo nepracuje, ať nejí!*" Ano,
> ale *co* je práce? *Být věrný svému nezištnému údělu* –
> nebo být prodavavačem odpustků
> či horlivým topičem v krematoriu,
> zavádět teploměr do konečníku války
> nebo musit zpívat při vinobraní
> na důkaz, že nejíš hrozny
> [. . .]
> nebo i pod ztrátou hrdla přepilovat pouta
> a raději si vyloupat oči,
> aby neviděly ty dnešní hrůzy,
> a přece ještě zaslechly ty dávno mrtvé,
> ale svobodné zpěváky? . . . [27]
>
> (*Noc s Hamletem*, written 1949–1956 and 1962, published 1964)

"He that will not work shall not eat!" True,
but *what* is work? *To be faithful to one's lot, unselfishly* –
or to sell indulgences
or become a zealous stoker in a crematorium,
stick a thermometer in the rectum of war
or have to sing at the vintage[28]
to prove you don't eat grapes
[. . .]
or on penalty of death to file off your fetters
and rather force your eyes out
than look at the horrors of today,
and yet still hear the singers
dead long ago, but free . . . ?[29]
(*A Night with Hamlet*)

The poem *Noc s Hamletem* (see p. 29) was first introduced in the Prague wine-cellar *Viola* in November 1963 with the musical accompaniment of Marek Kopelent when it was still in manuscript. It was presented by Vladimír Justl, the literary historian and long-time editor of Holan's work, and this exceptional production was repeated in *Viola* at least a hundred and fifty times up till the end of the eighties. Much later, the poet and translator Michael March wrote: "Though *A Night with Hamlet* is not on everyone's lips, its violence and sexuality could draw a crowd. A seminal work of the 20th century, it bears comparison with *The Waste Land* and *Howl.*"[30]

At the same time as the "reappearance" of the older generation and the rise of the younger generation (see pp. 94–98), the work of the middle generation reached full maturity. By the early sixties more epic and narrative poetry with a wider range of imagery was being written. Vladimír Holan's older work, which had now been published, had an influence on this epic poetry, as did the poems of Robinson Jeffers in Kamil Bednář's translations (*Mara*, 1958, and some of his subsequent books). Karel Šiktanc's (→ Profiles) poem *Heinovské noci* (Heine's Nights, 1960) was epic in character. This poem made Šiktanc's name in Czechoslovakia – until then, he was one of the less well known poets around the review *Květen* (May, see pp. 45–47). Unlike the variegated, diverse and ever-changing Šotola, Šiktanc's poetry was centripetal – returning again and again to the same basic situations and moral values. Even in the sixties it was imbued with fragments of "ordinary" reality, significant recollections of childhood and a kind of fictional memory of family and society, as, for example, in *Adam a Eva* (Adam and Eve, 1968). František Hrubín's *Romance pro křídlovku* (Romance for Flugelhorn, 1962, see p. 71) completed the picture. All these works were a development of prewar and wartime epic poetry with the addition of a strong element of lyricism.

On the other hand, shorter narrative poems were still realistic and unsentimental, like the earlier work of *Group 42* (see pp. 15–16). Such were Josef Kainar's (→ Profiles) *Lazar a píseň* (Lazarus and the Song, 1960), Jiří Kolář's *Vršovický Ezop* (Aesop from Vršovice [a Prague suburb], which was written in the mid-fifties, published in part in 1966, but did not appear in full till 1993) and the work of Jan Zábrana, which was also partly written in the fifties. Jiří Kolář (→ Profiles) called his own work authentic poetry, and in fact his poems are real or fictional documents analogous to his graphic art work.[31] For example in the section called *Černá lyra* (The Black Lyre) there are stories of human cruelty and shame from concentration camps going back to ancient times. In the section which bears the same name as his book *Vršovický Ezop* Kolář experiments with common Czech and Prague slang. Like Bohumil Hrabal in his texts and Josef Kainar in some poems in *Lazar a píseň*, it is as if he had a hidden microphone recording the speech of peripheral characters.

Even in the mid-fifties the question of whether the contemporary poet had the "right to grieve when coming in contact with death" was still being seriously debated. Recurrent themes in Czech poetry around 1963 were death, destruction and anguish, and the Romantic poet Karel Hynek Mácha's "eternal nothing". Vladimír Holan's vision of the world substantially added to this debate – he saw life as a miserable existence, a darkness penetrated only by occasional bright memories of childhood, pure love and poetry.[32]

Vilém Závada, in his book of poetry *Jeden život* (One Life, 1962), attempted to return to his old style of poetry from the twenties and the thirties but with increasing soul searching and more disquieting questions. Once again the poet moves away from superficial to deeper meanings, "to dig in the seams of one's own soul". The poet continued to develop these ideas till they culminated in his following book, *Na prahu* (On the Threshold, 1970, see also p. 140), which was the most impressive work he wrote after 1945. František Hrubín (→ Profiles) also takes death as the leading theme of his *Romance pro křídlovku* (Romance for Flugelhorn, 1962), which became famous in the remarkable film version by Otakar Vávra.

> Už dnes láska a smrt křižují se ve mně,
> noc lásky a smrti žíhá jasně a temně
> mých dvacet let, těch dvacet zlatoploutvých ryb.[33]
>
> Already love and death are crossing inside me,
> a night of love and death tempers brightly and darkly
> my twenty years, these twenty golden swimming fish.

With *Romance* the poet returned to a subject he had treated long before, a student's love for a girl who died young, "the eternal fosterchild of fleeting summertime". The poem has striking epic and dramatic features; several periods of time are interwoven in it: holidays in 1930, fairs in Lešany (a village in Central Bohemia where Hrubín spent his childhood) in 1933 and 1934, and the year 1961. The language ranges from lyrical metaphor to colloquial expressions and common Czech. Nevertheless, as in his early collections written in the 1930s, Hrubín deliberately keeps the range of his language narrow without Holan's extremes and complicated coded meanings. The style of the poem depends above all on sophisticated repetitions and variations.

Love is represented as twofold: sensually physical in the character Tonka, and in Terina, the girl from the merry-go-round, as intoxicating, ravishing beauty, "everything that stops the heart". Even death is twofold: it means the completion of life as in the death of the grandfather, but also premature frustration – the beloved girl's death that the hero learns of only by chance and many years later. So love and death cut across each other in many different ways. Human life is perceived as delirious thrills of joy but also as oppression beyond the strength of man to bear.

Hrubín developed a vision analogous to that in the *Romance* in his final poetic works, *Černá denice* (The Black Morning Star, 1968), a cycle of poetic dreams where the world of the living blends with the world of the dead, and *Lešanské jesličky* (The Lešany Nativity Scene, 1970), which is set at the end of the poet's childhood in First World War. The story of the ferryman Joseph, his wife Mary and their child, in danger but saved, is an allusion to the gospel, and once again the author introduces his own distressing experiences. "I remember / daddy going away to war and waiting / for him to come back, I was nearly five and from that time on / I would always be waiting for something and always / be waiting for someone."[34]

Death and anguish were also dominant themes at the beginning of the sixties in the collections, *Záznam o potopě* (Chronicle of the Flood, 1963), *Nebožka smrt* (The Deceased Death, 1963) and *Co a jak* (What and How, 1964) by Miroslav Florian, Karel Šiktanc and Jiří Šotola respectively, all poets connected with *Květen* (see pp. 45–46).[35] MIROSLAV HOLUB's (see pp. 46–47 and → PROFILES) work casts doubts on optimistic faith in modern science and technology in spite of the influence of a stay in the United States. Nevertheless, while he was there he did complete the collections of poems *Beton: Verše z New Yorku a z Prahy* (Concrete: Poems from New York and from Prague, 1970) in addition to writing accounts of his travels (*Anděl na kolečkách* [An Angel on Wheels], 1963; *Žít v New Yorku* [To Live in New York], 1969). Holub's trust in progress disappeared, as is illustrated most effectively in his book *Ačkoliv* (Although, 1969), which includes not only poems but also lyrical micro-essays and aphorisms. Another selection was published in English in 1971 entitled *Although*.

> Ačkoli báseň vzniká tehdy, když už nic jiného nezbývá, ačkoli báseň je posledním pokusem o řád, když neřádu jest už až po krk,
> ačkoli básníků je nejvíc zapotřebí, když je nejvíc zapotřebí také svobody, vitamínu C, komunikací, zákonů a terapie hypertenze,
> ačkoli "být umělcem je selhat a umění je věrnost selhání", jak praví Samuel Beckett, není báseň z posledních, nýbrž z prvních věcí člověka.[36]

> Although a poem arises when there's nothing else to be done, although a poem is a last attempt at order when one can't stand disorder any longer,
> although poets are most needed when freedom, vitamin C, communications, laws and hypertension therapy are also most needed,
> although "to be an artist is to fail and art is fidelity to failure", as Samuel Beckett says, a poem is not one of the last but one of the first things of man.[37]

At the same time words regained their importance in poetry and verbose free-flowing verse disappeared. JAN SKÁCEL (see pp. 44–45 and → PROFILES) reached the pinnacle of his achievement in the mid-sixties with the collection *Smutěnka* (Little Sadness, 1965). The poet's economy of words, but words rich in meaning, his deliberate pauses and his lack of rhetoric are reminiscent of Karel Toman, a Czech poet of the early 20th century, or the concise Chinese or Japanese lyric. Statistical analysis of Skácel's poetry has shown that there are fewer words of purely grammatical significance than nouns and verbs, that is, words charged with meaning. In particular attributive adjectives, signs of adornment, have been intentionally omitted. At the same time some expressions have a mysterious, almost magical effect. For example, the reader never does discover what the oft-repeated word *smutěnka* (in English approximately "little sadness") really means – is it the voice of nature? human grief? echoes of ancient myths? The very uncertainty, the deliberate ambiguity, is characteristic of Skácel's approach. It is in harmony with the wider trends in literature, moving away from the "illusion" of realism and a rigid scale of values.

Skácel's poetic world, created out of the basic certainties of childhood and the Moravian countryside, remained unchanged, but in the course of the sixties and seventies there was an increase in darker references to pain and death.

IVAN DIVIŠ (→ PROFILES), a contemporary of Skácel and Holub, moved in a different direction. The title of one of his books, *Chrlení krve* (Spitting Blood, 1964), typifies his vision of the world – he sees agitation, constant tension and aggression, and to portray it he uses rich metaphors and deformation of language in the manner of Holan. Like Holan, Diviš looks at the world with passion; he sees sharp contrasts, purity and innocence on one hand, guilt, evil and vulgarity on the other. Gradually he found a belief he could hold on to in the absolute of Christianity. The lengthy poem *Thanatea* (Thanatea, 1968), written in Baroque style, is a dialogue with death, personified by a woman.

The change in JAROSLAV SEIFERT'S (→ PROFILES) work surprised his readers. Before the war, lyricism, melody and regular versification were established features of his poetry. Even after the February 1948 coup the same characteristics were evident in the books *Píseň o Viktorce* (The Story of Viktorka, 1950, see p. 35), *Maminka* (Mummy, 1954) and other poems. In them, melancholy and the hardships of life are offset by idyllic melody. In the mid-sixties, after a period when he was unable to write because of a serious illness, the poet made an uncompromising change in his whole attitude to poetry: "Away with that poetic rubbish, metaphor and rhyme," he wrote, "life is sometimes chillingly bleak."[38] Free verse now replaced rhythm and rhyme. There was less poetic expression, less use of metaphor, the language became less refined and more prosaic. In *Koncert na ostrově* (The Concert on the Island, 1965) there are certainly well-known Seifert characteristics, memories of childhood and youth, the attraction of women, the magic of Prague, but everything is seen through "the black mirror" of death to which the author had twice come very close. From this perspective when "the bat time / with its webbed wings destroys everything", hardly anything rises above futility. It might be art, that "concert on the island", but it is certainly love that leaves "its footprints / on human skin".[39] Jaroslav Seifert's new creative period continued with more collections including *Morový sloup* (The Plague Column), written between 1968 and 1970. It came out in samizdat in 1973 but was not published in Prague in book form till 1981. In English it was published as *The Plague Column* in 1979 and a new translation as *The Plague Monument* came out in 1980. It also coincided with widespread changes in Czech poetry. Seifert might have been inspired by Jiří Kolář and Vladimír Holan to move from poetic language to harsh realism. This concept of time and history, sceptical in its lack of illusions, had an analogy in poetry, drama and eventually in the novel.

At the end of the sixties individual Christian authors began to make their voices heard to a greater extent.[40] Catholic literature in particular had been drastically hit by the Stalinist purges. Two great figures of a past generation, Jakub Deml and Jaroslav Durych, did not live to see the change as both died at the beginning of the sixties. The first thing their contemporary BOHUSLAV REYNEK (see p. 29) was allowed to do was to work in graphics but he could not publish any poetry till 1969. JAN ZAHRADNÍČEK (→ PROFILES) suffered a cruel fate. After five years in prison he received permission to visit his home where he learned the sad news of the death of two of his children. Although he had been promised a pardon, he had to go back to Mírov prison and was kept incarcerated for another four years. This finally broke him. He was not in fact released till the great amnesty in May 1960 by which time he had only a few more months to live. Zahradníček's unpublished texts – like the poems of Václav Renč and Josef Kostohryz – could not be published at home till the end of the sixties. *Znamení moci* (The Sign of Power, see pp. 29–30) appeared in 1968 in the radical review *Student* (The Student) and was recited in public by Radovan Lukavský in St Thomas's Cathedral in Prague. Other poems that Zahradníček had written in prison were arranged by Bedřich Fučík, his friend and fellow prisoner, but the only book to reach the public was *Čtyři léta* (Four Years, 1969). That same year saw the publication of VÁCLAV RENČ's *Setkání s Minotaurem* (A Meeting with the Minotaur), manifestly the most impressive collection by that sophisticated translator, dramatist and poet.

The Christian authors of the war generation, contemporaries of Jiří Orten and Ivan Blatný, were a little better off. One of them, Ivan Slavík, called them "the generation of the dispersed". Their progress was delayed by the war and disrupted after 1948. Many of them suffered years of persecution. The poet ZDENĚK ROTREKL, who was first sentenced to death and then had his sentence commuted to life imprisonment, spent thirteen years in the uranium mines and prison camps. His intricate poetry, full of imagery, a continuation of the Baroque, was not published in Bohemia for four decades. The collection *Sněhem zaváté vinobraní* (Snow-covered Vintage) did not appear till 1991. The Catholic priest and poet FRANTIŠEK DANIEL MERTH was arrested in summer 1948 straight from the confessional. In his five years in prison he too made the acquaintance of the notorious mines at Jáchymov; for twenty years he could not publish anything. The majority of his poems were published for the first time in samizdat in the eighties. Their inspiration is the natural beauty of the Bohemian Forest (Šumava) in the southwest border regions of Czechoslovakia where the author lived, but their aspiration is abstract spirituality. LADISLAV DVOŘÁK also suffered persecution; his studies were interrupted, he worked as a labourer, and it was not till 1967 that he obtained a position as an editor. Dvořák's *Obrys bolesti* (Profile of Pain, 1966) is an example of his succinct verse, harsh rather than pleasing to the ear. His poetry, like his prose, which is also condensed in style, deals with poverty with an existentialist sub-text. Dvořák's characters, failures and outcasts are very similar to Bohumil Hrabal's. Behind them often lie the author's own terrible experiences, most evident in the later stories *Šavle meče* (Sabres Swords) that appeared in samizdat and were later published in exile in London in 1986. But the most outstanding figure of that generation was IVAN SLAVÍK. For many years he too could work only as an essayist and translator. Most notably he was able to translate and interpret the poetry of the Mayans and Aztecs. He also worked as a publisher editing the poetry of the early 20th-century author Richard Weiner, a writer who suffered from an identity crisis and Kafkaesque anxiety, and who had a great influence on him. From his first work *Snímání* (Taking Down from the Cross, 1947) his characteristic view of the world is evident in the challenging antitheses and constant contemplation of the poet's self and the world around him. Some of his poetry brings him very close to the poetics of *Group 42* (see pp. 15–16). Unlike them, however, Slavík seeks miracles of creation and the road to eternity. This may well be the meaning of the poem *Každodenní* (Everyday) from the collection *Osten* (The Thorn, 1968), but perhaps it is more striking in the poem *Podmínka* (Stipulation):

Mluvit o radosti
A neznat bolest
Útočit na svět
A neuklidit sám v sobě
Získat lehko
A vyhnout se tíži
Je zatemňování smyslu
[. . .]
Ve všedním dni
Začíná věčnost[41]

To speak of joy
And not to know pain
To attack the world
And not to put your own house in order
To achieve what is easy
And avoid what is difficult
Is the extinction of all reason
[. . .]
Eternity begins
In the everyday world.

(*Stín třtiny* [The Shadow of a Reed], written 1947–1948, published 1965)

2. Changes in Prose

The changes in the sixties radically transformed prose. In 1960 Antonín Jelínek wrote in *Plamen* (Blaze) that the question of whether to go along with socialism or against it had ceased to have any meaning for young writers. Much more urgent for them was the question of personal and social morality. The critic was reprimanded by the dogmatists for speaking in these terms, but of course it did affect the actual state of affairs. By then the novel about "building socialism" was already on its last legs. The perfect, bloodless heroes were being replaced by people that were more alive, fallible and sceptical. At the end of the fifties and the beginning of the sixties, novels and short stories were showing signs that they could aptly be called works of the mid-life crisis, which, of course, in the Czechoslovak context of the time, was primarily associated with politics. Alexandr Kliment's *Marie* (Mary, see pp. 53–54) was followed by Jiří Fried's *Časová tíseň* (Pressure of Time, 1961), the description of the mental crisis of a chess master,[42] and Jan Trefulka's two-part story *Pršelo jim štěstí* (Happiness Rained on Them, 1962;[43] the title is of course ironic), which was also interesting for its method of presentation. The story is told by three different narrators reflecting three different points of view. Trefulka's novellas contain autobiographical elements. The scene in which Karel is expelled from the party and has to leave the university had its prototype in real life in 1950 when three students, including Jan Trefulka and Milan Kundera, were expelled from the Faculty of Arts in Prague. Later Milan Kundera described this episode somewhat differently in *Žert* (The Joke, see p. 84).

In his novel *Hodina ticha* (An Hour of Silence, 1963), set in Eastern Slovakia, IVAN KLÍMA (→ PROFILES) was also writing from personal experience. He too, borrowing from Karel Čapek, used different methods of narration. After the characters' stories have been told there follows an intermezzo, a study in depth of the innermost soul of the main hero. The action is deliberately presented "in leaps", fragmented, not smoothly progressing. The belief in a single "objective world" that had dominated the novel of previous years was shaken. In *Hodina ticha* we find a situation typical of the novels which extolled "building socialism" but here the situation is turned on its head. Martin Petr, a civil engineer, goes to a backward part of the country to prepare for the building of a big waterworks. As the story unfolds more and more questions arise. "What was the point of that?" Martin asks himself. "Great thoughts and aims that had driven him to go there in the first place were now gradually fading away."

Disillusion is also a characteristic of the heroes of JAN PROCHÁZKA. His stories often go back to the liberation of 1945, the fifties and to the countryside of South Moravia, where the author came from. He makes full use of dramatic descriptions of actual places, most of which were used as backgrounds for films by Karel Kachyňa. *Ať žije republika* (Long Live the Republic) came out in 1965, the same year as the book. The film *Noc nevěsty* (Bridal Night) was made in 1967 from the book *Svatá noc* (Holy Night)[44] published in 1966. (Procházka's children's books, published in English, were *The Carp* [1977] and *Lenka* [1981].)

The critic Milan Jungmann called Klíma's *Hodina ticha* a novel with a new vision. Jiří Opelík wrote that it was a work of transition from faith to knowledge. However, Přemysl Blažíček, whose views were nearer those of the rising generation, thought that in many ways Klíma was entrenched in the old ideas.

In the novel, the clear distinction between light and shade was becoming blurred. Behind the illustrious façades it was apparent that all kinds of unseemly things were happening. The "bird's eye view" of the thick volumes of the fifties, in which a man existed only as a representative of his social class and had no importance as an individual, was gradually replaced by the "worm's eye view" and subjective interpretations and values. The personal responsibility of the individual was now the issue. Milan Suchomel wrote: "History and objective conditions do not constitute an alibi, they do not absolve man of responsibility. He is also answerable for them."[45]

War and the Nazi occupation were the themes that united another group of novelists. For that reason they were sometimes spoken of, for example by Aleš Haman in 1961, as the second wave of war writers, lumping together Norbert Frýd and Jan Otčenášek and the works of Arnošt Lustig from the end of the previous decade (see pp. 54–55). In the meantime the picture of war had changed. Spectacular heroism and the consciousness of a great historical mission had gone, as it had from Grigorii Baklanov in Russian literature, from Vasil Bykav in Belorussian literature and from the works of Vladimír Mináč, Rudolf Jašík and Ladislav Ťažký in Slovak literature. The Czech novel continued along the lines begun with Jiří Weil's *Život s hvězdou* (Life with a Star, see p. 17). It concentrated chiefly on the lot of the Jews.[46] Exceptional, extreme situations are placed within everyday, "dormant" totalitarianism, reminiscent of Kafka's writing where violent acts are unexceptional and take place casually.

Jiří Weil's (→ Profiles) last novel, *Na střeše je Mendelssohn* (1960, published in English as *Mendelssohn Is on the Roof*, 1991), did not come out till after his death and then with cuts by the censor. In it the author expanded several themes from his earlier works. The bizarre scene at the beginning is typical. The German *Reichsprotector* in Bohemia, Heydrich, on a visit to the Rudolfinum concert hall in Prague in 1941, noticed the statue of the German composer Mendelssohn-Bartholdy, a man with Jewish ancestors. The statue was to be removed immediately, but the German official who was to carry out the order, expecting to be promoted to the rank of the SS, was unable to identify it from the others. Judging their "Jewishness" by the length of the statues' noses, he would also have removed the statue of Richard Wagner, a composer loved by Hitler and the Nazis. Eventually a scholarly Jew had to help by giving a detailed description.

Arnošt Lustig (see pp. 54–55 and → Profiles) also continued to write. His best-known novella from the sixties is *Modlitba pro Kateřinu Horovitzovou* (1964; published in English as *A Prayer for Katerina Horovitzova*, 1973, and filmed for television by Antonín Moskalyk in 1965. It was based on an incident from 1943, when the Nazis in Italy interned some rich Jewish businessmen with American passports. They promised to release them on payment of a ransom. Later, however, when they had gained control of their bank accounts the Nazis had them murdered in Auschwitz. Lustig of course made many adaptations to the original subject. The novel is very cleverly constructed. From various hints the reader suspects the inevitable tragic outcome, while the victims live in blissful hope till the last moment. The eponymous character, a beautiful Jewish girl, is the only one who has the courage to resist: when she has to go naked to the gas chamber and a German officer looks insolently at her, she attacks him with a buckle on her bra, seizes his gun and shoots him. Lustig drew a portrait of another Jewish girl in the novel *Dita Saxová* (1962; published in English as *Dita Sax*, 1966; new translation as *Dita Saxova*, 1979, filmed with Lustig's cooperation by Antonín Moskalyk, 1967). Dita is the only one of her family to survive the concentration camp, but she is so distressed in the postwar world that she commits suicide.

Other authors to write on Jewish subjects were HANA BĚLOHRADSKÁ in *Bez krásy, bez límce* (Without Beauty, without a Collar, 1962; filmed with Bělohradská's cooperation by Zbyněk Brynych as *A pátý jezdec je Strach* [And the Fifth Rider Is Fear], 1964), JOSEF ŠKVORECKÝ in *Sedmiramenný svícen* (The Menorah, 1964) and LADISLAV GROSMAN, whose *Obchod na korze* (The Shop on Main Street, 1965)[47] is situated in Slovakia. The latter was made into a film by Jan Kadár and Elmar Klos and a year later won the first Oscar for Czechoslovakia. Ivan Klíma and Ladislav Fuks both wrote on subjects similar to Lustig's *Kateřina Horovitzová*, in fact Fuks became the most outstanding writer on the fate of the Jews, which he saw as a parable of the general threat to mankind.

In LADISLAV FUKS'S (→ PROFILES) novels, unlike Lustig's, there is very little action, the emphasis is on the inner state of mind of the characters, and subtle nuances of thinking and experience. The reader is aware of a strange ambiguity and disjointedness; many things are deliberately not explained. Fuks was attracted by fantasy and mystery even in his literary debut, the novel *Pan Theodor Mundstock* (1963; published in English as *Mr Theodore Mundstock*, 1968). It was not published till Fuks was in his forties and it became an immediate success. The critics rated it one of the best contemporary novels and the book was eventually published in seventeen countries.

The subject is similar to Weil's *Život s hvězdou* (see p. 17). Mr Mundstock is also an outsider, alone, an undistinguished clerk who is waiting to be taken to the Theresienstadt concentration camp. He tries to find his salvation by thinking out and perfecting strategies for surviving the German concentration camp. "He is in training" for getting into a convoy, for hunger, for being beaten, even for his own death. However, as he is approaching the assembly point for the convoy, keeping to his prepared strategy and changing his little case from one hand to the other, he is knocked down and killed by a German car.

The author of *Pan Theodor Mundstock* tries to reproduce the tragic, absurd situation of the Jews during the occupation, and at the same time to give a picture of the plight of man in general. The story is told in the third person but almost everything is seen through the eyes of the central character. The real and fantastic elements merge directly into each other; for example, Mr Mundstock's alter ego Mon is depicted as an actual being until the thirteenth chapter when we realize that he exists only in the hero's imagination. The metaphorical impact is heightened by the repetition of words and key motifs (dust, star).

The aim of official prose in the fifties was to convey an unambiguous message. Fuks's works on the contrary are based on confusion, impenetrability, and a host of complex meanings. In the novel *Variace pro temnou strunu* (Variations for a Dark String, 1966), the view of the world is even narrower and more bizarre than in Mundstock. The narrator is Michal, a grammar school pupil, a morbidly sensitive boy, the son of a highly placed police officer. The sentence "life is a prison and an illusion like the whole world" gives an early indication of the sinister atmosphere immediately before the occupation and war. In the author's next books, *Spalovač mrtvol* (1967; published in English as *The Cremator*, 1984; made into an outstanding film by Juraj Herz, 1968) and *Myši Natálie Mooshabrové* (Natalie Mooshabrová's Mice, 1970), the characters and settings become ever stranger and the style, based on allusion and repetition, more complex. These books are somewhere on the borderline between horror stories and thrillers.

In the course of the sixties, prose writing developed on different lines and in different directions. New genres appeared and new-old genres reappeared: after the science fiction of Josef Nesvadba and Ludvík Souček following on perhaps from Jakub Arbes and Karel Čapek, there was a kind of sophisticated detective fiction in the works of Karel Michal, Edvard Valenta, Hana Prošková and Josef Škvorecký. A wide range of popular and light literature that had once been completely suppressed by officialdom flourished again. More than ever before the cultural climate was created by films. Musicals and westerns were shown in the cinemas. Satire, fantasy, entertainment, subjective soul searchings and harsh realism were all now possible subjects. There was a more extensive range of narrative techniques, subjective time, the story told from the point of view of the individual or different individuals. The language itself went from the extremes of slang and colloquial syntax to artistically stylized expressions, metaphor, poetism and formal speech. The former uniformity of imagery and style that made everything equally dull was now replaced by individuality, greater charm and colour.

JOSEF ŠKVORECKÝ (→ PROFILES) began publishing his texts again in 1963, after a break caused by the scandal surrounding the publication of his novel *Zbabělci* (The Cowards, see pp. 51–52). In the 1960s, he published his older work as well as some new texts, such as the short novel *Legenda Emöke* (1963; published in English as *Emöke*, 1977). This is a novel about a wasted opportunity for the development of a deep emotional relationship, and about the clash of an authentic, honest attitude to life with a conformist attitude. Then in 1967 Škvorecký brought out *Bassaxofon* (translated as *The Bass Saxophone* in 1977), a homage to the greatness of jazz music as a metaphor for the creative process, which turned out to be his most successful work in the USA and Canada; it later served as an inspiration for the composer John Robby to write a jazz opera. At this time, Škvorecký also published a collection of short stories, *Sedmiramenný svícen* (The Menorah, 1964), which included the highly sophisticated short story *Eine kleine Jazzmusik*. Film director Miloš Forman wanted to make a film based on this story but the Communist president Antonín Novotný prevented him from doing so, mistakenly believing that Forman wanted to shoot *The Cowards*. In the 1960s, Škvorecký also ventured for the first time into an entirely new genre: the detective story. He created his own character out of the slightly bumbling, timid investigator Lieutenant Borůvka (Bilberry), *Smutek poručíka Borůvky* (1966; *The Mournful Demeanour of Lieutenant Boruvka*, 1973). He published literary essays about the genre of detective fiction. From the 1960s onwards, Škvorecký's work was deeply influenced by the Anglo-Saxon literary tradition and by the work of the interwar Czech author Karel Čapek.

BOHUMIL HRABAL (→ PROFILES) was the most outstanding figure in contemporary fiction. By age he belonged to the war generation, being ten years older than Fuks. After many years spent writing only for a few friends or without hope of being published, from 1963 to 1968 he produced at least one book a year. His work aroused admiration, astonishment and enthusiasm but also a great many protests from conservative readers. The author himself, unabashed, said that "a real book is not for helping the reader to get to sleep, but to make him jump out of bed in his long johns and run and sock the writer on the jaw".

Hrabal's prose writing upset accepted ideas about literature in several different ways, beginning with his texts in *Perlička na dně* (The Pearl in the Deep, 1963). Most of these texts were written in the 1950s and published in English in *The Death of Mr Baltisberger* (1975). Poetic metaphors appear alongside obscene pub expressions. Non-traditional narrative methods were another new departure. Instead of connected action, Hrabal used a mosaic of situations or a flow of ideas as occur in speech. Hrabal's vision did not reflect ideology and was totally without any hierarchy of values. The narrator or speaker shows the same amount of interest in trivia as in significant, strange or terrible events. To make this clear, Hrabal uses the device of a long series of subordinate clauses with the conjunctions "and" and "but" connecting unconnected facts. The novella *Taneční hodiny pro starší a pokročilé* (1964; published in English as *Dancing Lessons for the Advanced in Age*, 1995) goes furthest in this direction. It is composed of a single sentence that keeps acquiring additions and is left unfinished.[48] Other characteristics of Hrabal's style are exaggeration and the use of colourful eye-catching detail.

> " . . . once an old woman stopped and asked me what company her son was in, she'd made some cakes for him, and suddenly up rode Count Zelikowski on his stallion and roared, Who told you you could talk to that hag, you whoreson! and gave me a taste of his crop and leaped clear over the woman on his stallion at twenty degrees below zero, and once I was on guard duty, I was twenty-one at the time and so full of energy I could have lit Prague for a week, why, even now I'm a holy terror when I see that safeguard of marital bliss, a well-developed female body, and back then I was a member of the Sokol Gymnastic Society and had a Sokol curl and a Sokol uniform that fit me like the president's fit him, and there was a whole field full of Sokols and flags waving in the trees, a row of white horses, a row of red horses, and two beauties tearing each other's blouses to shreds over me . . . "[49]

Akin to Bohumil Hrabal were Jaroslav Hašek, Ladislav Klíma, the later surrealists, *Group 42* (see pp. 15–16) and James Joyce in *Ulysses*; Hrabal was also strongly influenced by modern plastic arts. The word *pábitelství* (palavering) could well be applied to one aspect of Hrabal's prose. It was actually the 19th-century Parnassian Jaroslav Vrchlický, who was the first to use the word *pábit*. Used by the poet František Hrubín and his friends, it did not become famous till Hrabal's book *Pábitelé* (1964, Palaveres; most of these texts were also written in the 1950s and published in English in *The Death of Mr Baltisberger*, 1975). *Pábitelé* are unconventional people, outsiders and charismatics (not in the religious sense), crazy visionaries possessed by their dreams and constantly amazed. Dialogues play an important part in Hrabal's work. Sometimes they are overheard conversations among people who have a gift for vivid original speech, and sometimes they are tragic-comic and absurd, divorced from reality. A film version of Hrabal's shorter texts from the sixties, *Perličky na dně* (The Pearls in the Deep) was made by a group of young directors (Jiří Menzel, Jan Němec, Evald Schorm, Věra Chytilová, Jaromil Jireš). Thus these stories of Hrabal became a manifesto of the forthcoming "New Wave" of Czech cinema (see p. 91).

The author chose a more traditional method of presentation in his novel *Ostře sledované vlaky* (1965, *A Close Watch on the Trains*, 1968; also translated as *Closely Watched Trains*, 1968) in which he combined two of his manuscripts from the years after the February 1948 coup. The film version by Jiří Menzel, with Václav Neckář in the main role, made the book famous. The script by Menzel and Hrabal was published in English as *Closely Watched Trains* (1971) and, also in 1971, as *Closely Observed Trains*. The next collection of short stories, *Inzerát na dům, ve kterém už nechci bydlet* (Advertisement for a House I Don't Want to Live in Anymore, 1965) was filmed by Jiří Menzel as *Skřivánci na niti* (Larks on the String) in 1969. Set in the early fifties, it was banned and had its premiere in 1990. It is not, however, primarily a criticism of the social system. The stories arise out of everyday situations which show up the latent poetry, cruelty and absurdity of life. The hallmarks of the author's style are still there but the zany sprightliness has been replaced by black humour.

The story *Ingot a ingoti* (Ingot and Ingots) from the same book begins with a girl shrieking "Let me liiiiiive!" as she is thrown out of a pub. At the end after the girl has been raped in a workman's hostel and thrown out, her voice from beneath the window wails, repeating the sentence "Let me liiiiiive! let me liiiiiive!"[50]

3. Novels of Disillusionment

In the middle of the decade large-scale prose works, chiefly novels, began to attract attention. The main subjects were again personal failure and disillusionment, which now spilled over into a more general picture of the age and into speculation about the place of man in history.[51]

"Everything was more or less pared to the bone," said František Hrubín (→ Profiles) in 1967. People did not know what mattered or where they stood, they were losing their identity. They were trying to get rid of externally imposed systems, they were turning inwards and reminding themselves of the basic meaning of life. It was part and parcel of the attempt to return to youth and childhood, to their original and more genuine convictions. "Jan tried to walk on his hands. Somehow or other he leaned back and remained lying on the ground. It was some time before he managed to stand up and find his bearings; he received no instructions from anywhere, neither from Earth nor from the universe . . . "[52] This is the symbolic beginning to Hrubín's lyrical novel *Zlatá reneta* (The Golden Apple, 1964, filmed by Otakar Vávra, 1965). Jan, at a crisis, was aware of the triviality of much of his life.

There was even more profound scepticism in the novels of the "May" generation, *Smrtelná neděle* (Fatal Sunday, 1967)[53] by Jaroslav Putík, *Sekyra* (1966; published in English as *The Axe*, 1973) by Ludvík Vaculík, Milan Kundera's *Žert* (1967; published in English as *The Joke*, 1969, with a new translation in 1982, filmed with Kundera's cooperation by Jaromil Jireš, 1968), and Jaroslav Putík's second novel *Brána blažených* (The Gate of the Blessed, 1969). They were, according to Milan Jungmann, "tales of a dreadful time when the vault of heaven collapsed", and were the bitter confessions of heroes who believed in a clear sense of history and in their own great mission as its architects. Kundera and Vaculík had completed their next works by the end of the sixties but then they could no longer have them published.

The background to all this was disillusionment with Communist ideals. There was, however, no attempt at reforming them, "rectifying a wrong direction" as in some other contemporary novels. Not only was Stalinism called into question but so was any kind of predetermined planning of people's lives. Published works dealt with contemporary matters, especially politics. They went "right to the bone" – of course in the spirit of Hrubín's words. They dealt with everyday problems, with the alienation of man from man and from his environment, with wilful and inadvertent acceptance of pretence and role playing, with seeking one's own "self", with the results of our interference in world events and the guilt it causes us, and with the relationship of the individual to history.

So eventually the Czech novel mostly returned to the tradition of the polyphonic prose of the thirties. This is particularly true of Ludvík Vaculík and Milan Kundera whose many-faceted works are composed of texts, structured in different ways, each one indicating a different avenue of thought.

LUDVÍK VACULÍK'S (→ PROFILES) *Sekyra* is notable first of all for its language. Jiří Opelík distinguished six different lexical levels, from literary Czech and the old-fashioned style of the father's letters to Moravian Wallachian dialect. Unlike dialect in older texts, dialect and other non-literary expressions are not used to indicate character. Language is not simply a means of revealing what the characters are like. Even the narrator uses dialect and non-literary expressions, especially regarding word order and syntax. In the novel, in a single paragraph, even in a single sentence, the style can change from one level to another.

In *Sekyra* levels of time also overlap closely. In the very first sentence the narrator says he is going to visit his brother. In trying to say something about the brother, he describes their childhood, their parents and finally his own and his father's later life – and does not reach the visit to the brother till the end of the novel. These reminiscences, "returns" to the past and prospects, and "excursions" into the future occur unexpectedly: "'Don't go.' Mother pleaded a quarter of a century ago." "'We'll have to regulate the stream again,' Dad said, and as he spoke, the fish vanished; 'and straighten that path,' and the line of apple trees toppled to the ground, 'and one day, maybe, we'll lay a branch line on the other side to the factory,' he said, and a hideous embankment of slag bulged over the mill-race."[54]

The time changes in the story and the variations in style give the text a dynamic quality. Dialogue will suddenly interrupt the narrative, and alternate with meditations, descriptions of the countryside and humorous scenes. In this story presented "at random" like a stream with many springs, the narrator describes the life of his family from an East Moravian village, particularly his relationship with his father. After the war his father, a penniless villager, and obstinate idealist, becomes an active Communist Party official who eventually does no more than blindly follow the party line. The son, a journalist in Prague, comes into conflict with the corruption and obtuseness of the authorities. At this crisis he returns home to the values of his childhood – being true to yourself and rebelling against ruined personal relationships – the values his father represented for him. A scene at the end of the book illustrates this idea. In spite of the fact that it is forbidden, the narrator and his brother remove a tree from the wood. This scene is an analogy with the one at the beginning where the son and the father go out secretly stealing apples.

Important historical events are marginal to the novel. *Sekyra*, an openly autobiographical novel, is not primarily an attack on ideology. Nevertheless it develops into a fundamental criticism of the age, of the national character and of a civilization too rapidly becoming dependent on technology. Thanks to its style and vision of the world, it has become Vaculík's key work.

Unlike Vaculík, MILAN KUNDERA (→ PROFILES) presents his stories in strictly logical order. This is evident as early as *Směšné lásky* (Laughable Loves, 1963), to which additions were made in 1965 and 1968 (published in English as *Laughable Loves*, 1974). The final selection dates from 1991. The heroes want to escape from the excruciatingly dull responsibilities of normal life. They are, however, overtaken by the developments they themselves set in motion. For example, the lovers in *Falešný autostop* (The Hitchhiking Game) start playing at being a callous motorist and an insolent hitchhiker, pretending they have met by chance. The game completely fascinates them; however, it turns serious and brutal, and in the end they cannot throw off the roles they have assumed because the game has revealed some unpalatable truths to them about each other. "After a moment he heard her sobbing quietly. The girl's hand diffidently, childishly touched his. It touched, withdrew, then touched again, and then a pleading, sobbing voice broke the silence, calling him by his name and saying: 'I am me, I am me . . . ' [. . .]"[55]

In 1960 Kundera's story *Já, truchlivý bůh* (I, the Mournful God, filmed with Kundera's cooperation by Antonín Kachlík in 1969) was published in the review *Plamen* (Blaze). In 1963 it was included in the book *Směšné lásky* (Laughable Loves), but the author omitted it from the final version published in Brno in 1991. In it we find the following: "Life is a paradox. What we do acquires the opposite meaning from what we originally intended."[56] This sceptical admission on the part of the narrator about failure in love is repeated in other words in the novel *Žert* (The Joke), but it does not refer only to the hero's own world. It is a projection of the more general relationship of the individual to history and questions the supremacy of man as the creator of history.

The joke in the title of the novel has many meanings. Initially it refers to the postcard making fun of dogmatic Marxism that the twenty-year-old Ludvík sent as a joke to a girl student. The affair snowballs; the postcard is considered a hostile act. After an "incriminating" speech by his friend Zemánek, Ludvík is expelled from the party and the university and sent to an army penal corps. Years later, to avenge the ruination of his life, Ludvík attempts another "joke". He decides to seduce Zemánek's wife Helena. However, he very soon finds out that her husband no longer loves her. He has become a popular "reformist" teacher at the university and has an attractive young girlfriend. The joke once again turns on its perpetrator. Ludvík, who in his youth thought he was "at the wheel of history", and who later tried at least to think up a suitable revenge, ends up bitterly disillusioned, embarrassed and ridiculous. History is actually a huge ironic joke at the expense of man.

The main narrative is filled out with a network of accounts of the lives of many other individuals, composing a picture of Czech society from 1948 to the mid-sixties. Within this network the construction is equally complex. Besides Ludvík there are three other narrators, who, as the critic Milan Blahynka has pointed out, tell the story in exactly measured proportions. Ludvík narrates two thirds of the text, Jaroslav one sixth, Kostka one ninth and Helena one eighteenth. Each of them uses a different style, each one has a different inner world and each has different illusions. In this way different perspectives cast doubt on a single supreme truth and show that reality has many faces.

In 1984 Milan Kundera wrote: "If I look back at *Žert*, I find in it everything I have been aiming at in my later novels." This is a reference to the use of many different narrators in his novels, to variations and mirror images, but above all to the key themes in his work. These are, as they appear in *Život je jinde* (published in English as *Life Is Elsewhere*, 1974), "the age of lyricism", cheap revolutionism, the embodiment of immaturity in man and society. In *Kniha smíchu a zapomnění* (published in English as *The Book of Laughter and Forgetting*, 1980) the theme is the dominance of forgetfulness, life without historical memory or responsibility. In *Nesnesitelná lehkost bytí* (published in English as *The Unbearable Lightness of Being*, 1984) it is the crisis of language, ritualism and systems that alienates people from each other, and the impossibility of reaching understanding between people.

The historical novel, the jewel in the crown of literature after the February 1948 coup, now also acquired a new look. The books of FRANTIŠEK KOŽÍK, a skilful writer of historical biographies, can be taken as an example. Compared with *Josef Mánes* (Joseph Mánes, 1955),[57] a work about the Czech painter, his biographical novel about well-known musician Leoš Janáček *Po zarostlém chodníčku* (On an Overgrown Path, 1967) is a much more complex piece of work. The language varies in style and is more colourful. The characters talk to themselves and different periods of time merge into each other.

In the fifties this fashion gave rise to the historical chronicle and with it an "objective" picture of history – although in truth it was more like a free version of history. Contemporary prose treated historical subjects generally as analogies for power, morals and conscience. The rejection of schematic models was reflected also in the choice of subjects. Instead of the 15th-century Hussite movement and the 19th-century National Revival, the pre-Hussite Middle Ages and the Baroque were now preferred. VÁCLAV KAPLICKÝ, for example, one of the oldest traditional novelists, in his *Kladivo na čarodějnice* (The Witch Hunt, 1963; filmed by Otakar Vávra, 1969), gives an account of the Inquisition trials in North Moravia at the end of the 17th century. The very word "trials" sounded ominous; readers remembered the atmosphere of fear and injustice at the beginning of the fifties and assumed the novel was really intended as a parable. OLDŘICH DANĚK chose to set his novel *Král utíká z boje* (The King Flees the Battle, 1967; filmed by the author as *Královský omyl* [The King's Blunder, 1968]) at the time of the Luxembourg kings in the 14th century during the conflict between John of Luxembourg and Jindřich (Henry) of Lipé. The novel deals with power and the abuse of power. The past does not create "great history", it is not a review of a succession of heroic deeds and wise aphorisms – on the contrary it is made up of deeds full of self-interest and intrigue. To remove any illusions the author deliberately stresses the fact that the novel is a work of fiction. He continued in the same vein in the works that followed, *Král bez přílby* (A King without a Helmet, 1971) and *Vražda v Olomouci* (Murder in Olomouc, 1972). In the latter, the historical background had become merely a framework for a detective investigation into the murder of Václav III, the last Czech king from the Przemyslide dynasty, and a vehicle for reflections on truth and power.

JIŘÍ ŠOTOLA tended to favour the epic style in his poetry but in 1967 he tried his hand at historical drama in the television play *Waterloo*. This surprised his readers in spite of the fact that he had written an extensive novel *Tovaryšstvo Ježíšovo* (The Society of Jesus, 1969,[58] set in the time of the Counter Reformation. The main character in the novel is the scholarly Jesuit Vojtěch Had (*had* = snake) who dutifully carries out the tasks entrusted to him. In a remote corner of Bohemia he has to build a chapel, get a legacy from a rich widow and establish a cathedral. Gradually, however, his enthusiasm wanes. He realizes he is doing something shameful by becoming an instrument of the authorities and he ends up in despair. "We have won. We have power, we have the gospel, we have property. And with all that we have nothing."[59]

The novel, whose chief characters are authentic historical figures, represents the negative aspect of the restoration of Catholicism after the defeat of the Czech Protestant nobility's uprising against the Habsburgs in 1620, at the beginning of the Thirty Years War in the 17th century, and the failure of any triumphant ruling ideology. Father Had is in fact the antithesis of the physically dying, but spiritually victorious, missionaries in František Křelina's novel *Amarú, syn hadí* (Amarú, Son of the Snakes) and in JAROSLAV DURYCH's tetralogy *Služebníci neužiteční* (Wicked Servants), Part 1 of which was published in 1940. The work in its entirety was published in Rome in 1969. Šotola also uses poetic language and symbolism.

Incidents are repeated and rearranged for dramatic effect but the lofty spirituality of Durych and Křelina is missing. Like Putík, Vaculík and Kundera, he takes man's involvement in history with a large measure of scepticism.

The rising generation of writers was most radical in breaking down the barriers traditionally separating different genres. The novel *Čest a sláva* (Fame and Honour, 1966; filmed by Hynek Bočan in 1968) by KAREL MICHAL shows the dark side rather than the bright side of history. In it the usual themes and style of historical prose come in for ironical treatment. The noble knight Rynda from Loučky and Poříčany is more like a peasant farmer than an aristocrat. And Rynda's declaration of war against the Habsburgs at the very moment when a peace treaty was bringing the Thirty Years War to an end firmly establishes the tragi-comic aspect of the characters.

The most important historical novelist of the younger generation was VLADIMÍR KÖRNER. He was also important as a film writer, especially in collaboration with the director František Vláčil, one of the greatest 20th-century Czech artists, in the films *Údolí včel* (The Valley of the Bees, 1967) and *Adelheid* (Adelheid, 1969). He also uses "film" techniques in his literary works – the dialogue is crisp and the descriptions and highlights are reminiscent of the cinema. Like Karel Michal in his *Čest a sláva* Körner rarely uses authentic historical personages. If they do appear they are presented with none of the conventions that usually apply in historical novels and films. In the introduction to his *Písečná kosa* (Strip of Sand, 1970) the author points out that it is "not a historical novel". Körner does not concentrate on "how things were" but aims at portraying the existentialist, timeless problems of man. The heroes of his books are lonely and vacillating people in search of something. The commonest themes are violence, fanaticism and pillage, ending inexorably in tragedy. All these features are to be found in the gloomy tale *Písečná kosa*, set in the 13th century, and in *Adelheid* (Adelheid, 1967), set in the weeks following the Second World War. *Adelheid* is the story of the dramatic love-hate relationship between people from different worlds – a Czech officer who had returned from the Western front and a German girl whose father and brother were Nazi criminals.

Vladimír Körner makes use of the same material as Václav Řezáč once did in *Nástup* (The Line-Up, see p. 24). However his outlook is competely different. He views the world three-dimensionally, concentrating on portraying the complex inner life of his characters. JAROSLAV DURYCH chose a similar subject for his novella *Boží duha* (God's Rainbow), written in 1955 and published posthumously in 1969. Set at the border immediately after the war, it is also a love story. This novella is the best of Durych's postwar work. It describes the strange love of a Czech – in this instance an elderly man – for a German girl. The horrors of the day, the putrefying corpses in the church, the killing of the girl's parents and her rape are presented only as isolated incidents but they are described in the graphic terms and horrific detail typical of Durych. The story is meant to be first and foremost a parable of guilt, punishment and reconciliation. The child the German girl is expecting is a glimmer of hope at the end of the book, and the rainbow surrounding the two main characters represents God's mercy.

In his first novel *Cesta ke hřbitovu* (The Way to the Graveyard, 1968) OTA FILIP broke with tradition in his portrayal of recent history and Czech–German relationships. Ludvík Vaculík wrote of it:

> "In Filip's view, the Czech nation under the German occupation consisted of workers making weapons for the Nazis, of cowardly timeservers and officials. Besides them there was a handful of fighters in the mountains who were however a danger to both sides. And within all these groups were informers and traitors. Only individuals show any heroism, honour or responsibility . . . "[60]

Cesta ke hřbitovu foreshadows the view of history in the author's largest work *Nanebevstoupení Lojzka Lapáčka ze Slezské Ostravy* (The Ascension of Lojzek Lapáček from Silesian Ostrava). This came out in exile and in samizdat in 1974 but it had already appeared in a German translation a year earlier. "Great" history is seen from the point of view of the "little" man who has no desire to be a hero and is not interested in ideology but in his own everyday world. It also foreshadows several other works with elements of fantasy that strip the glamour from the distant past, the war, the liberation of 1945 and the expulsion of the Germans.

If the heroes of Ota Filip's two novels try with all their might to preserve their natural world in the turbulence of history, VLADIMÍR NEFF in *Trampoty pana Humbla* (The Trials and Tribulations of Mr Humbl, 1967)[61] portrays the negative aspects of the "little Czech". His Humbl is a servile creature, willing to adapt to any regime from Austria to Communism and ready to flatter any superior. He is even prepared to drive a man to death, a man who had helped him but who could have prevented a furthering of his career. The author conceived his novel as Humbl's "confession", which allowed him to adopt a style revealing Humbl as regretful, servile and at the same time aggressive. In the end he concludes that "there are many of us Humbls and the fact that we exist is beneficial and desirable, for we make history".[62]

Writing about the times after the 1948 Communist takeover from the point of view of the victims of Stalinism was a new departure in domestic literature.[63] ARNOŠT LUSTIG described the appalling conditions in the work camps in his story *Bílé břízy na podzim* (White Birches in Autumn, 1966). Towards the end of the sixties the prisoners themselves began to write about their experiences – KAREL PECKA in his novel *Horečka* (Fever, 1967) and in his short stories *Na co umírají muži* (That's What Men Die Of, 1968), JIŘÍ MUCHA, an experienced journalist and writer, in his semi-fictional diary *Studené slunce* (The Cold Sun, 1968; published in English as *Living and Partly Living*, 1967) and JIŘÍ STRÁNSKÝ in the stories in *Štěstí* (Happiness). Stránský's collection *Štěstí* was dated 1969 but most of that edition was destroyed and a new edition without the censor's cuts was not published until 1990. Karel Pecka's short story collection *Na co umírají muži* had been written as early as the fifties in the camp at Bytíz where Pecka served part of his eleven-year sentence for editing an underground journal after the Communist takeover. Pecka's fiction was highly effective even later, whenever it was true to documented facts and the testimony of witnesses. Thus *Motáky nezvěstnému*

(Messages to Missing Persons), his wide-ranging picture of the life of political prisoners in the fifties, came out in Canada in 1980, in samizdat in Prague 1978 and in Brno in 1990.[64]

4. Literary Criticism

Concurrently with developments in literature a remarkable revival took place in criticism and literary thinking. Oleg Sus, Jiří Brabec, Milan Suchomel, Jiří Opelík, Zdeněk Kožmín, Aleš Haman and Jan Lopatka became well known as critics. The critics of the middle generation, Sergej Machonin and Milan Jungmann from *Literární noviny* (Literary News), who had shown decided leanings towards dogmatism after the February 1948 coup, began to change their committed attitudes to literature. Ladislav Štoll and a few other individuals maintained the positions they had adopted in the early fifties and gradually became isolated in spite of the support of the party ideologists.

Literary scholarship also saw the return of the older generation. VÁCLAV ČERNÝ (→ PROFILES) came out of seclusion and returned to literary work. Another scholar who had begun as a critic and essayist before the war was the literary historian from Olomouc OLDŘICH KRÁLÍK. The breadth of his vision and his provocative hypotheses were astonishing. His books and studies attempted to interpret and reconstruct the creative process. A representative volume of his literary essays came out in 1995 as *Osvobozená slova* (The Liberated Words).

After years of being banned the Prague structuralist school also ceased to be regarded as "the movement that absorbed everything characteristic of the corruption of art in imperialist capitalism". Structuralism first revived in linguistics and stylistics – in the works of Bohuslav Havránek, Pavel Trost, Karel Hausenblas and Lubomír Doležel, and then in the theory of versification and the theory of translation – in the works of Brno scholars Josef Hrabák and Jiří Levý. These branches of literature had been allowed to continue almost completely without interference. The precision of structuralism – the attempt to establish the exact meaning of a text – worked as an antidote to the vagueness and licence of the fifties. The idea of a work of art as something original and independent gradually infiltrated literary thinking and virtually meant the rejection of the official "reflection theory". An important step forward was the publication in 1966 of the treatises of JAN MUKAŘOVSKÝ from the thirties and forties. *Studie z estetiky* (Studies in Aesthetics) was followed in 1971 by *Cestami poetiky a estetiky* (Along the Pathways of Poetics and Aesthetics). Some of these works were published in English in collections of Mukařovský's work *The Word and Verbal Art* (1977), and *Structure, Sign, and Function* (1978). The work of FELIX VODIČKA, who applied his structuralist method to the history of literature, was highly influential in this field. His collected studies *Struktura vývoje* (The Structure of the Literary Process) was published in 1969.[65] After many years ROMAN JAKOBSON, co-founder of the Prague Linguistic Circle and Czech structuralism, was able to speak in public again in Czechoslovakia. He returned as a world-famous scholar, and at the end of a symposium in Prague he proposed a toast:

> "I propose a toast to the beauty of the Czech land that has delighted me for nigh on fifty years and that I have been able to recapture today. [. . .] I should like to pay my respects to the land where more than anywhere else culture is indigenous, where the great majority of people think for themselves and only an insignificant few are not capable of independent thought. Unfortunately elsewhere the reverse is still true." (Toast at the closing of the symposium in Prague on Constantine the Philosopher, 1969)[66]

Some younger theoreticians, the aestheticians Robert Kalivoda and Květoslav Chvatík, the stylist Lubomír Doležel, the literary theorists Miroslav Červenka and Milan Jankovič, formed a group round Mukařovský and Vodička. Many others developed the ideas of structuralism. Most of them collaborated in *Struktura a smysl literárního díla* (The Structure and Meaning of a Literary Work, 1966), a collection to celebrate the seventy-fifth birthday of Mukařovský.[67]

From 1966 the bi-monthly review *Orientace* (The Way to Go) was the platform for the new structuralists and other authors who had originally gathered round *Květen* (May, see pp. 45–47) proclaiming the anti-ideological conception of art. In the introductory number Miroslav Červenka wrote: "In the fight against dogmatism (i.e. Communist authoritarianism) we realized what huge potential there was in our attempts to produce general accounts of Man in his predicament. Such accounts were in themselves strong enough to offer human experience as an antidote to ideological reductionism."[68]

From the end of the fifties the work of literary historians and literary lexicographers was revitalized. Volume 2 of the scholarly *Dějiny české literatury* (The History of Czech Literature) was published in 1960. This was a collective work produced in Mukařovský's Institute of Czech Literature and dedicated to the National Revival. The chief author and editor was Felix Vodička. The final volume, Volume 4, dealing with the literature of the first half of the 20th century, was finished in 1969 but was not published till 1995 when it was edited by Zdeněk Pešat and Eva Strohsová. *Slovník českých spisovatelů* (A Dictionary of Czech Writers, 1964), edited by Rudolf Havel and Jiří Opelík, made a significant contribution to lexicography. It recorded the names of many hitherto suppressed writers, such as Jan Čep, Jakub Deml, Egon Hostovský, Jan Zahradníček and others. An even greater achievement was the monumental *Lexikon české literatury* (A Lexicon of Czech Literature) with Vladimír Forst and Jiří Opelík as chief editors, on which scholars worked for several decades (see p. 180).

Besides structuralism, other movements injected new life into literary thinking. The conception of art inherent in phenomenology and existentialism was related to the philosophy of human life especially as developed by Martin Heidegger and in Czechoslovakia by JAN PATOČKA(see p. 65 and → PROFILES). The work of the Polish aesthetician, philosopher and phenomenologist Roman Ingarden was also highly regarded. Following in his footsteps ANTONÍN MOKREJŠ analyzed various philosophical questions in his book *Umění, skutečnost, poznání* (Art, Reality and

Perception, 1966). Both phenomenology and structuralism stressed the importance of autonomy and the independent nature of art. Literature should not merely represent an idea, an author's opinions or historical events. According to Patočka it is "the creation of works which have meaning in themselves, like an experience that cannot be transferred to anyone else" (1966).[69] It has therefore a unique role and nothing can take its place. It upsets established means of communication and perception and enables us to see things we are incapable of seeing for ourselves in our daily lives.

At first it was difficult for structuralism and phenomenology to enter into the argument against ideology. It was even more difficult for Catholic critics, such as Bedřich Fučík (see pp. 155–156) and Miloš Dvořák, to return to literature. "The years of mercy" 1968–1969 did not last long enough for them. The majority of their books and studies, although ready for printing, were not published.

The Sixties Generation

1. The Development of the Younger Generation

Literary life was considerably enlivened by the rise of the younger authors, the third successive generation of outstanding writers after Vítězslav Nezval's avant-gardists and Jiří Orten's wartime generation since the inauguration of the First Republic in 1918. As usual it was the poets who first came to the attention of the public. Between 1961 and 1962 *Mladá fronta* (Frontline Youth) published poems by Josef Hanzlík, Ivan Wernisch, Petr Kabeš and Jiří Gruša. Antonín Brousek and Pavel Šrut had their first slim volumes of poetry published by *Československý spisovatel* (Czechoslovak Writers' Publishing House) between 1963 and 1964. More or less at the same time dramatists were producing some remarkable works. Josef Topol's *Konec masopustu* (The End of the Carnival) and Václav Havel's *Zahradní slavnost* (The Garden Party) were published in 1963, and Milan Uhde's *Král – Vávra* (King – Vávra) came out a year later. Jan Schmid, the main contributor to the *Ypsilon* ("Y") Theatre, did perhaps the most important work in the theatre at this time.

In the sixties literature and films were very closely connected. Young film-makers, Miloš Forman, Jiří Menzel, Věra Chytilová, Jan Němec, Juraj Jakubisko and others regularly collaborated with writers. The poetic quality of their films also had a great deal in common with the poetics of contemporary literature. The work of the film-makers came later to be designated as the "New Wave" of Czechoslovak cinema.[70]

At the heart of this generation were the authors born in the late thirties and at the beginning of the occupation. The war, the liberation in May 1945 and postwar enthusiasm were not such formative influences for them as they were for the younger war generation, those associated with *Květen* (May, see pp. 45–47), Pavel Kohout, Ludvík Vaculík, Milan Kundera and Ivan Klíma. They took no part in the February 1948 coup either as victors or losers. As children they immediately clashed with Stalinism which was masquerading as the joyful building of a new world.

> "They said to us: This is how we denied ourselves, this is how we bled; but then they put us in a little car and we drove round all the attractions of the fair – at every turn there was a dead body. And when we recoiled and closed our eyes, or simply vomited, they said to us: after all it's for you, yes, *in spite of everything* this is socialism." (Jiří Gruša, 1982)[71]

So Gruša and his contemporaries were spared many illusions. Unlike Kohout, Kundera and Klíma, they had no need later to come to terms with their illusions.

In the eyes of the regime of course this was the first generation for whom the "better tomorrow" was built. The official (and the only permitted) youth organization, the Czechoslovak Union of Youth, was supposed to be a means of educating young people, giving them an insight into and promoting the Communist Party of Czechoslovakia. In fact young people were largely indifferent to this youth organization; the number of members decreased and other interest groups sprung up spontaneously. The students were particularly disenchanted. During the traditional rag days in university towns – especially in Prague when many young people aged about twenty gathered round the monument to the Romantic poet Karel Hynek Mácha on the first of May – there were processions and speeches expressing discontent. There were also scuffles with the police. In 1965, at the conference of the unions of university students, Jiří Müller gave vent to bitter criticism: he demanded autonomy and the right to have an opposition to the party. He won the support of the majority of those present but a year later he was expelled from the union and from the university and called up to the army. In common with other student union leaders he could not take part in public life again till the time known as "the Prague Spring".

Young writers were also sceptical about official propaganda and frequently had absolutely no faith in the socialist utopia. For that reason we do not find any great proclamations, passion or self-confidence in their works. Their work does not try to change the world. These writers are more concerned with getting through life with integrity, looking behind the artificial layers of ideology and the shell of civilization for the fundamental realities of human existence and the natural order of things.

> a najednou se v nás něco hroutí,
> padají balvany a možná koktáme,
> ale musíme to říci –
> chladná a čistá voda, spodní pramen,
> vytryskne . . . [72]
>
> and suddenly something in us crumbles,
> boulders fall and we may stumble,

> but we have to say this –
> cold, clear water, an underground spring,
> will gush out . . .
>
> (Petr Kabeš, *Čáry na dlani* [Lines on the Hand], 1961)

Their perception of values is in many ways similar to Jiří Orten's and the war generation's. They have in common an interest in the existentialist view of life, in the work of Vladimír Holan, František Halas, the original Catholic author Jakub Deml, Richard Weiner and Ladislav Klíma, an early 20th-century predecessor of modern underground poets, and also the Baroque. At the same time as the younger writers were having their first works published, older writers, in particular Vladimír Holan, Jiří Kolář and Bohumil Hrabal (all → PROFILES), were also having works published most of which had been written during the previous decade. Zbyněk Hejda and Jan Zábrana, both now thirty-five, also had earlier works published. Common to all was the younger generation's poetics and vision of the world. Post-February 1948 underground literature now appeared openly and became part of the current literary scene.

Living in a totalitarian state led the young, as their elders had done during the war, to stress moral responsibility and to emphasize the independence of literature. In 1962 Josef Hanzlík wrote in *Literární noviny* (Literary News) that "only 'a pure poem', *ein Gedicht an sich* can be truly modern", and was promptly reprimanded for such a view. In 1964 JIŘÍ GRUŠA (→ PROFILES) caused the ideologues to react angrily when he said in an essay entitled *Realismus jako mravnost* (Reality as Morality) that an author's responsibility is personal and cannot be transferred to any group or institution.[73] Simultaneously he caused another outcry by his reaction to VLADIMÍR MEDEK'S article *Verš pro Stalina* (Verses for Stalin) in *Plamen* (Blaze, 1964). With reform in mind Medek criticized the cult of Stalin in Czech poetry and its cosmetic changes. Jiří Gruša, in his polemical *Verš pro kočku* (Verses Good for Nothing) in *Literární noviny,* went further and argued that Vítězslav Nezval's poem *Stalin* (Stalin) was not a slight deviation but the logical result of the way Nezval had developed since the thirties. Gruša saw the danger in accepting an impersonal, institutionalized truth, be it Stalinist or anti-Stalinist.[74] In the same year, in his collection of poetry *Světlá lhůta* (A Lucid Interval), Gruša permitted himself an ironic answer to Jiří Wolker, the well-known left-wing post-First World War poet. To Wolker's famous lines "miluji věci, mlčenlivé soudruhy" (I love things, silent comrades), he responded provocatively "nenávidím věci – mlčenlivé soudruhy [. . .]" (I hate things – silent comrades [. . .]).

Ladislav Štoll, Jiří Taufer and others then headed a campaign in the Communist daily *Rudé Právo* (Red Rights) against this author. A government clampdown followed. Gruša was forced to leave the editorial staff of *Tvář* (Countenance), was prosecuted for subversion, and for two years he was unemployed. Arguments about the views of the young poets spread even to *Literární noviny* where it was stated that it was better "to err with the party" than perhaps to be right and oppose the party. On the other hand in the same paper Jiří Šotola and Milan Kundera made a critical reappraisal of their own intolerant radicalism after the February 1948 coup.

At first the young writers published in established reviews, the Brno *Host do domu* (A Guest in the House) and the Prague *Plamen* (Blaze). Later they acquired their own reviews, *Tvář* (Countenance, 1964–1965 and 1968–1969) and *Sešity* (Notebooks, 1966–1969). Of course these were not "merely" platforms for this generation of writers. The disruption that had been forced on literature meant that conflicting literary theories were now being promulgated at the same time by various age groups and different schools of thought.

This would perhaps be best illustrated by naming some of the authors associated with *Tvář* in 1964 and 1965. The youngest were Jiří Gruša, Ivan Wernisch, Antonín Brousek, Jan Lopatka and Bohumil Doležal. Václav Havel and Věra Linhartová were a little older – both had connections with underground literature in the fifties. At the age of thirty Emanuel Mandler, Zbyněk Hejda and the philosopher and essayist Jiří Němec – who introduced the work of Jakub Deml and Ladislav Klíma into *Tvář* – were equally important to the review. Josef Jedlička and Ladislav Hejdánek, both thirty-five, were also to some extent involved. Some mature but not established writers, like Bohumil Hrabal, Jan Patočka, Jiří Kolář and others, were also published in *Tvář*. The review carried works of the Surrealist Group from the fifties, texts from the Jan Hanč diaries (see p. 111), translations of the philosophers Martin Heidegger and Pierre Teilhard de Chardin, who had both previously been considered unacceptable.

> "In the past many literary traditions have been broken and much of value has been summarily discarded. Reviving them and bringing them to the attention of the literary world cannot, in our opinion, be done in a single issue, but it will be an essential part of the work of our review." (Editorial in the first number of the review *Tvář*.)[75]

Jiří Gruša, Emanuel Mandler, Jan Lopatka, Bohumil Doležal, Antonín Brousek, Zbyněk Hejda, Václav Havel and others wrote fundamentally critical articles for *Tvář*.[76] Consistent rejection of government ideology and support for reform led to the review being banned at the end of 1965. However, the group around it continued working and contributed to the collections *Podoby* (Resemblances, 1967) and *Podoby II* (Resemblances II, 1969). After being closed down by the censor, the review was published again for a short time from the autumn of 1968.[77] In the seventies and eighties the *Tvář* writers played a significant part in creating samizdat and unofficial literature.

2. Poetry

Right at the beginning of the sixties Josef Hanzlík published his first work *Lampa* (The Lamp, 1961). In it there were several recurrent themes: children coming into contact with war, descriptions of nature, the future, the purity and earnestness of youth as an antidote to spineless conformity.

> vždyť to prý stačí: zaplatit
> a dostat za to svoje,
> být klidný, hrát a nebát se,
> nemít nic, co bys projel,
> vždyť to prý stačí: nevadit
> a říkat vida, vývoj –
> a pít si život po lžičkách
> a jako vlažné pivo,
> vždyť to prý stačí.
> Cožpak je to pravda?[78]
>
> after all it's supposed to be enough: to pay
> and get what you've paid for,
> to be calm, to play and be unafraid,
> to have nothing you should have lost,
> after all it's supposed to be enough not to hinder
> and to say you see, evolution –
> and drink in life in spoonfuls
> like warm beer,
> after all that's supposed to be enough.
> How on earth can that be right?
>
> (Smutná báseň pro Lenku [A Sad Poem for Lenka])

Lampa is characteristic of the early poetry of the sixties generation. In IVAN WERNISCH'S (→ PROFILES) first slim volume *Kam letí nebe* (Whither Are the Heavens Flying, 1961) we find similar melodious word pictures of nature, meadows, dandelions; the world is seen through the eyes of a naïve, eager youth. In places it is reminiscent of Fráňa Šrámek, an early 20th-century poet, celebrating youth and life, of naïve boyish poems in Jiří Wolker's *Host do domu* (A Guest in the House, 1921) and of the early Jiří Orten.

Hanzlík went on to develop this vision of the world in his following books but the majority of the sixties generation gradually developed along different lines. The characteristic tender intimacy gave way to a harsher note of reality which might even be described as ironical anti-lyricism. The magic of Fráňa Šrámek has now become something to be parodied in the plays of Václav Havel and Milan Uhde.

In his later works Wernisch turned the artless lyrical "self" into a deliberate mockery of ingenuousness. The poet leads us into magically beautiful regions but promptly "stigmatizes" them as unreal and artificial. He quotes snatches of folk songs and fairground songs or paraphrases well-known texts – but overall he creates an atmosphere of mockery. He uses bizarre names and epithets. By the end of the sixties beautiful visions more often turn into apparitions, flower-covered meadows change to "the stink of flowers from neglected gardens", "little worms in apples / white and crawling", "my love, / flies will be our kisses / and rats / our horses . . . " (*Dutý břeh* [The Barren Shore] 1967)[79]. The concept of an empty paradise of masks and puppets, everything bathed in a grotesque, sinister light, became widespread.

JIŘÍ GRUŠA (→ PROFILES) went through a similar phase in his poetry in which evil was found to be lurking even in children's games.

vedou mi nevěstu
a ta má
ta je má
[. . .]
zblízka jednonohá
zdálky rozvedená
odboku střelená
nevěstinka moje[80]
(*Cvičení mučení* [Practice Torture], 1969)

they are leading bride for me
and she is mine
she is mine
[. . .]
one-legged from near
divorce from far
nuts from the side
my sweet little bride

Vítězslav Nezval's poetry and sensuality, in particular the book of love poetry, had a greater influence on ANTONÍN BROUSEK than on any of his contemporaries. This can be particularly seen in the love poetry which forms a part of Brousek's collection *Spodní vody* (Underground Waters, 1963). But from the very beginning there was another distinct side to him. He was attracted to the work of Viktor Dyk, an early 20th-century poet of irony and disillusionment, and aimed at precision of meaning and economy of expression. He wrote poems on topical subjects that reacted critically to contemporary events. This aspect of his work gradually assumed greater importance. In his second collection *Netrpělivost* (Impatience, 1966) he expresses his disappointment and disillusionment not only with public life as before, but also with eroticism, as in the cycle of poems *Z nemilostné lyriky* (The Non-love Poetry). The conflict between the external world and the poetic intensifies: "Den je noc a noc je den / Večer začíná již ráno / Vydýcháno Nevětráno / Někdo za mne kýval ano / Někým jsem byl podveden"[81] (Day is night and night is day / Already in the morning evening is setting in / Polluted Stuffy / Behind me someone nods yes / Someone has made a fool of me).

The poet JIŘÍ KUBĚNA also belonged to the circle connected with *Tvář*. He was the author of thirty books in manuscript, only fragments of which were published at the end of the sixties. A representative selection appeared in samizdat in 1986 under the title *Hvězda a Kříž* (The Star and the Cross). A cross-section of his work was presented in 1995 in the extensive volume *Krev Ve Víno* (Blood Into Wine).

Kuběna's poetry is exalted, introspective and difficult to assess. At times it borders on verbalism and at other times it combines majesty and dignity with pithiness and flippancy. It has several features in common with the elaborate, experimental lyric poetry of Věra Linhartová or Miloslav Topinka (see p. 110) but it diverges from them in tending to uphold traditional Catholic spiritual values. Here too the power of ancient myth is brought to life and the most intimate, even erotic experiences (often of a homosexual nature) of the lyrical subject become general statements about the nature of man.

The poets Jan Zábrana and Zbyněk Hejda, both in their thirties, now, belatedly, had their work published for the first time alongside the texts of the younger generation. JAN ZÁBRANA published *Utkvělé černé ikony* (Fixed Black Icons, 1965), poetry written in the fifties, whose style ranged from flowery and decorative to harsh and austere. The first of ZBYNĚK HEJDA's collections of poetry to be published had also been written at the end of the fifties. They have a rustic setting but are far from being the classic rustic idyll. The reader finds himself in a sombre, almost nightmarish atmosphere filled with sensuality. "Po hrdlech zvířat přejížděly nože / Té muziky! A bez hlásku!"[82] (Knives were moving along the throats of animals. / So much music! In total silence!) is a typical quotation from the first poem in Hejda's book *A tady všude muziky je plno* (And All Around Music Fills the Air, 1963). The author expanded this idea in the volume of poems *Blízkosti smrti* (The Nearness of Death) and in other works that he was not able to publish. *Blízkosti smrti* was written in the early sixties but was published for the first time in samizdat in 1978, and was revised and published in Prague in 1992. He also elaborated on this idea in his most impressive work, *Lady Felthamová* (Lady Feltham), a collection of poems and prose, records of dreams, which had been written at the end of the sixties and the beginning of the seventies. It was published in samizdat in 1979 and in Prague in 1992. Pictures of gloomy, ghostly regions and morbid motifs are recurrent. The poetic hero is plagued by horror and anxiety, vaguely aware of the existence of something higher and invisible and of the impossibility of achieving peace of mind and salvation.[83]

Pláč
úlevný nebude seslán.

Ani nepřijde děvka,
hebká,
děvka pro štěstí,
s nohama od pelesti k pelesti.
[. . .]
Obrazy z dávných dob
mizí.

Pán se nezjeví,
sklízím.[84]

No alleviating weeping
will be sent down.

Nor will any silken,
long-legged whore come,
a whore for luck,
with her legs spread wide across the bed.
[. . .]
Pictures of ancient times
vanish.

The Lord will not reveal himself.
I reap the harvest.

Most of the young poets rejected the flowery lyrical poetry of the post-1948 era. At the same time they rejected just as firmly the mainstream Czech "song-like" tradition found in symbolism, avant-gardism, most of Hrubín's poetry and even in Seifert's poetry up to the mid-sixties. Now "pretty pictures", musicality and extravagant metaphor linking distant concepts by association disappeared. The ideas of František Halas and Richard Weiner, the ideas prefered by *Group 42* and to a certain extent by *Květen*, came back into favour. Restraint and moderate scepticism replaced enthusiasm; stylistically, economy of expression and irregular, staccato versification became the dominant features.

VÁCLAV HRABĚ's poetry was not inspired by current events, it was something apart, on the fringe of the world of Czech poetry. In his work there are traces of Czech avant-garde poetism, American beatniks, jazz and rock music. Typical of this generation was the rejection of conformism and a sympathy for all those things "co nelze vyhandlovat / v Tuzexu[85] / nabiflovat přes noc / získat protekcí" (that cannot be bought / in the Tuzex shops / or cannot be learned by swotting overnight / cannot be obtained from friends in high places). These poets loved authenticity and the reality of life: "Vyjmenovat své lásky / a bude-li to třeba / nechat se zabít / pro ně"[86] (Make a list of one's loves / and if necessary / let oneself be killed / for them) – from *Báseň skoro na rozloučenou* (A Poem on Nearly Parting). Hrabě's flaunted nonconformism and his premature death in 1965 at the age of twenty-five contributed to his veneration and his becoming something of a cult figure. Hrabě's first volume of poems came out in 1969 under the title of *Stoptime* (Stoptime). His poetry appeared in its most complete form in *Blues pro bláznivou holku* (Blues for a Crazy Girl) in 1991.

3. Drama and the Theatre, Prose

This generation of writers also made their names in drama and the theatre, especially in the little theatres typical of the day. At the beginning of the sixties most of the traditional "stone-built" theatres, generously subsidized by the state, were suffering from a crisis of diminishing audiences. On the other hand the smaller theatre companies that had developed from the initiatives of enthusiasts, and which had difficulty in keeping going in the face of the disapproval and lack of encouragement of the state, were rapidly capturing the interest of audiences. In fact these fringe or studio theatres were an important factor in creating the special atmosphere of the sixties. Like some of the reviews, their influence transcended the theatre and expanded to focus on the wider range of social and cultural issues.[87]

These fringe theatres were able to continue the kind of avant-garde theatre of the years between the wars and of the immediate postwar *Divadlo satiry* (Satirical Theatre). Above all they continued the kind of theatre of Jiří Voskovec, Jan Werich and Jaroslav Ježek in *Osvobozené divadlo* (Liberated Theatre) in 1927–1938. They were often also "authors" theatres, that is to say, the authors of the plays were at the same time the actors on the stage. Their poetic theory provided an antidote to descriptive realism in the theatre, obligatory in Czechoslovakia after the February 1948 coup. This meant that the theatre had to reflect life accurately, to conform to certain sterotyped norms and to try to create a perfect illusion of reality. In the *Realistic Theatre* in Prague this meticulousness even went as far as to have roses growing over the balcony of the Capulets' palace so that Shakespeare's Juliet could say: "What's in a name? that which we call a rose / By any other name would smell as sweet." On the other hand, in the performances at the *Semafor*, the *Zábradlí* or *Večerní Brno*, hyperbole, slapstick and short spontaneous improvisations were the order of the day. Authors, directors and actors happily combined different genres and situations – stage dialogues, songs, satire, revue and pantomime. Members of the audience did not get the impression they were watching a perfectly crafted piece of work but felt they were being addressed, interested or provoked personally and were being drawn into the play as collaborators in its creation.

> "Dear audience, you are spectators [. . .]. In our grandmothers' day very little was required of an audience like you. To sit, have two eyes, or at least one eye, similarly to have ears, or one ear [. . .]. But we demand discipline and intelligence from our audience [. . .], there's to be no whispering or chattering, and there's certainly to be no necking here [. . .]. The theatre is not some sleazy dive [. . .]. Now the theatre of the Middle Ages, that was theatre! [. . .] To say nothing of the theatre of the Far, Farther and the absolutely Farthest East, which is so far that it, in fact, becomes the theatre of the Near West."[88]

Vyskočil's theatre work and his prose writing are both based on the "logical" development of an apparently ordinary situation or idea as the point of departure. It was his encouragement that led gradually to the formation of several theatrical companies. In 1957 and 1958 he arranged "text appeals" with Jiří Suchý at the *Reduta club* in Prague and afterwards he was one of the founders of the *Theatre on the Balustrade* (*Divadlo Na zábradlí*). In 1962 he left the *Balustrade* and returned to the *Reduta* where he found new collaborators in Pavel Bošek and Leoš Suchařípa. It was then that he conceived his idea of *nedivadlo* ("non-theatre"; this was also called *nedělní divadlo,* which is a pun combining the twin meaning of *neděle,* i.e. "Sunday" and "non-work"). This meant that a work was deliberately left unfinished, a performance not fully rehearsed, but it could be changed by constructive improvisation on the stage – rather like jazz improvisation. *Malé hry aneb Maléry* (Playlets or Mishaps, 1967) is an example of this "non-theatre". *Studio Y* in Liberec, founded in 1963, developed along similar lines. Its organizer and chief contributor was Jan Schmid. "*Ypsilonka*" (Studio Y), which moved to Prague at the end of the seventies, became famous for, among other things, a collective, deliberately chaotic improvisation *Tzv. večer na přidanou* (So-called Evening with Encores) first staged in 1966. Some of the audience had to come on stage and were forced, for example, to play various musical instruments. On other occasions the audience was offered potato pancakes and fish, with the addendum: "Stuffing yourself like this in the theatre for free, yes, we know, you like that. [. . .] But what about showing what you can do . . . "

The best known of these theatres was unquestionably *Semafor*. Unlike Ivan Vyskočil's rather intellectual humour, it continued in the tradition of night clubs, cabarets and the slapstick of the silent films. In *Semafor* the song-writing duo Jiří Suchý and Jiří Šlitr, the popular singers Waldemar Matuška, Eva Pilarová, Karel Gott and Hana Hegerová played important roles – for example, in *Zuzana je sama doma* (Zuzana Is Home Alone, 1960).

JIŘÍ SUCHÝ, born in 1931, belongs to the era between the *Květen* group and the sixties generation. His songs and writing for the theatre form a kind of bridge between the poetry of the everyday (see pp. 45–47) and the poetics of Wernisch and Šrut. They are based on everyday life but employ hyperbole and fantasy, making fun of big words and extravagant emotions. At the same time they enthuse about "a little poetry". Banality, burlesque and black humour run all through his work. However, they are always directed more towards the joyful side of life rather than the dark side.[89]

In the course of time the fame of Jiří Suchý and Jiří Šlitr increased, not only as authors but also as actors and performers in original sketches – Suchý wearing a white straw hat in the character of a gawky, boastful romantic, Šlitr in a black bowler hat as a slow-witted fusspot pouring cold water on his partner's enthusiasm. This is how they appeared for the first time in the play *Jonáš a tingl-tangl* (Jonah in the Music Hall, 1962), a sequence of sketches, cabaret acts and musical numbers. It ran for two hundred and fifty performances and was followed by other successful plays and films – for example, *Kdyby tisíc klarinetů* (A Thousand Clarinets), the second Czech film musical made in 1965 from an older play by Suchý and Vyskočil. The first Czech film musical was based on Vratislav Blažek and Ladislav Rychman's show *Starci na chmelu* (Old People Hop-picking, 1964). Later other literary figures appearing in *Semafor* included the duo Jiří Grossmann and Miloslav Šimek, famous for their sketches and short stories (*Návštěvní den*, Visitors' Day I–III, 1967–1971). At the end of the sixties the company suffered a serious blow with the death first of Jiří Šlitr and then of Jiří Grossmann.

In the sixties outstanding dramatists like Uhde, Havel and Topol were also connected with the fringe theatres. The versatile MILAN UHDE, who wrote novels, screenplays, criticism and poetry collaborated with *Večerní Brno* (Evening Brno), a theatre presenting predominantly satire, where his "nonstop nonsense" *Král – Vávra* ("continuous nonsense" King – Vávra) had its first performance in 1964. A play with songs, loosely based on Karel Havlíček's *Král Lávra,* a 19th-century satirical poem inspired by an Irish fairy-tale about a king with donkey's ears, it ridiculed contemporary demagogy and conformism.

> Kukulín: Anyway King – Vávra has donkey's ears.
> Old Vrba: But Kukulín! That is a biased interpretation of reality.
> Kukulín: I see them as they are. You can't keep things quiet for ever. [. . .]
> Old Vrba: Yes you can. That's your job as secretary. If there was nothing to hide, you wouldn't be needed [. . .]. It's nothing to me if King – Vávra has donkey's ears, because he's the Supervisor of the Earth's Axis, isn't he? That's the question today.[90]

VÁCLAV HAVEL (→ PROFILES) wrote primarily for the theatre. In the sixties he was connected with *Divadlo Na zábradlí* (The Theatre on the Balustrade) mostly during its great years when Jan Grossman was the head of the drama section of this theatre. At that time the small building on the banks of the Vltava river was becoming one of Europe's most famous theatres. Sophisticated performances of existentialist and absurd dramas, such as Samuel Beckett's *Waiting for Godot* or Grossman's adaptation of Franz Kafka's *The Trial* were put on. It was Havel who created original Czech absurd drama in *Zahradní slavnost* (1963; published in English as *The Garden Party*, 1969) and in his later plays.[91]

Zahradní slavnost has features in common with Uhde's *Král – Vávra*, which was staged shortly afterwards. It also parodies the current use and constant repetition of empty words, showing them up as sterile and meaningless. Nevertheless Havel's play has a wider purpose: it is not merely a topical satire, but is also a more general parable of the threat to man of the loss of his human identity. Hugo Pludek, the main character in *Zahradní slavnost*, at the end of the play gives this answer to the question of who he actually is:

> "Me! You mean who I am? Now look here, I don't like this one-sided way of putting questions, I really don't! [. . .] What a rich thing is man, how complicated, changeable, and multiform. [. . .] In man there's nothing permanent, eternal, absolute [. . .] We all are a little bit all the time and all the time we are not a little bit; some of us are more and some of us are not more [. . .] besides, he who is too much may soon not be at all, and he who – in a certain situation – is able to a certain extent to not be, may in another situation be all the better for that."[92] (translated by Vera Blackwell)

The hero's speech contains statements that are in themselves basically logical and true – but in the actual scene in the play, they are ambiguous and comical. Havel uses the same technique in all his work. For instance, in *Vyrozumění* (1965; published in English as *The Memorandum*, 1967) the main theme is again the misuse of language and the disintegration of human personality.

JOSEF TOPOL was the only one of that generation to have begun publishing in the fifties. At the age of nineteen he wrote *Půlnoční vítr* (The Midnight Wind), a play about the early Middle Ages, which had its first performance in 1955. Topol began as, and still is, a poet and unlike both Uhde and Havel, there is a poetic quality in all his plays. What Uhde, Topol and Havel have in common is of course the departure from realistic illusion and also the rejection of a positive solution, even of any unambiguous ending. In this they all differ from the dramatic works of authors close to the "May writers", like František Pavlíček's *Zápas s andělem* (A Struggle with an Angel, 1961; revised in 1963) and Milan Kundera's *Majitelé klíčů* (The Owners of the Keys, 1962).

At the end of the fifties and the beginning of the sixties Topol collaborated with the *National Theatre* in Prague where Otomar Krejča and Karel Kraus were instrumental in introducing new plays. After their departure conservatism was again the rule, so Topol's *Konec masopustu* (The End of the Carnival), one of the great Czech dramas, was first staged in Olomouc in 1963. It was a year and a half later before it was put on in the *Tyl Theatre* in Prague under the direction of Krejča.

The action takes place in the countryside at the end of the fifties. The central figure is František Král – the name is symbolic (king) – the last private farmer in the village who refuses to join a Communist cooperative farm. To Král his fields are not just possessions, they have a moral significance, they are part of the moral code on which his life is based. At the same time *Konec masopustu* is not exclusively about social issues. Like all Topol's plays it works on many levels. The carnival masks that are stored in the coffin of Král's feeble-minded son Jindřich epitomize one level. At the end by an unhappy chance Jindřich does in fact get killed. The play can perhaps be put down as an investigation into guilt and the whole action as the conflict between impersonal, authoritative truth and responsible uncorrupted behaviour.

In the mid-sixties Topol, his closest collaborators, Otomar Krejča[93] and Karel Kraus and the actors Jan Tříska and Marie Tomášová, founded *Divadlo za branou* (Theatre beyond the Gate) in Prague. Compared with *Semafor* or the *Theatre on the Balustrade*, it was rather traditional, specializing in intimate, lyrical drama and tackling human problems like Chekhov. Topol's *Kočka na kolejích* (Cat on the Rails, 1965)[94] was the first Czech play to be premiered there. On the surface it was an ordinary love story. The lovers, Évi, a waitress, and Véna, a removal man, are waiting at night for a train in a desolate station. Of course certain situations also have a figurative or existentialist significance. For example their repeated unsuccessful attempts to light a damp match may be perceived as symbolic of the frustrations in their lives. (Évi – her name is derived from Eve, the first woman – finally manages to light a match but not to light a cigarette with it.) At the very end the two lovers are swallowed up by the approaching train, there is a "sharp discordant sound and everything suddenly goes dark". *Kočka na kolejích* is in the most general sense a parable of creation and the fall of man. In Topol's other works there are increasing signs of ambiguity and concentration on the inner life of the characters, for instance in *Hodina lásky* (An Hour of Love, 1968). At the beginning of the seventies, however, *Divadlo za branou* was closed and Josef Topol – like Havel, Uhde and many others – was officially banned from all cultural activities.

Poetic drama also used non-traditional means, as for example in Radim Vašinka's amateur theatre *Orfeus* (Orpheus). It was also loosely connected with the first "happenings", sketches that were acted in the street and shocked people. In Czechoslovakia towards the end of the sixties these were arranged by Milan Knížák and Eugen Brikcius.

The most interesting of the younger prose writers at the beginning of the sixties were Jan Beneš and Karel Michal, who was slightly older than the others. Novelists of that generation who began to write later were Vladimír Körner, who has already been mentioned (see p. 86), and the experimental author Věra Linhartová, who will be discussed later (see pp. 112–113).

KAREL MICHAL's short stories *Bubáci pro všední den* (Weekday Ghosts)[95] ranged from factual "reportage" to artistic invention. Their publication as early as 1961 was one of the first signs of the regeneration of Czech prose. In one of these stories, for instance, an ordinary man, an accountant, acquires a ring which makes it possible for him to turn into a bear. He tries to use it:

> "'Good morning,' said the accountant and turned into a bear. Then he took a few steps forward. To heighten the effect he growled as a sign that he was terrifying.
> The first to let out a shriek was the old woman with the shopping bag, she dropped her bankbook and, petrified, crossed herself. The two or three customers present flattened themselves against the wall."[96]

The author takes the reader to places as far as possible from the supernatural: to wages offices, military units, teams of roadworkers. In such a notoriously down-to-earth context miracles or supernatural beings are all the more surprising. These devices expose the absurdity of automatic responses to situations.

> "'You have to understand,' the lawyer tapped a pencil on the table, 'a man can change into a bear. Well, we've agreed about that. But so that we can offer the public value, real entertainment value, not just some kind of hyped-up technical trick, you have to make a bear do something exceptional, something that not every animal can do. Dance on a ball, do bar exercises or that kind of thing. Can you do that?'
> 'No, I can't,' Mikulášek replied gloomily. He could neither dance normally, let alone dance on a ball."[97]

JAN BENEŠ's short stories from the beginning of the sixties were different, rather like Hemingway in style. They were constructed like traditional stories but tended to relate facts with hardly a trace of sentiment. They are full of common Czech, military and prison slang. The author drew on his own experience of prison in other stories with similar themes. Beneš's short stories came out in English as *The Blind Mirror* (1969). In 1962, Beneš wrote the novel *Druhý dech* (in English *Second Breath*, 1969), which was published in Czech in the West in 1974.

His contemporary KAROL SIDON gave his two autobiographical novels, *Sen o mém otci* (A Dream about My Father, 1968) and *Sen o mně* (A Dream about Me, 1970), a different treatment. They are in the nature of a confession painfully baring the soul. Nevertheless there is doubt and uncertainty in the end: "Simply by being born a male, I was cursed. It means for ever seeking, for ever attacking, for ever dancing around the beginning and the end, snatching at truth [. . .]. Like Cain with the mark on his brow, with the mark of a gruesome intention, with guilt in his heart . . . "[98] Even in these first autobiographical novels the themes of existentialist doubt and Judaism provide the key to the author's work.

4. Singers and Songwriters

Vladimír Merta, Karel Kryl and Jaroslav Hutka were among the youngest of this generation. They were songwriters and singer-guitarists who wrote their own words and music. Like the protest songs of Bob Dylan and Donovan in the West and the Russian songwriter Vladimir Vysotsky in the East, their intention was to stir up protest rather than to entertain. They differed from the ordinary run of pop music in the deliberate simplicity of the music, often inspired by folk-music, and the unusual quality of the words.

> Potkala jsi chlapce krásného jako nedělní kapesník ráno
> shlíželi jste se navzájem v podobách ovoce
> zkřehlými prsty probíral v klíně sušená jablka
> zdálo se mi že tě zná že chci to co chce on
> a co mu bude dáno
>
> Tiché slavnosti božího těla
> měkké lenošky v divadle hudby
> malátná slabost – *toho jsem měla*
> posvátná samota kamkoliv kráčíš
> a smutný montgomerák nudy namísto trávy.
>
> You met a fellow as handsome as a Sunday handkerchief in the morning
> you looked down at each other in the likeness of fruit
> with numb fingers he probed the dried apples on his lap
> it seemed to me that he knows you and that I want what he wants
> and what will be given to him
>
> Silent glories of the Corpus Christi feast
> soft armchairs in the theatre of music
> languorous weakness – *I have had him*
> sacred solitude wherever you walk
> and a sad macintosh of boredom instead of grass.[99]

The singers and songwriters from the youth clubs and student colleges at the end of the sixties – like the beat and rock bands – found their way into the concert halls and broadcasting and their records became best sellers. For several months KAREL KRYL was famous for his songs on the record *Bratříčku, zavírej vrátka* (Brother, Close the Gate, 1968), which became the symbol of protest against the Soviet-led invasion of August 1968. Their biblical and historical themes were transparently a reference to the present time; the author's aggressive lampooning matched the prevailing tension and expressed with great urgency the despair and defiance. After August 1968, Kryl was unable to have any more of his texts or songs published and the author himself went into exile. His second LP *Rakovina* (Cancer) came out in 1969 in Germany. His songs, however, continued to be secretly copied and listened to and the name Kryl remained a symbol of resistance to the regime throughout the entire period of normalization.

JAN VODŇANSKÝ was another whose poetic ideas were very close to the songwriters. He came to prominence as part of a singing and acting partnership with the musician PETR SKOUMAL in *S úsměvem idiota* (With the Smile of an Idiot) in the *Činoherní klub* (Drama Club), which later appeared in book form in 1969. His texts are based on parody and nonsense rhymes.

The relationship of literature and modern music, jazz, pop, rock and folk music, would need a chapter to itself beyond the scope of this book. One thing is certain: from the latter half of the sixties aesthetics began to be perceived differently. This change had already begun to take place in the West in the fifties.The traditional role of poetry was largely being taken over by the texts of songs, – and signs of this can be seen even earlier, for example, in the interwar songs of Jiří Voskovec and Jan Werich. For young people, poetry, as traditionally understood, was losing the relevance and importance it had had for decades from the Romantic era. This might be explained as a manifestation of "ruggedness", the resistance to elegant versification that was obvious in poetry itself. From another point of view it could be the reaction to the complex sophistication of the work of Vladimír Holan and his numerous successors in the sixties – hence the change to simple, songlike, basic ideas. Czech literature had several times experienced a similar reaction, most notably between symbolism and the works of rebels and anarchists, František Gellner, Fráňa Šrámek and Viktor Dyk. A parallel development can be seen in some of the younger authors of the sixties, particularly in Karel Sýs and Jiří Žáček, also after 1970 in the samizdat underground. The change in the way Czech literature was developing – in technical terms the change of paradigms – was deeper and more fundamental than all the reasons advanced to explain it. In other words it was a process that was gradually taking place in various European and world literatures. Culture was shifting from "reading" to "listening" and "looking" – so to an audio-visual culture. It was as if poetry was returning to its original form as in ancient Greece when it was directly connected with recitation, dance and song. This process was commonly spoken of as a crisis of modern life and later as post modernity. There is no doubt that these changes of perception were connected with the expansion of the mass media, films, broadcasting, television, etc. and with the rapid development of modern technology. All these things create a speedier – and of course a simpler and more superficial – means of communication. More than ever spiritual depth on the one hand, and a historical dimension on the other, were missing from the culture of everyday life. People concentrated their attention on the "here and now", on living in the present, on material well-being (at its worst mere consumerism), on the purely personal aspects of their lives, on irrationality, on the nature of man, on sensuality – erotica and violence. Attempts to renew spirituality in a different way, without the traditional elements of European thought, metaphysics, a sense of history and the idea of progress led to an interest in Asiatic thought, especially Zen Buddhism and yoga. Later in the sixties this found expression in Věra Linhartová and Eva Kriseová and others of their generation, and in the eighties in Zuzana Brabcová and her generation of writers.

The Experimental Era

1. Poetry

One of the principal demands made on "socialist literature" was popularity, in the sense that it should be understood by the greatest number of people. In practice this meant the lowering of artistic standards and returning to well-established means of communication. Pluralization and fewer restrictions allowed the arts to use a wider range of techniques. Monotonous rhythm and rhyme ceased to be the only valid model for poetry to follow. A number of poets also rejected melodiousness and metaphor. In prose there was greater use of fantasy and imagination, the story was told from the point of view of different narrators, and various levels of language were used. The inventive poetics of the fringe theatres took shape. Original lyrical-existentialist and absurd drama was created.

Between 1963 and 1966 and especially at the end of the decade experimental poetry became increasingly important. Works aiming primarily at formal effect and seeking new language and stylistic means were published. Understandably there are no clearly defined limits to "experimental" literature. Every important work of art is a unique attempt at a new vision of reality, so by its nature it is an experiment. For example, the stories of Ladislav Fuks and Bohumil Hrabal, Václav Havel's plays and many other works already discussed are on the borderline of experimental literature.

Surrealism and Concrete Poetry in particular belong to this genre. The surrealists began to return to mainstream culture in the mid-sixties. In 1964 an exhibition of surrealist graphic art from the years 1930–1950 was arranged but it was soon closed down. Two years later, in Prague, there followed an exhibition including contemporary works entitled *Symboly obludnosti* (Symbols of Monstrosity). It was accompanied by cultural evenings at which members of surrealist groups were present.

Vratislav Effenberger was still the chief organizer and theoretician of the group (see pp. 33–34). Between 1953 and 1962 he edited *Objekt* (Object), five manuscript anthologies by a number of authors.[100] Besides middle generation writers, like Effenberger himself, the poet Zbyněk Havlíček, the painter and poet Mikuláš Medek, some young and some very young writers, like Petr Král, Stanislav Dvorský, Věra Linhartová and Milan Nápravník, published their work in these anthologies. These younger writers in fact made up the third wave of surrealists. The group introduced itself through the book *Surrealistické východisko* (The Surrealist Point of View, 1969) and in several other texts that were published at the end of the sixties. A typical example of the vision of the younger surrealists was MILAN NAPRAVNÍK'S story *Předmoucha* (A Preliminary Fly) from his book *Moták* (Secret Message, 1969) which was written in dactyls and with internal rhyme: the unabridged version, *Kniha Moták* (The Secret Message Book) was published in 1995.

In his youth OLDŘICH WENZL was close in outlook to another surrealist group, *Skupina Ra* (Group Ra), which was active shortly during and after the war. His poetry – a more sophisticated variation of surrealism – could not be published till after the mid-sixties when the author was already seriously ill. *Yehudi Menuhin* was published in 1964, but the collection *Veškerá poezie* (Complete Poetry) was published through the good offices of Ludvík Kundera, although not till 1982, after the poet's death.

Wenzl's contemporary EMANUEL FRYNTA, another of the war generation, was "unclassifiable". He was famous as an essayist and translator from seven languages. Based on nonsense and an apparently unconnected association of words and ideas, his prose works could not be published either during the sixties. Sometimes they are like childish puns, for example, the poem *Angličané* (Englishmen) from the posthumous collection *Písničky bez muziky* (Songs without Music, 1988)

Angličané jsou námořníci
a slečny oslovují Miss
co o nich ale musím říci –
že neumějí pravopis.

Už jejich první omyl je ten
že píšou I – a čtou to aj!
To jako kdyby psali květen
a vyslovovali to máj.

Je mi jich líto, hlavně dětí,
co ty s tím mají za dřinu –
já musel napsat jen tři věty
a myslel jsem, že zahynu.

Ta hrůza, než se naučíte
pár slovíček, a natož stran!
A u nich každé malé dítě
musí být rovnou Angličan.[101]

Englishmen all go to the sea,
and girls as "miss" address.

But the thing that most surprises me
is that their spelling is a mess.

Their very first mistake is that
they write "I" but speak it "ay".
It's almost as if they wrote down "cat"
and pronounced it "butterfly".

I feel most sorry for the kid
who has such effort to apply.
Three sentences are all I did
and thought that I would die.

Learning a few words is no joy,
let alone a page's worth.
But in their country every little boy
must be an Englishman from birth!
(translated by Keith Brandon)

In another of Frynta's stories, *Máte bratra?* (Have You Got a Brother?), a student answers his English teacher's question, Have you got a brother? in the affirmative after vainly trying to answer in the negative. He adds that his brother is a plumber. Because his teacher needs the U-bend in a pipe repaired, the student has to disguise himself as his brother, learn to be a plumber and so on.[102]

According to Frynta the poetics of nonsense "introduce absurdity in order to bring to light the nonsense and absurdity concealed in unthinking language, illogical reasoning and the usual automatic reactions to the world around".[103] The nonsense works by Lewis Carroll, author of *Alice in Wonderland*, Edward Lear, another Englishman, and the German poet Christian Morgenstern are recognized classics. In the sixties this type of literature was represented also by the works of Ivan Vyskočil and Václav Havel.

A movement in modern literature pursuing a completely different course from either absurd literature or surrealism was Concrete Poetry. It also continued several avant-garde initiatives, such as dadaism, but in a different way. The very name is somewhat misleading; Concrete Poetry is in fact a parallel development to abstract painting, plastic op-art and computer graphics. Concrete Poetry is based on a rational approach, every work being constructed according to a precise plan, but there is also room for chance and plays on words. The resultant poem is not the expression of any emotion or lyrical attitude, but something made from the language itself. One type of Concrete Poetry, so-called visual poetry, for example JIŘÍ KOLÁŘ'S (→ PROFILES) *Básně ticha* (Poems of Silence), is a special arrangement of graphic characters. These poems were written at the end of the fifties and the beginning of the sixties but were not published unabridged till 1994. There is frequent use of "alternation", the fusing of various types of text – parts of a newspaper editorial might be inserted between parts of a classic poem. The texts affect each other, challenge each other and multiply. Another method of writing Concrete Poetry is to use one text as a point of departure and introduce variations on it. And lastly the most extreme method is the use of the formal rules of grammar to produce works with the help of a computer, so-called "machine texts".

Some texts were intended for inclusion in the Czech experimental poetry anthology *Vrh kostek* (A Throw of the Dice) which was ready for publication at the end of the sixties, but did not reach the reading public till 1993. It was edited by JOSEF HIRŠAL and BOHUMILA GRÖGEROVÁ, innovators and organizers of this movement in Czechoslovakia. Their own work was published in the book *Job-boj* (Job-Fight, 1968).

So Concrete Poetry does not create what is basically understood as poetry. It creates "artificial" poetry purely by the way the texts are constructed. Its authors sometimes go to the other extreme and produce works completely devoid of style. They seize upon fragments of raw fact, quotations, documents, especially relating to city life – as an analogy with graphic pop art, American hyperrealism, and so on. JIŘÍ KOLÁŘ's *Vršovický Ezop* (Aesop from Vršovice, see pp. 70–71), and some of JOSEF HIRŠAL's texts in *Soukromá galerie* (Private Gallery, written between 1947 and 1954, published in 1965) belong to this school.

Distrust of ready-made, smoothly flowing language was manifested in various ways. Some of the younger poets even experimented with language invented for the purpose. In their work they revived the mannered style that was a legacy from the Baroque and carried on from Vladimír Holan's poetry of the thirties and Josef Palivec's poems during the Second World War. The language was very similar to the ingenious poetry of the Russian futurists, where the words do not express the mood of a lyrical subject, or refer to any outward reality but are themselves the subject matter, creating original worlds completely transcending normal means of communication. Connected with this movement were VĚRA LINHARTOVÁ (→ PROFILES), who abandoned surrealism in the sixties and whose unabridged poems were published in the nineties, and to a certain extent, IVAN WERNISCH (→ PROFILES) and two other younger authors of the sixties, JOSEF PETERKA and MILOSLAV TOPINKA. Topinka's *Krysí hnízdo* (Rats' Nest) was published in 1971 but the whole edition was destroyed. In it synonyms and discordant connecting words with the sound "r" and "u" pile up: "V krčmě / za krchovem, v charouzně, pazderně, / krčím se v krysím hnízdě. / [. . .] / V uších mi hučí, kňučí, skučí . . . "[104] (In the tavern / behind the graveyard, in a ramshackle hut, a rough cabin, / I cower in a rats' nest. / [. . .] / My ears hum, thrum, drum . . .) The same play on the sound of words and synonyms is to be found in Linhartová: "Smrkáč ti rubáš tká / mračně se kolem smráká / rty semklé pootvírá stálý smích / trs makovice strmí výš než strom."[105] (A guttersnipe is weaving your shroud / cheerless darkness all round / lips half open pressed into an everlasting laugh / a cluster of poppies towering higher than a tree.) This quotation comes from *Dům pro mé lásky* (A House for My Loves), published in the review *Tvář* in 1968 and in book form in 1993. In his remarkable book of poetry *Krušná* (Grim, 1970) Josef Peterka exploits the many complex levels of meanings of folk sayings that become mysterious, ambiguous ciphers when used in unaccustomed contexts.

2. Prose

Two main approaches to experimental prose can also be distinguished. One approach aimed at genuine, authentic "news", like the renowned films of Miloš Forman, Ivan Passer and Jaroslav Papoušek. The other approach again tended towards stylization, ingenuity and innovation. It used fantasy but was intellectually demanding like the films of Jan Němec, Věra Chytilová and Juraj Jakubisko.

The work of JAN HANČ, once a member of *Group 42* (see pp. 15–16), represents the extreme position of the first approach. Most of the entries in Hanč's notebooks date from the early sixties but nothing of his literary output could be published from 1948 to his death in 1963.

The outstanding feature of his work is his antagonism to established literary conventions, especially poetic ornamentation. It is deliberately harsh and critical and, like his *Nápisy na záchodech* (Lavatory Writings), it delves into areas usually avoided by art. It is also highly personal and often linked to sensual experiences:

> "I show life as it really is. Is it my fault it does not fit in with their fucking notion of what it is and what they are pretending it is? They think they're free not to give a damn about what I'm forced to give a damn about. A fart is a fact even if according to Dr. Guth-Jarkovský[106] it is something regrettable because it does not go with evening dress." (Sešit číslo 4 [Notebook no. 4], written in 1962)[107]

By looking at life as it appears on the surface and also examining its underside, Hanč does not merely intend to be offensive or shocking. Moving abruptly from reportage to banality, from contemplation to sarcasm, his views have a basic aim – to expose the kind of human existence hiding behind an artificial protective covering. Beside the works of Jakub Deml, Bohumil Hrabal and Jiří Kolář (Hrabal and Kolář → PROFILES), Hanč's notebooks became the inspiration for a whole branch of literature in the seventies and eighties. They were mainly distributed in samizdat, especially in the so-called underground. They were based not on stories where the plot unfolded smoothly nor on traditional poetics but on uncompromising, direct descriptions of events and phenomena, on abbreviations, on reflections, on vulgarity alternating with lyricism.

VLADIMÍR PÁRAL'S (→ PROFILES) novels give the impression of playing ironically with scientifically precise "information" and so form a contrast to Hanč's harsh realism. In fact his novel *Soukromá vichřice* (A Private Gale, 1966; filmed by Hynek Bočan, 1967) has the apposite subtitle "laboratorní zpráva ze života hmyzu" (laboratory notes on insect life). The author's style is related to the "programmed" type of Concrete Poetry, in the sense that Páral's texts are made up of sentences, themes and situations, frequently repeated with only slight changes. They are deliberately terse – with copious enumerations and occasionally omitting the verb:

> "Late as usual, Express no. 7 from Bucharest, Budapest and Bratislava, was just pulling into Platform One at Brno Main Station. It was Wednesday, April 1, and there was the usual confused rush of travellers who lacked reservations but were

> trying, as a matter of principle, to board the middle cars of the train, even though these cars were intended (likewise as a matter of principle) for those who had reservations. In the midst of this rush Jacek Jošt (33/5' 9", oval face, brown eyes and hair, no special markings) took in the always unexpected sequence of numbers on the middle cars until, sufficiently amused, he finally caught sight of his own car, no. 52, hooked up between nos. 34 and 38.
>
> In compartment E two unpleasant surprises: First, Jacek's seat, no. 63, the second from the window, was just being occupied. Second, and even more unpleasant, its occupant was the loathsome Trost, like himself from Ústí, in fact from the apartment house opposite his own. In the window seats, nos. 61 and 62, two women stopped talking, as if scandalised by the two newcomers actually venturing to sit down in an otherwise empty compartment, right next to them.
>
> [. . .]
>
> Late as usual, Express no. 7 from Bucharest, Budapest and Bratislava, was just pulling into Platform One at Brno Main Station. In the midst of the usual confused rush of travellers Jacek took in the always unexpected sequence of numbers on the reserved cars until, sufficiently amused, he finally caught sight of his own car, no. 53, hooked up between nos. 28 and 32.
>
> In compartment F by the window on seat no. 67 a fat old man looked up, we have no. 68 across from him, Jacek put his travelling satchel up into the net, hung his beige iridescent raincoat beneath it, and when he'd sat down, another passenger entered the compartment with a seat ticket in hand, he had the odd number 69, next to the fat man, he put his suitcase up into the net and he hung beneath it his blue-gray raincoat of the same material and cut as Jacek's." (*Katapult*, in Czech 1967; in English, 1989)[108]

Páral's novels from the sixties all have similar subjects. They are set in the industrial area of North Bohemia, in the fictitious chemical plant Kotex. The people are like clockwork dolls, easily interchangeable, as suggested by their names: Áda – Ida, Jožka – Joska, Jošt – Trošt. In the end eroticism and sex, regarded by some characters as an exciting adventure, turn into boring routine. In the same way single-minded pursuit of a career ends up as arid stereotyped behaviour.

This is how Páral drily describes consumerism as a way of life that can find nothing worthwhile outside itself. In his extensive novel *Milenci a vrazi* (1969; published in English as *Lovers and Murderers*, 2001; filmed by Viktor Polesný, 2004) the author attempts to find a philosophy of this life in the fortunes of the residents of a house in the North Bohemian city of Ústí, "the reds", that is, the Conquerors. They are greedy but possess nothing, but gradually take over the positions of the "blues", who are rich and powerful but overrefined. Years later they themselves lose all initiative, become degenerate and new "reds" attack their positions.

Experimentalism is particularly strongly featured in VĚRA LINHARTOVÁ'S (→ PROFILES) work. Her novels have no set subject, no firm plot, yet at the same time her prose is refined and sophisticated with many cultural allusions. On the borderline between imagination and reality, it is at the opposite end of the spectrum from the austere prose of Jan Hanč.

Věra Linhartová published her first three books, finished by the end of the fifties, in the course of a few months between 1964 and 1965. What sets this author apart is her technique of gradually undermining her story and casting doubt on its validity. Sometimes, after beginning a sentence, the narrator does not even manage to continue but goes on to explain various circumstances and contingencies in detail, then reflects on these versions of events and about himself and the story remains unfinished. Elsewhere doubt is cast on the finished narrative. Thus in the story *Co nejvíc šedé* (As Much Grey as Possible), from her collection *Mezipr̊uzkum nejblíž uplynulého* (Intersurvey of the Nearest Past, 1964), the narrator murders Prosper but immediately says: "And so it would have been much better for me if I really had killed Prosper, if in fact Prosper had really existed. If all that had really been true and not just a story . . . "[109] There are also startling changes of narrator, changes from third to first person narrative, even changes in the gender of the narrator (the masculine is replaced without comment by the feminine and vice versa). Finally some characters apparently come to life for the first time after their names had explained what they were – born in fact out of the language, the lexical exchanges, puns and spoonerisms.

Linhartová is linked mainly with the work of Richard Weiner, an interwar writer who suffered from an identity crisis, and Milada Součková (→ PROFILES) by the use of all these techniques that disrupt established methods of narration and dispel all illusion of reality. They emphasize the unreality of the narrative and direct attention to the text as an artificially created piece of fiction. The systematic breaking of literary conventions causes uncertainty in readers. So we are, as Milan Suchomel wrote, firmly against "facile, automatic certainty" in the interpretation of the nature of man and in our perception of language.

In her next collections, chiefly in *Dům daleko* (A House in the Distance, 1968) and *Chiméra neboli Průřez cibulí* (Chimera, or a Cross Section of Onions, which was written in 1967 but not published till 1993), she experiments to an even greater degree. The narrative becomes less and less coherent, turning into a series of situations, reflections, allusions and neologisms till it finally disintegrates. These novels were followed by her departure into exile where she began writing in French.

Intellectual games, fantasy and a disrupted story line with digressions and reflective passages, form a link between Linhartová and IVAN VYSKOČIL (see pp. 49–50 and pp. 99–100). Unlike Věra Linhartová's difficult texts, Vyskočil's stories are more easily understood and livelier. They mostly date from the time when the author was working in the theatre and are inspired by the influence of stage and audience on each other.

Vyskočil does not, like Linhartová, put the "predictability of the world" in doubt by rational analysis but by humorous hyperbole. For example, in the first story in the collection *Kosti* (Bones, 1966), he derives the next stage of the concept special school (a school for mentally handicapped children), the special grammar school, for pupils who have finished the special school, and correspondingly "special university", "special doctor", and finally a complete "special life":

> "First of all we thought that the special grammar school and indeed all special secondary schooling was established because those who finished the normal special school insisted on the right to further education suitable for them. It is in fact unthinkable for anyone to be deprived of the right to continue his studies and the chance to get a professional post simply because he is mentally not up to it. Especially if he shows appropriate effort and diligence and knows the right people. (Knowledge also comes from the word know. It's just a matter of adding 'ledge'. And as alphabetically know comes before knowledge, knowing the right people should take precedence over knowledge.) If that is the case then certainly there should also be special business schools, special universities and special technical colleges from which special engineers would graduate and get suitable special jobs. (Special jobs? What next? Could it reach the point, let's say, when a special doctor replaces a doctor because . . . , does the reason matter anyway? But because he is not up to it he is handed over, let's say, to the normal doctor who is up to it, and who as his subordinate does everything for him as some kind of special assistant to the special doctor.)"[110]

In Vyskočil's texts the world is comically topsy-turvy and horrifyingly bizarre, in some ways in fact very like the world as it is. His novels are not just references to the manipulative practices of contemporary society but pointers to the kind of danger that in varying degrees threatens any society at all.

Nineteen Sixty-Eight

1. Writers in Conflict with the Communist Party

> "In the sixties Czech literature had an unusually wide influence, beyond the normal sphere of literature. Writers were almost as popular as our national hockey team or rock singers. However the writer who was to come up to 'national expectations' had to have something of the showman and popular singer and he also had to have the fighting spirit of an international hockey player." (Jiří Kratochvil)[112]

In the late sixties there was increasing discontent among the people, including reforming Communists. At the 13th Congress of the Communist Party of Czechoslovakia in 1966, the economist Ota Šik said that economic reform could not be achieved without political change. That same year it was openly stated in *Hospodářské noviny* (Financial News) that "the illusion of a rise in the standard of living as an automatic consequence of socialism" was a product of party propaganda; however, the party central office, the seat of power, continued to function as before. It did not of course depend on zealous advocates of the regime like in the fifties but on a class of privileged bureaucrats. In comparison with the fifties there was much greater public freedom – but sharper criticism was suppressed and the critics persecuted. In January 1967 a new press law was passed legalizing censorship, the institution responsible for it being euphemistically called Ministry of the Interior Central Publication Administration. Ministry officials very frequently used their powers. For example, an ordinary party member, the chairman of a local organization, said in an article in *Literární noviny*:

> "You know, I wonder what we are really like. We Communists. In what, if anything, are we better than other people. Work? Character? Knowledge? I know many non-party members who are better in all these ways. What does that mean for us Communists? That we have party cards? That we pay our contributions? That we go to meetings? That we are disciplined? I know what the party's mission

> is – but I keep asking myself, what kind of people we are as individuals. And if our continued membership of the party is not simply a licence to reach higher positions and gain prosperity before we've earned it, considering our work, character and knowledge. And if in fact it is nothing but a licence . . . "

Typically this particular passage was cut out by the censor. Similarly, Bohumíra Peychlová's article on prostitution was published, but only after protracted argument and with deletions, for during socialism prostitution did not officially exist. Some numbers of *Literární noviny* had up to a third of the contents cut by the censor.

The new constitution of 1960 declared that socialism had been fully established in Czechoslovakia. It also considerably restricted the rights of independent Slovak institutions. Dissatisfaction was rife in Slovakia, especially when Antonín Novotný himself, the president and first secretary of the party, acted with contempt towards the Slovaks. He personally ordered the banning of the book *Ako chutí moc* (published in English as *The Taste of Power*, 1967; in Slovak and also, in a separate edition, in Czech, 1968) by the Slovak journalist and author Ladislav Mňačko, in which he spotted references to himself and other leading figures in the party. In the summer of 1967 Mňačko was one of the writers who protested mildly at the slanderous anti-Israeli campaign carried on by the media at the time of the Arab–Israeli war. He also expressed his opinions while on a visit to Austria. This was immediately regarded as treason and Mňačko was deprived of his citizenship. The Slovak Writers' Union was forced to condemn him not just as a citizen but also as a writer.

In fact it was people engaged in the arts, especially writers, who most frequently came into conflict with the powers of bureaucracy. They tried to make it possible to have a free exchange of ideas and challenged the increasing censorship of political criticism. Ferdinand Peroutka (→ Profiles), the most important interwar Czech liberal journalist, who had been living in exile in the West since 1948, had declared in 1966: "Literary reviews can now print political, sociological and financial articles, so writers have decided with good reason to become citizens. Being a citizen means taking an interest in and taking part in public affairs."[113] But it was not till a year later that the main conflict with the government occurred at the 4th Congress of the Union of Czechoslovak Writers in June 1967.[114]

Milan Kundera (→ Profiles), whose responsibility it was to give the opening address, set the tone of the session. He deliberately dispensed with the customary long-winded rhetoric and came straight to the point. He said that Czech culture, long isolated from the rest of the world, first by the Nazi occupation and then by Stalinism, was threatened by the loss of a sense of history. "People living only in the immediate present, without being aware of being part of history and without culture, are turning their native land into a wilderness, without beauty, where nothing is remembered of the past."[115] Kundera quoted H. G. Schauer, a critic close to T. G. Masaryk, who had raised the question of the purpose of Czech national existence, asking whether it was so valuable and beneficial internationally to be worth preserving. This issue was raised in Schauer's article "Naše dvě otázky" (Our Two Questions) from the end of the 19th century: What is the role of our nation? What is our role in the history of mankind? What is the nature of our national existence? Are we as secure in our own house as we think we are? Is our national existence really worth the effort? Is its cultural value really so enormous?

Kundera recalled that contemporary Czech education was losing its European dimension. He protested bitterly at any form of censorship:

> "Any form of suppression of ideas [. . .] is directed at the suppression of truth because it is possible to reach the truth only by the free and equal exchange of ideas. Any attack on freedom of speech and thought, however discreet the technology and whatever name censorship goes under, is a scandal in the twentieth century and a shackle for our literature preventing its diversification."[116]

The speech that followed by Jiří Hendrych, then the second man in the state, secretary of the Central Committee of the Czechoslovak Communist Party, with all the official rhetoric, seemed to belong to another world. He called the writers to fight against bourgeois ideology, demanded that art should be "socialist" and "realistic". He criticized the Writers' Union for its tendency to endorse "the pluralism of ideas". The gulf between the two papers, one immediately after the other, reflected the difference between the sharply critical mood of the huge majority of the writers and the conservatism of the top party officials. The reforming authors continued to attack. PAVEL KOHOUT and IVAN KLÍMA (both → PROFILES) spoke about censorship and demanded, in accordance with the constitution, freedom of the press and freedom of speech. "An author's special relationship with his work will always be at odds with official doctrine," said ALEXANDR KLIMENT. He spoke of Solzhenitsyn's bitterly critical letter to the congress of Soviet writers. Immediately afterwards, by general agreement, the letter was read out condemning Soviet cultural policy and censorship as illegal and unconstitutional.

The party leaders were not accustomed to this kind of criticism. The delegation from the Central Committee led by Hendrych ostentatiously walked out. The main shock, however, did not come till the following afternoon when LUDVÍK VACULÍK (→ PROFILES) took the floor. In his novel *Sekyra* (see pp. 82–83) he had described a scene, obviously with many autobiographical features, when at a meeting the hero publicly refused to say he had been lying, and instead of the obligatory self-criticism openly said what he thought. Now the situation in the novel was being repeated in reality. Vaculík claimed he was going to speak only about what was common knowledge among those present: society was governed by a handful of powerful men, a spirit of submission was being fostered among the people, democracy and justice were being systematically suppressed:

> "... for twenty years not a single human problem has been resolved – from straightforward needs like schools, housing, and economic prosperity to more subtle needs that undemocratic systems cannot satisfy, – the feeling of having an effective part

> to play in society, that ethical criteria should supersede political decisions and belief in the importance of the ordinary man and his unheroic work, the need for trust among people, the advancement of education for all. And I am afraid we have not reached the level of the rest of the world and I have the feeling that our republic has lost its good reputation. I realize we have not given mankind any original thought or good ideas [. . .], we are repeating the mistakes of East and West, our society has no institutions that could attempt to look for a faster and a more efficient alternative to our noisy and smoky lifestyle."[117]

This kind of forceful criticism had not been heard in public since the Communist takeover in February 1948. Understandably, the reaction to Vaculík's speech and the whole congress was the imposition of sanctions. At a meeting of the Central Committee three writers were expelled from the party. In addition Vaculík was accused of disparaging the republic, which was a punishable offence. *Literární noviny* was taken out of the control of the rebellious Union of Czechoslovak Writers and as a result was nearly closed down. No material from the congress could be published apart from individual speeches by writers "faithful to the party" which the Communist daily *Rudé Právo* (Red Rights) published. Completely in the spirit of the usual propaganda, the party press disseminated disinformation about the congress and argued and "struggled" with opposition writers who were denied in advance the chance of defending themselves.

Soon, however, many copies of Vaculík's speech were circulating and the Writers' Congress became the compass that pointed the way to the spring of 1968. The "Strahov incident" in the autumn of 1967 was another pointer. Students from the Strahov residence in Prague, angered by constant power failures, gathered in a spontaneous demonstration. In the procession they carried lighted candles and chanted various rather jokey slogans like "We want light!" The police considered it a political protest and concluded that the small groups of students were heading for the Castle where at that very moment some kind of meeting of party leaders was taking place. So in Neruda Street the procession was brutally attacked and dispersed which led to further anger and discontent.

2. "The Prague Spring"

The government, having lost much of its power, was unable to resolve the growing crisis. At stormy sessions of the Central Committee of the Czechoslovak Communist Party in December 1967 and January 1968, Antonín Novotný, the first secretary, was deposed and his place taken by the Slovak Alexander Dubček. Although a dedicated Communist, he was, however, open to reform and discussion. He had personal charisma and spoke a different language from previous leaders. Abroad he became famous for his aphorism about the need for "socialism with a human face". His informal behaviour, openness and warmth won him popularity. At the same time, however, he was characterized by indecision, naïvety and trust in the Soviet Union and its leaders.

All these characteristics were reflected in the reformers in the leadership of the Communist Party during the "Prague Spring". Censorship was virtually abandoned, some elements of a market economy were introduced, plans were being made for federalization which was to bring equality to the Slovaks; rehabilitation of the victims of repression after the Communist takeover of 1948 was speeded up and compromised officials were gradually removed.[118] There was to be no ideological supervision of science and the arts. In addition frontiers with the West were to be opened. However, the reformers intended these changes to take place within the framework of the existing political organization. The party was to retain its leading role.

In 1968 mass media, press, radio and television played a key role in the democratizing process. Writers and journalists gained enormous popularity and with it greater influence than ever before. Former editors of *Literární noviny* re-launched the journal under the title *Literární listy* (Literary Gazette). It became an arts periodical with a circulation of 300,000, the largest in Europe. Banned again after August 1968, it reappeared under a third title, *Listy* (Gazette). The radical wing was represented by the politically oriented *Reportér* (The Reporter) and *Student* (The Student) in which the poem *Znamení moci* (The Sign of Power, see pp. 29–30) by Jan Zahradníček was published.

A series of articles in *Literární noviny* by the philosopher Karel Kosík called *Naše nynější krize* (Our Present Crisis), referring to T. G. Masaryk's well-known late 19th-century work, which had defined a new political programme for the Czechs, and seeking ways to democratize Marxist socialism prompted Ivan Sviták to write a reply, *Vaše nynější krize* (Your Present Crisis).[119] It was obvious that besides the handful of conservative Communists who simply rejected any change, and besides reformers supporting Dubček's leadership, another movement was becoming established among the Communist intellectuals who were sceptical about reforms controlled by the party and ultimately about any chance of regenerating the existing regime.

Thanks to freedom of speech, non-Communists could after two decades express their views in public. Besides organizations like Kan (Association of committed non-party members) and K 231, an association of former political prisoners, a circle of independent writers was founded. It brought together about sixty members including, Bedřich Fučík, Alexandr Kliment, Václav Havel, Petr Kopta, Josef Hiršal and Jan Vladislav. It strove to promote democratic values and worked calmly and unemotionally. The poet Jaroslav Seifert was elected to head the committee of the Czechoslovak Writers' Union for the redressing of wrongs – it investigated 168 cases of persecution of literary figures after the Communist takeover of February 1948 – and to fight for legal rehabilitation. The publishing houses planned to publish books by hitherto banned authors, living at home or in exile, like František Křelina, Jan Zahradníček, Josef Palivec, Ivan Blatný and Jan Čep. In 1967 for the first time Egon Hostovský was published. Professors Václav Černý and Jan Patočka returned to the Arts Faculty at Charles University and could lecture again after twenty years. At the same time in the second half of 1968 the review *Tvář* appeared again. In it even an article by Ladislav Hejdánek which had been suppressed in 1965 was published. This was an argument with Zdeněk Mlynář on the subject of intervention by the authorities in controversies about ideas and the arts.

> "Attempts by the authorities to intervene in controversies about ideas and control their results will certainly be repeated again and again also in socialist societies; what matters is that this should be taking place in the open. That is to say people have to be informed about every matter of importance so that any citizen who has anything to say can say publicly what he thinks about every such case [. . .]. When there are conflicting ideas, different, mutually inconsistent, contradictory views must necessarily confront each other. [. . .] should anyone maintain that open discussion would threaten the basis of our society, he is simply admitting that he fears debate out of some kind of weakness."[120]

Although democratization in Czechoslovakia was limited, it aroused worldwide interest. From the twenties Communism had suffered from anti-democratic tendencies that it had never been able to shake off. At a time of political crisis in the West – student revolts in France and Germany, the anti-Vietnam war movement in the USA – where the "New Left" appeared to be an alternative, and when it was not clear which of the two superpowers would gain predominance, the Czechoslovak attempt to combine Marxist socialism and democracy was followed with great interest. The Soviet leadership, in sharp disagreement, also followed developments carefully, fearing the spread of the reforming movement into other socialist countries.

In summer 1968 it was obvious that the public's renewed interest in public affairs was outstripping the ideas of the reforming party and the leading politicians. Committees were set up to prepare for the establishing of a social democracy; in business, workers' councils were formed; the religious organization *Dílo koncilové obrody* (Implementing the Second Vatican Council's Reforms) rejected state control of the church and worked for dialogue in the spirit of the Vatican council. The call for free unions and free elections became stronger. At the end of June Ludvík Vaculík's manifesto *Dva tisíce slov, která patří dělníkům, zemědělcům, úředníkům, vědcům, umělcům a všem* (Two Thousand Words That Belong to the Workers, Farmers, Officials, Scientists, Artists and Everyone, in English, *From Stalinism to Pluralism*, ed. by Gale Stokes, New York and London, 1991, pp. 126–130) appeared in the daily press and in *Literární listy*. He criticized the slow tempo of change and turned to the public with an appeal to establish "independent committees of citizens and commissions" which would have no links to official organizations. In a short time this appeal was signed by hundreds of important people; 120,000 signatures were gathered in all.

Dubček's party leadership rejected Vaculík's manifesto. At the same time, however, it reacted unenthusiastically to appeals from the Soviet Politburo and other "fraternal parties", particularly the notorious demagogues of East Germany, demanding the suppression of "revisionism" among the Communists of Czechoslovakia and the suppression of "antisocialist forces". There was no lack of provocation either, for example, the discovery in North Bohemia of arms allegedly belonging to the West "in preparation for the counter-revolution"; of course it was proved that the arms from one of the containers were of Soviet manufacture. Alexander Dubček, Parliamentary Speaker Josef Smrkovský, Prime Minister Oldřich Černík and others found themselves in a dilemma. On the one hand, they needed the support of the public to combat the conservatives at home and to win support abroad; on the other hand, they were being pressed by the public for more democratization, which they feared, hypnotized by "the menacing sphinx of the USSR and also by their own past".[121]

Even before the planned extraordinary Congress of the Czechoslovak Communist Party and before the elections, five countries, with the Soviet Union in command, occupied Czechoslovakia. It was the biggest military operation in Europe since the Second World War. On the 21 August there were 750,000 foreign troops in Czechoslovakia – according to a contemporary joke "after 2,000 words, 2,000 tanks" – of course there were three times as many tanks as that.

Bratříčku nevzlykej
to nejsou bubáci,
Vždyť už jsi velikej
To jsou jen vojáci
přijeli v hranatých
železných maringotkách.[122]

Little brother do not weep
they are not bogey men
After all you are a big boy now
They are only soldiers
they have come
in big iron caravans.

The spontaneous peaceful resistance of the population caught the occupying forces off guard. The unity and the determination of the people to defend democracy in August 1968 was reminiscent of the atmosphere during mobilization in September 1938 before Munich. At that time writers and artists also played a decisive role both by improvising radio and television broadcasts and by distributing leaflets with news and by their work at an extraordinary party congress. The hundreds of slogans written on walls in Cyrillic script, saying things like "Lenin arise, Brezhnev has gone mad" and "Soviet circus back in Prague", were remarkable manifestations of popular humour. Václav Havel, who had spent the last week of August with the actor Jan Tříska in Liberec, North Bohemia, recalled these days:

> "We worked in the broadcasting station there. I wrote a commentary every day, Honza read them on the air, and we even appeared on television, in a studio that was rigged up on Ještěd.[123] We were also part of the National Committee chairman's permanent staff [. . .]. Things were never more efficient than they were then. The print shop could put out a book in two days, and all kinds of enterprises were able

> to do almost anything right away. I remember a typical story: The scourge of Liberec and environs was a gang of about a hundred tough young men called 'Tramps' who would go on weekend forays into the countryside. For a long time, the town officials hadn't been able to put a stop to them. The leader was a fellow they called the Pastor. Shortly after the invasion, the Pastor showed up at the chairman's office in the town hall and said, 'I'm at your disposal, chief.' [. . .]. Thus arose a strange collaboration, one result of which was that for two days members of the Pastor's gang wore armbands of the auxiliary guard, and three-man patrols walked through the town: a uniformed policeman in the middle with two long-haired Tramps on either side."[124]

3. Defeat of the Reformers

The August invasion caused hundreds of deaths, but the consequent damage was incomparably greater. The Czech and Soviet leaders agreed to legalize the "temporary" presence of the occupying army. At first there was still hope that reform could continue for Dubček and his supporters were still in office. Moscow, however, exerted ever more pressure on them to step down. At home there was a "healthy nucleus" of Communists supported by the Kremlin and prepared to take power. The atmosphere of appeasement, well known from the autumn of 1938, when France and Britain, after Munich, accepted Hitler's demands and forced Czechoslovakia to give up its border regions, manifested itself in the people, convinced that through no fault of their own they had been sold down the river to a stronger power.

Just as in 1939 it was the young people who showed resistance. In November 1968 there was a strike of university students. All the Czech universities were on strike. Many businesses, and above all the intellectuals, showed solidarity with them. In January 1969, in protest against growing apathy, the Prague student Jan Palach set fire to himself, and in February Jan Zajíc followed his example. These deaths shook the public at home and shocked Western Europe. Some poems by Josef Kainar, Miroslav Holub, Jan Skácel and Karel Šiktanc, and songs by Bohdan Mikulášek and Vladimír Merta on the subject of Palach's death, bear witness to this sense of shock.

> Ani tak nehořím
> Já plynu
> Ze žhavých úst jak verš
> Jako verš o svobodě
> Verš který zmarní spálí udusí
> A přece svého dojde
>
> Ani tak nehořím
> Já spíš celý vlaji
> Ptáci mě nebesům
> Celého odevzdají[125]

But I am not so much on fire
As flowing
Out of an incandescent mouth like verse
Verse about freedom
Verse that lays waste burns chokes
And in fact comes into its own

But I am not so much on fire
As I am waving like a flag
To the heavens
Birds will hand me over whole

(Bolest ať mi poví [May I Be Delivered from Pain])

Palach's death[126] did not prevent the number of reforms being gradually reduced. It did, however, become a permanent memorial which had the power to move people even many years later, for example, Josef Šimon's poem in his collection *Vyvolávač* (The Town Crier, 1988) and demonstrations on the twentieth anniversary of his death in January 1989 that foreshadowed the November revolution.

Early in 1969 there was a dispute between two leading authors, Milan Kundera and Václav Havel. In the Christmas number of *Listy* MILAN KUNDERA (→ PROFILES) published an essay *Český úděl* (Our Czech Destiny) in which the year 1968 was rated highly as having made an impact world-wide. He said that resistance in the face of the August occupation indicated a new stage in our history and that "the Czech autumn was perhaps of even greater importance than the Czech spring"; so hope was not lost for further developments from the events of January.[127] In expressing this view Kundera might be thought to be reacting to his recent scepticism in these matters, as seen in the novel *Žert* (see p. 84) and his speech quoted at the writers' congress in 1967, or as typical of the position of reformist Communists who still considered socialism to be of unquestioned value. VÁCLAV HAVEL (→ PROFILES), however, took a sharply opposing view. He did not consider attempts to reintroduce law and order and freedom after many years as the way to become the centrepiece of world history, but simply as setting out on the road to "the normal, healthy functioning of the organism that is society". In *Český úděl?* he called Kundera's accolade self-regarding delusion and a danger to further development, as it could lead to camouflaging the actual very critical situation.[128]

Kundera, supported by the philosophers Karel Kosík and Lubomír Nový, replied to this article personally. Emanuel Mandler in *Tvář* and Jaroslav Střítecký in *Host do domu* took Havel's side. Basically this was a clash between reforming Communists and the young sixties generation of writers.

After "the ice hockey week" in March 1969, when thousands of people came out on to the streets in Prague and elsewhere after the second victory of the national team over the USSR, the Soviet leader Brezhnev decided to dispose of the reformers once and for all. With the country occupied by tanks, Alexander Dubček was forced to step down, and another Slovak, Gustáv Husák, became leader of the party. Husák had originally been one of the advocates of reform but after August he changed sides and joined the pro-Soviet faction.

Two years after the 4th Writers' Congress in June 1967, which was the prologue to the revivalist trend, there was a meeting of the constituent congress of the national writers' organizations, the Czech and Slovak unions. Most of the Slovak writers meanwhile welcomed Husák for they expected him to fulfil their national aspirations. As early as 1968 Vladimír Mináč, Vojtech Mihálik and Laco Novomeský had coined the phrase "first federalization, then democratization". The Czech writers loudly voiced their disagreement with this political line, which was pushed by Husák. In May 1969 Otomar Krejča, director and head of *Divadlo za branou* (Theatre beyond the Gate) said: "As long as we have live souls in the auditorium we shall not be isolated and we shall be stronger than the authorities who have no support other than themselves and who are cut off from the elite of the nation as what has happened in society in the past year has shown."[129]

The Congress of the Union of Czech Writers in June 1969, however, turned out to be the epilogue to the hopes of revival. Jan Procházka's words in the opening address caught the mood of the conference when he said that they were meeting at a time "when liberties are decreasing again and overnight the bailiffs in charge of them are increasing".

For the first time after twenty years – and for the last time for another twenty years – the congress took place without delegations from the Communist Party and without the party taking an active interest beforehand. One of the first documents the new session produced was a bitter protest at the shutting down of the journal *Listy*. The state agencies did not however react to the protest. The state authorities never approved the registration application of this Union of Writers and gradually other reviews were closed down.

On the first anniversary of the invasion, 21 August 1969, people, chiefly in Prague and Brno, gathered spontaneously in the streets. The government brought in the police, the People's Militia, the Communist Party's private army, and the regular army with tanks. People lost their lives, there were numerous wounded and many demonstrators were arrested. Afterwards the last representatives of the reformers were forced out of public life. It meant the end of any hope of continuing or at least partly retaining any democratic changes.

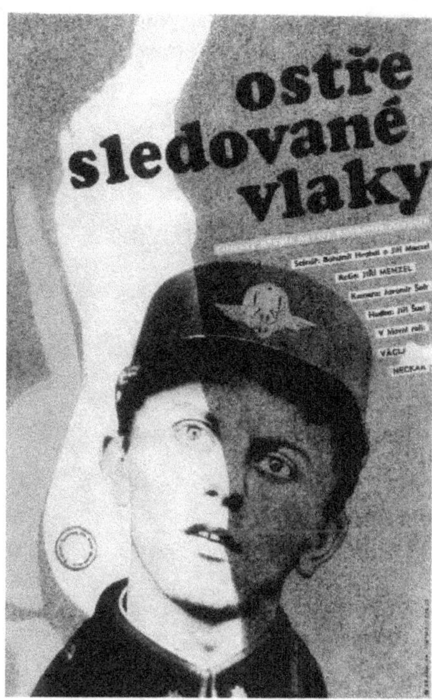

15 A poster for *Ostře sledované vlaky* (Closely Watched Trains), a film by Jiří Menzel (1966) inspired by Hrabal's story (František Zálešák)

17 Milan Kundera (1929) in 1967 (Dagmar Hochová)

16 A poster for *Skřivánci na niti* (Larks on a String), a film by Jiří Menzel (1969) inspired by Hrabal's stories *Inzerát na dům, ve kterém už nechci bydlet* (Advertisement for a House I Don't Want to Live in Anymore) (Alexej Jaroš)

18 Milan Kundera by Adolf Hoffmeister (1968)

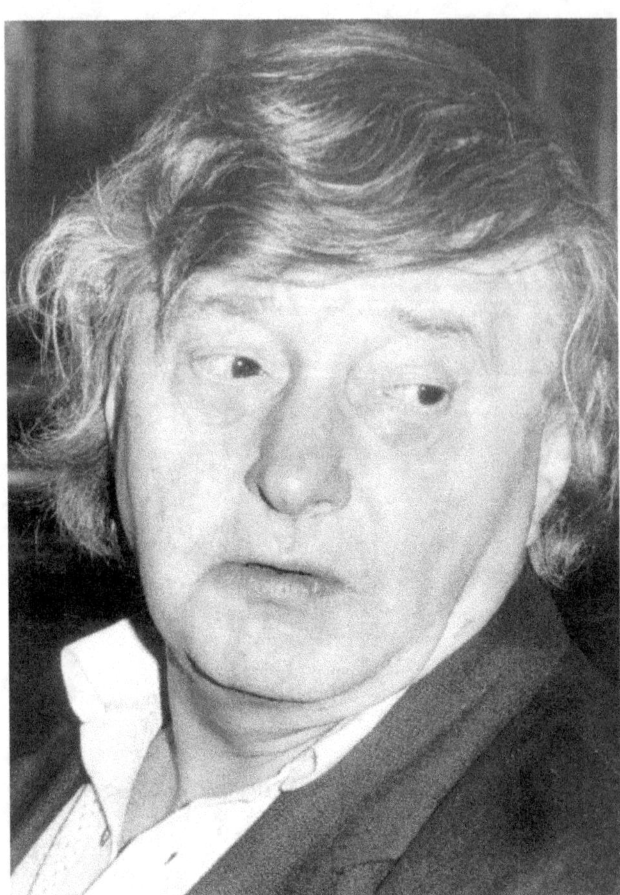

19 Ladislav Fuks (1923–1994) in 1977 (Milan Jankovič)

20 Ivan Klíma (1931) in 1988 (Viktor Stoilov)

21 Pavel Kohout (1928) in 1967 (Dagmar Hochová)

22 Ludvík Vaculík (1926) with his son in 1988 (Viktor Stoilov)

23 Věra Linhartová (1938) in 1998 (Dagmar Hochová)

25 Ivan Diviš (1924–1999) in 1990 (Viktor Stoilov)

24 Jiří Kolář (1914–2002) in early 1970s (Milan Jankovič)

27 Jan Mukařovský (1891–1975) in the 1930 (author of the photograph is unknown)

26 Karel Šiktanc (1928) in the 1970s (Milan Jankovič)

28 Jan Patočka (1907–1977) in the early 1970s (Milan Jankovič)

29 Václav Havel (1936) in 1989 (Viktor Stoilov)

30 Sylvie Richterová (1945) in 1997 (Dagmar Hochová)

31 Daniela Hodrová (1946) in 1997 (Dagmar Hochová)

32 Jáchym Topol (1962) in 1997 (Dagmar Hochová

The Seventies and Eighties

"Today more cellulose is turned into denunciations, Acta Pilati and anonymous letters than into books, and the much hated Čehona, archetype of the conservative Czech loyal to the monarchy,[1] has returned to tend Moscow's stables. Today ambitious judges slap together ideological trials against anyone who dares to think, and Josef K., having committed yet another non-crime by signing the Manifesto of Two Thousand Words, tries in vain to convince the pettifoggers of his innocence; the house in Hrabal's stories dealing with the absurdities and pitfalls of the Stalinist period, Advertisement for a House I Don't Want to Live In Anymore, is today as it was then: narrow, stuffy, full of snares . . . "

(Angelo Maria Ripellino)[2]

NORMALIZATION

1. Restoring "Order"

Public resistance to normalization was crushed by force. The authors of the petition *Deset bodů* (Ten Points, August 1969), including Ludvík Vaculík and Václav Havel, who demanded that what remained of democracy should be kept, were sued for "subverting the republic". Organizations that refused to submit to normalization, for example Seifert's Union of Czech Writers (Svaz českých spisovatelů), were called "pressure groups" in the officialese of the new men in power and disbanded. On radio, television and in the press, smear campaigns were carried on against the "agents of counter-revolution", Václav Černý, Jan Procházka, Pavel Kohout, Ivan Sviták and Václav Havel. They were silenced and could not defend themselves in public. The Socialist Movement of Czechoslovak Citizens, whose manifesto for 28 October 1970 contained the words "let us lead a struggle for a socialist, democratic, independent, free Czechoslovakia", and the conspiring Revolutionary Marxist Party attempted to form a political opposition but their efforts were speedily crushed. Their representatives, Jiří Müller, Jaroslav Šabata, Milan Hübl, Petr Uhl and others ended up spending many years in prison. The secret police, which doubled in strength between 1968 and 1970, relentlessly pursued any "anti-socialist" bias in the arts. In 1971 some writers, actors and musicians from Ostrava, including Ivan Binar, Petr Podhrázký and Josef Frais were arrested and a year later were convicted of sedition and slandering the state. The pretext for these arrests was a production in the *Waterloo Theatre* of Valentin Katayev's Soviet classic *A Son of the Regiment* as a musical.[3]

There was a purge of hundreds of thousands of Communist Party members. So the party rid itself of reformists and thinking and creative people in general who refused to be part of the new totalitarianism. Purges followed in the civil service, the army and the police, the universities – Václav Černý and Jan Patočka were again dismissed from the Arts Faculty in Prague where they had returned in 1968 – the schools and editorial staffs. There was a great shake-up in radio and television broadcasting; news broadcasts were full of empty rhetoric. The purpose of the media was again not to provide but to withhold information and to disseminate propaganda.

Up to half a million were sacked from their jobs. About 120,000 Czech citizens remained abroad after August 1968. Among them were many well-known authors: Josef Škvorecký, Arnošt Lustig, Josef Jedlička, Ludvík Aškenazy, Jan Beneš, Karel Michal, Věra Linhartová, Ivan Diviš, Antonín Brousek and many publicists. Throughout the seventies and eighties many others followed – Milan Kundera, Jiří Kolář, Pavel Kohout, Jiří Gruša, Jan Vladislav, Jaroslav Hutka, Vlastimil Třešňák and Karol Sidon. The total number of Czechoslovak nationals who went to the West between August 1968 and November 1989 is estimated at 300,000. By the autumn of 1969 it was no longer possible to cross the frontier at will. If anyone wanted to go to "a capitalist foreign country" they had to go through a complicated procedure explaining their reasons. Once again non-party members came up against a ceiling. They were not allowed to remain in positions of responsibility. People were forced into humiliating self-criticism or into unskilled jobs. Editors, critics and scientists became stokers, night-watchmen and window cleaners.

> "Most of all I enjoy central-heating control rooms, where men with higher education, chained to their jobs like dogs to their kennels, write the history of their times as a sort of sociological survey and where I learned how the fourth estate was depopulated and the proletariat went from base to superstructure and how the university-trained elite now carries on its work. My best friends are two former members of our Academy of Sciences who have been set to work in the sewers, so they've decided to write a book about them . . . "[4]

The extent of these purges had no parallel either during the Nazi occupation or after the February Communist takeover. The "enlightened despotism" of Antonín Novotný before January 1968 now appeared idyllic. Young people wore badges on their jackets with the inscription "Sorry, Tony".

Understandably the bans affected freedom of speech more than anything else. From the time of J. K. Tyl and Karel Havlíček in the 1830s and 1840s, if not before, Czech literature had developed in conjunction with the cultural reviews and magazines which had been a powerful influence in its development. Literary arguments were conducted in them preparing the way for the next generation. Never before, as at the beginning of normalization, had all literary journals in existence been banned at the same time. After *Listy*, *Tvář* and *Sešity*, it was the turn of *Plamen* (Blaze), all the important regional journals, such as *Dialog* (Dialogue), *Texty* (Texts), *Červený květ* (Red Flower), even the bland journal *Impuls* (Impulse); the Brno *Host do domu* and the Prague *Orientace* (The Way to Go) held out for quite a long time, their last issue appearing in 1970. In Slovakia one of the first to be "killed off" was *Kultúrny život* (Cultural Life), a weekly paper that had made it possible in the sixties for Gustáv Husák to be freed from prison and return to public life. All these politico-cultural journals were replaced by *Literární měsíčník* (Literary Monthly) published by the official Writers' Union. The politico-cultural

Tvorba (Creations), with Jiří Hájek in charge, echoed its views. Only authors who had been "vetted" could be published in it and they could write only on "permissible" subjects. So most writers were beyond the pale; as far as public institutions were concerned, it was as if they had ceased to exist. Ideological debate and literary polemics disappeared. Reviewers outdid each other in praise of average and below average authors approved by the "upper echelons", such as Josef Rybák, Jan Kozák, Ivan Skála, Jiří Taufer, Ladislav Štoll. While banned authors Milan Kundera, Ludvík Vaculík, Václav Havel and others were not spared hard-hitting criticism, it was always obligatory to praise members of the union. In the eighteen years of its existence, *Literární měsíčník* did not once publish a negative criticism of any approved writer from the ranks of the official union. So it became widely accepted that criticism was to be avoided, and those who had achieved certain positions tried to defend them at all costs.

Secret instructions about the withdrawal of books from libraries affected hundreds of authors. In all about a million volumes were withdrawn. Bans were applied in varying degrees: some authors were allowed to publish occasionally, but nothing could be written about their books; others were allowed only to translate; others were not even allowed to translate. Unlike during the sixties, censorship had no firm base in law. Instead it gave rise to a network of approval and specious disapproval so that vigilant control was maintained both through the collusion of responsible editors in newspapers, reviews and publishing houses and a form of self-censorship which removed in advance any sensitive themes or undesirable expressions.

The bureaucrats seemed to have copied some practices from George Orwell's novel *Nineteen Eighty-Four* and from the actions of his famous "Ministry of Truth". For example even Soviet books that might prove to be provocative were suppressed. Before the congress of the Communist Party of Czechoslovakia the publication of an innocuous book entitled *Chalupa na spadnutí* (The Tumbledown Cottage) was banned. Some titles were published in ridiculously small editions, for instance Aloys Skoumal's historic translation of James Joyce's *Ulysses*, came out in 1976 in an edition of 7,000 but it practically never reached the bookshops and readers queued in vain to buy it. Other works by officials of the union or approved party activists were published in incredibly large editions and remained unsold in spite of all the publicity. Nevertheless, new editions were immediately prepared.

Superficially, the atmosphere after the Communist takeover of February 1948 was repeating itself. However, the radical enthusiasm of the postwar period was completely absent. Normalization was jokingly called "Stalinism with a human face". Unlike in the fifties, when the regime committed a large amount of judicial crimes, in the seventies only certain individuals and groups were singled out for persecution. The regime, whose hallmark was careful conservatism, strove to retain the status quo. Not one of the premiers of Czechoslovakia since 1918 had remained in office as long as the seventies moderate normalizer Lubomír Štrougal, previously a 1968 moderate reformist. For many years there were only negligible changes in the top echelons of the party.

From the ordinary citizen the state demanded only passive loyalty; in return he or she was guaranteed peace and a relatively decent standard of living. In any case even the majority of Communists did not believe that the party and the people were firmly united. Nor did they believe that socialist Czechoslovakia was flourishing and that 99.7 per cent of the votes were cast for the National Front candidates. Ideological slogans were delivered ritually and colourlessly, more or less without enthusiasm and without the conviction and fire of the post-February Communist takeover. There were frequent references to debased Czech "realism" and to material advantages. Those who wielded power went about their business without much ado, wrote Milan Šimečka. "An era of materialism had arrived."[5]

> Proč asi myslíte, lidi, že žijete,
> a jak to podivně s žitím nakládáte
> [. . .]
> Co s tím naděláme, to všechno musíme
> [. . .].
> Děláme pouze to, co je nutně třeba,
> abychom náhodou nepřišli o chleba.[6]
>
> Why do you think you are living, folks,
> and how strangely you go about life
> [. . .]
> What we are doing with it is all we can do
> [. . .].
> We are doing only what is necessary
> so that there is no chance of losing our bread and butter.
>
> (Jaroslav Hutka, Abychom náhodou [So that we would not by chance . . . , 1972])

The attempt not to lose one's "bread and butter" led to people playing two roles, publicly pretending to be acquiescent citizens obediently keeping all the rules and regulations and privately conducting their lives according to their own moral code. Private life was of course tainted by this perversion. This is what Milan Pávek attacked in his novel *Simulanti* (Dissimulators), which was published in 1983 but then banned, although a limited number of copies were allowed to be sold three years later. In Pávek's novel, life is based on hypocrisy and pretence. Boundaries between truth and lies disappear. *Simulanti* might be set in a Utopian future, but it was transparently a picture of contemporary society. The theme of "a pact with the devil" appeared to a certain extent in literature published with official approval, but chiefly in samizdat, in novels by Ivan Binar, Karel Pecka, Jiří Gruša, in poems by Svatopluk Karásek and Ivan Martin Jirous, and in dramas by Václav Havel, Jiří Suchý and Daniela Fischerová. It was a reaction to the dangerous double game of trying to outwit the authorities, to appear to be dutiful subjects while at the same time taking advantage of the benefits offered. Like a pact with the devil, this leads to moral and physical decline. It seems that the evil threatening man comes not only from outside. It penetrates as far as we ourselves allow it to, through our apprehension about being victimized, and our fear for our place in society. "If the devil exists, then above all he exists within our own selves!" says one of Havel's characters in *Pokoušení* (1985, Prague in 1990; English translation published as *Temptation*, 1988). This Czech devil-tempter goes on to say, "I [. . .] wouldn't be able to move you an inch if you hadn't secretly dreamed about moving in that direction yourself long ago!"[7] When the actor spoke this line in Jan Grossman's 1991 production of *Pokoušení* in the *Theatre on the Balustrade* after the Velvet Revolution, he turned not to his fellow actor, as the text of the play dictated, but to the auditorium and spoke to the audience, and instead of using the singular form of dreamt (*nesnil*) he used the plural (*nesnili*). In this way he emphasized to them this type of "normalized" behaviour.

2. Literature Divided

It is obvious from official proclamations that writers did not collaborate with the normalizing regime to the same extent as after the February 1948 takeover of the Communist Party. As early as June 1970 a resolution of the Central Committee of the Communist Party of Czechoslovakia stated unequivocally:

> "In the past, especially in 1968 and 1969, the cultural front was one of the areas most affected by right-wing opportunism, nationalism and hostility towards the Soviet Union. In this, many exponents of the right who had succeeded in getting into positions of authority played a decisive part [. . .]. As a result of this influence and by means of the most varied demagogic slogans and under the guise of defending freedom and the interests of art, they succeeded in maintaining a false political unity until the May 1969 plenary session of the Central Committee of the Communist Party of Czechoslovakia and possibly even for some time after that."[8]

The resolution *Poučení z krizového vývoje ve straně a společnosti po XIII. sjezdu KSČ* (Lessons Drawn from the Crisis Development in the Party and Society after the 13th Congress of the Communist Party of Czechoslovakia) followed in January 1971. A stinging attack in this "analysis" gave ideas from the fifties a new lease of life: the Soviet invasion was "international assistance", it provided the opportunity for the country's political and economic recovery; on the other hand, attempts at reform were a threat to socialist achievements and were a preparation for counter-revolution. Writers and publicists were again first to be branded "evil-minded counter-revolutionaries".

The founding congress of the new Union of Czech Writers did not meet until mid-1972. The president of the union, Jan Kozák, told his audience in the main speech what they already knew from *Poučení*, namely, that writers between the years 1968 and 1969 were "the brain droppings of the beginning of the counter-revolution". What was new of course was the literary output from the sixties being described as works from "a time of great travesties, such as had never before existed in the history of Czech literature".[9] This time the speech made by the secretary of the Czechoslovak Communist Party was no different from the main speech and the delegation from the party stayed till the end of the congress.

In 1969 the union over which Seifert presided had almost 500 members including translators. In spite of all the propaganda and the material advantages, Kozák's "regenerated" union did not attract more than 115 authors – of those the important ones were Vilém Závada, Norbert Frýd, Jiří Marek, Václav Kaplický, František Kožík, Miroslav Florian and Josef Hanzlík. It was symptomatic that at its inception there were no former ardent supporters of the Communist regime, such as Milan Jariš, Adolf Hoffmeister or Jan Otčenášek.

From the end of the war Slovak and Czech literature had developed along similar lines. Slovak poets who had supported Husák's rise to power were given political posts: Laco Novomeský became one of the leaders of the party, Vojtech Mihálik became Parliamentary Speaker and Miroslav Válek became Slovak Minister of Culture. The Union of Slovak Writers was not officially disbanded, but "merely" subjected to purges. The majority of those expelled, Ladislav Ťažký, Peter Karvaš, Katarína Lazarová, Anton Hykisch, Ján Johanides and Pavol Števček, could be published officially again after a few years.

The progress of normalization and their own disadvantaged positions caused difficulties for the "writers in liquidation", as Bohumil Hrabal called himself and his colleagues. Heinrich Böll branded the situation in Czechoslovakia "a cultural graveyard".[10]

However, the writers who had been silenced began to defend themselves. In 1971 three Czech publishers set up in business abroad. Two of them, *Sixty-Eight Publishers* in Toronto (Zdena Salivarová-Škvorecká and Josef Škvorecký) and *Index* in Cologne (Adolf Müller and Bedřich Utitz), became the chief centres for exiled literature during the seventies and eighties and published authors banned at home. In Toronto more than 200 titles and in Cologne up to a 170 titles were published.

Immediately authors at home made their voices heard. In December 1972 thirty-six Czech writers signed a petition to the president for the release of political prisoners. At the same time Ludvík Vaculík and friends made a typewritten samizdat literature series of it that he later called *Petlice* (Padlock).

Czech literature split into three parts: domestic "approved", domestic unpublished, that is, samizdat, which was edited but still in manuscript, and foreign, that is, exiled. The fact that literature was split up like this was not in itself surprising, it had been divided for years at home and elsewhere, especially in Russia, with domestic samizdat, and exiled "tamizdat". Divisions in Czech literature had been recorded since the time of Munich 1938, although the size of each branch relative to the others had changed. Until 1970, Czech unpublished literature and Czech exiled literature had been in the minority, limited to a few focal works and by no means comparable in its scope to approved literature. Widespread purges at the beginning of the seventies, bans on publishing on a massive scale at home and mass departure into exile created a different situation. The majority of important writers, including many who had taken part in the building of the post-February state, found themselves beyond the bounds of official culture. Another factor causing change was the liberalization of relations between the West and the East. Frontiers were not as impassable as before and modern technology made communications easier. Authors who could not publish at home gradually found they could be published abroad, both in Czech and in translation. Financial and material assistance flowed in from the opposite direction; works published in exile, foreign newspapers and later photocopiers and computers were smuggled in.

The Three Worlds of Literature

1. Literature Published in Czechoslovakia

Each of the three literary movements in the seventies and eighties functioned under different circumstances and aimed at different classes of readers. Approved and samizdat literature within Czechoslovakia and literature in exile all gradually created an "atmosphere" special to themselves, their own circle of authors, journals, publishers and standards of aesthetic values. At home in particular, differences between "official" and "unofficial" works sometimes reached a point where it seemed that people living in the same country, even in the same town, came from different worlds.

In the late seventies the samizdat essayist Milan Šimečka observed, " . . . what I read in the various books and journals seems like news from another world which probably exists, but about which I know nothing. I live in a different world."[11] Ten years later Václav Havel wrote:

> "Think of all the new samizdat books and publishing ventures, think of how many anonymous and improbable people are copying them out and distributing them, think of all the attention this is enjoying with the public! [. . .] You would feel that the young people you see there live in their own world, a world very different from the one that breathes on us from the newspapers, from TV and the Prague radio. These two worlds simply fail to connect . . . "[12]

The "union" authors also had the feeling they were different. Of course this was a difference of another kind that they spoke about in private. In public only a few particularly aggressive individuals put it into words when they wrote about the authors who had emigrated and the samizdat writers at home as if they were the ones who had cut themselves off from Czech literature. Karel Sýs for instance used this argument at the end of the seventies in *Literární měsíčník* (Literary Monthly) in an article on poetry and the position of Antonín Brousek and other unofficial poets.

In Slovakia normalization took a "milder" form. The majority of the most important writers remained within the framework of approved literature. Only a few individuals, Ladislav Mňačko, who published in German from the seventies onwards, the short story writer Jaroslava Blažková and the poet Peter Repka, left for the West. Blažková and Repka published almost nothing from the 1970s onwards. So Slovak literature in exile continued to be based on writers who, as supporters of the Slovak semi-fascist state, had left Czechoslovakia immediately after the war. Samizdat literature in Slovakia was more important than Slovak literature in exile, although there was much less Slovak samizdat of it than Czech samizdat. Slovak samizdat writers included the novelists Dominik Tatarka, Ivan Kadlečík and Hana Ponická, the essayists Milan Šimečka (who wrote mostly in Czech) and Miroslav Kusý. They all had connections with the Czech samizdat system. At the end of the seventies and the beginning of the eighties some of the younger generation formed a group around the Bratislava journal *Kontakt* (Contact), which later incorporated *Fragment* (Fragment) and *Fragment K* (Fragment K). This group was very close to Brno and Prague samizdat.

So Slovak literature did not, like Czech literature, develop into three main branches. In Slovakia there was in force a system of cultural repression, bans and censorship. However, as the literary historian Peter Zajac claims, literature developed mainly round approved literature at home. The fact that during normalization the Minister for Culture and spokesman for Slovak literary policy was Miroslav Válek, whose name meant something, unlike that of the Czech normalizer Jan Kozák,[13] made a significant difference.

At first sight, literature published by the state publishing houses and accessible in the libraries seemed to occupy the most favourable position of the three branches of literature. Writers had no subsistence problems because they had salaries from the state and could devote themselves to their work. They did not have to fear persecution or, like the samizdat authors, be afraid of the police, who had the power to remove and destroy manuscripts. Compared with writers in exile, they had greater opportunities to make contact with their readers. Their works could be published in large print runs – unlike samizdat works that came out in editions of two dozen copies and the few hundred copies published in exile. There was also, at least in theory, feedback from public criticism.

"Official" authors, however, lacked one thing essential for art: the freedom to publish whatever they wished. Two vetting processes, censorship and self-censorship, were applied to the subject matter and to some parts of an author's work; even his poetics had to be "cleaned up" and peculiarities of style and language suppressed. Lively texts often turned into conventional pieces of work perfectly produced as if they had come off a conveyor belt, but without life.

It would be an oversimplification to say that in the seventies and eighties only second- and third-rate writers were published within Czechoslovakia. At the end of the sixties and the beginning of the seventies before the final victory of normalization in literature, some remarkable works came out. Miroslav Florian's collections *Svatá pravda* (Absolute Truth, 1969, completed 1971) and *Iniciály* (Initials, 1972), Vilém Závada's last great work *Na prahu* (On the Threshold, 1970), Vladimír Páral's *Profesionální žena* (A Woman by Profession, 1971; published in English as *The Four Sonyas*, 1993), Ladislav Fuks's *Příběh kriminálního rady* (The Case of the Senior Police Investigator, 1971), and Norbert Frýd's *Císařovna* (The Empress, 1972) were all published. Younger members of the sixties generation, the poets Karel Sýs and Josef Peterka, the poet, short story writer and novelist Petr Prouza and the short story writer Vojtěch Steklač began promisingly. All these writers were part of the "official" branch of literature in the seventies, and in some cases also in the eighties. They were able to go on publishing and producing further works. However, there was a definite decline in the literary quality of their work. For example, Ladislav Fuks and Vladimír Páral changed their vision of the world. Both authors stopped asking disturbing questions and drawing pictures of bizarreness and stupidity and accepted social conformity. At the beginning of the seventies VLADIMÍR PÁRAL (→ PROFILES) wrote a story about some people living in an isolated creek on the Slapy lake in Central Bohemia, an allegory of the rise and abuse of power. The novel, *Tam za vodou* (Beyond the Water), however, was banned and not published till a quarter of a century later in 1995. His next works are without satire and lack his penetrating vision of the world; Páral's heroes even acquire an enthusiasm for work, for example in *Mladý muž a bílá velryba* (The Young Man and the White Whale, 1973).[14] LADISLAV FUKS (→ PROFILES), in whose cryptic prose there are only brief spells of external reality, wrote a straightforward story about 1948, the year of the Communist takeover, *Návrat z žitného pole* (Return from the Field of Rye, 1974). VILÉM ZÁVADA, one of the oldest generation of poets, did not go quite as far. Yet even he seemed to take fright after the cruelly probing poetry in his book *Na prahu* (On the Threshold, see also p. 71). Here motifs of anxiety recur, the lyrical hero compares himself with Job from the Bible. In his next book *Živote, díky* (Thanks, Life, 1977) Závada went back to mild middle-of-the-road optimism. The poetry of MIROSLAV FLORIAN, a contributor to *Květen* in the 1950s, deteriorated to such an extent that at its best it was merely clever virtuosity.

This was the time when the work of many writers again became reminiscent of the political output from the era after the February Communist takeover of 1948, illustrated by the work of such individuals as Vítězslav Nezval, Josef Kainar, Václav Řezáč, Marie Pujmanová and Jan Drda. In the seventies, once again the demand for "clarity of ideas" was exerting pressure. Writers who wanted to continue to publish had to endure very tight restrictions to be accepted as official literature. Willingly or unwillingly they changed their poetics, forced in Vladimir Mayakovsky's metaphor "to trample on the throat of their songs". At the end of the sixties Jan Lopatka came up against this dilemma when, in connection with the enforced changes in Hrabal's works, he wrote that a text issued by a publishing house must not appear too strange, must not be too complicated, should not be seen as an allegory of life under socialism, should not be "merely" playing with words; of course even less should it be provocative or have unsuitable allusions and so on. In short "the demands made on an author are superhuman" (the collection *Podoby II* [Resemblances II], 1969).[15]

In comparison with the hard-and-fast norms of the fifties, the situation in the seventies was a little more relaxed. Clearly defined plots, black-and-white conflicts and superficial descriptions were no longer used and subtler value judgments were possible. More flexible methods of construction were allowed. In novels, for example, it was possible to dispense with the "omniscient" narrator. In general there was much greater interest in personal life, matters of an intimate nature, family problems and erotica – which corresponded to the social mentality of the normalizing era. The popular television series by Jaroslav Dietl, *Nemocnice na kraji města* (Suburban Hospital, 1978–1979, sequel 1982, in book form 1988), was typical. This series, which was incidentally also popular in West Germany, managed skilfully to combine an attractive subject with credible everyday details. In general, it aimed at presenting an idealized picture of the world. The novels by the women authors Valja Stýblová, Jaromíra Kolárová and, in the later seventies and eighties, Zdena Frýbová, performed a similar function, supplying traditional light reading. Frýbová was the first writer to use the methods of West European bestsellers. The publishing houses and critics however presented their writing, which superficially criticized small-town mentality and attempted clumsy psychological study, as valuable analytical works. Light literature of a more sophisticated nature was Vladimír Neff's romantic trilogy *Královny nemají nohy* (Queens Have No Legs, 1973 etc.), in which he wrote about the exploits of the knight Petr Kukaň at the beginning of the 17th century.

Undemanding entertainment was uppermost in humorous writing. Satire had all but disappeared. The works of Miroslav Skála in particular, the one-time collaborator in the satirical cabaret of *Večerní Brno* (Evening Brno) was well above the average in this genre. His *Cesta kolem mé hlavy za 40 dnů* (Around My Head in Forty Days, 1979, a title inspired by Jules Verne)[16] is set in a mental hospital and combines wit and elements of fantasy and farce. It also makes humorous use of language.

The departure of the hero to the unspoilt countryside introduced another kind of escape. The novel *Když v ráji pršelo* (When It Rained in Paradise, 1972),[17] by the experienced Jan Otčenášek, was the first of a succession of novels on this theme. In it a young couple, a philosopher and his teacher wife, leave Prague for Šumava (Bohemian Forest) to restore a dilapidated mill. The official critic, Vladimír Dostál, rightly reproached the author for giving no reason for the couple leaving Prague and "avoiding more important social problems". An author who wanted to publish but at the same time had no intention of adopting the ideas of the normalizers in his writing was forced to use this type of subject. Several younger writers, Jiří Medek, Jan Kostrhun, Jiří Navrátil, followed Otčenášek's example. In mildly symbolic or artless stories, in simple analogies between man and nature, they were seeking something to prevent them from being obliged "to describe the improvements of socialism realistically". A chapter in Milan Kundera's *Nesnesitelná lehkost bytí* (in Czech 1985; published in English as *The Unbearable Lightness of Being*, 1984) is a parody, perhaps unintentional, of such works. The chief characters Tomáš and Tereza leave Prague for the country in despair but country life turns out to be a trap and not the idyll they imagined.

JAROMÍR TOMEČEK, one of the oldest generation of writers, in his *Hora hoří* (A Mountain on Fire, 1984), continued to present a more profound look at nature. The picture of nature threatened by human predators is at the same time a picture of a threat to human relationships. A similar theme provided the inspiration for the works of the one-time friend of Catholic writer Jakub Deml, STANISLAV VODIČKA, who did not begin writing till the seventies. His short works explore the events of the natural world, its secret rhythms and inner timing. "Sit on a tree stump or a rock and listen to the silence. Suddenly something will snap. As if someone had broken a thin dry twig. After a while it will snap somewhere above your head. That is the beginning of the great concert of silence." (*Tam, kde usínají motýlové* [Where the Butterflies Fall Asleep], 1978).[18]

It was also possible for writers to escape the iron control of official standards by resorting to complex literary forms. From time to time authors who had not "compromised themselves" in the sixties and had managed to avoid direct complaints were able to publish carefully constructed prose. VLADIMÍR MIKEŠ published *Zednická novela* (The Mason's Story) in 1974, KAREL MILOTA brought out *Noc zrcadel* (Night of Mirrors)[19] in 1981 and STANISLAV ZEDNÍČEK published poetry with a spiritual theme in the book of poetry *Větrná zátiší* (A Windy Retreat) in 1974.[20]

Besides Miloslav Topinka, who was "dismissed" as editor when *Sešity* was shut down, there were two other young poets of outstanding ability in the late sixties and early seventies, Josef Peterka and Karel Sýs. JOSEF PETERKA'S intellectual poetry changed to embrace the required "positive values for life". Nevertheless his penetrating scepticism was still evident in his *Autobigrafie vlka* (Autobiography of a Wolf, 1980). This was the picture of a man being split into opposing roles, a clear reference to the current situation. As a result of the criticism of this book, however, there followed the completely conformist *Autobiografie člověka* (Autobiography of a Man, 1984). KAREL SÝS'S first books were refreshing as a reaction to the gloomy, melancholy, metaphysical poetry written by Holan's imitators in the sixties. However the titillating voluptuousness and sensuality of his first book, *Newton za neúrody jablek* (Newton When the Apples Did Not Ripen, 1969), and the Nezval-like playfulness of the poetry that followed had become empty and routine by the end of the seventies.[21]

JIŘÍ ŽÁČEK was close to Sýs in his poetic vision of the world. He also contrasts abstract meditation with personal experience, the joys and sorrows of everyday life, the complex structures of free verse with simple poetic forms. In his collection *Anonymní múza* (The Anonymous Muse, 1976) a street girl who persuades the poet to accompany her for a pub crawl through the "darkest night" is the embodiment of poetry. Humour, texts of songs and poems for children, *Aprílová škola* (The April Fools' School, 1978) and many other books form an important part of Žáček's work. Four-line stanzas of rhyming iambics are characteristic of his poetics.

PETR SKARLANT, who was a few years older than the others, may be counted as one of the younger members of the sixties generation. He is the author of a book of love poems *Hebká kůže* (Silken Skin, 1972), and *Věk slasti* (The Age of Bliss, 1977), a prose collection of reminiscences of his youth in the sixties in which he also mentions the poet Václav Hrabě (see p. 98). A very similar poet was PETR CINCIBUCH, who, besides being involved in other professions, was also an ambulance driver. He was able to write knowledgeably in *Veterán rallye* (Veteran Rally, 1976) because of his fascination with the world of motorcars. Cincibuch's poetry is more concerned with the inner life than the poetry of Sýs or Žáček, concentrating more on ethical problems; rejection and lost love are typical themes. A subject of lifelong interest to JOSEF ŠIMON, the youngest of the "thirty-year-olds" as they were called in the seventies, was the world of the modern big city, a world he sometimes viewed harshly and wrote of critically as he did in *Pouštní pták* (Bird of the Desert, 1981).

At first these authors were more or less tolerated in approved literature. The quality of their work was fundamentally different from the verse of Josef Rybák and Karel Boušek. In the course of time, however, they themselves largely accepted official standards. Casualness, flippancy and the intimate nature of their poetry often became a stereotype. Josef Šimon, in his collection *Vyvolávač* (The Town Crier, 1988), was the most successful in overcoming this tendency.[22]

2. A Grey Area

What was distinctive and worthwhile in the literature that reached the public did not come from the richly subsidized and highly praised authors belonging to the Writers' Union but from the "fringe" authors in the shifting grey area between approved and banned literature. Jiří Šotola and Vladimír Körner continued to produce historical novels that fell into this category. JIŘÍ ŠOTOLA'S (see p. 85) characters are usually pawns on the chessboard of history. For them events have no higher significance, their ideals are regularly shattered, and in the end they themselves, like the vagabond actor Matěj Kuře (in Czech *kuře* = chicken) during the Napoleonic wars in the novel *Kuře na rožni* (Chicken on a Spit), are simply engaged in a struggle to survive. This book had a history. It appeared first in a German translation;[23] two years later it came out in samizdat in *Petlice* (Padlock) and two years after that, in 1976, when the author's "self-criticism" had appeared in the politico-cultural weekly paper *Tvorba*, it was published by the Czechoslovak Writers' Publishing House. Šotola's unique style and language are characterized by very short "chopped-up" sentences, crisp dialogue and the use of archaisms and irony. Man crushed by history is also the subject of other tragic tales by VLADIMÍR KÖRNER (see p. 86). His novels, set in various different periods, always appear to be allegories of the present day. The novel *Lékař umírajícího času* (Doctor in a Dying Age, 1984) was about the life of the doctor and humanist Jan Jessenius, who was put to death in the Prague Old Town executions of 1621 after the Czech Protestant nobility's uprising against the Habsburgs. It was serialized for television and a film was made from the novel in 1990.

KAREL MICHAL had earlier written a historical novel on non-traditional lines in his *Čest a sláva* (Fame and Honour, see p. 86) and then he produced his "historical apocrypha". Apocrypha originally meant biblical texts that the church did not recognize as authentic. Modern literature uses the term for works interpreting famous subjects differently, perhaps by showing them in a new light or by treating them with irreverence and irony like Karel Čapek's *Kniha apokryfů* (posthumously 1945, Book of Apocrypha; in English *Apocryphal Stories*, 1949). Michal's apocrypha were written at the end of the sixties but the book *Rodný kraj* (Native Land) was not published till he was in exile in 1977. VÁCLAV ERBEN, the author of the well-known detective stories with Captain Exner, tried his hand at a similar type of novel in *Paměti českého krále Jiříka z Poděbrad* (Memoirs of the Czech King George of Poděbrady).[24] This was a longer work in three parts, published between 1974 and 1981. In it he cleverly makes use of the gaps in historical sources and allows the Hussite leader Prokop Holý to escape from the Battle of Lipany.[25] The title character himself loses the traditional nobility of a "Hussite king", instead he is portrayed as the embodiment of callousness and power.

Lekce jízdy (A Riding Lesson, 1987), by one of the younger exiled authors, PETR KOUBA, also reads like an ironic attack on the romantic respect accorded to history.

The novels of Bohumil Hrabal and Ota Pavel were on the fringes of official literature. BOHUMIL HRABAL (→ PROFILES) of course was always a special case. In the mid-seventies he gave an interview to the official weekly paper *Tvorba* in which he expressed a certain degree of loyalty to the regime. From then on he became an officially approved writer and his works – after many revisions by the censor – could be published at home. The three areas most affected by deletions and alterations were politics, erotica and passages containing existentialist and religious ideas. At the same time, however, the author's uncensored texts were appearing in samizdat and abroad. One of the important novels, *Obsluhoval jsem anglického krále* (published in English as *I Served the King of England*, 1989),[26] was not published by the Czechoslovak Writers' Publishing House till fifteen years after its 1974 publication in samizdat in *Petlice*. In the meantime, it had successfully conquered half of Europe where it had been hailed as an important work.

The interview with *Tvorba* aroused a storm of indignation among some samizdat writers. However most of the banned authors questioned about it by the journalist Jiří Lederer, who was also banned, in the book *České rozhovory* (Czech Interviews, samizdat 1978, Index, Cologne, 1979, published in Prague 1991) did not condemn Hrabal's behaviour. They were of the opinion that an author must be judged solely on the literary value of his work.

So Hrabal's texts reached the public in various forms. It was easier for works to be published officially if they were based on the magic of nostalgia and days gone by, such as *Postřižiny* (in English *Cutting It Short*, 1993),[27] which appeared in *Petlice* in 1974 and was published in Prague in 1976. On the other hand, there were three versions of the harrowing *Příliš hlučná samota* (in English *Too Loud a Solitude*, 1990),[28] Hrabal's key work written between 1973 and 1976, and published in samizdat in *Expedice* (Dispatch) in 1977. In 1981 it was published only in the censor's adulterated version,[29] the unabridged version did not appear till 1989.

By then Hrabal's style did not seem as shocking as it had done earlier. It concentrated on variation and the repetition of key words and ideas, such as "smetiště dějin" (the rubbish heap of history), "hlučná samota" (loud solitude), and "nerozlišující pozornost" (indiscriminating attention). Themes of sadness, emptiness and depression now appeared in Hrabal's work alongside exhilaration.

At the same time Bohumil Hrabal remained true to his perspective "from below". He said of his hero Haňťa in *Příliš hlučná samota*, "He lives at the bottom in a kind of sewer but he looks upwards." Haňťa compacts waste paper in a Waste Paper Recycling Centre – work that Hrabal himself did from 1954 to 1959. For years he reads avidly many books intended for destruction, becoming "educated against his will". He is to be transferred to a modern mechanized plant but he cannot adapt to the work there and decides to commit suicide in the hydraulic press. Hrabal's major theme in this period is the trauma of being forced actively to collaborate with destructive impersonal forces because one lacks the power and heroism to fight against them.

Three versions exist of *Příliš hlučná samota*. The first was written in verse in colloquial Czech, the second in "ordinary" prose, and the final one was again in prose, but it has the same lyrical and rhythmic structure as the first version. In this last version Haňťa's death is not a reality. It is something he dreams about in a drunken stupor while lying on a park bench. The novel represents a creative human being enmeshed in the consumer society. The mass destruction of rare books, the persecution of intellectuals, the war of the rats in the underground sewers, all symbolize the fate of culture in an age without culture. The hero's *angst* is projected into the idea of a gigantic press that is gradually swallowing up the whole of Prague. This disaster theme is similar to the deluges and floods in Egon Bondy's *Invalidní sourozenci* (The Disabled Siblings) and Ota Filip's *Nanebevstoupení Lojzka Lapáčka* (The Ascension of Lojzek Lapáček, see p. 87), samizdat novels contemporary with Hrabal's, and in the later works by the authors Zuzana Brabcová, Petr Placák and Vít Kremlička writing (see pp. 184–185) in the eighties.

OTA PAVEL's highly original collections of stories, *Smrt krásných srnců* (The Death of the Beautiful Hinds, 1971)[30] and *Jak jsem potkal ryby* (How I Met Fish, published posthumously in 1974), made him a natural successor to Hrabal's "palavering" (*pábitelství*, see p. 81). Pavel's works were staged and filmed many times; probably the most remarkable is the TV film *Zlatí úhoři* (1979, Golden Eels, made by Karel Kachyňa). Above all it is the character of the narrator's father, the "funny dad" who is the "palaverer". He is boastful and romantic, a man who loves rivers and fishing. The mixture of comedy and tragedy – the departure of the father and brothers to the concentration camp, the father's postwar disillusionment with Communism in *Běh Prahou* (in English *A Race Through Prague* in *Cross Currents*, 1983) – are also reminiscent of Hrabal. Pavel's informal, conversational style, for example, "Before the war my mum was dead keen on going to Italy," his typical naïvety and nostalgia, are of course much less pronounced than Hrabal's.

The author writes frankly about himself and his family, adding a wealth of corroborating detail. The main subject of both books is nature, in particular the Czech countryside around the Berounka river in Central Bohemia. Nature is seen as the primordial manifestation of life, both beautiful and cruel, as paradise and as some kind of higher impartial justice.[31]

Even the poetry of the masters Jaroslav Seifert, Oldřich Mikulášek and Jan Skácel was not considered acceptable literature during normalization. Their poetry was published in samizdat and in exile, and it was not till the end of the seventies and the beginning of the eighties that new works began to be published by the state publishing houses, and then only in limited editions with deletions by the censor. The published works were subsequently ignored by the critics. JAROSLAV SEIFERT (→ PROFILES, see pp. 35, 73–74) was one of the first to sign *Charter 77*. Officials of the regime persuaded the eighty-year-old poet to promise he would take no further part in any protest campaign. However, Seifert repeatedly broke this promise and so found himself again out of favour. Not till 1984, after the award of the Nobel Prize, was the Communist government forced to recognize him and they even attempted to arrogate him to themselves. A few years earlier the authorities had taken Jiřina Šiklová to court for sending abroad the manuscript of Seifert's memoirs *Všecky krásy světa* (All the Beauties of the World, see p. 156) and other documents in a bid to negotiate the Nobel Prize for him.

The continually shifting relationship between "judgment" and "mercy" is the essential idea behind OLDŘICH MIKULÁŠEK'S (→ PROFILES, see pp. 44, 69) late work. *Agogh* (Agogh), his greatest achievement, is a book of great dramatic tension. It was written at the end of the sixties and the beginning of the seventies and for a long time was available to readers only in samizdat. In 1980 it was published in exile but it was not published in Czechoslovakia till 1989. The title probably refers to the stories of Saul in the Old Testament, to the name of the defeated and murdered king who to the last believed in his power and inviolability. Of course the poet was also attracted by the similarity in sound to the word "agogh" (it may be connected with the English "agog"); some stanzas sound like an invocation, in some there is ingenious artificially created language, and at the other end of the scale blasphemy and vulgarisms. The colour symbolism is striking, especially the colours red and white, the colours of blood and wine. Eroticism and the themes of dying and futility dominate the work but there are also suggestions of self-mockery in sentences like "I hobble ahead on two crutches". The whole collection is intensely personal, but at the same time it is an indictment of the sterility of contemporary civilization. In this way it is reminiscent of Jaroslav Seifert's books of poetry, *Koncert na ostrově* (The Concert on the Island) and

Morový sloup (The Plague Column), and Vilém Závada's *Na prahu* (On the Threshold, see pp. 140, 71, 74).

Although pain and bitterness increase in Mikulášek's poetry, the poet himself never ceases to be entranced by beauty. The "mad" streak in his poetry is there right up to his last years. "Všichni se jednou zeptají: / A co je pravda? / Tiše jim odpovím: Ach, Eloáh! / A oni zeptají se, kdo je to Eloáh? / Tišeji odpovím: / nevím, jaká je jeho dráha."[32] (They all ask one thing: / What is truth? / Quietly I answer them: Oh, Eloah! / And they ask, Who is Eloah? / More quietly I answer: / I don't know what his way of life is.) – from *Čejčí pláč* (The Cry of the Lapwing, 1984).

The most important features of JAN SKÁCEL's (→ PROFILES, see pp. 44–45, p. 73) poetic vision also remained unchanged. Compared with Seifert and Mikulášek, the poet himself is less often the subject of his poetry. Now, more often than in his earlier works, isolation and evil are present. Death is seen as a fearful threat but also as the culmination of life giving it its ultimate meaning. On the other hand memories of home and childhood act as sure and certain positive values. Specially significant are the pictures of the countryside, which seems to speak to man in a primaeval voice and change the time and place of the poems into a mysterious magic world.

> ve stodolách schne zavěšené ticho
> medvědi snů mých úly vybrali
> čas zastavil se v dávné budoucnosti
> za humny býval navždy bývalý[33]

> silence is hanging up and drying in the barns,
> bears from my dreams have stripped the hives,
> time stands arrested in the distant future
> and on the threshing floors remain our bygone lives[34]

In his poems, in places, Skácel leaves fairly long spaces between words within the lines of a poem. By so doing he marks significant shifts in ideas and distinguishes different semantic content within the poem. Unlike his earlier poetry, both rhyme and rhythm – dactylotrochees with occasional iambs and regular verse forms, the sonnet and especially four-lined stanzas – are distinctive features of his mature work. The cycle of a hundred four-lined stanzas, *Chyba broskví* (The Flaw of the Peaches), came out originally in samizdat in 1975; later the poet included it with another similar cycle of poems, *Oříšky pro černého papouška* (Nuts for a Black Parrot), in the collection *Naděje s bukovými křídly* (Hope with Beechwood Wings, 1983).

It was not till the mid-eighties that LUDVÍK KUNDERA, another Moravian and contemporary of Jan Skácel, could once again publish openly. Versatile and innovative, Kundera began as a poet inspired by surrealism in the *Skupina Ra* (Group Ra, see p. 108), and then worked as a journalist, as organizer of the arts in Brno and as an essayist. He was an exponent and defender of František Halas's work, he wrote plays and was outstanding as a translator from the German of Bertolt

Brecht, Georg Trakl, Gottfried Benn and others. His book of poems, *Hruden* (1985; the ancient Slavs used the word *hruden* as the name of the thirteenth month which occurred in a leap year), was a selection taken from unpublished collections written after the sixties. It is evident that Kundera's poetry is imbued with avant-garde imagination. Light-hearted fantasy is of course much more restrained in Kundera's mature work and is complemented by intellect and irony. It was not until after November 1989 that other collections by Ludvík Kundera gradually began to be published. *Malé radosti* (Small Pleasures) and others came out in 1990.[35]

3. The Creation of Samizdat

Samizdat became the new phenomen of the age. While attempts were made after 1948 to preserve unpublished texts and prove that it was not possible for creative work to be completely wiped out, samizdat was striving for something more; it was to be circulated among readers creating an alternative means of communication and it was to function as part of independent culture and independent thought.

Samizdat is a word taken over from Russian. It means an independent publishing house. In Poland, where samizdat was most widespread in all the Communist countries, the expression "the second circulation" (*drugi obieg*) was used.[36] Czech samizdat literature in the early seventies began in a small way. The organizers proceeded carefully; they were usually not even known to each other. The best known of the samizdat publications was *Petlice* (Padlock) but others existed and others had preceded it. One of these was the Olomouc *Texty přátel* (The Writings of Friends) that carried works by Moravian poets and essayists. *Petlice* was run by Ludvík Vaculík with the help of Sergej Machonin and Milan Jungmann, his former colleagues from *Literární noviny* (Literary News, see p. 57), and his younger friends Jiří Gruša, Petr Kabeš and Jiří Müller. The idea was mooted in the autumn of 1972 at a meeting of banned authors where they read their manuscripts to each other. The original name was *Vzdor* (Defiance), an acronym from the first letters of a sentence at the beginning of every text – "**V**ýslovný **z**ákaz **d**alšího **o**pisování **r**ukopisu" (Copying of manuscript expressly forbidden). The name *Petlice* did not appear till later as a joking allusion to *Klíč* (The Key), the name of the official series. *Petlice* was not intended as an opposition arts enterprise. A few typewritten copies, twelve at first and twenty-four at the second copying on the typewriter, could not compete with the print runs, comprising tens of thousands of copies, produced by the Prague state publishing houses. Besides, the authors received no royalties – bound typescripts were sold at a price covering operating costs, the cost of paper, manual typing and binding; so they were much more expensive than books produced in the usual way.

First-hand evidence about *Petlice* came from, among others, Vaculík himself in his novel *Český snář* (A Czech Dreambook).

> "Wednesday 24th January 1979
> Again spent the afternoon running around after the books. Took one parcel to the author for him to sign the title pages, put the photographs in with the texts and then took them myself to various places to have them bound. I ask how long it'll take. Well . . . when he does these photos . . . I take the hint, the fellow has no money to buy the materials: must give him six hundred in advance. Then by tram to the other end of town where I have to pick up the bound almanacs today. A glance at my watch, however, tells me I haven't enough time because shortly I have to go to the Rudolfinum to meet Zdena who is to give me more typed copies. [. . .]
> We drive through the centre of Prague, the streets, covered in salty slush, are half empty and I can watch the cars behind us fairly easily. 'How did it go?' I ask. Zdena has taken the day off to go to various doctors. 'You know what,' she said, hitting the steering wheel with her hand, 'let's not talk about it. We're alive and that's the main thing!' She spoke enthusiastically and pointed to the traffic lights as if they were a meadow in bloom. [. . .] We drive to the bookbinders for the almanacs. Zdena is perfect there because R., who had handed them in for binding, had, for some unknown reason, given a fictitious female name. So if I, whom they know, had come for them, this deception could have bothered some innocent people."[37]

By 1989 there were 410 volumes of *Petlice*. A copy of Ludvík Vaculík's *Morčata* (published in English as *The Guinea Pigs*, 1973) was one of the first works to be included. This novel, which was published abroad in more than ten languages, was rejected by the Czechoslovak Writers' Publishing House. Similarly rejected was Jaroslav Seifert's best late work *Morový sloup* (published in English as *The Plague Column*, 1979, and in a new translation as *The Plague Monument*, 1980). Incredibly, as stated in the written report, it was rejected "on artistic grounds". So *Morový sloup* came out in samizdat in *Petlice* and from there found its way into the world, followed by the works of Ivan Klíma, Pavel Kohout, Karol Sidon, Oldřich Mikulášek, Jan Trefulka, Jiří Šotola and Bohumil Hrabal . . .[38]

Petlice was famous but it was far from being the only samizdat series. By the mid-seventies two other important series had been founded: *Kvart* (Quarto) managed by the translator and poet Jan Vladislav and *Expedice* (The Dispatch) begun by Václav Havel and the critic Jan Lopatka. *Kvart*, started by the group of authors round Jiří Kolář, specialized in poetry, translations and essays. About a hundred works had appeared in it by the beginning of the eighties when Vladislav went into exile. Shortly after his departure *Kvart* folded. *Expedice* reached a total of nearly three hundred volumes and, like *Kvart*, introduced new names to samizdat: authors associated with the former review *Tvář* (see p. 94) and the underground. Another innovation in *Expedice* was that technical details, that is, the name *Edice Expedice*, the name of the author and the work were all stated beside every contribution and the number of the volume and the signature Václav Havel were added. In this way it was different from the "undisciplined samizdat" of the early years when typescripts were not acknowledged and errors abounded in the copies. It was also a sign of the growing self-confidence of the organizers of independent culture that they no longer wished to remain anonymous.

The rapid spread of samizdat at the end of the seventies was connected with the publication of *Charter 77* and the effect it created. The human rights movement *Charter 77* developed from concepts similar to the first Czechoslovak president's (T. G. Masaryk) "civic activism" (*nepolitická politika*) – from the determination to resist force with humanity and from the conviction that political interests should not have precedence over moral principles. This community of ideas brought together writers of divergent ideological and artistic views: there were former Communists (Pavel Kohout, Ludvík Vaculík, František Pavlíček, Sergej Machonin, Eva Kantůrková and Jiří Brabec), opponents of post-February 1948 politics of culture (Václav Černý, Vratislav Effenberger and Ladislav Hejdánek), the foremost authors of the war generation (Jiří Kolář, Josef Hiršal and Zdeněk Urbánek), the sixties generation (Václav Havel, Josef Topol, Jiří Gruša, Petr Kabeš, Karol Sidon, Jiří Kratochvil and Jan Lopatka) and the youngest chartists, the songwriters and representatives of the underground (Jaroslav Hutka, Vlastimil Trešňák, Svatopluk Karásek and Ivan Martin Jirous).

According to JAN PATOČKA (→ PROFILES), the purpose of *Charter 77* was to stand outside the sphere of power politics. It was inspired by the realization that people cannot be controlled by success and fear alone; that there are other higher values. The *Charter* was "the solidarity of the shaken"; citizens who voluntarily took upon themselves the duty of speaking out against injustice.

> " . . . today people are once again aware that there are things worth suffering for! That the things they might suffer for are the things that make life worth living. [. . .] art, literature, the arts etc. would be mere empty shells without these values and life would never rise above mere mechanical existence." (Jan Patočka, Co můžeme očekávat od Charty 77? [What can we expect from Charter 77?], 8 March 1977)[39]

The Catholic priest and theologian JOSEF ZVĚŘINA wrote that *Charter 77* put tolerance, respect and love for one's neighbour in place of the ideology of hate that had held sway in the Czech nation since the Second World War: "It was discovered that a man is a man whether he belongs to the party or to anything else. That much more than ideology and party unites man with man" (from the volume *O svobodě a moci* [On Freedom and Power], Index, Cologne, 1980).[40]

After the Western press at the beginning of January 1977 printed *Charter 77*, the founding declaration that pointed out that in Czechoslovakia international agreements on basic human rights guaranteed by the establishment were not being observed, the regime mounted a bitter campaign. The signatories were branded "wreckers and usurpers" and "agents of imperialism". The Communist daily *Rudé Právo* (Red Rights) stated boldly, "In a socialist state counter-revolutionaries will never be given space for their scheming, class enemies will never be given democratic liberties." The text of the *Charter* was never made public, yet the media daily published dozens of angry protests against it. A great "Anti-Charter" of artists was produced and signed by most well-known officially recognized actors, writers, publicists, playwrights, etc. At the same time chartists began to be harassed by the police. As early as January Václav Havel and Jiří Lederer were arrested.

Lederer was sentenced to three years in prison for sending works of Czech writers abroad. On 13 March 1977, after many hours of questioning by the police, the seventy-year-old Jan Patočka died of a heart attack.

The unexpectedly severe reprisals caused arguments within the *Charter*. It was obvious that a direct fight with the ruling powers would mean self-destruction and that dialogue with representatives of the regime to promote gradual change, as had happened in Hungary, was an avenue closed to them. This was the situation that gave rise to the idea of a "parallel society" (*paralelní polis*), which is a parallel community, as Ladislav Hejdánek called it in September 1977 in *Dopisy příteli* (Letters to a Friend). Václav Benda made it a reality in May 1978. It involved taking samizdat as a model and extending it to other branches of the arts and, as far as possible, to other spheres of civil life: beginning to create an alternative educational system, a new informational organization, new political structures and trade unions, etc. Thus samizdat literature took on a more important role becoming part of a wider "second culture" and a "parallel society" beside independent concerts, visual arts exhibitions, theatre in flats, private lectures and underground universities, video journalism and other activities.[41]

New publications began to appear. At the end of 1977 the poet Jaromír Hořec started the series *Česká Expedice* (Czech Dispatch). The graphics in the books were perfect; sometimes there were even original woodcuts. At the same time Vladimír Pistorius founded *Krameriova Expedice* (Kramerius Dispatch). All these names, *Edice Expedice*, *Česká Expedice*, *Krameriova Expedice*, made deliberate reference to the dissemination of Czech books at the beginning of the Czech National Revival at the time when Bohemia had been a part of the Austrian monarchy. V. M. Kramerius was a Czech patriot, journalist and founder, in 1790, of the *Česká Expedice* publishing house, whose publications were distributed in the Czech countryside by selfless activists. Samizdat publications were disseminated in exactly the same way in the 1970s and the 1980s.

The Brno circle of authors produced *Studnice* (The Well). Unlike the above titles that indicated a connection with the Czech National Revival, there were facetious names of publications like *Mozková mrtvice* (Brain Death), *Jitrnice* (White Pudding) and *Popelnice* (The Dustbin). The editor Jiří Gruntorád wrote about *Popelnice*:

> "So in 1978 I began to type out a copy of Seifert's *Morový sloup* (The Plague Column) with one finger on an old Remington and bound it in black canvas covers. I asked my friend Václav Benda to take it to the great man to be signed, however, before long police officers confiscated the signed copies from him. I did not let this setback discourage me, but I did not get another batch of copies of *Morový sloup* signed. Šiktanc's *Český orloj* (The Czech Clock), Skácel's *Chyba broskví* (The Flaw of the Peaches) and seventeen other works, both prose and poetry followed [. . .]. The next year twenty-five more titles were published [. . .]. That year my house was searched twice by the police and for the first time I was sent to prison for fourteen days as a warning. The year 1980 brought thirty more titles and a prison sentence of two and a half months. [. . .] At the end of the year I was sent to prison for four years for subversion of the republic. When I got out

I discovered that thanks to our friend Oleg Hejnyš, another twenty-eight titles had been published in *Popelnice* . . . "[42]

Towards the end of the seventies other literary and cultural publications aimed at the wider public were founded. *Spektrum* (Spectrum) was the first sophisticated journal intended to represent "the alternative culture". However only three numbers were published. *Vokno* (The Window),which was, however, an idiosyncratic platform for underground culture, had a much longer life. Several hundred issues were published from 1970 till the mid-nineties – with a break at the beginning of the eighties when the editorial staff were sent to prison. In 1981 two quality journals, *Obsah* (Contents) and *Kritický sborník* (Collected Criticism), were founded. The monthly *Obsah* tried to continue the tradition of *Literární noviny* (see p. 57) to some extent, but its circle of authors was expanded to include, for example, Catholic writers. It carried fiction, essays, articles – Ludvík Vaculík's regular essay on yellow paper was famous. The authors transcribed their own contribution in the required number of copies and then distributed them among themselves so that they all had a complete copy of every issue. A selection from every complete volume of *Obsah* was then published in *Petlice*. Unlike *Obsah*, the editing of which had been improvised, the quarterly *Kritický sborník* was meticulously prepared for publication. The man behind its establishment was the literary scholar and novelist František Kautman and the editing was shared by the critics Josef Vohryzek and Jan Lopatka, the political scientist and linguist Luboš Dobrovský, the linguist and critic Karel Palek and the Protestant minister Miloš Rejchrt. *Kritický sborník* concentrated on the arts, especially literature, and reviewed not only samizdat but books published in exile and "official" literature at home. There were sometimes bitter arguments between groups, personal quarrels and jealousies. Most samizdat authors, however, managed to remain unbiased in the matter of ideology. The Chartist "solidarity of the shaken", the coming together of people of different opinions in the common resistance to totalitarianism, led to tolerance and openness. Discussion meant open dialogue and not the suppression of other points of view.

The individual samizdat journals and series had their standard format and layout. They had a circle of authors and regular subscribers. They also became the focal point for wider cultural activities, for example, *Vokno* introduced a range of books, arranged concerts and exhibitions (regularly closed down by the police). Later *Voknoviny*, a newssheet in the form of leaflets, was published and even a Videomagazine of Vokno was launched. Besides becoming more deeply involved in other cultural activities, samizdat literature also separated into groups representing different literary trends and different views of a more general nature: Christian-Catholic, socialist, conservative, liberal, underground, etc.

Well-known older and middle-aged authors who were forced by normalization into the "ghetto" of samizdat were joined by young and very young writers, many of them voluntarily because they wanted nothing to do with state-controlled culture. In the seventies these included Karol Sidon, Jiří Kratochvil, Ivan Martin Jirous, Eda Kriseová, Iva Kotrlá, Pavel Řezníček, Jaroslav Hutka and Vlastimil

Třešňák. In the eighties the group associated with the revue *Revolver Revue*, Jáchym Topol, Vít Kremlička and Petr Placák, and others, including Zuzana Brabcová and Václav Jamek, also published in samizdat.

Collaborating with exiled writers abroad was now of much greater importance than in the fifties and sixties. For both sides the exchange of information and material meant a great deal. For samizdat it meant material and moral support. More and more literary manuscripts were finding their way to the West, for example, all three numbers of *Spektrum* were published in London, some numbers of *Svědectví* (Testimony) were produced in Paris, having been prepared for publication in Czechoslovakia, and the impressive almanac *Hodina naděje* (The Hour of Hope) was published in German and Czech.[43] Some foundations and committees were set up in support – like the František Janouch Foundation of Charter 77 and the Hus Foundation. The Jaroslav Seifert Prize and the Jan Palach Prize were instituted.

Contacts with officially approved literature published at home developed much more slowly than collaboration with exiled writers. The connecting link between "official" and "unofficial" culture was the so-called "grey area" (see p. 143), those writers who were on the borderline between being banned and approved. Some critics and writers published in samizdat under pseudonyms, while other banned writers, such as Milan Jungmann, Lumír Čivrný, Milan Uhde, Jiří Brabec, František Pavlíček and Pavel Landovský, used assumed names when their works were being officially published. There was frequent collaboration in the realm of drama and the theatre, for example the samizdat *O divadle* (About Theatre)[44] was not very different from the "official" *Scéna* (The Stage). The playwrights Karel Steigerwald, Daniela Fischerová and Přemysl Rut (see pp. 191–192), like the creators of the studio theatres and the critics Václav Königsmark and Vladimír Just, had much more in common with the banned authors than with the artists' unions. It was the same with many songwriters and folk and rock singers.

To a greater extent samizdat writers were able, without much risk, to become translators. Some, like Pavel Šrut and Ivan Wernisch, were allowed to publish their translations, while others, like Josef Hiršal and Lumír Čivrný, published translations under assumed names. Literature in translation played an important part in the literary developments of the seventies and eighties. Translation was not as strictly censored as works by Czech authors, so it took over some of the functions of original literature, for instance the cultivation of style. Besides the well-known translators from the sixties, there were now many more people translating, especially from English, like Josef Jařab, Michael Žantovský and Jiří Josek. Jindřich Pokorný and Hanuš Karlach translated from German and Václav Daněk, Ludmila Dušková and Zdeňka Psůtková from Russian. Postmodern works by Kurt Vonnegut, E. L. Doctorow and Umberto Eco were introduced, and the nonconformist Soviet writers Vasili Sukshin and Bulat Okudzava were highly acclaimed. The Prague publishing house *Odeon* remained the quality vehicle for publishing translations.

In the course of the eighties fringe culture suffered less persecution. The 1986–1987 legal action against the *Jazzová sekce* (Jazz Section), which brought out works by Jindřich Chalupecký and Bohumil Hrabal, was a case in point. This persecution produced an unprecedented wave of solidarity throughout the world. The accused were finally given relatively lenient, mostly suspended, sentences.[45]

According to Jiří Gruša, usually 130–150 people read one copy of an original text (each of them was published in twelve to fourteen typed copies) in *Petlice*. So assuming a minimum of two manually typed editions, at least three hundred people would read every contribution.[46] These figures show that samizdat literature was not as exclusive a branch of culture as it might appear to the uninitiated, although since it functioned in abnormal circumstances, there was a danger of the "greenhouse effect". Some texts were a code in themselves accessible only to the initiated; so a special kind of hermetic sealing developed. In other cases the stumbling block was the threat of "oppositionism", the state of mind that opposes everything, or even the opposite phenomenon, "oppositional conformity". Works appeared and were acclaimed as acts of civic bravery rather than as works of high aesthetic value.

Nevertheless, it was through samizdat that a new conception of literature began to gain ground from the end of the seventies. Since the 19th century, Czech writers had traditionally fulfilled non-literary functions and had assumed responsibility for national enlightenment. It was incumbent upon them rather than on politicians to give expression to contemporary thinking. Between 1967 and 1969 the notion that the writer's mission was to act as spokesman for the nation was at its height. But some authors, particularly those of the sixties generation, including Antonín Brousek, Jiří Gruša, Karol Sidon and Jiří Kratochvil, felt it necessary to distance themselves from this idea. According to them the writer as a citizen could and should involve himself in public affairs but literature must remain his profession.

> "Compared with books published in this country in the sixties, the standard in *Petlice* was considerably higher. The relentless confrontation with reality revived Czech writing to such an extent that it began a period of reassessment and of necessity took a good look at itself as something not to be taken for granted [. . .]. We have broken free from the spell of the sixty or seventy years of the human life span and have discovered ourselves in the waves of time, history, and eternity. The Czech writer has been deprived of his part in the revival and reforming of society, but has begun at last to look after himself." (Karol Sidon, 1976)[47]

4. Samizdat Literature

One *Charter 77* document was entitled *Právo na dějiny* (The Right to History, 1984). Its essential thesis was that for decades the Czech nation had been deprived of its history. Many historical facts had been consistently suppressed. All traces of Catholic culture, German literature in Bohemia and the democratic tradition of the First Czechoslovak Republic had been wiped out.

"Every man and every nation lives through memory that creates and preserves individuality. Destruction of memory, whether it be by accident or design, means the destruction of the individual and the whole of society. [. . .] only people with no recollection of the past, with no special sense of identity, can allow themselves to be dominated without justification, without resisting and without attempting to live with dignity according to their own ideas and not in accordance with any prescribed plan." (Jan Vladislav, 1985)[48]

The samizdat and exiled writers consistently opposed this "government by forgetting" as Milan Kundera called the normalization era. They therefore became active in various different ways, creating a "parallel society" and an "alternative culture" by reminding people of democratic, conservative, Christian ideals, by refuting the system of values disseminated by the official establishment, and stressing historical traditions and awareness of their own culture.

The focus of conservatism in the eighties was the samizdat review *Střední Evropa* (Central Europe). It came out in two editions, one in Prague and one in Brno. After 1989, the Brno *Střední Evropa* changed its name to *Proglas*.[49] In the seventies Milan Kundera, Karel Kosík and the exiled philosopher and essayist Václav Bělohradský,[50] had tried to revive the democratic and liberal tradition in Central Europe.

There was a resurgence of Christianity, especially Catholicism, organized by secretly ordained bishops and priests. Young people were attracted to the faith by its concentration on mental and spiritual idealism, qualities that were signally lacking in the regime. Of the many Christian periodicals in samizdat, *Komunikace* (Communications) is perhaps the one that is remembered. The most outstanding of the Catholic writers was the Brno poet and essayist ZDENĚK ROTREKL. He was of the same war generation as Jiří Orten. He spent thirteen years in prison, and throughout the entire Communist regime from 1948 to 1989 not one of his books was published. Rotrekl is the author of a collection of short biographical sketches, *Skrytá tvář české literatury* (The Hidden Face of Czech Literature, samizdat 1977, Toronto, 1987, Brno 1991), and a book of meditations, *Barokní fenomén v současnosti* (The Phenomenon of the Baroque in the Present Day, samizdat 1985, Prague, 1995), that traces Baroque elements in Czech literature up to the present time. Rotrekl's complex, sophisticated poetry is specially remarkable for its Baroque imagery.[51]

A literary event that made an impact beyond samizdat literature was the publication of BEDŘICH FUČÍK's memoirs in essay form about prominent figures in the culture of the First Republic. The shorter version, *Sedmero zastavení* (Seven Stations of the Cross, samizdat 1977, Munich 1981), later expanded to *Čtrnáctero zastavení* (Fourteen Stations of the Cross, 1984) was published in Prague in 1991. Bedřich Fučík, a contemporary and friend of František Halas, Jan Čep and Jan Zahradníček, worked from the end of the twenties as critic for the reviews *Tvar* (Form), *Listy pro umění a kritiku* (Art News and Criticism) and *Akord* (The Chord).[52] In the thirties he was the managing director of the publishing house *Melantrich* and after the war of *Vyšehrad*. Under his management *Melantrich*[53] in particular became a top publishing house. February 1948 meant the end of his connection with official literature. After ten years in prison he was allowed to translate for a year or two but only between 1967 and 1969 was he allowed to publish any of his work. However, it was *Čtrnáctero zastavení* that first showed the greatness of Fučík's personality, his firm but tolerant Catholic faith, his fundamental humility, his readiness to accept new ideas and his artistic discrimination. He agreed with the view of Josef Florian[54] that the paths of truth and love are not those of political ideology. The almost eighty-five-year-old author ends his memoirs with the following:

> "All past defeats, wrongs and suffering have now lost their bitterness because they have found their true meaning and value; trees are more beautiful and every single leaf is more precious; the hydrologic cycle resembles a wonder above all wonders; light and dark and the structure of matter are more and more mysterious and more alluring; the epitome of order: millions of stars go about their business in a rhythm breathtaking in its precision.
>
> And what about man in the midst of all these marvels? What about his mysterious body? What about his spirit, soul and heart? Can he identify with these secrets? What about his free will and the mystery of the highest justice? Despite the menace of the atom, despite all kinds of totalitarianism and tyranny, despite every menacing evil, all we can do is hope and believe that life is good and sweet, as all the poets on our small planet have sung in their hymns, amen."[55]

Besides Fučík's there were two other brilliant books of memoirs by the oldest of this generation of authors, Václav Černý and Jaroslav Seifert. VÁCLAV ČERNÝ'S (→ PROFILES) extensive three-volume *Paměti* (Recollections) was first published in Toronto between 1977 and 1983, then in Brno between 1992 and 1994. JAROSLAV SEIFERT'S (→ PROFILES) memoirs, *Všecky krásy světa* (All the Beauties of the World), after many samizdat editions, was published simultaneously in 1981 by two publishing houses abroad, *Index* in Cologne and *Sixty-Eight Publishers* in Toronto. A censored version came out in Prague in 1982. The two books were of course totally different in conception. Seifert looks back with a nostalgic smile and treats the grimness, even the cruelty, of life with benign forbearance. By contrast Černý, always scathing and confrontational as a critic, is an impassioned judge of the age and of the shortcomings of so many Czech public figures. His *Paměti* unleashes a vehement denunciation of the immorality of the Communist system and all who promote it.

A great many samizdat works, manuscripts and works written in exile were somewhere on the borderline between memoirs, essays and fiction. ZDENĚK URBÁNEK'S *Ztracená země* (The Lost Country, samizdat 1986, Prague, 1992) and JOSEF JEDLIČKA'S family chronicle *Krev není voda* (Blood Is Thicker than Water, published posthumously in 1991) come into this category. The two volumes of JAN ZÁBRANA'S *Celý život* (A Whole Life), also published posthumously in 1992, were in diary form as was *Let let* (Years and Years), tales from the fifties and sixties by JOSEF HIRŠAL and BOHUMILA GRÖGEROVÁ. *Let let* was published in samizdat between 1987 and 1988 and in Prague between 1993 and 1994. Earlier Josef Hiršal had published his memoirs from the thirties and forties. The book by EVA

KANTŮRKOVÁ, a novelist of the middle generation, *Přítelkyně z domu smutku* (samizdat 1984, Prague, 1990; published in English as *My Companions in the Bleak House*, 1987) was also based chiefly on fact. As a television series in 1992 it was directed by Hynek Bočan. On the basis of her own experience of ten months in the Prague prison Ruzyně, accused of subverting the republic by her activities in independent culture, the author drew remarkable portraits of her fellow prisoners, their behaviour and their mental states. The picture of prison life became transformed into a picture of the whole of society, a "world of undisguised manipulation where it is easy to control people".

Factual evidence contradicts the false picture of the past and present given out by state propaganda and officially approved literature. The most famous underground work of literature is IVAN M. JIROUS's *Magorovy labutí písně* (The Swan Song of a Crackpot). This collection of poems was written during the author's five year term of imprisonment and published in samizdat in 1985 and in Prague in 1990. The harshness of everyday life (he was held in a high security prison, in the company of murderers) is interspersed with memories of family and friends and, surprisingly, with a dialogue with God.

Služební psi na dvoře vyjí
a Radim slaví eucharistii.
[. . .]
Krásná je hora Mt St Michel
já nejdál do Valdic jsem přišel
moje básně jsou samý klišé
na hubě vyrazil mi lišej.[56]

The police dogs howl in the yard
and Radim celebrates the eucharist.
[. . .]
St Michael's Mount is beautiful
the farthest I came is the Valdice Prison
my very poems are cliches
eczema attacked my mouth.

The form of this stanza goes back to František Gellner, an early 20th-century rebel poet, and to the 1950s "Total Realism" of Egon Bondy's (see p. 32). Its provocative vulgarity and the theme of "life at the bottom" makes it a work typical of Czech underground culture of which Jirous was organizer and spokesman. The underground movement originated in the West and was strongest in the USA at the end of the sixties. The movement was closely associated with rock and beat music. Its philosophy evolved from the poets of the beat generation, Jack Kerouac and Allen Ginsberg, from the "New Left" and from the students' revolt of 1968. The underground movement flaunted its differences from the consumer society and from absolutely all conventions in style of dress, behaviour, sexual freedom and the use of drugs. The 1969 Woodstock pop festival in the state of New York, attended by half a million people, was an enormous demonstration of underground culture.

Two notable poets, besides Jirous, who belonged to the Czech underground in the seventies and eighties were MILAN KOCH and SVATOPLUK KARÁSEK. Koch was influenced by the beatniks and died prematurely in 1974. Svatopluk Karásek, a Protestant clergyman, wrote the lyrics for the band *Plastic People*. They shared the underground affinity with modern nonconformist music, attempted to stand "outside culture" and protested bitterly against the political establishment. The situation in Czechoslovakia at the time meant that the Czech underground had no left-wing tendencies, except for Egon Bondy, the forerunner and literary model for the movement; in fact it tended to the opposite direction, often being attracted to mysticism and religion. The rock group *DG 307*, for example, was inspired by Gregorian chant in its album *Opustil mě anděl* (I Was Forsaken by an Angel).

Actuality also became a feature of novels and short stories. The texts by the songwriter VLASTIMIL TŘEŠŇÁK have strong affinities with the underground. They are usually autobiographical, set in the area round Prague, especially in Karlín where he was born; social outsiders, for instance the Romany people, appear in these texts.[57] In his extensive novel written in exile, *Klíč je pod rohožkou* (The Key Is under the Mat, 1995), Třešňák describes the bitter experiences of a Czech emigrant in the West. Reality in ZDENA SALIVAROVÁ'S prose work is stark and brutal. One novel, the remarkable *Honzlová*, dates from the end of the sixties. *Honzlová* was published in Toronto in 1972, and in 1973 came out in English as *Summer in Prague*.[58] IVAN KLÍMA (→ PROFILES) also makes skilful use of fact in his short stories *Má veselá jitra* (samizdat 1978, Toronto, 1979; published in English in 1985 as *My Merry Mornings*). *Moje první lásky* came out in samizdat in 1981 and was published in Toronto in 1985. The English translation came out as *My First Loves* in 1986. *Moje zlatá řemesla* was published in English as *My Golden Trades* in 1992. All three were published in Prague in 1990. His longest novel, *Soudce z milosti* (in English *Judge on Trial*, 1990), was also in part autobiographical in character. It was first published in German in 1979, in Czech in London by *Rozmluvy* in 1986 and then in Prague in 1991; the original version, entitled *Stojí, stojí šibenička* (There's a Gallows on the Hill), was published in samizdat in 1978. Against the background of change in modern Czech history, it asks the question of how basic honourable ideas have become debased and where the responsibility of the individual begins and ends. EDA KRISEOVÁ, in her book *Křížová cesta kočárového kočího* (A Coachman's Way of the Cross), a study of people undergoing psychiatric treatment, alternates fantasy with objective reality and psychological sensitivity. The work, finished in 1971, was published in samizdat in 1977, by *Sixty-Eight Publishers* in Toronto in 1979 and in Brno in 1990. Some of PAVEL KOHOUT'S (→ PROFILES) novels mix realistic plots with elements of fantasy. The most successful was *Katyně* (in English *The Hangwoman*, 1981), the tale of a lovely angelic girl Lízinka who received her schooling in the Central Academy for Hangmen. It was first published in German in 1978, then in samizdat in 1978, then by *Index* in Cologne in 1980, and in Prague in 1990. The Czech title also refers to a place in Poland where one of the biggest mass executions of the Second World War was carried out.

Here *popravnictví*, execution as a science, is described with terrible thoroughness, not as a loathsome profession but as a serious vocation. With blasphemous exaggeration, it is suggested that evil and all manner of perversion be legalized. The author reinforces the shocking impact by omitting the last word of a chapter and putting it at the beginning of the following chapter.

LUDVÍK VACULÍK (→ PROFILES) had always written from personal experience but during the seventies and eighties his texts became more autobiographical. His novel *Český snář* (A Czech Dreambook) was published in samizdat in 1981, by *Sixty-Eight Publishers* in Toronto in 1983, and in Brno in 1990.[59] It is in the form of a diary of the year from January 1979 to February 1980. He appears in it himself as Ludvík Vaculík along with his family, friends and acquaintances, including Jiří Gruša, Karel Kosík, Karel Pecka, Václav Havel, Ivan Klíma, Karol Sidon, Eva Kantůrková. He describes his work for samizdat, everyday conversations and meetings, police interrogations, his indecision about continuing with the manuscript, his dreams and daydreams, his relationship with nature which puts the trivialities of civilization into perspective, and his romantic attachment to Helena, which ended when she emigrated. Yet, the work hovers on the borderline between fact and fiction – hence the tension within.

Český snář describes many situations so frankly that after its publication it aroused the indignation of some of the people described in it. It also caused fears that Vaculík, by his candour, might have betrayed to the police things that should have been kept quiet.[60] The diary form is a protest against the romanticizing of reality: "já se nebudu omývat, ať jsu od krve, chci!" (I will not wash, I will be covered in blood, I will!). In it, the threats to his life, his successes and failures, and his attempt to retain his personal integrity are all described.

Remembering the past was a favourite theme of some poets of the middle and older generations. Often authors previously considered second rate now came to the fore. Such were Jiřina Hauková, Emil Juliš and most outstandingly Karel Šiktanc.

In *Český orloj* (The Czech Clock) KAREL ŠIKTANC (→ PROFILES) wrote one of the great works of Czech poetry. It came out in samizdat in 1974, in Munich 1980–1981, and was published in Prague in 1990. Collections of "calendar" poems, covering the period by individual months from January to December are relatively common in Czech literature. Karel Toman and Jaroslav Seifert had also written this type of poetry, but the poems in this book are set in a primitive, natural, mystical, "organic" time. At the same time the lives of the three generations of the lyrical hero, who has autobiographical features, his father and son also form an important element.

From the sixties, Šiktanc's poetry was concerned with historical and tribal memory: "Mnémosyné! // Mé neštěstí! / Má bohyně! / Uchraň nás trestu na svobodě této!"[61] (Mnemosyne! // My misfortune! / My goddess! / Save us from the punishment of freedom!) is the ending of the poem *Modlitba k bohyni paměti* (Prayer to the Goddess of Memory) in the collection *Adam a Eva* (Adam and Eve, 1968, see p. 70). In Šiktanc's essentially epic poems, he introduces a village in Central Bohemia, its traditional way of life, Christian symbols and an even greater number of recurring pre-Christian mythical symbols.

Tady ta zem,
to je srdeční krajina světa.
Tady to bolí, jako by zamrzala
krev.
Po bezrukých tu sem tam hůl.
Po němých sem tam holá věta.
A proto slavíci voláni
k výslechům,
kde peří k dostání
kde se bere
zpěv.

Betlémy nezvěstné.
Jen občas spatřeno uprostřed oceánů
v proutěném košíku
jezule umrlec.
Tak umírá se na psí čas.
Anebo na marihuánu.
Dřímá svět u kamen, nohy má
v peklíčku –
a mžourá skrz komín,
kde v nebi prázdná
klec.[62]

This land here
it is the heart of the world's landscape.
Here it hurts, like freezing
blood.
After amputees, here and there a cane remains.
After mutes, here and there a simple sentence.
And that's why nightingales are summoned to
interrogations
where feathers are made available
and where you can get
songs.

Bethlehems are missing.
Only occasionally sighted in the midst of oceans
in a wicker basket
baby Jesus's corpse.
That's how we die of a dog's life.
Or from marijuana.
The world dozes by the stove, its feet in
a mini-hell –
and squints up through the chimney
at an empty cage
in heaven.[63]

(*Tanec smrti* [Dance of Death], written 1974–1975)

Snatches of popular speech, sayings and vulgarisms are mixed with sophisticated metaphors and a great many classical references and other stylistic changes. The author uses a complicated form of versification: iambs of different lengths alternate with trochees, the lines are divided in such a way as to interrupt the rhythm and the lines do not always correspond to the sound rhythms of the poem as a whole. Rhyme is used unconventionally and with great skill. The result is the overlapping of many layers of meaning.[64]

Karel Šiktanc developed his distinctive style in the cycles of poems connected to each other by many motifs and having the same semantic orientation. Five poems in *Pro pět ran blázna krále* (Damnation and a Mad King; published in samizdat in 1978 and in Prague in 1991), are loosely connected by aphorisms relating to the life and death of the Romantic poet and rebel K. H. Mácha and the "madman" theme: the theme of a man outcast and threatened. There is an even greater degree of menace in the book of poetry *Srdce svého nejez* (Don't Eat Your Heart Out, samizdat 1988, Prague, 1994). Throughout the work the themes of tragedy and anxiety are repeated with the death of the father and strange Kafkaesque interrogations set within the framework of a grim picture of Bohemia and Prague "se zmítala na hřbetě sloužících / jako chalcedonová rakev"[65] (tossed on the crest of lackeys / like a chalcedony coffin).

The theme of "timelessness" that "sneers at eternity" and the theme of "lousy time" that has "lost its way" is also to be found in the poetry of Šiktanc's friend and contemporary Miroslav Červenka, a literary theoretician, critic and poet. In the sixties he specialized in literary theory, and during normalization he published specialist works and poetry abroad and in samizdat. His poetry was collected in the volume *Strojopisná trilogie* (A Typewritten Trilogy) and published in samizdat in 1985, and in Prague in 1992. Even after 1989 this dualism continued; clarity of thought and the search for absolute values while investigating memory frequently coexist.

Already in the fifties and sixties Jiřina Hauková, once of *Group 42* (see pp. 15–16), was beginning to abandon harsh realism and move towards the use of metaphor. Her poetry was becoming more delicate, natural and lyrical. Compared with the complexity of Šiktanc's poetics, Hauková's stylistic effects were achieved by more traditional means, but even here the great themes of time and memory predominate. In a poem dedicated to her seventy-year-old husband Jindřich Chalupecký are the words, "Viděli jsme děs v jasném oku / ještěrky na zdi v Pompejích, / stejný děs doby je v našich očích: / sváry a hádky, pustošení světa [. . .]. / Bezčasá paměť země všechno ví. / Od trilobitů, dinosaurů / po nesytku a skřípinec jezerní."[66] (We have seen terror in bright eyes /of the lizard on a wall in Pompeii, / the same terror of the age is in our own eyes: / arguments and quarrels, the devastation of the world [. . .]. / The timeless memory of the earth knows everything. / From trilobites, dinosaurs, / to butterflies and lake plants.) This quotation comes from *Světlo v září* (Light in September) published in samizdat in 1984 and in Prague in 1995.

Similar views about memory in nature and the earth are to be found in Emil Juliš. "Jdeme s proudem všichni, jsme současníci, / i my, kteří nejsme 'všichni', ačkoli jsme tu / někdy od třetihor. Snad máme na krku / jiný amulet a budeme proto snědeni . . . "[67] (We all drift with the flow, we are contemporaries, / even those of us who are not 'all', although we have been here / sometime since the Tertiary age. Round our necks we may have / different amulets and for that we may be consumed . . .) *Blížíme se ohni* (We Are Approaching the Fire) was first published in Munich in 1987 and revised in North Bohemian Ústí nad Labem in 1988. Emil Juliš, noted for his experimental Concrete Poetry (see p. 109), lived for decades in cultural isolation in Most in the devastated industrial landscape in the North of Bohemia. It was undoubtedly this depressed area that caused the change of focus in his work to ecology in its widest sense including the "ecology" of the human heart and the moral values lacking in the modern world.

The generation of the poets of the 1960s, including the exiled Antonín Brousek (see p. 168), distrusted ornamental style and figures of speech in general, they "distrusted words". Set phrases acquired new ironic meanings. In IVAN WERNISCH'S (→ PROFILES) samizdat collection *Prasinec* (The Pigpen, 1982; *prasinec* also referred to *prosinec*, "December", in Czech "the pleading month") irony reached a chilling intensity. The name of Wernisch's collection, *Pojízdný hřbitov* (The Travelling Graveyard, samizdat 1984), was typical. At the other end of the scale there was Wernisch's humour, naïveté and absurd writing, particularly on Russian themes.[68] ANDREJ STANKOVIČ exploited rhythmic and contextual cliches and especially platitudes as a basis for his poetics, bringing him close to Wernisch and Brousek on the one hand and to the underground on the other. The result is often nonsense. PETR KABEŠ, another poet of the sixties, used an original form of composition in his books of poetry, *Obyvatelná těla* (Habitable Bodies, samizdat 1974, Liberec, 1991), and *Skanseny* (Folk Museums, samizdat 1978, Brno, 1991), and in the works that followed these. In his work, fragments of events, bits of quotations and sentences are jumbled together, and in places the result is effectively a compilation of ciphers and magic incantations. The book *Těžítka* (Paperweights, 1994), most of which was published in the samizdat *Obsah* in the eighties, was made from an arrangement of absurd sayings, quotations from documents and plays on words.

Unlike official literature, samizdat literature focused fairly successfully on the social novel and the role of the individual in society. In these novels the lives of the chief characters epitomize life in general and history. These authors were younger members of the war generation of writers. They often entered the postwar age as enthusiastic young Communists and later experienced disillusionment and disappointment. Amongst them were Eva Kantůrková, Jan Trefulka, Mojmír Klánský, Alexandr Kliment, Ivan Klíma and Jaroslav Putík. EVA KANTŮRKOVÁ wrote *Černá hvězda* (The Black Star) in 1974, when it was published in samizdat. It was written after her *Smuteční slavnost* (Funeral Rites) of 1967, which was adapted for the screen by Zdeněk Sirový, though the film was banned in 1969 and not shown till 1990. JAN TREFULKA'S *O bláznech jen dobré* (Speak Nothing but Good of Madmen) was published in 1973 in samizdat, by *Sixty-Eight Publishers* in Toronto in 1978 and in Brno in 1990, and MOJMÍR KLÁNSKÝ'S *Vyhnanství* (Banishment) came out in 1975 in samizdat, in *Index*, Cologne in 1976, and in

Prague in 1990. ALEXANDR KLIMENT'S *Nuda v Čechách* (Boredom in Bohemia) was also published in Prague in 1990 having first appeared in samizdat in 1978 and in Toronto in 1979. JAROSLAV PUTÍK'S *Muž s břitvou* (Man with a Razor) came out in 1984 in samizdat, in Cologne in 1986, and was published in Prague in 1991. These works – including IVAN KLÍMA'S *Soudce z milosti* (Judge on Trial, see p. 158) – continue the literary principles created by the most famous novels of the sixties. The narrative is usually based on the life and circumstances of the main character. The story is not necessarily told in the first person; it projects a more general view. There is an obvious connection with the unofficial fiction of the fifties, for example, with Josef Škvorecký's *Zbabělci* (The Cowards, see pp. 51–52) and works by Bohumil Hrabal and Josef Jedlička (see pp. 32, 33). Like the earlier novels, it is the mind of the central character that gives these works their perspective, opposing the idea of an omniscient narrator. These works are not "objective". The world certainly does not fit into a prearranged pattern, bearing the stamp of ideology, suitably retouched and prettified. It is seen from the point of view of the lower orders; "from the rubbish heap of history", as Hrabal says, reality as seen by the individual. These works are confessions and personal testimonies. They deal with what officially encouraged literature never managed to accomplish. They define openly and in specific terms their heroes' rebellion against the conformist environment – their inner, sometimes open, revolt against the role they were expected to play in society. "The first sin I committed," confesses Kliment's hero with the characteristic name Mikuláš Svoboda (Freedom), "was to accept stultifying slave labour without rebelling." Trefulka's more enterprising hero, Cyril Duša (Soul), wants "to abandon my personal feeling of social security, for the first time in my life to rebel and go to places where no one has ever been, to lose myself, to find myself . . . " In both works, and also in all of Klíma's novels, eroticism and illicit "turbulent" love affairs have a significant part. Another recurrent theme is madness – as in Kriseová and Šiktanc, and in official literature in Miroslav Skála – the kind of madness of Don Quixote, the madness of those following their own whims regardless of what is "reasonable". So free love and madness are a manifestation of inner freedom, an attempt to free oneself from the shackles of everyday life.

The younger writers advanced themes similar to those relevant to writers in the sixties but one theme crucial to the preceding generation was absent, disillusionment with Communist ideology. Their artistic ideas were also different: links between parts of the plot are left unclear or omitted, the interplay of fact and fiction is more frequent and more complex, the historical context of a novel is not made clear, nor is it misrepresented, and the action is seen from various points of view. JIŘÍ GRUŠA'S (→ PROFILES) *Dotazník aneb Modlitba za jedno město a přítele* (samizdat 1976, Toronto, 1978, Brno, 1990; translated as *The Questionnaire, or, Prayer for a Town and a Friend*, 1982) is the very best of works of this type. Václav Černý called it "one of those lovely surprises, that our fiction readers [. . .] get only very seldom".[69] The ostensible subject is the questionnaire that the hero has to fill in when, at the beginning of normalization, he is trying for the sixteenth time to get a job (he never manages to get one). Jan Chrysostom Kepka gives such complete answers to the questions about his parentage, his past, his opinions, and so on that he is prompted to think back to his childhood, his birth and about his relations and their lives as far back as the 18th century. At the same time events described like newspaper reports and strange anecdotes mix with the concept of "Great History", the prosaic is mixed with gentle humour and the magic of the supernatural. Sensuality is fundamental to Gruša's view of life. Sensual, particularly erotic experiences have an equally important place in his picture of the world. *Dotazník* and the author's next novel, *Mistr Panny aneb Ackermann aus Behaim*[70] (Master of the Virgin or Ackermann from Behaim),[71] which was published in Prague in 1992, can be interpreted as the hero's search for inner discipline. In his ancestral past and within himself he struggles against the circumstances of his life, against control and manipulation. He fights to maintain his personal integrity, which he finds above all in the world of imagination.

The exiled novelist and essay writer SYLVIE RICHTEROVÁ (→ PROFILES) also develops the theme of memory and has a similar approach to poetics in *Návraty a jiné ztráty* (Homecomings and Other Casualties), which was published in samizdat and in Toronto in 1978, and *Místopis* (Topography; samizdat 1981, Cologne, 1983). Both these texts have been included in the volume *Slabikář otcovského jazyka* (Father's Language Primer) published in Brno and Prague in 1991. At the same time her work is more obviously autobiographical and less idiosyncratic than Gruša's. Yet even here the narrative is broken up, questions and changing aspects of reality assume a greater importance than a conventional smoothly flowing story. Here too the rhythm comes from the person of the narrator, who alternates between the feminine and masculine genders, and whose state of mind changes at a particular moment. In *Slabikář otcovského jazyka*, in the story of the same name, the story line is even more disrupted by microstories, reflections and essays on literature. Klíma, Putík and others, however, keep to the traditional method of presenting the reader with a fictitious world in which they set their texts. Occasionally Richterová's, Kratochvil's and Hodrová's (Kratochvil and Hodrová see pp. 189–190) narrators do not conceal the fact that they are inventing a world that is incomplete, that there are "holes" in it – typically Sylvie Richterová's next work bears the title *Rozptýlené podoby* (Vanished Images, samizdat 1979, Prague, 1993).

Gruša's contemporary KAROL SIDON (see pp. 103–104) also develops similar themes in his stories. Rather than fantasy and whimsy, his recurrent themes are the precariousness of human existence, depression, feelings of guilt and isolation. "Things are simply quite different from what I thought and believed. I myself am different from my picture of myself [. . .] I have to look steadfastly and remorselessly inside myself. Every one of us has his own story which leads us on to death"[72] (*Brány mrazu* [Gates of Frost], samizdat 1977).

In Sidon's novel *Boží osten* (God's Barb, samizdat 1975, Prague, 1991) and in his novella *Brány mrazu*, published in samizdat in 1977), the theme is Jewishness and there are references to the old Jewish books. The autobiographical scenes from his earlier works are now missing; dreams and fantastic ideas and even life after death form a kind of secondary plot that leads straight into scenes from real life.

In the novels of Gruša, Richterová and Sidon, and also in those of Jiří Kratochvil and Daniela Hodrová (Kratochvil and Hodrová see pp. 189–190), the characters have to come through difficult circumstances in their lives; they are battered by repression and blunder through the tedium of everyday living. However, we would look in vain in them for any historical progress, or at least for any development or "education" in the sense of enlightenment or hope of salvation in the Christian sense. We find only a cycle of repetitions and variations. The traditional idea of historical progress has gone, to be replaced by personal and collective memory.

5. Literature in Exile

Czech authors in exile, like authors officially published at home, enjoyed somewhat easier working conditions, and at the same time they were free to write as they pleased, uncensored and without having to censor themselves like samizdat writers at home. Compared with officially published and samizdat authors, they had richer sources of information. The opportunity to travel and make contacts opened up the world to them and broadened their horizons.[73] Of course, with a few exceptions, writers in the West did not attract the same attention, favourable or otherwise, as at home. Literature was not an outlet for expressing public concerns. People were free to enter the world of politics or economics and culture so that the variety of entertainment available reduced the influence of literature.

The exiles also had the special problem of their readership. In spite of the increase in the number of publishing houses and new magazines, the Czech public abroad was necessarily limited. For example, the largest publishing house in exile, *Sixty-Eight Publishers* in Toronto, produced an average of 1,500–2,000 copies of each novel and between 500 and 1,000 copies of each volume of poetry. Daniel Strož's Munich publishing house, *Poezie mimo domov* (Poetry Abroad), published considerably smaller numbers, between 250 and 400 volumes. The publication that broke all records in exile was Škvorecký's *Tankový prapor* (The Tank Battalion; translated as *The Republic of Whores*, 1993),[74] reaching a total of five editions of 9,000 copies. When *Tankový prapor* was published in 1990 in Prague by the publishing house *Galaxie* (Galaxy) more than 150,000 copies were printed.

It was therefore natural that Czech authors in exile did not achieve success until their works were translated. In this way, the loss of their Czech, rather stifling environment, was compensated by their gradual adaptation to their foreign surroundings.[75]

> "When you have been away for two, three or even five years, it is easy to go back. But twenty years is a quarter of your life or half an adult's age. There are new commitments, new friendships, the place you have emigrated to has become your new home, even your beloved home [. . .]. In the course of twenty years I have read very few Czech books. Do not be angry with me on that account. No one can live

> completely in two cultures. Even though I speak nothing but Czech with my wife, I am surrounded by French books, I live in a French environment [. . .]. One day this had to influence my decision with regard to which language I write in."[76]

The pressure to assimilate of course affected everyone differently. It could be an exceptional source of new material for exceptional works. It could stop an author writing altogether. Karel Michal gave up writing when he was no longer living in his native cultural environment. Some authors took up different careers. Karol Sidon studied Hebrew in Germany and became a rabbi. Others "crossed over" into different languages. Ludvík Aškenazy and Ota Filip wrote in German, Věra Linhartová in French and Jan Novák in English. Some wrote in two languages; Jiří Gruša also wrote in German, Petr Král and Milan Kundera in French, František Listopad in Portuguese, Viktor Fischl and Ladislav Grosman in Hebrew.

Just as some authors gravitated naturally to samizdat and some became samizdat authors through force of circumstances, so there were many different reasons for writers choosing to go into exile. Some were afraid of political trials, some of anti-Semitism, some left for financial reasons, some from the desire for self-realization. Some were forced to go to escape persecution after *Charter 77*. Jiří Kolář and Pavel Kohout were even illegally prevented by the Czechoslovak authorities from returning home and so were made exiles against their will. Just as some authors found a kind of freedom at home in "banned" literature, so some like Josef Škvorecký and Ota Filip considered exile a relief and a benefit. In exile Milan Kundera found new creative freedom. For others like Jaroslav Vejvoda and Ivan Diviš, it was a traumatic experience. Věra Linhartová made a distinction between exile as "something to be endured", when after going abroad, time and everything related to the past stood still, and exile as "experience transformed", when you no longer expect to return:

> "I chose, then, the place where I wanted to live and I also chose the language I wanted to speak. [. . .] A writer is not imprisoned by one language. [. . .] my sympathies lie with nomads. I do not have the character to be sedentary. I can say truthfully that my own 'exile' was the fulfilment of what had always been my most ardent wish: to live *elsewhere*."[77]

For these reasons there was a considerable artistic and thematic diversity in literature in exile. There were also quite significant differences between the two waves of emigrants, after the February 1948 coup and after August 1968. The numbers involved in the second wave were greater and many of those who emigrated at that time stayed "away" even during the seventies and eighties. The relations between the two groups, who had quite different life experiences, were not exactly ideal. In Jan Novák's book of stories, *Striptease Chicago* (Toronto, 1983), which was published in Prague in 1992, the narrators used common Czech and Czech-American slang and the stories were explicitly erotic. This caused outrage in the older emigrants.

These differences were exacerbated by the convictions of various groups: the socialism of the circle round the Rome review *Listy* (Gazette), the centrist liberalism of the journals *Svědectví* (Testimony) in Paris and *Proměny* (Metamorphoses) in New York, the Catholicism of the journal *Studie* (Studies)[78] and the publishing house *Křesťanská akademie* (Christian Academy) both of Rome, and the Munich *Opus bonum* (Good Work), the conservatism of the London journal *Rozmluvy* (Dialogues) and the underground values of the Vienna journal *Paternoster*.

Literature in exile was also understandably fragmented territorially. While samizdat was being organized in Prague, and also to a lesser extent in Brno, Olomouc and in North Bohemia, in exile several equally important centres of culture, a considerable distance from each other, were being set up: firstly in Germany and Austria and also in German-speaking Switzerland where A. P. Pašek founded in Zurich the publishing house *Konfrontace* (Confrontation); secondly in France and Italy; thirdly in Britain; and finally and fourthly across the ocean in the USA and Canada. All these activities were linked by respected periodicals, like *Svědectví* and *Listy*, which regularly published the literary yearbook *Čtení na léto* (Summer Reading) edited by A. J. Liehm from 1980, and *Proměny*. From 1977 *Studie* also broadened its outlook and allowed non-Catholic views to be expressed in it. Publishing houses, especially *Sixty-Eight Publishers*, played a key role. In the course of the seventies and eighties, other publishing houses sprang up and the number of journals and reviews and supporting cultural organizations increased. Gradually more and more contacts with home were established, leading to a situation that had never previously existed, in which foreign and domestic publications entered into fruitful interaction. An important event in the mid-eighties was the founding of the *Dokumentační středisko československé nezávislé literatury* (Documentation Centre for the Promotion of Independent Czechoslovak Literature) in Scheinfeld in Germany. It was founded with the support of Prince Schwarzenberg, the Janouch Foundation of Charter 77, and other individuals and institutions. Under the direction of the historian Vilém Prečan, exile and samizdat literature was systematically collected and edited for publication. Through all these agencies, exile literature, like Polish exile literature, achieved much greater importance and also become respected at home.

It is therefore difficult to assess the development of Czech literature in exile. Both official literature and samizdat were produced within a unifying cultural framework which did not exist to the same degree for literature in exile. The difficulty is all the greater in that books banned at home and published by Czech publishing houses in the West form part of literature in exile where they had their readers and critics. On the other hand works by exiled writers were circulated and reveiwed at home in samizdat.

It is said that if writers in exile continued to write in Czech, they generally continued in more or less the same style they had developed at home. This is true of the novels of Škvorecký, whose main novel written in exile, *Příběh inženýra lidských duší* (published in English as *The Engineer of Human Souls*, 1984), continues the "saga" of Danny Smiřický. It is true also of Milan Kundera's great novel, written abroad, *Nesnesitelná lehkost bytí* (published in English as *The Unbearable Lightness of Being*, 1984),[79] and also of the work of Jan Beneš, Pavel Kohout and Vlastimil Třešňák. Two poets of the sixties who continued to write in the same style as before were Ivan Diviš (→ PROFILES, see p. 173) and Antonín Brousek. In his poetry Brousek continues his characteristic playing on stock phrases and cliches. Irony and self-mockery reach a peak in the books of poetry *Zimní spánek* (Hibernation), which was published in Toronto in 1980 with a second version published in Prague in 1991, and *Vteřinové smrti* (Momentary Deaths), 1987 with an expanded edition published in Prague in 1994.

Some authors first began to realize their literary potential in exile. JAROSLAV VEJVODA and JAN NOVÁK (an author of scripts for some Miloš Forman films) were two of the younger authors who did so. Both describe the life of emigrants, Vejvoda in Switzerland[80] and Novák in the USA.[81] They describe their illusions, their disillusionment and their conflicts with their new environment. A common device of Novák and Škvorecký is the use of a mixture of Czech and American English.

As in samizdat, some outstanding works were written in the form of life stories that give at the same time a broader picture of the culture and society of the past. The foremost interwar liberal journalist FERDINAND PEROUTKA (→ PROFILES) lived and worked in exile after the Communist takeover. His first novel *Oblak a valčík* (A Cloud and a Waltz) was published in 1976 but it was not published in Prague till 1991. The novel, based on the play of the same name performed in the Prague *National Theatre* in 1947, returned to the time of the German occupation. By means of a changing patchwork of scenes the author succeeded in creating a panorama of the era. It is full of the "small" and "great" events of history, the tragedy and absurdity of lives lived in stormy and destructive times. In *Oblak a valčík* as well as in his second novel, *Pozdější život Panny* (The Later Life of the Virgin, posthumously Toronto, 1980, Prague, 1991), which examines the question of what would have happened if Joan of Arc had not been burned at the stake, the author used the same straightforward style and precise language found in his journalism.

Another panoramic novel followed only a year later, although it was not till 1992 that it was published in Brno. The title of JOSEF ŠKVORECKÝ'S (→ PROFILES) *Příběh inženýra lidských duší. Entrtejment na stará témata o životě, ženách, osudu, snění, dělnické třídě, fízlech, lásce a smrti* (1977; in English *The Engineer of Human Souls. An Entertainment on the Old Themes of Life, Women, Fate, Dreams, the Working Class, Secret Agents, Love and Death*, 1984) refers to Stalin dubbing writers "engineers of human souls". Unlike Peroutka, who uses the impersonal third person form, Škvorecký chooses to write in the first person. The narrator is Danny Smiřický, the main hero of *Zbabělci* (see pp. 51–52) and of other works (for instance *Mirákl*, 1972, translated as *The Miracle Game*, 1990), who is now, like his creator, a professor at the University of Toronto. He describes his experiences at the university and in the émigré community, but most of the time he returns to the past, especially to his youth during the war in the small Czech town of Kostelec. The novel is made up of dozens of tragic and farcical situations divided into a great number of episodes. The scenes at the university illustrate the vast differences in Danny's situation from that of the students from the West, who have no experience of totalitarianism and cannot comprehend the reasons for the lack of freedom under Communism. Humour and irony play an important part in the letters that appear throughout the narrative. One of the letter-writers is the "Czechoslovak" Lojza, who has the capacity to live happily whatever regime is in power. As can be seen, he is not particularly literate:

> "Karlsbad
> 7 March 1942
>
> Dear Dan,
> I adres you with these few lines to let you know I am well and hope you are enjoying the same blesing at present. I am here at the Karlsbad spa for a week and doing fine, on a special deal for workers laid on by Rinehard Hydrick. In the old days only the rich came here but now its for workers to. We get 4 meals a day, breakfast is bread with artaficial honey or marmalade and for dinner we get meat 3 x a week ant then tea and a roll in the afternoon and a tart on sundays and for supper they give us as much as the noon meal. Its all laid on for workers by the Reich Protecter Rinehard Hydrick. Herr Schilink picked me to go because Dr Selich told him I got shadows on my lungs so they sent me off on this Rinehard Hydrick thing I wouldn't come down with TB. I am doing fine. Are you still working on Mesershmits? After this Rinehard Hydrick thing is over I wont be coming back to the plant because I volanteerd to work in the Reich they need skilled bakers and besides the pays better where they work nights. [. . .]
>
> 25 July 1967
>
> Dear Dan,
> I adres you with these few lines to let you know I am well and hope you are injoying the same blesing at present. Im writing you this leter form a cultural tour in the German demokratish republik. [. . .]
>
> In Dresdin we was in the Pina Kotex where they have paitings by old masters and also an exibision called Terrorangrif an Dresdin about the Amerikan imperialist airaid on Dresdin where more than 200,000 inocent people died. We got took round by our German comrade who described the airaid in detale because he was in Dresdin at the time as a soldier [. . .]. This comrade spoke about how the people of Dresdin was longing for peace but the Amerikan war mungers sent huge squadrins of airplanes and flying fortresses and dropped more than 500,000 tons of fire and explosiv bombs on the city. It was a inhuman crime against the peace loving people of the German demokratish republik by the war mungers who started the second world war and other wars sinse the like Koria for example and Vietnam and against Egypd in Izrail. [. . .] When the German comrade spoke about the sufering of the people who only wanted peace which the Amerikan imperialists had not use for one man punched him in the face without no provokation. He was a tourist from Ostria and I guess he was a Kike he had this funny nose and bushy eyebrows and he shouted that the people of Dresdin had it comin to them and they had to hold him back and then take him away because he got real historical. Our comrade tour directer said he probly was mentaly ill [. . .]."[82]

The experience of living under totalitarianism also plays a fundamental part in MILAN KUNDERA'S (→ PROFILES, see pp. 83–84) novels. It is not surprising that from the early eighties, when he lost his Czech citizenship and became a French citizen, his work has more and more reflected French culture.

Kundera wrote about the time when he was first in exile: "I was in regular contact with a well-known film director who signed many petitions on behalf of Czechoslovakia. One day I discovered he thought we were writing in the Cyrillic alphabet and that we were orthodox." As a result of meeting people with such ideas, Kundera stressed that Bohemia and Moravia were not part of Eastern Europe but were part of Western civilization, particularly of the culture of Central Europe. According to Kundera, what particularly distinguishes the Central European novel, by writers such as Robert Musil, Franz Kafka, Jaroslav Hašek, Hermann Broch and Witold Gombrowicz, is scepticism and the way it exposes all myths.[83]

Milan Kundera's novel *Nesnesitelná lehkost bytí* (*The Unbearable Lightness of Being*, in English 1984) became the most highly rated Czech novel among the best-sellers in Europe and America. It was first published in French in 1984 and in 1985 it was published in Czech in Toronto. The novel consists of several interrelated stories and various themes. The narrator, who has no part in the story, comments freely on events. After *Žert* (The Joke, see pp. 83–84) Kundera stopped writing in the first person, a form to which he did not return till the nineties. The novel is set in Czechoslovakia in the sixties and during normalization but the action also largely takes place in the West. It is centred round two couples; the first are Czech, the surgeon Tomáš, who is the embodiment of lightness and is always on the lookout for new erotic adventures, and his wife Tereza, who represents seriousness and who, unlike her husband, believes in faithfulness in marriage; a Czech sculptress, Sabina, and her Swiss lover, Franz, make up the second couple. One of the main themes of the novel is kitsch, which, like the totalitarian regime it closely resembles, is superficially appealing and poses no questions. To get away from it Sabina escapes from Czechoslovakia, but in the West she finds a new kind of sterility; no one understands her and she herself sinks into acceptance of the kitschy ideas of the East. Franz represents the foolish notions of Western left-wing intellectuals.

> "In the realm of kitsch, the dictatorship of the heart reigns supreme.
>
> The feeling induced by kitsch must be a kind the multitudes can share. Kitsch may not, therefore, depend on an unusual situation; it must derive from the basic images people have engraved in their memories: the ungrateful daughter, the neglected father, children running on the grass, the motherland betrayed, first love.
>
> [. . .]
>
> The brotherhood of man on earth will be possible only on a basis of kitsch.
>
> [. . .]
>
> Those of us who live in a society where various political tendencies exist side by side and competing influences cancel or limit one another can manage more or less to escape the kitsch inquisition: the individual can preserve his individuality; the

artist can create unusual works. But whenever a single political movement corners power, we find ourselves in the realm of *totaliarian kitsch*."[84]

Kundera's characters are not intended to be figures of "flesh and blood" but embodiments of ideas, images and theories. The authorial narrator reveals that he invented them himself. The same holds good for the following novel, *Nesmrtelnost* (*Immortality*, 1991), published in French in 1990 and in Czech in Brno and in Toronto in 1993, where a woman whose graceful gesture is the catalyst for the plot is the real heroine. This work is set completely outside Czechoslovakia, but the philosophical element and essay-like qualities that had been present in Kundera's work from the beginning are even stronger, including the reflections on "imagology", that is, the art not of being and trying to achieve something, but of creating illusory, eye-catching images through advertising.

The theme of remembering also appears in the poems of Milada Součková, Ivan Blatný, Ivan Jelínek and in the novels of Viktor Fischl, writers who emigrated after the February 1948 coup.

In her last poems in exile, MILADA SOUČKOVÁ (→ PROFILES) continued to write on the themes she had developed in her sophisticated poetry of the fifties and sixties: returning home, nature, thinking back to her forefathers and her childhood. The theme "down memory lane" was most fully exploited in *Sešity Josefíny Rykrové* (Josephine Rykrová's Notebooks, first published in 1981, postscript by Roman Jakobson; with an expanded edition published in Prague in 1993). The atmosphere at the beginning of the 20th century was built up by a succession of details about the daily life of the time, interspersed with many comments in English, Czech and other foreign languages. "Verše k obrazu ve Zlaté Praze, / tak že by psala Josefína? / ve třídě za ní sedí Buňatová / z pomologické zahrady v Troji / přes řeku, přes Stromovku do školy, / to nebyl most, přeprava pramicí, / Máj, Zlatá Praha / zjara, kdy v Troji jdou ledy / slýchal je v noci Vrchlický, / Buňatová dnes přijde pozdě." [85] (Verses to illustrate a picture in the magazine Golden Prague, as Josefína might have written them? / behind her in class sits the girl Buňatová / we walk from the pomological garden in Troja / across the river, across Stromovka to school, / there was no bridge, a ferry made the crossing, / the magazines May, Golden Prague / in spring, when the ice is melting in Troja / the poet Vrchlický heard it in the night, / Buňatová will be late today . . . , *Přívoz v Troji*, The Ferry in Troja).

For a long time nothing was known about what happened to IVAN BLATNÝ (→ PROFILES, see p. 16), a member of *Skupina 42*, who remained in Britain after March 1948. As a result of loneliness, health worries and the fear of Communist agents he became mentally ill. From the mid-fifties Blatný was in psychiatric clinics in England. Later it appeared that he had probably been writing poems all the time and that the British nurses thought they were nonsense and had thrown them out with the rubbish. In the 1970s, a nurse who happened to have some friends in Czechoslovakia began to collect them and finally sent them to the Toronto publishing house *Sixty-Eight Publishers*. Blatný's last two collections were compiled by Antonín Brousek from a selection of these texts, *Stará bydliště*

(1978, The Old Homesteads) and *Pomocná škola Bixley* (Bixley Special School, 1987, another version in samizdat, Prague, 1982).

Typical features of these poems are the audacious association of ideas, shifting from Czech into various foreign languages, English, German, French,[86] and quotations and allusions. In this way they form a kind of topography of memory.

> Je neděle Mám volno
> pacienti očekávají své návštěvníky
> chodím mezi budovou nemocnice a farmou
> snad budu mít také nějakou návštěvu
> snad mě najdou
> snad se na cestě objeví Brušák
> anebo Listopad
> anebo Dresler
> jsou tady v cizině léta a ještě jsem je neviděl
> mám připraveny básně
> budeme mluvit o literatuře
> svět bude zase plný života[87]
>
> It is Sunday I have a day off
> the patients are waiting for their visitors
> I walk between the hospital building and the farm
> perhaps I'll have visitors too
> perhaps they'll find me
> perhaps Brušák will appear on the road
> or Listopad
> or Dresler[88]
> they have been here in a foreign land for years and I still haven't seen them
> I have poems ready
> we'll talk about literature
> the world will be full of life again

It was not till the seventies and eighties that IVAN JELÍNEK, who was ten years older than Blatný, composed his best works. A poet keenly interested in language itself, he wants to penetrate "Tam dolů ke kořínkům řeči, / do hlubokosti. / V svit bílých kostí / slov šeptaných do nářečí." [89] (Down to the roots of speech, / to the very depths. / In the light of the white bones / of words whispered in dialect.) Jelínek, like Josef Palivec and Zdeněk Rotrekl (see p. 74), is a scholar of great erudition and a past master with words. He deliberately chooses words with complicated semantic and sound associations.

The poet and novelist VIKTOR FISCHL moved to Israel in 1949, and as an Israeli diplomat worked in many countries. After almost thirty years he went back to literature. In 1975 he published the novel *Kuropění* (Dawn, Zurich, 1975), which came out in Prague in 1991. In an interview he said, "I think I am one of those people to whom the words of the psalmist apply, 'In old age they are also fruitful!'"[90] His works are not hampered by political awareness or by stylistic experimentation. They are written in an elegant, mildly archaic language and embrace several themes; *Kuropění* deals with the laws of nature and human existence. The fate of the Jews during the war is the subject of the novel *Dvorní šašci* (Court Jesters), which was published in Hebrew in 1982 and in Czech in Cologne in 1985. An expanded edition was published in Prague in 1991.

A similar kind of poet who emigrated after the February 1948 coup and later worked in the Library of Congress in Washington was JIŘÍ KOVTUN. The poems he had been writing from the fifties were first collected in the book *Hřbet velryby* (The Whale's Back), which was published in Prague in 1995. They are unpretentious and distinguished by a kind of muted luminosity through which the mysterious affinity with the world can be perceived. Kovtun's prose works, the novel *Pražská ekloga* (Prague Eclogue), which was first published in Munich in 1973 and in Brno in 1992, and the novel *Zpráva z Lisabonu* (News from Lisbon, Zurich, 1979, Prague, 1999) are more complicated in structure and sometimes have gripping plots. Nevertheless in spite of the tension prevalent at the time, traditional moral values are convincingly upheld.

The hardest thing about exile was "the divorce of home and the natural world" as Rio Preisner described it. This is manifest in various ways. In IVAN DIVIŠ'S (→ PROFILES, see p. 73) collection of poems *Odchod z Čech* (Departure from Bohemia, Munich, 1981, Prague, 1990), the love-hate relationship with Bohemia and exile in general is viewed, to put it in existentialist terms, as an inhibiting, limiting situation for the artist. For Diviš, the poetic absolutist, spiritual bleakness and brutality are present in every aspect of everyday life, and in double measure during normalization in Czechoslovakia. His language is also aggressive, stretching meanings to a dangerous limit. In *Obrať koně!* (Turn the Horse!, Munich, 1988, Prague, 1992) he writes, "Proč žiju, nevím, / ani kde to jsem, / ale jsem zařazen! / Zařazen, a proto dostanu nažrat."[91] (Why I am living, I do not know, / nor where I am, / but I've been put into a slot. / Put into a slot, and that's why they'll feed me.) He finds a possible way out of this situation in the revival of national life, the renewing of eternal values, especially the relationship to God. Diviš's impressive work, written in the course of several decades, is *Teorie spolehlivosti* (The Theory of Reliability), which consists of diary entries, meditations and aphorisms. It was published in Prague in 1994 and in it he goes back to his key themes, the passages about death being particularly powerful.

6. Drama and the Theatre

In the seventies and eighties, because of the elimination of the majority of the prominent writers of the preceding era, only some major works were produced in the theatre. Just as novelists escaped into the past, so playwrights, like Jiří Šotola and Oldřich Daněk, succeeded in escaping into the past by writing historical plays. One such remarkable drama is OLDŘICH DANĚK'S *Vévodkyně valdštejnských vojsk* (The Duchess of Wallenstein's Troops, 1979) in which a single character multiplies into two or three different actors. Good plays on contemporary subjects were the exception, like ANTONÍN MÁŠA'S plays in collaboration with *Laterna magika* (The Magic Lantern, see p. 50). Earlier works by prominent playwrights, such as Josef Topol, Václav Havel, Milan Uhde, Pavel Kohout, František Pavlíček, Milan Kundera and Ivan Klíma were banned. These authors might write new plays but they had only a faint hope that they would be put on abroad or for the benefit of a few people in "theatres in flats". They found themselves in an even more precarious position than the banned poets. The lack of any direct connection with the theatre meant that their work was considerably restricted if not rendered completely impossible.

> "With a poem or a piece of fiction you can curl up anywhere, you can be alone with them. But a play belongs on stage. It is three-dimensional. Without actors it is not even half a play. An audience – not just someone reading in bed, in the tram or on holiday – gives a play its third dimension."[92] (Josef Topol, 1976)

Nevertheless Václav Havel and Pavel Kohout in particular managed to write plays which, although banned at home, enjoyed success abroad. By the end of 1988 fifty different translations of Havel's plays had been made. Kohout's plays had 450 first performances in the West and about 11,000 performances in all.

At the beginning of the seventies, absurd and lyrical-existentialist drama was still the predominant genre in the theatre. At that time KAROL SIDON (see pp. 103–104) wrote several important plays. Only one of them, *Latríny* (Latrines, 1972), was put on and even then it only had a few performances. Some plays, including *Shapira*, a play about betrayal and conscience, which was written in 1974 (a revised edition was published in Prague in 1990) were known only to samizdat readers. VÁCLAV HAVEL'S one-act play *Audience* (in English as *Conversation* in *Index of Censorship* 5, [1976], no. 3)[93] appeared in samizdat in 1975. The author originally wrote it simply to amuse his friends during their regular social evenings. The play was exceptionally successful in "alternative culture" circles. It was soon followed by other one-act plays, such as *Vernisáž* (translated as *Unveiling. Private View*, in *Selected Plays, 1963–1983*, 1992) and *Protest* (translated as *Protest*, in *Selected Plays, 1963–1983*, 1992), published in samizdat in 1975 and 1979. The Austrian Minister of Education and Culture issued an official invitation to the author to come to Vienna for the first night. The Czechoslovak authorities, however, refused him a passport and commented that "Václav Havel does not represent Czechoslovak culture." *Audience*, *Vernisáž* and *Protest* had features that gave an obviously factually accurate and authentic picture of the day. In the main character of the dissident writer Vaněk, it is not difficult to recognize attributes of the author himself.

> *Brewmaster*: In point of fact, what the hell was this stuff you been writin' – if you don't mind me askin'?
>
> *Vaněk*: Theatre plays –
>
> Brewmaster: Theatre plays, huh? So that played 'em in some theatre somewhere, or what?
>
> *Vaněk*: Yes.
>
> *Brewmaster*: Oh, yeah, yeah – So theatre plays, huh? Listen, that bein' the case,

> you oughta write somethin' about our brewery here. Somethin' like about somebody like Bureš – D'you know Bureš?
> *Vaněk*: Yes – (. . .)
> *Brewmaster*: But anyway, I betcha this never even crossed you mind, right?
> *Vaněk*: What do you mean?
> *Brewmaster*: Well, that you gonna end up rollin' em in a brewery one day –
> *Vaněk*: Well – (*noncommittal*).
> *Brewmaster*: Them is the paradoxes of life, right?[94]

Audience gave rise to a series of similar plays with Ferdinand Vaněk as the main character. Havel himself went on to write *Vernisáž* (*Unveiling. Private View*) and *Protest*; Kohout added *Atest* (*Permit*), which was premiered in Vienna in 1979, *Marast* (*Morass*) and *Safari* (all published in English in *The Vaněk Plays*, 1987); *Morass* was first performed in Göttingen in 1982. Both *Atest* and *Marast* were edited in Prague in 1990. Actor and occasional playwright PAVEL LANDOVSKÝ wrote *Sanitární noc* (Closed for Cleaning) which had its first performance in Germany in 1976. It was published in Czech in the collection *Jiné komedie a Sanitární noc* (Closed for Cleaning and Other Comedies) in Toronto in 1982. His *Arest* (in English *Arrest* in *The Vaněk Plays*), also featuring Vaněk, was staged in Vienna in 1981. Even JIŘÍ DIENSTBIER, journalist, dissident and Czechoslovak Foreign Secretary after 1989, wrote a Vaněk play *Příjem* (translated as *Reception*), that was published in samizdat in 1978 and also in *The Vaněk Plays*.[95]

Other banned dramatists also took their subjects from actual events. FRANTIŠEK PAVLÍČEK wrote *Dávno, dávno již tomu* (Long, Long Ago) a monodrama (a play for a single actor) based on the life of Božena Němcová, which was staged in a private flat in 1979 and in Prague in 1990. The lives of 19th-century classic Czech writers called to mind similarities with the contemporary situation in the arts. MILAN UHDE was inspired by a strange episode in the lives of Marx and Engels to write *Zvěstování aneb Bedřichu, jsi anděl* (*The Annunciation or Friedrich, You Are an Angel*)[96] which was published in samizdat in 1987 and had its first performance in Zagreb in Croatia in 1988. In 1990 it was staged in Prague. *"Ecce Constantia!"* ("Ecce Constantia!"), PAVEL KOHOUT's unconventional treatment of the religious 15th-century Council of Constance was published in exile in 1989 and in Prague in 1990. Unlike previous versions of the subject of the 15th-century religious reformer, Jan Hus does not appear on stage when he is condemned to death as a heretic by the Council. The play is only partly concerned with the case of Jan Hus. It is about the possibility of cleansing the church and getting back to its original message. If, in the struggle for power, the cold pragmatist prevails over the convinced and skilful reformer, we can take this as an indication of the author's scepticism about reconstructing history, comparable with the disillusionment evident in the novels of his contemporaries.

In the seventies and eighties, the so-called "studio theatres" (fringe theatres) became more influential, compared to traditional drama and the great theatres, than they had been in the sixties (see pp. 98–99). The desire of contemporary playwrights to associate themselves with the prewar Jiří Voskovec's and Jan Werich's

Osvobozené divadlo (Liberated Theatre) was demonstrated in May 1977 with a gala performance celebrating the fiftieth anniversary of the premiere of its famous comedy *Vest Pocket Revue*, where Jan Werich appeared and performed to a packed house in the Lucerna Hall in Prague. The small "studio" theatres managed to free themselves from the bureaucracy surrounding the arts more easily than the state-subsidized theatres. Their performances, often based on improvisation and a splendid rapport with the audience, could get round difficulties with the censor more easily than plays with a fixed "classic" plot.

In various theatres and clubs IVAN VYSKOČIL with a few collaborators gradually developed his "non-theatre" (see pp. 99–100), which meant constantly evolving theatre. In 1980, in collaboration with Leoš Suchařípa and Vlasta Špicnerová, he wrote *Haprdáns neboli HAmlet, PRinc DÁNský* (Haprden, or Hamlet, Prince of Denmark). Vyskočil's version of the classic play differed from Shakespeare's by including scenes that he supposedly omitted. Some characters talk like men of the present day, for example, Claudius as a moderate reformer and Polonius as a pragmatic politician. Hamlet suffers from "oppositional tendencies", which are cured by psychotherapy, and turns into a perfectly respectable citizen. So the tragedy does not take place. According to Vyskočil's words, Hamlet is changed into a "normal" play. Apart from anything else the play is an allusion to the situation during normalization in the seventies. "Now who could cavil at that? Now that everything is fine and stable?! Who would benefit? What good would it do anybody? – Not the audience certainly." The play was in part a puppet show with kitchen implements; Claudius was represented by a cooking spoon, Polonius by a strainer, Hamlet by a whisk, and so on.

In 1972 *Semafor* put on its most successful play, *Kytice* (A Garland of Flowers) by JIŘÍ SUCHÝ. It was based on the classic Karel Jaromír Erben's 19th-century ballads and had a run of six hundred performances in which the actor Josef Dvořák appeared. However, without Jiří Šlitr and Jiří Grossmann, the theatre was no longer the unique attraction it had been in the sixties. The collaboration of Jiří Suchý with the comedienne Jitka Molavcová, gave it fresh life, for instance, in his play *Jonáš, dejme tomu v úterý* (Jonah, Let's Say on Tuesday, 1985), a sequel to his famous *Jonáš* (Jonah, see p. 100).

Studio Y produced its impressive works in the seventies and eighties. Collective improvisations and the linking of plays, music and song made it totally unlike the "stone-built" theatres, that is the established theatres. The head of this theatre, JAN SCHMID, often charged onto the stage and admonished the audience, the actors exchanged roles and so on. Some of *Ypsilon's* works, in particular Schmid's plays *Život a smrt K. H. Máchy* (The Life and Death of K. H. Mácha, 1978) and *Třináct vůní* (Thirteen Fragrances, 1975), were devoted to problems of the Czech character, a favourite theme of the studio theatres. The play *Třináct vůní* came closest to the current ideas about drama. The guest producer in *Ypsilon* was Evald Schorm, the well-known director of New Wave films in the sixties, who became a leading theatrical producer when he was banned from making films. *Třináct vůní* is a series of bizarre pictures of a small Czech family from 1937 to 1945 seen through the eyes of the now grown-up Maruška. Portrayals of national characteristics ("We'd better not draw attention to ourselves," her mother keeps repeating), were also fairly transparent references to the present day.

The character of a self-taught, unrecognized, ineffectual genius who always fails was the basis on which the *Jára Cimrman Theatre* was founded. The main writers for the theatre (LADISLAV SMOLJAK and ZDENĚK SVĚRÁK) created a successful hoax which was at the same time satirical and entertaining. The performance consisted of introductory "scholarly" lectures on Cimrman's life and work, and in the second half of the evening there was a "reconstruction" presented in a non-theatrical, wooden fashion. The character of Jára Cimrman parodied among other things several national characteristics, parochialism, the ability to work hard with no practical result, amateurism. It also ridiculed the exhortative type of pseudo-scholarly public education.

> "Cimrman was an excellent impersonator but his impersonations did not meet with the kind of reception they deserved. This could have been due to the fact that Cimrman imitated people unknown to the public, for example his sister Louise or the hunchbacked barber Kalous, so that it was impossible to judge how accurately Cimrman had caught their mannerisms and their way of speaking."[97] (Cimrman kabaretiér [Cimrman the Cabaret Artist], 1981)

The fame of two Moravian theatres, the Brno theatre *Husa na provázku* (Goose on a String) and *HaDivadlo* (HaTheatre), which started up originally in Prostějov but moved to Brno in the late seventies, extended far beyond Moravia.

Husa na provázku was named after the early 20th-century author Jiří Mahen's 1925 book of film libretti. After the Communist Party leader Gustáv Husák (*husák* = male goose) came to power at the beginning of normalization in the 1970s, the name was considered unsuitable and the theatre was renamed *Divadlo Na provázku* (Theatre on a String). It was famous for burlesque clowning, mostly by BOLESLAV POLÍVKA, who was exceptional as an actor and also as the author of *Trosečník* (The Castaway, 1977) and *Poslední leč* (Hunters' Feast, 1981). Besides Polívka, whose performances also won acclaim elsewhere in Europe, the theatre was famed for adaptations of older works; for example LUDVÍK KUNDERA's adaptation of the 17th-century theologian and pedagogue Jan Amos Komenský (Comenius) in *Labyrint světa a lusthauz srdce* (The Labyrinth of the World and the Summerhouse of the Heart,[98] 1983), and the musical based on themes from Ivan Olbracht's novel from Carpathian Ruthenia, *Nikola Šuhaj loupežník*,[99] *Balada pro banditu* (Ballad for a Bandit, 1975). *Balada pro banditu* was made into a film in 1978. The musical was written – anonymously – by the banned playwright Milan Uhde.

ARNOŠT GOLDFLAM also occasionally appeared on stage in *Divadlo Na provázku*, where from the late seventies he worked with distinction as a producer. Since then he has also written plays for *HaDivadlo*. His perspective is surreal but at the same time it is almost brutally realistic. Once again the themes are family, family discipline of the wrong kind and meaningless rituals. So it is in his first work *Horror* (Horror, 1981), in which attention is focused on the younger son, who, unlike the rest of the family, is a dreamer and a thinker. The other members of the family regard him as the black sheep and decide to cure him. First of all he is forbidden to go for walks, then he is tied up and given electric shocks. Finally they kill him. However, this unnatural care and aggression does not stop there. In the end the elder son, who has always conformed, is threatened with the same fate.

Divadlo Na okraji (The Fringe Theatre) in Prague was also established on the basis of adaptations of other works. Unlike the entertaining improvisations of *Ypsilon* and *Divadlo Na provázku*, which were more like folk street theatre, ZDENEK POTUŽIL's productions were carefully and precisely devised. *Divadlo Na okraji* had its greatest success in 1977 with the adaptation of Bohumil Hrabal's *Postřižiny* (Cutting It Short, see p. 145). Potužil's adaptation of Hašek's well-known novel was also ingenious. He called it *Švejci* (Švejks) and in it four performers, two actors and two actresses "lend themselves" to the chief character.

7. Literary Criticism

Literary theory was badly affected by the silencing of the most outstanding critics, Oleg Sus, Milan Suchomel, Jiří Opelík, Zdeněk Kožmín, Vladimír Karfík, Aleš Haman and Jan Lopatka. It was also affected by purges in the universities, in the Academy of Sciences, among newspaper and review editors and eminent scholars, such as Felix Vodička, Jiří Brabec, Miroslav Červenka and Milan Jankovič. Work on the history of literature was discontinued and Volume IV of the *Dějiny české literatury* (History of Czech Literature), edited by Zdeněk Pešat and Eva Strohsová, was banned. It was not published till 1995, a quarter of a century after completion. Literary theory was supposed to rid itself of structuralism, phenomenology and other "damaging trends". So-called "allegiance to Marxism", "class orientation" and "popular appeal" should once again be the basis of literary theory. Ladislav Štoll, who became director of the Czech and World Literature Institute for the second time, published *Básník a naděje* (The Poet and Hope), a revised version of his *Třicet let bojů za českou socialistickou poezii* (Thirty Years of Struggle to Create a Czech Socialist Poetry, an expanded version published in book form, 1950, see p. 21), the notorious collection of post-February dogma. Milan Blahynka advanced Štoll's views further in his concept of *pozemská poezie* (poetry of the real world), in which he included approved authors of the past S. K. Neumann, Vítězslav Nezval, Josef Kainar, and "living classical" authors like Miroslav Florian. He also unhesitatingly included the younger poets Karel Sýs, Jiří Žáček and Michal Černík.

As in other branches of the arts, a semi-official literary fringe movement grew up alongside official literary scholarship. Representatives of this movement were the critics Vladimír Macura and Vladimír Novotný, who wrote in the arts column of *Zemědělské noviny* (Agricultural News), Milan Jungmann, whose articles in the daily *Práce* (Work) appeared under a pseudonym, and Jan Lukeš writing in the daily *Svobodné slovo* (The Free Word) in the eighties. Several books that did not conform to the criteria of ideology were published including *Josef Čapek*, JIŘÍ

Opelík's epoch-making innovative monograph of 1980, and Vladimír Macura's 1983 study of the Czech National Revival *Znamení zrodu* (Signs of Rebirth), which was inspired by the Russian-Estonian semiotician J. M. Lotman, and Jan Lehár's *Nejstarší česká epika* (The Oldest Czech Epic, 1983). Lehár followed this with his essays for his anthology *Česká středověká lyrika* (The Czech Mediaeval Lyric, 1990). The trend continued with the monograph about the Baroque scholar *Bohuslav Balbín* (1983) by the authors Jan P. Kučera and Jiří Rak and the work of Jaroslava Janáčková, Zdeněk Pešat and others. Přemysl Blažíček's *Poezie Karla Tomana* (The Poetry of Karel Toman) and his *Haškův Švejk* (Hašek's *Švejk*), inspired by a phenomenological existentialist approach to art, remained unpublished (they came out after the fall of Communism in 1995 and 1991).

Obviously in exile and in samizdat there was only a limited amount of criticism possible. Moreover, critics were constrained by consideration for banned authors. Adverse criticism of their works would play into the hands of official propaganda, which claimed that "alternative" literature was worthless. Nevertheless, these were the very critics who were able to express independent judgments. Milan Jungmann at home published *Cesty a rozcestí* (Roads and Crossroads) in samizdat in 1986 with an expanded version published in London (1988). Abroad Antonín Brousek and Josef Škvorecký published a review of official poetry and prose in *Na brigádě* (Teamwork, 1979). Other critics working in exile were Helena Kosková and Jiří Kovtun, and in the eighties Květoslav Chvatík.

Literary scholars inspired by structuralism continued their work in obscurity. Oleg Sus and Zdeněk Kožmín worked in Brno; Miroslav Červenka, Mojmír Otruba, Alexandr Stich and Milan Jankovič in Prague; Lubomír Doležel in Canada; František Svejkovský in the USA and Květoslav Chvatík in Germany. Their methodology is usually known as neo-structuralism, but in many ways their views are vastly different from the original Prague School of the thirties. Miroslav Procházka and Marie Kubínová in Prague and Sylvie Richterová in Italy are younger scholars associated with the neo-structuralists.

Scholars and essayists not sponsored by the state considered it their first duty to challenge officialdom's notions of the past. The essays of Václav Černý, Bedřich Fučík, Zdeněk Rotrekl (see pp. 156, 155, 74) and some of the essays in Jan Vladislav's *Tajný čtenář* (The Secret Reader) in particular, bear witness to this belief. The publication of the dictionary of unofficial authors, in which Jiří Brabec, Jan Lopatka, Jiří Gruša and Petr Kabeš collaborated, was an event of great significance. The dictionary first appeared in samizdat in 1978 entitled *Slovník českých spisovatelů* (Dictionary of Czech Writers). It was an attempt to reconstruct the history of Czech literature from 1948 to 1978. An expanded edition with the additional collaboration of Igor Hájek came out in Toronto in 1982. In 1991 it was published in Prague under the title *Slovník zakázaných autorů* (Dictionary of Banned Authors). It contained information about hundreds of authors whose work had been completely or partially suppressed, clearly demonstrating the extent of interference in the arts during normalization.

Lexikon české literatury (A Lexicon of Czech Literature) was compiled with basically the same purpose – the reconstruction of the history of literature minus ideology. Part I of what was the largest dictionary of its kind at that time was published in 1985, part II in two volumes in 1993, Part III also in two volumes in 2000. In all, four volumes were planned. Work on it had begun in the seventies in the state institute Ústav pro českou a světovou literaturu (Czech and World Literature Institute). The scholars who contributed to it, Mojmír Otruba, Jiří Opelík, Zdeněk Pešat, Vladimír Forst, Eva Taxová, Ludmila Lantová and Květa Homolová and others, were mostly on the fringes of official literary life. The dictionary is a comprehensive survey of authors, anonymous works, reviews, almanacs and publishing houses from the beginning of Czech literature till 1945.

The Eighties Generation and Postmodernism

1. The Eighties Generation

Just as it was after February 1948, the only youth organization in existence in the seventies and eighties was the SSM (Socialistický svaz mládeže – The Socialist Youth Association). However, circumstances had now changed. After the war a good many young people believed in Communist ideology, but in the sixties this belief had evaporated and after August 1968, to all intents and purposes, ceased to exist. During normalization it was common to pay lip service to Communism and simply advance one's own career. The youth organization still existed formally but the heart had gone out of it. Activists in the organization proclaimed loyalty to the regime but groups of musicians, friends of the earth and other groups with no official motivation sprang up within it.

In 1983 the military commanders in the Warsaw Pact decided to deploy Soviet nuclear warheads in Czechoslovakia. The media, which had previously carried angry protests against NATO warheads in Western Europe, now began a campaign in support of these "defence" warheads. Reasonable people were understandably infuriated. *Charter 77* pointed out that peace as an aim is inseparable from human rights and that, above all, responsible government and freedom of information are a prerequisite for reduction in tension. Young people who gathered on Kampa in Prague near the Vltava river on 8 of December each year at a symbolic tomb of John Lennon made their views known, played guitars and sang. In 1984 these groups of young people filled Charles Bridge. The police dispersed them by force using truncheons and dogs. A year later part of the crowd surged out from Kampa and made for the Castle shouting the slogans, "Give peace a chance!", "No rockets means peace!", "Down with the army!". A hastily devised written protest followed: "We do not agree with the deployment of any nuclear weapons on either side of Europe!"

About this time the thirty-year-old Ivo Šmoldas wrote the poem *Maria* with the English subtitle "The Day After":

Ve výhni třesku slunce potemnělo.
Praskla jí voda. A pak první stah
hnul hrbem břicha, co tu čnělo
z rozvalin, na něž padal prach.

Kruh popálenců na ni civěl.
Štětky vlasů z oloupaných hlav
stlaly se na zem jako seno v chlívě –
tomu, co přijde, na pozdrav.

Do louže krve mezi stehny
vyklouzl tvor. A jeho křik
v chuchvalcích vlasů *byl tak něžný*,
až se jí ze střev zvedl vzlyk.

Však v ústní díře zkroutil se a řachl
do tiché vrstvy aktivního prachu.

In the ruin of the boom the sun darkened
The waters broke. And the first contraction
moved the mound of the belly, as it rose up
from the ruins, where the dust fell.

A circle of burnt humanity gaped at them.
Bristles of hair from shaven heads
scattered on the ground like hay in a cowshed –
as a greeting to what will come.

Into the pool of blood between the thighs
the creature slid out. And its cry
in lumps of hair was *so feeble*
it brought a sob from the very guts.

Yet it twisted in the mouth and thundered
into the silent layers of radiation dust.[100]

(*Zimní srst* [Winter Coat])

This poem and others like it expressed the feelings of a generation that had grown up in a time of social stagnation, lack of freedom and closed frontiers. Rock and punk music, capable of expressing the harshness and cruelty of the world around, and the sentiments of individuals, continued to exercise an influence on this generation. Their feelings of sterility, the ironic relationship between the world and themselves, were expressed by the music of the groups of the so-called

New Wave, such as *Pražský výběr* (The Prague Blend), *Jasná páka* (Clear Gear), *Garáž* (Garage), and *Visací zámek* (Padlock). Young people met in sports clubs, in pubs, they met as religious groups and as friends of the earth. They were seeking a different direction in their lives from the rigid path they were expected to follow.

The intellectuals of this generation, most of whom were born in the late fifties and in the sixties, found their way into samizdat, into the grey area of the arts and to some extent into official literature. Moods of scepticism, isolation, obsessive visions of catastrophic floods, walls, alcoholic dependency, insanity and mental homes, prison and dreamlike images of levitation were typical themes. More than the generation of Ivan Wernisch, Jiří Gruša and Antonín Brousek, young people felt closer ties with the poets of the war generation, especially with Jiří Orten, who died in 1941 at the age of twenty-one. Orten's poetry, which concentrated on the individual and existence, danger and depression, inner purity and vulnerable tenderness, was very much alive. Other topically relevant ideas were the suspicion of optimism, great gestures and fine words, a distrust of politics and all officialdom. This wariness (and the general scepticism of the eighties generation) obviously had its roots in the state of contemporary society but it went deeper than that. It arose from a distrust of modern civilization and its consequences. Věra, the narrator in Zuzana Brabcová's (see p. 185) novel *Daleko od stromu* (Far from the Tree, 1984), says, "National Revivals, invasions of foreign armies, the fall of governments, the differences between the Eastern and Western blocs, held no interest for me."[101]

Už na to seru, protože to mám za pár (I Don't Give a Shit, because I'm to Be De-mobbed, 1985), the title of an anthology of poetry by young samizdat authors arranged by Andrej Stankovič, was typical. In it we find two outstanding poets (and novelists), Jáchym Topol and Petr Placák. Both were contributors to the review *Revolver Revue* (see p. 153) and were also connected with nonconformist rock music. Topol wrote texts chiefly for his brother's band *Psí vojáci* (Dog Soldiers). Placák's brother Jan was also a well-known rock musician.

JÁCHYM TOPOL (→ PROFILES), son of the dramatist Josef Topol (see p. 102), gathered three of his first books of poetry into the collection *Miluju tě k zbláznění* (I'm Madly in Love with You), which was published in samizdat in 1988 and in Brno in 1991. It and another book of poems, *V úterý bude válka* (On Tuesday There Will Be War, 1992), contain features typical of this generation: internal and external threats, high-flown emotional expressions together with aggressive language, vulgarisms, sometimes alternating with a literary, bookish style. The outside world appears repugnant, bleak and abominable; the lyrical subject takes on the role of castaway and outlaw. Perhaps the only positive emotion is the sympathy for "others under threat", whether they be Indians, the white whale or "my beautiful sister".

2. Prose and Postmodernism

This last motif, suggesting some kind of mystical love that has been lost and is being sought after, is only hinted at in the poems. However, it became one of the main themes in Topol's long novel *Sestra* (1994, Sister; translated as *City Sister Silver*, 2000). Themes also developed in it are the author's sensitivity to cruelty, his grim view of contemporary civilization and his apprehensive expectation of the end of the world, the apocalypse. The book deals with the adventures of a group of young people in Prague after 1989. The arrangement and style of the narrative is unusual; lyrical passages, sometimes in the nature of incantations or litanies, are interspersed among descriptions of the world, "the text rolls on like an overflowing river" as Josef Vohryzek wrote.[102]

> "With Little White She-Dog I was no one again, a shape born of vapor, wind, moisture. She stroked nerves I didn't know I had, my face took on a new appearance, I started to feel my body. I started to dance. For a cripple, just stretching your hand is a dance. She drew me in, forming me, and that in turn shaped her nature.
>
> As the well-mannered little girl walked to her lesson in classical languages with the former priest, at the time a stock clerk because he hadn't signed out of fear of the Devil, or to the church of the priest who had signed because only the Church is eternal and every regime eventually topples, ending up on the bottom like grains of sand in the infinite ocean of grace . . . in her mouth she could still taste the seed of the little man of her tribe, because not even the Church is older than the tribe, and we were closer to each other than to those broken-backed families of ours. The present, which our families felt was a world built on falsehood, and the period prior to the invasion, which they clung to, were both the same gobbledygook to us. We weren't afraid of anything. We didn't care about blood and lineage, just like Romeo and Juliet."[103]

Medorek (Young Medor), the first novel by PETR PLACÁK, who was two years younger than Topol, appeared in samizdat in 1985 and was published in Prague in 1990. It brought the twenty-one-year-old author to the notice of the unofficial critics and has remained his most important work to date. The stories about Medor, who starts working in a factory at the age of sixteen, have more realistic plots than Topol's. But Placák also works within a very free format. There are dreamlike, fantastic scenes and he makes use of satirical hyperbole. For example, right at the beginning of the story when the hero goes to work for the first time, he writes:

> "At the gatehouse he asked where his department was. He went up the stairs and knocked at a door. The bitch Kareninová was sitting in the office. However at the time he did not know her.
>
> 'Good morning,' he said.
>
> She raised her toad-like head from her desk and snapped, 'What do you want?'
>
> 'I'm supposed to start work here.'
>
> 'What's your name?'
>
> 'Medor, Karel Medor,' he said.
>
> 'Oh you're Medor,' she grinned but immediately her gob contracted. 'Where have you been, may I ask; we expected you a month ago! We were about to get the police!'

several acclaimed authors, such as Karel Sýs and Josef Peterka (see pp. 140, 142). On the other hand he had a high regard for the nonconformist songwriters Vladimír Merta, Jiří Dědeček and Jan Burian. In place of direct political commitment he demanded intellectual and moral responsibility. It was the duty of the writer to be true to reality. He even wrote that contemporary literature lacked the compassion of some of the authors of the sixties. Lukeš's book did not totally reject "socialist literature" but it did attempt to widen its concept. It became the target for unexpectedly harsh criticism. Josef Peterka called it "a lampoon with a malicious political purpose". The author was accused of the basest "sins", in other words, according to Vítězslav Rzounek, he was resurrecting ideas from the sixties and opposing "the process of normalization and consolidation". For some time to come this campaign prevented other attempts to widen the concept of official literature.[108]

The slight, temporary liberalization at the end of the seventies and the beginning of the eighties brought about the return of some important authors from samizdat to the state publishing houses. After Jaroslav Seifert, who was published again in 1979, in 1981 publishing houses took the risk of publishing new books by Jan Skácel and Oldřich Mikulášek. Works by Miroslav Holub followed in 1982, and somewhat later, in 1985, works by Ludvík Kundera. In 1982 the novelist JIŘÍ MUCHA became famous for a new version of his book about his father, the turn of the century Art Nouveau painter. The book originally called *Kankán se svatozáří* (Cancan with a Halo, 1969) was now given the title *Alfons Mucha* (the English translation entitled *Alphonse Mucha. His Life and Art*, 1966). Publication of his other novels followed, including one that stood out from the rest, *Podivné lásky* (Strange Loves, 1988), a work that was almost purely based on fact. Mucha's works always drew on his own colourful life and he tended to use factual material. At the same time his novels were mysteries with exciting plots. This is true of *Podivné lásky*, which makes use of memoirs and letters to portray real people and events in Bohemia and France between 1939 and 1940. The principal character is Vitka Kaprálová, Mucha's first wife, a gifted composer who died prematurely. Many years after her death, the author goes back to her correspondence and surprisingly reveals a previously unknown side to her, particularly her strange love affairs with various men, including the composer Bohuslav Martinů.

At the end of the seventies and the beginning of the eighties the novelists Vladimír Páral and Ladislav Fuks (both → PROFILES and see pp. 111–112, 78–79,) went back, with some success, to their former style of writing. VLADIMÍR PÁRAL did so chiefly in his *Generální zázrak* (An Absolute Miracle, 1977) and LADISLAV FUKS in *Obraz Martina Blaskowitze* (The Picture of Martin Blaskowitz, 1980; an excerpt in English appears in *Panorama of Czech Literature*, 4 [1982], pp. 30–40) and more consistently in *Vévodkyně a kuchařka* (The Duchess and the Housekeeper, 1983; an excerpt in English appears also in *Panorama of Czech Literature*, 6 [1984], pp. 49–72). This extensive, coded novel could also be taken as a contemporary parable about the threat of the destruction of humanity.

In *Vévodkyně a kuchařka* and in other novels of the day, particularly in the novels of Milan Kundera and Pavel Kohout, there are obvious features of postmodernism. Postmodernism originated in North America and then appeared in West European culture sometime in the sixties. It was a reaction to various avant-garde trends, such as functionalism and surrealism, which claimed to be the only true modernism with a coherent system of stylistics supporting social progress. Questions were now being asked about the idea of progress. There were doubts about utopian, social engineering and about metaphysics and the idea of one constant valid truth. The leading theorist of postmodernism, Jean-François Lyotard, challenged the implications of "great stories" that unambiguously explain the meaning and course of history:

> "What was that happy ending to the story told by the Marxist Left? The removal of injustice. Well then, what is it we keep hearing from those countries where this scenario, stubbornly maintained by governments, is the official reality for millions of people? Thousands of insignificant little stories recently told in Solzhenitsyn's books and in the testimony of dissidents and visitors to these lands [. . .]. They make it possible for those who finally now listen to these stories and to pass them on, stories with no author's name that were being acted out in Prague in 1968 and in Budapest in 1956 at the same time as they were being invented." (1977)

The postmodernists see the contemporary world as multicultural, coming from various cultures and civilizations, not only from Europe and traditional European thinking, emphasizing plurality, acknowledging the uniqueness of the world and the phenomena that cannot be defined by a single, universal meaning. Much of this was foreshadowed in Czech literature, in the work and philosophy of the Čapek brothers and of the idiosyncratic writer and painter Josef Váchal. The idea of the "small events of history" has already been noted in regard to the works of Ota Filip, Jiří Šotola, Jiří Gruša (→ PROFILES and see pp. 87, 143, 163–164) and can be further traced in the essays of Milan Šimečka and others.

The decline of "great stories" also had an effect on style. Melody and harmony were not necessary, not even desirable. The postmodernists take their inspiration from the theories of the Austrian-British philosopher Wittgenstein, according to whom there are many language games, each with its own rules. These games interact. In this way diversity of style and play on words triumph. A typical technique is the quoting from and "re-writing" of older works, films and novels, so that two levels of text evolve. Mirrors, disguises and labyrinths are favourite devices connected with this technique. The postmodernists prefer their work to be comprehensible and entertaining rather than exclusive like the avant-garde but even here two levels of meaning have to be taken into account. Most works can have several interpretations; they can be read as exciting stories behind which there are more profound philosophical messages. They use the techniques of advertising, "pulp fiction", popular culture and sometimes even parody.

Postmodern authors revel in describing bizarre situations and, like in the famous films of David Lynch, sexual perversions. In prose writing, essay-type passages are part of fiction, reflections and interpretations of the plot interrupt the plot itself. The works of the Argentinian Jorge Luis Borges and the Italian Umberto Eco are examples of this trend. In Czech literature this is typical of the work of Václav Jamek, Vladimír Macura (see p. 216), Jiří Kratochvil, Daniela Hodrová and of Jan Křesadlo (see pp. 215–216), whose work is more on the level of light reading.

In the eighties, while still unknown as an author, JIŘÍ KRATOCHVIL (→ PROFILES) wrote two novels. One of them *Medvědí román* (Bear Novel) was finished in 1985 and was published in samizdat in 1988 and in Brno in 1990. The other novel *Uprostřed nocí zpěv* (Singing in the Middle of the Night) was published in Brno in 1992. Later *Avion* (Avion, 1995) completed the trilogy, which is one of the best prose works of recent times. Nevertheless, it took a long time for Kratochvil's work to reach the public and it met with difficulties on the way. His age makes him a sixties generation author but, caught up in normalization, he could publish only in literary journals. His first book of short prose was banned after 1968. As a more or less unknown author living in Moravia he was not even the centre of interest in unofficial culture. By the time he was first published officially in 1990, he was fifty.

The style of Jiří Kratochvil's novels is highly original. Metaphor and grandiose expressions are cheek by jowl with vulgarisms and Brno slang. The construction of the narrative is also unconventional. In fact it is the negation of any systematic narrative construction: the narrator embarks on an exciting story that he promptly interrupts, pointing out that it is pure fiction. He teases the reader, inveighs against the normal techniques of novel writing, quotes, parodies and gives cryptic hints about its meaning.

In *Uprostřed nocí zpěv* and *Avion* there are in fact two separate narrators and two narratives, although at first we do not realize this. Specific places, Brno streets and buildings and episodes very close to real events, such as the experiences of the author himself and other children of emigrés in the fifties, alternate unexpectedly with bizarre comedy and scenes of horrific brutality.

Such poetics in many ways closely resemble the "magic realism" of the Latin American novel, expecially the work of the famous Argentinian Jorge Luis Borges. Kratochvil shows great affinity with him in his use of spoofs and the favourite devices of *doppelgänger*, mirrors and photographs, but above all in the constant challenge of the meaning of it all. Everything is repeatedly weighed up, looked at from every possible point of view, questioned and left open to doubt.

DANIELA HODROVÁ (→ PROFILES) has much in common with Kratochvil. In the eighties she was even less well known than him, for her novels were not published either officially or in samizdat but remained in manuscript. Like him her first novel was not published till long after it was written. Although *Podobojí* (In Both Species) was mostly written between 1977 and 1978, it was published only in 1991 when the author was forty five. Excerpts also appeared in English in *Prairie Schooner*, 66, no. 44 (Winter 1992), pp. 36–45, and in *The Prague Review*, 2, no. 2 (Winter 1996), pp. 67–91. *Kukly* (polysemic title: Pupae/Masks/Puppets), written between 1981 and 1983, was also published in 1991. Immediately afterwards in 1992 *Théta* (Theta),[109] the last novel forming a kind of trilogy, was published. By now, at the end of the eighties, the gap between the writing of the novel and publication was very much shorter.

Daniela Hodrová is also a writer whose inspiration is learned and theoretical. Like Kratochvil she plans out her work with precision, she writes essays on literature and is a professional literary researcher specializing in the theory of the novel. This duality is shared with her contemporaries Sylvie Richterová (see p. 164) and Vladimír Macura (see pp. 179, and 216). It is therefore not surprising that her novels are very sophisticated. Every one is created from an intricate network of allusions, repetitions, variations and recapitulations. The narrative keeps changing perspective; sometimes it focuses on a narrow horizon of perception, at other times an omniscient narrator with knowledge of the future emerges. Here fantasy and the supernatural take over. Puppets and twins are recurrent themes; men change into animals and, from beyond the grave, the dead enter the world of the living. At the end of the novel *Théta*, Hodrová herself comes into the story, both as a character and as the author. In this way, the pendulum swinging between fantasy and realism in the novel comes to a full stop.

If Kratochvil turns Brno into a city of magic as well as a real city, Daniela Hodrová does the same for the Prague districts Vinohrady and Žižkov. Prague itself is "a precarious, seductive, disturbing place". Her style is the epitome of doubt and uncertainty. The meaning of the events related is consistently rendered ambiguous as the novel proceeds. The accepted picture of modern Czech history, the Nazi occupation, the Prague Spring, normalization and the return to a free society, is challenged, although at first sight these events are not apparently central to the novel.[110]

Officially published prose in the second half of the eighties also lagged behind unofficial prose in importance. Of course some interesting works were produced by novelists of the middle and younger generations, in particular the second of the two novellas within the single book *Duely* (Duels, 1988) by ANTONÍN BAJAJA, the novels *Půlnoční běžci* (Midnight Runners, 1986) by ZDENĚK ZAPLETAL and *Zdi tvé* (Your Walls, 1988) by MICHAEL TŘEŠTÍK. In them the same questions are raised about personal responsibility, moral identity and life and death as in the novels of samizdat and authors in exile. Another remarkable work, also published belatedly, was ALEXANDRA BERKOVÁ'S first book, *Knížka s červeným obalem* (The Little Book with the Red Cover, 1986).[111] At the end of the story *Velké šuby-duby* (The Big Rave), the initiated might recognize the allusion to Josef Škvorecký's *Zbabělci* (see p. 51) and its recurring themes and famous ending.

> "The zootsuiters were dancing in front of the bandstand, kids I liked and whom I'd be leaving within the next few days since I'd be going away, going somewhere or other again, so I played for them and I thought about the same things I'd always thought about, about girls and about jazz and about that girl I was going to meet in Prague."[112] (Josef Škvorecký)

> " . . . I'm thinking about the boy I'm going to meet in Prague, damn, where did I read that?"[113] (Alexandra Berková)

This was a greeting across the ocean to the exile in Toronto, a sign that official and unofficial literature were once more becoming closer.

3. Drama and the Theatre

In the late seventies[114] two outstanding dramatists aged about thirty, Karel Steigerwald and Daniela Fischerová, first came into the grey area on the fringe of official and unofficial culture. Understandably, they had more in common with fringe and experimental theatre than with traditional theatre. The director Ivan Rajmont staged Steigerwald's plays, *Dobové tance* (Period Dancing) in 1980 and *Foxtrot* (Foxtrot) in 1982, in the regional theatre in Ústí nad Labem in North Bohemia but two of his other plays had to wait till 1988 for their first performances. Director Luboš Pistorius even brought DANIELA FISCHEROVÁ and her play *Hodina mezi psem a vlkem* (The Small Hours, in English as *Dog and Wolf*, translated by A. G. Brain [Alice and Gerald Turner], in *Czech Plays*, 1994, pp. 141–224) to the Prague *Realistické divadlo* (Realistic Theatre) but it had to be taken off after four performances and the author did not see her works performed for another seven years. *Hodina mezi psem a vlkem* is set in mediaeval France. Its subject is the life of the vagabond poet François Villon. The subject would not in itself have been an obstacle if the trial of Villon had not been portrayed as the struggle with the authorities of a man striving for freedom, and had not been patently a reference to the present day. Later at the end of the eighties, in "*Ecce Constantia!*" ("Ecce Constantia!"), a play about the Middle Ages, PAVEL KOHOUT used a similar kind of updating by introducing reporters and contemporary mass media. Again the director was Luboš Pistorius with Jitka Pistoriusová in the television production of 1992.

Fischerová also chose historical subjects for other plays in which she developed the themes of responsibility, honour and conformity, as in Faust's pact with the devil in *Báj* (The Myth), which had its first performance in 1987. There are also "devilish" themes in the screenplay of *Vlčí bouda* (The Wolf's Lair), which was made into a film by Věra Chytilová.[115] In comparison, KAREL STEIGERWALD is more realistic, less enigmatically allegorical, more like situation comedy or farce. Nevertheless, *Dobové tance*, a play in which the action is set in the Czech countryside after the defeat of the 1848 revolution directed against Austrian feudal absolutism, is not concerned with historical accuracy. It is a typical modern dispute. As in N. V. Gogol's *The Government Inspector*, the play begins with the arrival of a high official from the capital. Everything in the play, the behaviour of the nervous "patriots", pouring scorn on their own pasts, ingratiating themselves with the new masters, incriminating everyone else while trying to remain uninvolved and defending their stance on moral grounds, is reminiscent of the tragically comic confrontations of normalization. In a wider sense it is an eternally topical theme. The characters talk to try to cover up the real issues and, in so doing, unwittingly give everything away.[116] Steigerwald's use of this technique brings him very close to Václav Havel in his dialogues, the councillors remind one of Brewmaster in *Audience* (see pp. 174–175). In the same way Fischerova's "pact with the devil" reminds one of Havel's *Pokoušení* (Temptation, see pp. 134–135). This shows how close both dramatists were to samizdat literature.

Many writers for the studio theatres, like Ivan Vyskočil, Jan Schmid and

Arnošt Goldflam (see pp. 99–100, 176–178), who have already been mentioned, adopted the same approach. *Takový beznadějný případ* (Such a Hopeless Case), by Vyskočil's text-appeal collaborator Přemysl Rut, was staged by a group of the author's friends in 1986 in a small dramatic club in Prague. It enlivened the Czech variety of absurd drama by adding a touch of humour. The chief character, the simpleton Hejhula, has lost his home, his memory and his past and is trying to regain them. In his pocket he finds a key which he tries in the doors of various houses to no avail. He comes to a door marked Veřejná bezpečnost (Public Security, i.e. Communist police) and, trusting naïvely, thinks he has found safety and security. However, the police arrest him and put him in a cell . . . In this way the author points out the falsehoods on which the regime is based. At the same time it raises a more general problem which constantly recurs in every human society: the difference between the names given to things and what they actually stand for.

Tomáš Vorel and Otakar Schmidt Štětináč were authors of the eighties who made a contribution to the theatre. They were connected with the Prague theatre *Sklep* (The Cellar) and appeared in the 1989 film *Pražská pětka* (The Prague Five) with other theatre companies. Their crazy humour has the characteristics of post-modernism. In 1985 Petr Lébl, an outstanding theatrical director of the nineties, had his first production, an adaptation of Kurt Vonnegut's *Slapstick* (in Czech *Groteska*) staged by the Dramatic Society of the Prague Transport Company. Jan Antonín Pitínský began in the Brno Amateur Dramatic Club and after 1989 he was a co-founder of the Brno theatre and the cultural centre *Kabinet múz* (The Chamber of Muses). He found fame with his original play *Matka* (Mother, 1988) in which he linked motifs from the anti-Nazi play by Karel Čapek (in English *The Mother*, 1939) and the classic socialist-realist novel of the same name by Soviet writer Maxim Gorky. In the nineties he also published tongue-in-cheek novels that were as crazy and offbeat as the works of the *Sklep* theatre and his own pieces for the theatre.

News of Gorbachev's reforms in the second half of the eighties reached Czechoslovakia only as distant echoes. "Perestroika" in Czechoslovakia could be approprately characterized in the words of Voskovec and Werich's satiric song from the thirties paraphrasing Lenin, "one step forward, two steps back". In the period before November 1989, writers who, as young writers in the seventies, had become established in the arts during normalization obtained key politico-cultural posts. The poet Michal Černík became president of the Writers' Union in place of Ivan Skála, the poet Jaroslav Čejka replaced Miroslav Müller as the head of the Culture Department in the Central Committee of the Czechoslovak Communist Party, and a third official poet, Karel Sýs, became the editor in chief of the weekly literary paper *Kmen* (Stem). But in spite of that (or rather precisely because of that) literature took longer than other branches of the arts to become free.

Slovak writers were noticeably better off in this respect. In the later eighties, the review *Romboid* (Rhomboid) frequently managed to avoid the restrictions imposed by normalization, particularly in *Dotyky* (Contacts), a supplement for young writers that finally emerged as an independent journal. From Slovakia there were also rumours that more incisive criticism was being allowed. At the writers' conference, the poet and translator Lubomír Feldek said openly, "For eighteen years now our literature has been fighting to have some connection with freedom of conscience." And even before November 1989 the dissident Dominik Tatarka began publishing in the literary review *Slovenské pohľady* (The Slovak View).

In Bohemia and Moravia, on the other hand, the most those claiming to be official critics would admit, even at their most indulgent, was that the novels of the exile Milan Kundera might have a place in the second stream of Czech literature. Places in the "main stream" were reserved for officially permitted and acclaimed authors. In 1989 Jiří Hájek was still maintaining that barely a dozen names had disappeared from literature (that is, state-permitted literature) and of these "only a few were of any worth". At that time, even within the Writers' Union, there were some reformers like Petr Prouza and Ondřej Neff who obviously had contacts with exile literature. Milan Jungmann took issue with Hájek's disparaging comments and the policy of "faint praise" in the samizdat monthly *Lidové noviny* (The People's Paper) which had a much wider circulation:

> "By now the destructiveness of normalizing politics in the arts is obvious to all who are not blinded by fanaticism [. . .]. Removing the ideology that chases people of a different persuasion to the 'fringes of society' is the only solution to the problem of integrating Czech literature and restoring true artistic values."[117]

At the end of the eighties, student journals, such as Martin Mejstřík's *Kavárna* (Coffee House) and Monika Pajerová's *Situace* (Situation), which had more in common with samizdat than with the official line, played an important part. The meetings of the Brno debating club, *Otevřený dialog* (Open Dialog), and the re-establishment of the Pen Club in Prague, contributed to the rapprochement of official and unofficial culture between 1988 and 1989. The review *Most* (The Bridge), with its editors Milan Uhde, Petr Král and Jiří Gruša, and other reviews were also a contributory factor. Uhde wrote in the foreword:

> "Most, the bridge on which we meet, is metaphorical. It is the review that tries to reach beyond barriers, of which there are quite a few, no matter who has erected them. There are barriers between those who left Czechoslovakia and those who stayed, between those who could not publish in Czechoslovakia and those who could; barriers between those who died and were almost or completely forgotten and those who long to restore broken contacts . . . "[118]

Gradually even officially approved writers came to be publicly criticised. For example, in March 1989 in the Brno daily *Rovnost* (Equality), Jiří Trávníček published a criticism of the book of poetry *Havran nepřilétá s květinou* (The Raven Does Not Fly with Flowers) by the hitherto untouchable Ivan Skála. The very title of Trávníček's review, *Vypelichaný havran* (The Moulting Raven), contained a wealth of meaning.[119] In September 1989, the first lecture by the previously banned literary scholar Jiří Brabec took place in a Prague youth club. Brabec refuted the dubious theory of the "main stream" and its gradual spreading of allegedly "peripheral phenomena". He claimed that all authors who wrote in Czech belonged to one Czech literature regardless of anything else. At the same time he warned against admiring everything that had been banned in previous years; that would constitute the same ideological attitude, only in reverse.

4. Poets and Songwriters

Towards the end of the eighties the main change in official literature once again took place in the peripheral "grey area". Apart from the theatre, it came chiefly from the rise of young poets who were not followers of the poetics of Karel Sýs, Jiří Žáček and Michal Černík (see pp. 142–143) and who felt in general that the position of social conformity of these writers was not for them. They were joined by some who had come late to the arts, like JIŘÍ RULF with his down-to-earth approach, and his exact opposite, the imaginative MICHAL AJVAZ. Ajvaz is also a novelist of note whose 1993 novel *Druhé město* (The Second City)[120] may be ranked beside Kratochvil and Hodrová. He is also the author of scholarly essays on philosophy. JOSEF ŠIMON, who once shared Sýs's poetics, came very close to them in his 1988 collection *Vyvolávač* (The Town Crier), which contained the poem *(. . . hranice . . .)* [(. . . pyre . . .)] inspired by the death of Jan Palach (see p. 122).

An important centre for the development of the arts in the eighties was the Prague club *Rubín* (Ruby) where a regular programme of discussions and recitations called *Zelené peří* (Green Feathers), organized by Mirek Kovařík, took place. Kovařík also organized similar literary evenings outside Prague. This programme of discussions and recitations, like other gatherings in theatres and factory clubs, was in fact replacing the exchange of ideas and polemics in journals. *Zelené peří* was also the title of an anthology by young authors (1987) that Kovařík had introduced in his programme. Anthologies and almanacs founded in the seventies (such as the *Omega* series published by the publishing house *Mladá fronta*) were now also taking the place of first works in book form.

Petr A. Bílek called the young writers of the eighties "the generation of lonely runners".[121] In this generation there were several talented writers of verse, such as the harsh and completely unsentimental SVATAVA ANTOŠOVÁ. She began writing in the North Bohemian Czech underground journal *Pako* (The Loony). She also wrote for the rock group *Mimo zákon* (Outside the Law) and for other groups. The title of her second book of poetry, *Ta ženská musí být opilá!* (The Woman Must Be Drunk!, 1990), is typical. Another emancipated young woman, SYLVA FISCHEROVÁ, caused a sensation with her first work *Chvění závodních koní* (The Tremor of Race Horses) in 1986.[122] It is mainly characterized by a tendency towards intellectualism and complicated imagery. IVO ŠMOLDAS, who like Fischerová is also from Olomouc, has already been mentioned. In *Zimní srst* (Winter Coat, 1988), he used concentrated František Halas-like language; nouns and verbs stand on their own without ornamentation and with practically no adjectives or adverbs. Grey and black, suitable for expressing feelings of *angst*, are the prevailing colours. In *Názorný přírodopis tajnokřídlých* (The Natural History of the Crypto-wing Animals, 1989), which appears on the surface to be a scientific textbook of zoology, the slightly older MIROSLAV HUPTYCH goes deeply into a limited range of ideas. The author was inspired by the poetic technique of Jiří Kolář (→ PROFILES) and his graphic work: he accompanied his verse with his own collages. Huptych and Kolář share the same interest in ethics:

Bejvávalo
že když si smrt brousila kosu
básník jí plival do ksichtu
nikoliv na brousek

Time was
when death sharpened his scythe
the poet would spit in his face
not on the whetstone

"The lonely runners" stressed the links between the ethics of writing and the ethics of living. For them, intellect, introspection and existentialist questions were more important than metaphor, subtlety and facile melody. This was in fact a parallel with the reaction of the poets concentrating on the issues of human existence, like František Halas, Vladimír Holan and Jan Zahradníček, to the avant-garde at the end of the twenties. Language: complex sound sequences, plays on words, neologisms and tongue twisters, was also of prime importance in LUBOMÍR KASAL's first work *Dosudby* (Entering Fate, 1989). This unconventional style, where the author attacks the reader, somewhat like Ivan Diviš's, is a revolt against the established norms of behaviour: "Je všední den / hlasitě mlčíme / mlčenlivě hlasujeme / proces demokratizace proběhne i kdyby byli všichni proti / A nejdůležitější je stát oběma nohama na zemi"[123] (It is a week-day / we are loudly silent / we vote silently / the process of democratization will go ahead even if all are against it / but the most important thing is to keep both feet on the ground). The quotation comes from a poem *Televizní noviny* (Television News) in *Dosudby*.

The links with unofficial culture in the works of this generation were now quite clear. This is particularly true of songwriters, rock groups like the Brno groups of Petr Váša, and folk singers. Folk music was related to movements concerned with nature and basic moral principles. Wabi Daněk and Jiří Žalman Lohonka were the foremost folk authors. Songwriters besides the older Vladimír Merta were Jan Burian, Jaromír Nohavica, Václav Koubek, Jim Čert and Dagmar Voňková, who was also inspired by folklore, and there were some others.[124]

Radostná nálada před chvíli na mě padla
a zatím ne a ne mě opustit.
Jdu s myslí mrtvoly, co ještě nevychladla,
a šťastným smíchem ruším noční klid.

Plazím se ulicí jako šnek po obrně,
kterej už navíc není nejmladší,
a je mi veselo tak jako chcíplý srně,
když na řeznickým válu skotačí.

Já bych snad ani nedoved
vypadat sklesle v elektrickým křesle.
Vždyť život je tak růžovej!
Jak čerstvě vyvražděný jesle.

A joyful mood came over me a short while ago
and now will not leave me.
I go with the thought of a dead body, still not cold,
with happy laughter I disturb the peace of the night.

I crawl along the street like a paralysed snail
that is no longer very young,
and I am as happy as a dead deer,
romping about on the butcher's block.

Perhaps I would not even
seem depressed in the electric chair.
After all life is as rosy!
As freshly slaughtered infants.

(Růžovej život [A Life of Roses])[125]

Before November 1989 people had begun to recover their self-respect. Under Gorbachev, the Czechoslovak Communist regime no longer had such strong support from the other "fraternal lands" and the Soviet Union and had begun to lose faith in itself. In December 1987, again only a few dozen people turned out on Prague's Old Town Square to demonstrate on the Day of Human Rights. The following year, however, things changed. In March 1988, a savage attack on a peaceful religious gathering in Bratislava caused an outrage. Nearly half a million people took part in a campaign for religious freedom.[126] The way was being prepared for the canonization of Anežka Česká (Agnes of Bohemia), a princess from the royal house of the Przemyslids in the 13th century, and a follower of St Francis of Assisi.

Besides *Charter 77* there were other civic associations demanding dialogue with representatives of the authorities, and freedom for all. An *Independent Peace Association* and *A Movement for Civic Freedom* were founded and *A Society for a More Cheerful Present* organized regular runs through the Political Prisoners Avenue in Prague (the name of the avenue, of course, commemorated the victims of the Nazi regime, not the Communist one) and an outing to a village whose name was Bezpráví (Injustice). Mass demonstrations began in Prague in August and October 1988 and continued with the "Palach week" (Jan Palach see p. 122) in January 1989, culminating in a huge, mainly student, demonstration which took place on 17 November 1989, marking the anniversary of the 17 of November

1939.[127] The days of the "Velvet Revolution"[128] are counted among the great events of Czech history, like the autumn of 1938 and August 1968. Unlike them, however, they did not end in the defeat of democracy but in its victory.

The Nineties and the Early Twenty-First Century

"We did not even curse, and from the closed world where an infelicitous word could have you hunted down or even arrested, we have escaped into a world where words have lost their power and their magic."

(Milan Jungmann, 1996)[1]

Literary Life without Barriers

1. Change of Function

Our judgment of contemporary literature can only be limited. One article on contemporary literature says that exploring it is like walking on a fresh lava field; its appearance keeps changing and only occasionally do we notice that it is moving and that anyone entering it is in danger of getting burned. Indeed, it is alive and knows no restraints. It is therefore hard to label, define or categorize.

The fact remains that the 1989 revolution brought not just political, social and economic change, it brought to an end a whole era of Czech culture and literature. The changes caused by the democratic revolution and the liberalization of society swept away the hierarchy which had been established by force and also got rid of the division of literature into official and unofficial. In the nineties, official, samizdat and exile literature all came together in a single stream, no matter how much they retained, for a time, their own characteristics. Now they were all basically equal as regards the business of communication.

Interference and banning for political reasons have disappeared, censorship is gone and the state no longer exercises control over the arts as it did in various forms almost constantly from the end of the thirties. Since 1989 literary life has been able to develop without artificially created barriers. The Union of Czech Writers (Svaz českých spisovatelů) with its nonsensical dogma of "Socialist Realism", its horde of paid officials and untouchable "national" and "honoured" artists, has been abolished. The Council of Writers (Obec spisovatelů), a professional organization bringing together authors of differing convictions or artistic leanings, has been formed. There are now also other writers' associations: PEN, whose activities were previously severely restricted, groups of writers drawn together by their areas of interest, for example non-fiction, science fiction, writers from the same region, those of the same political persuasion. People compromised by having been servants of the regime have given up leading posts in publishing houses, the Ministry of Culture and elsewhere. Firms that had published books and journals in exile either transferred their activities to the homeland or ceased functioning. For instance, Karel Jadrný's publishing house *Arkýř* (Oriel) now sometimes brings out books in cooperation with publishers at home, *Listy* (Gazette) is currently a political and cultural periodical, edited in Olomouc. Other publishing houses, such as *Sixty-Eight Publishers*, *Index* and the review *Svědectví* (Testimony), closed down voluntarily, but a few others continued to function abroad in suitable circumstances as centres of Czech national culture. One of the best-known publishers in exile, Daniel Strož, surprisingly changed direction and began publishing works by eminent poets of the Communist regime, for example Florian and Sýs, because he argued that they could no longer find publishers in the new circumstances. Yet hundreds of new publishing houses started up. Early in the 1990s these, just like existing publishing houses, overwhelmed readers with huge numbers of hitherto banned books, from living writers like Ludvík Vaculík, Václav Havel, Josef Škvorecký and previously banned classic authors, now deceased, such as Jakub Deml, Jaroslav Durych, Ferdinand Peroutka, Egon Hostovský, to the adventure novels of Jaroslav Foglar and the sentimental stories of Vlasta Javořická. There was also an ever-widening range of popular, unpretentious literature of no great value. Quite a few hitherto "serious" or "official" authors, such as Vladimír Páral, Josef Frais and Zdena Frýbová, have written works that fall into this category.

Of course the vast majority of the new publishers survived long enough to publish only a few works. Unable to compete in the market, several established publishing houses, *Odeon* and *Československý spisovatel* (Czechoslovak Writers' Publishing House), for example, also closed. Some of the new firms that came into being in the nineties publishing good Czech literature also later stopped publishing. They included *Pražská imaginace* (Prague Imagination), originally a samizdat publication for the benefit of Bohumil Hrabal and his circle, which ceased publishing in the latter half of the nineties. *Atlantis*, *Host* (Guest) and *Petrov* in Brno,[2] *Votobia* in Olomouc and in Prague *Torst*, *Argo*, *Akropolis*, *Paseka*,[3] the *Nakladatelství Lidové noviny* (The People's Paper Publishers), *Hynek* and *Triáda* were founded since the fall of Communism.

Literary and arts reviews have been shaken up in the same way. The official organ of the Writers' Union *Literární měsíčník* (Literary Monthly) and the political and cultural weekly *Tvorba* (Creations) disappeared shortly after the fall of Communism. *Kritický sborník*, *Prostor* (Space), *Revolver Revue*, *Host*, *Proglas* (the Brno section of *Střední Evropa* and other publications emerged from the samizdat underground. The literary weekly *Kmen* (Stem, see p. 192), edited by Karel Sýs under Communism, got rid of its compromised boss, reorganized itself and changed its name to *Tvar* (Form). Since 1994 it has been coming out fortnightly and has mostly been edited by Lubor Kasal. The surrealist review *Analogon* was resurrected. Its contributors include the theoretician and poet Alena Nádvorníková, the film director and graphic artist Jan Švankmajer and some much younger people. Also revived was the weekly *Literární noviny* (Literary News, see p. 57), first temporarily as a supplement to the daily *Lidové noviny* (The People's Paper), with its former editor and staff, including Ludvík Vaculík, Sergej Machonin, Milan Jungmann and Vladimír Karfík. However, neither they nor any of the other journals came anywhere near achieving the circulation and eminence they had in the sixties.

A publication that was of great importance for young writers in the early nineties was *Iniciály* (Initials), "a journal for new authors", but it closed down in 1994. In the later nineties its place was taken in Brno by *Host*, which included among its contributors Miroslav Balaštík, Jiří Trávníček, Tomáš Reichel, M. J. Stöhr and others, in Zlín by *Psí víno* (Woodbine) and in Vendryně near Třinec by *Weles*, a Moravian-Silesian publication. *Kritický sborník*, which had been edited by Karel Palek after the death of Jan Lopatka, closed down at the end of the nineties, but to a certain extent it was replaced by the Olomouc periodical *Aluze* (Allusion), edited from 1996 by Jiří Hrabal, which was similar in content with articles on aesthetics and philosophy that bordered on literature. Individual groups and periodicals continued to support different ideas as in the controversy between *Tvar*, represented by Pavel Janoušek and Vladimír Novotný, and Michael Špirit of the *Kritická Příloha Revolver Revue* (Critical Supplement of Revolver Revue), which had first appeared in 1995 and which espoused the radical views of Jan Lopatka (see p. 141). Petr Borkovec, Jan Jandourek, Martin C. Putna and other authors interested in religious matters affiliated to the important "Christian cultural review" *Souvislosti* (Context) founded in 1990. In contrast, fans of cyber punk, virtual reality and science fiction have had their magazine *Živel* (Element) since 1995. The periodical *Labyrint* (Labyrinth), originally founded to give information about the book market, changed to become a monthly and eventually an annual publication with extracts from Czech and world literature, essays, articles and interviews.

Literary prizes play an important part in the cultural life of the country, which is now much more varied than formerly. Besides the state prizes for original work and for translation awarded by the Ministry of Culture on the recommendation of an independent jury, there are two other important literary prizes: the Jaroslav Seifert Prize, originally awarded in exile, and the Magnesia Litera Prize. The Jiří Orten Prize is for young writers. For science fiction writers there is the Mlok Karla Čapka Prize (Karel Čapek's Newt Prize), for translators there is the Josef Jungmann Prize,[4] for authors with Prague connections the František Langer Prize, for journalists the Ferdinand Peroutka. The most recent prize for poets is the Jan Skácel Prize.

Criticism has a place in the journals already mentioned and in other publications. It figures prominently in the political weeklies *Respekt* (Respect) and *Týden* (A Week), less so in the daily papers, *Mladá Fronta Dnes* (Frontline Youth Today) with its supplement *Kavárna* (Café), *Lidové noviny* with *Orientace* (The Way to Go) and *Právo* (Rights) with its cultural supplement *Salon*. Besides the older generation of critics, including Josef Vohryzek, Milan Jungmann, Aleš Haman, who again became active in the arts after a period of enforced silence, there were also literary critics now in middle age, such as Vladimír Novotný, Vladimír Just, Jan Lukeš, Milan Exner and Pavel Janoušek. The younger generation was also producing notable personalities; in poetry criticism, authors, such as Jiří Trávníček, Petr A. Bílek, Miroslav Balaštík, Jan Wiendl, and in prose, critics, such as Pavel Janáček, Jiří Peňás and others.

Literary history also began to come to life again. Bibliographies of samizdat and exile literature, critical editions with commentaries, analytical studies and monographs on various authors are being published and at last serious specialist works have begun to appear, making possible an overview of the direction taken by literature in the last decade. An example is *Slovník české prózy 1945–1994* (Dictionary of Czech Prose 1945–1994), edited by Blahoslav Dokoupil and Miroslav Zelinský, published in Brno in 1994. Zdeněk Kožmín and Jiří Trávníček, also from Brno, compiled a history of postwar poetry, *Na tvrdém loži z psího vína* (On a Hard Bed Made of Woodbine, 1998). Dokoupil also edited *Slovník českých literárních časopisů* (Dictionary of Czech Literary Periodicals) covering the period 1945–2000, published in 2002, a reference book offering a valuable insight into the cultural life of the last half-century. *Slovník českých spisovatelů od roku 1945* (Dictionary of Czech Authors from 1945, Part I 1995, Part II 1998) is the work of the Institute of Czech Literature of the Academy of Sciences under the direction of Pavel Janoušek. An extensive history of Czech literature since the Second World War is being prepared by basically the same editorial group with some additional contributors.

Similar changes have also taken place in the theatre, film, television and other media. At last the banned dramatists Topol, Kohout (→ PROFILES), Havel (→ PROFILES), Uhde, Pavlíček (see p. 175) and others have returned to the Czech stage, but reduced state subsidies have threatened the continued existence of some theatres or have even led to the closure of others, like the resurrected *Divadlo za branou* (Theatre beyond the Gate; see p. 102). Postmodernism and the new poetics have made considerable inroads into the life of the theatre. The radical, naïve and at the same time grotesque plays of J. A. Pitinský, the theatre *Sklep* (The Cellar, see p. 192), the director Petr Lébl, who worked in the Prague *Divadlo Na zábradlí* (The Theatre on the Balustrade) till his untimely death, are all examples of this trend. Cultural contacts with the rest of the world were eagerly renewed and there was an exchange of information of all kinds. Among the huge amount of literature in translation in all fields there are works by authors who, like Vladimir Nabokov, Czesław Miłosz, the American beatniks and the complete works of Franz Kafka, had scarcely ever, or had never before been published. Paradoxically, at the same time, after the break-up of Czechoslovakia at the end of 1992 and its division into the Czech and Slovak Republics, contact was lost with the literature closest to home, Slovakian, with which Czech literature had had not only common historical roots but also two centuries of common cultural development. In Slovakia the changed situation led to the splitting up of the cultural scene and the association of authors. Writers with nationalistic tendencies formed the Association of Slovakian Writers (Spolok slovenských spisovateľov) that advocated "the total national and state sovereignty of Slovakia"; authors with more democratic views formed the Association of Writers' Organizations in Slovakia (Asociácia organizácií spisovateľov Slovenska).

The November 1989 revolution brought the return of traditional intellectual thinking and a flood of new ideas. It resulted in a revival of interest in spiritual matters and in Christianity. Interest in German and Jewish literature in the Czech lands, in Franz Kafka, Max Brod, Gustav Meyrink, Jiří/Georg Mordechai Langer and many others, reawakened. Lenka Reinerová/Reiner, born in 1916, is probably the last important author in Prague still alive, writing in German and remembering E. E. Kisch and other famous people.

Feminism came in slowly from the West. The foundation, *Gender Studies*, was established under the patronage of Jiřina Šiklová in 1991. Two years later in Bratislava the Czecho-Slovak feminist review *Aspekt* started up. It also started publishing books and lasted from 1993 till 2004. Among the leading literary figures embracing feminism are Eva Kalivodová-Věšínová, Blanka Čapková-Knotková and Libuše Heczková. Rather than some aggressive, provocative feminist texts, what is particularly stimulating about Czech feminism is a characteristic "feminine way of thinking", which studies the identity of woman and its role in the arts and society. It is in this respect that the novels of LIBUŠE MONÍKOVÁ are pioneering. She is a Czech who went to West Germany in the seventies and there won recognition with her novels and essays. The heroine in her first work *Eine Schädigung* (A Damaging Affair), published in German in 1981, is a woman in an unnamed totalitarian state. *Treibeis* (Drifting Ice, in German, 1992, published in Czech in 2001) contrasts the worlds of two Czech immigrants, an ageing man and a young girl.[5] The work of Milena Jesenská, an essayist and journalist between the wars, was also highlighted through feminism. Her work and the events of her life, her relationship with Franz Kafka, her activities in the resistance during the Nazi occupation and her death in a concentration camp, are of exceptional interest world-wide.[6]

The drawback to the liberalization of life in Czech society is the commercialization of the whole business of culture especially by the private media which often relegate worthwhile art to the periphery of public interest. The author LUBOMÍR MARTÍNEK, who went into exile and had experience of a number of countries, said in the review *Host* in 2001 after his return to the Czech lands, "I outlived Communism but I won't outlive [the popular crooner] Karel Gott. Even if I do survive him, his songs will still be played."[7] Pulp literature capitalizes on celebrities, such as actors, on erotica and sex, on suspense and fantasy. Science fiction is expanding at an extraordinary rate. Ondřej Neff, Josef Pecinovský and Vilma Kadečková specialize in this field. Fantasy writing following in the footsteps of the English novels of J. R. R. Tolkien and the Polish of Andrzej Sapkowski is expanding at an even greater rate. Science fiction has its specialist magazine *Ikarie* (Ikaria).

At the same time, however, there are critical voices raised against "postmodernism" seen superficially as mass consumerism. In 1997 JOLANA POLÁKOVÁ, for example, the author of the philosophical essay *Perspektiva naděje* (The Future of Hope) in *Tvar* stressed the importance of "an independent, responsible attitude to developments in the world" and "the defensive reaction of those who, raised as vigorous, ambitious Europeans, have no intention of giving up the pursuit of material well-being for transcendental values".[8] Many others have expressed the same views. Of these let us just mention JIŘÍ KRUPIČKA, one of the oldest natural scientists living in exile in Canada. In a book of contemplative essays entitled *Renesance rozumu* (The Rebirth of Reason, 1994) and in his following works he advocates unity based on a firmer footing than simply the advantage of the individual and the free market. The free market of ideas, formed on the lines of the free market in goods is, in his opinion, sure to lead to the destruction of democratic society. Not very many people listen to these exhortations.

So the freedom that several generations of Czech writers longed for had arrived. With it came cultural chaos; books from various periods and of different merit appeared on the market, with samizdat and exile publications and works that had been lying in drawers as manuscripts for ten years. Pavel Janoušek described this anarchy: "The old criteria no longer apply and as yet there are no new ones" (*Tvar*, 1990).[9]

Looking back after a few years it is obvious that literature has changed its function. The American author Philip Roth said in the eighties that in the West everything was allowed but nothing mattered. On the other hand in the East nothing was allowed and everything mattered.[10] So Czech literature had – even when banned and repressed, perhaps for that very reason – wide social impact. Writers and what they wrote took the place of much in the life of the people; literature, films and the theatre had a political and aesthetic function, fulfilling the roles that, since the nineties, have been taken over by various social institutions. One of the well-known persecuted Hungarian novelists, György Konrád, expressed exactly this when he wrote that man can no longer be a great evangelist nor a great heretic. Political dissent is no longer played out in literature. Criticism finds its place in parliament or in the press, it no longer needs to take place covertly in the theatre. According to Konrád the artist feels he has gone out of fashion. The state does not need him and at the moment the market cannot support him financially.

This situation is certainly also a result of the loss of the prestige that poetry and literature had enjoyed from the time of Romanticism till after the avant-garde movement. This has already been mentioned in the chapter on the sixties. The Central and Eastern European lands in the Soviet bloc preserved the special elite role of literature. In 1968–1969 Czech writers and journalists were the chief spokesmen for political reform. That non-literary role was confirmed by the persecution that followed, the rise of the dissident movement and samizdat works. After 1989, however, writers suddenly found that their profession was no longer regarded as special. According to Miroslav Petříček, a politically free society is a "media marketplace", and in the market in ideas and information, where the yardstick is success, writers have lost their elite position. Readers' interest in Czech literature reached its peak in the early nineties and has now sharply declined. Print runs of hundreds of thousands of copies of worthwhile Czech literature are remembered with nostalgia and books of literary value often have to be sold off cheaply.

So the idea that the Czech nation was unusually culturally mature has now been replaced by the actual state of affairs. Sophisticated art interests only a minority of the public and there is a much greater response to mass popular culture. Inferior and doubtful values are disseminated in picture magazines, by private and sometimes even public service television. However, the decline in interest in literature is also connected with the rise of new media, videos, computers, the internet, DVDs, all of which are based on the visual or audio-visual senses. Gradually the tradition of concentrating and taking time over reading, which was an essential part of European culture, is being lost.

> "Since the National Revival, Czech literature has been a literature with an aim and a mission. Over time, these changed only marginally. Literature has had to function as a 'national institution', it has been ordered to grow and expand to the greater honour and glory of the nation, it has had to serve various ideologies and, subject to almost military discipline, it has had to reflect reality and portray society until for a time it became a substitute for political opposition [. . .]. But after November 1989, an absolutely extraordinary situation arose in the relationship of society to writers and literature. Writers in general ceased being considered 'the conscience of the nation', a notion that suddenly sounds false and ludicrous. If some writers again find themselves at the centre of a reform movement, the nation will now want to see them in terms of reasonable politicians and not as writers of absurd dramas. The profession of writer has very rapidly fallen to the lowest rung of the social ladder. Never has Czech literature been as free as it is today. But it has remained only literature and it has only a handful of the most faithful readers [. . .]. Books have ceased to be regarded as holy 'cult' objects and are now merely goods . . . " (*Literární noviny*, 1992)[11]

That is how in 1992 the novelist and essayist Jiří Kratochvil summed up the situation of Czech literature. At the same time, however, he pointed out that the advancing chaos did not need to be confusion, it could mean the search for new opportunities. According to Kratochvil a new group of writers, different both from the former grey area writers and from the former opposition writers, was coming to the fore. It was the youngest of the new writers and some middle-aged authors who were refuting the concept of the author as spokesman for non-literary ideas and coming back, in the spirit of postmodernism in a wider sense, to literature as fiction. At the same time, using coarse language without circumlocution and the film techniques of intercutting shots taken from different angles, they varied the perception and interpretation of events. More than the sixties generation, they were even more deeply aware that there is no general criterion of value that can be applied without exception.

This analysis aptly identified the change in function of Czech literature in recent years. Of course its vehemence meant that it was one-sided, as Milan Jungmann pointed out when he argued in reaction that social and political commitment in literature was not exclusively a Czech national curse, for it has existed, and currently exists, in the literature of all nations. Therefore it is nothing artificial or superficial. Both the aesthetic and non-aesthetic functions are part of literature and need not be in conflict. According to Jungmann even a highly individualistic literary work, based on the principle of art for art's sake, can gain political importance in particular circumstances.

In the nineties Czech poetry and prose moved in both these directions, either stressing experimentation or communicativeness.

2. Poetry

Jiří Trávníček calls the early nineties a leap into "multi-reality" from the "pseudo-reality" of the eighties.[12] A great many trends, theories and poetic styles came back into Czech poetry. At last there were a complete editions of the works of Jan Zahradníček, Richard Weiner and Bohuslav Reynek and, at the beginning of the 21st century, the complete works of Jaroslav Seifert and the war generation poets, Jiří Orten, Oldřich Mikulášek and Jan Skácel. In the nineties the works of the great living poets, Ludvík Kundera, Karel Šiktanc, and later those of Zdeněk Rotrekl began to be published. The exiles Ivan Jelínek, Jiří Kolář, Ivan Diviš, Antonín Brousek and the Christian spiritual poets F. D. Merth, Zdeněk Rotrekl and Ivan Slavík, and the underground and surrealist poets, were again published as a matter of course in the Czech Republic. Ivan Blatný did not live long enough to see his work being published again in his native country. He died in England in Colchester in 1990.

Several distinctive influences affected the poetry of the nineties. One of those was JIŘÍ KUBĚNA (see pp. 96–97), more of whose multiform work was for the first time presented to the public. Kuběna was active in the arts world: he edited the review *Box*, arranged an annual meeting of poets in the Moravian castle Bítov, and encouraged younger poets. Yet the tranquil, and at first sight simple, poetry of Bohuslav Reynek (see p. 29), who died in the early seventies, had an even greater effect on contemporary poetry. It inspires by expressing a deep inner Christian faith and by its apparent simplicity. The poetry of ZBYNĚK HEJDA (see p. 97) represents the opposite tendency. The poems in his collection *Básně* (Poems), published in 1996, harsh and almost morbid, express unfathomable sadness and seek to uncover the mystery of death.

Poetry, like all the arts, shows regional differences. Besides Prague, important creative centres have been established in Brno, with the journal and publishing house *Host* and the publishers *Petrov*, in Olomouc with the publishing house *Votobia* and the review *Aluze*, in Zlín, where the review *Psí víno* focuses exclusively on contemporary poetry, and in North Bohemia and North Moravia. In this region of Ostrava/Silesia, the review *Weles* is published in Vedryně and the almanac *V srdci Černého pavouka* (In the Heart of the Black Spider), which was brought out in 2000, presented the work of local authors. One of these is the poet and novelist PETR MOTÝL, whose cycle of poems *Šílený Fridrich* (Mad Fridrich), written in 1989 and published in 1992, took up in a bizarre way the ideas of Petr Bezruč, the poet writing at the beginning of the 20th century of the humiliation and revolt of the Silesian region. Motýl personified the region as the mythical bard

Fridrich, "the illustrious scourge of the lords of Silesia and their followers" stalking through the streets and pubs of Ostrava. Coarse and vulgar, the poems are also highly imaginative. A poet of a completely different type is the introvert PETR HRUŠKA. He portrays a high-rise housing estate in Ostrava in his book *Obývací nepokoje* (General Unrest, 1995). One of the most talented contemporary poets is BOGDAN TROJAK (see p. 212), who comes from Těšín, where Czech and Polish are spoken.

KAREL ŠIKTANC (see pp. 159–161, → PROFILES) remains the greatest Czech poet of the older generation. After the great compositions of his earlier years he has given up writing cycles of poetry and prefers smaller formats. *Hrad Kost* (Castle Bone) was written between 1990 and 1994 and published in 1995.[13] *Šarlat* (Scarlet) was written between 1995 and 1998 and published in 1999. In these collections, there is a lot less pathos and more austere metaphor, but of course the intensity of expression and the characteristic themes remain, above all the theme of memory. The author alternates regular and free verse and has a wide range of styles at his command; he uses archaisms for ancient myths, invents neologisms for his original work, and uses slang and vulgarisms alongside them to suggest the animal nature of man.

Two writers, slightly younger than Šiktanc, who were late in publishing their poetry, were the well-known dramatist JOSEF TOPOL (see pp. 101–102) and VIOLA FISCHEROVÁ. *Básně* (Poems), Topol's extensive selection of his poetry from the fifties to the eighties, was published in 1997. Fischerová's collection of poems *Propadání* (Sinking) was ready for publication as early as 1957 but had never been published. *Zádušní básně za Pavla Buksu* (Requiem Poems for Pavel Buksa), dedicated to her husband the writer Karel Michal (see p. 103), were written in exile between 1985 and 1986 but not published till 1993. They are meditative poems and poems in prose, sometimes mere lists, at other times tender reflections or transcriptions of dreams.

Domovní dveře
vchod do otevřené rány
Schody se lesknou
Ani kapka krve
ani peříčko
Celý náš život
trval 16 let
a odehrál se ve třech pokojích[14]

Front door
way in to open wounds
The staircase is shining
Not a drop of blood
not even a feather
Our whole life
lasted sixteen years
and was played out in three rooms

Love and hope shine through the burden of life and the hopelessness of death. Other books of verse followed this successful collection. *Babí hodina* (An Hour in the Sign of Old Women) was written between 1986 and 1992 and published in 1995 with a bibliophile edition a year earlier.

Petr Kabeš (see p. 162), one of the poets of the sixties, arranged his works for publication, collecting his poetry from the sixties in the volume *Krátké letní procesy* (Brief Summer Actions, 1999), those from the seventies in *Kámen ze srdce* (A Stone from the Heart, 2000), and his poems from the eighties and nineties in *Pěší věc a jiné předpokoje* (A Pedestrian Affair and Other Antechambers, 1998). Jiří Gruša (→ profiles), who became ambassador to Germany and Austria after his return from exile and was then president of the International Pen Club, writes poetry and essays in both German and Czech. His Czech poetry from the seventies and eighties is collected in the book *Gruša's Wacht am Rhein*[15] *aneb Putovní ghetto* (Gruša's Wacht am Rhein or the Travelling Ghetto, 2001). Ivan Wernisch (see pp. 95, 162, → profiles) continues to write texts that play on conventional topics, genres and forms, combining great lyricism and irony, enigmatic unfinished phrases and bizarre nonsense, for example *Proslýchá se* (It Is Rumoured, 1996) and the works that followed. In these works the borderline becomes blurred between plagiarism, in the sense of paraphrasing or echoing other people's work, and his own texts. Pavel Šrut, another poet of the sixties, captured the imagination of the reading public with his "filmscript for a poem" *Zlá milá* (The Evil Beloved, 1997), parts of which were written in the seventies. In it there are several levels of style and meaning: metaphor, sophisticated allusions, calculated simplicity and descriptiveness. *Zlá milá* may be seen as the lyrical confession of a love affair and a life of despair but at the same time it can be viewed as an ironic dialogue with one of the most famous poems of Czech literature, Hrubín's *Romance pro křídlovku* (Romance for a Flugelhorn, see pp. 71–72) and with the traditional mission of poetry.

čekal jste smuteční chocholy?
romanci pro křídlovku?
koně vrané?
jejich zlatou moč
co epitaf
v bílém sněhu?

[. . . .]

tak dost
kdo kdy překřičel ticho

a ostatně:
je po zavírací hodině[16]

were you expecting sad plumes?
a romance for a flugelhorn?
raven black horses?
their golden urine

an epitaph
in the white snow?

[....]

well enough of that
who when he shouted down the silence

and anyway;
it's after closing time

The poets of the "lonely runners" (see p. 194) generation were now at the peak of their creative powers. In 1988 at the age of forty, an obscure poet, JIŘÍ RULF, officially published his first collection. An arts editor, working chiefly for the weekly *Reflex*, he published *Rádio Netopýr* (Radio Bat) in 1992 and *Maloměstské historie* (Stories from a Small Town) in 1999. An outstanding feature of his poems is his restrained approach and understated language. For him poetry is not only the untrammelled creation of word pictures or the revelation of intimate feelings but also responsible intellectual communication. Using traditional themes of death, eternity and love, he points out the danger to man of being lost in a society solely intent on getting and spending.

In contrast, word games and imagination play a large part in LUBOR KASAL's collections *Vezdejšina* (i.e. vezdejší věc – An Everyday Affair, 1993) and *Hlodavci hladovci* (Rodents, Hungry Animals, 1995 – in Czech the title is a play on words). In particular he uses euphony and alliteration; at the same time his poetry is provocative: "Toto jsou verše pro zedníka Petra / který mne naučil pohrdat vším / krom jeho vypaseného břicha" (These lines are for the brickie Peter / who taught me to despise everything / except his fat belly) – a travesty of a famous poem from the sixties by Václav Hrabě (see p. 98). The poem *Jám* (1997) is a social protest, in places almost a cosmic vision of metaphysical void. Apart from other things, it is an allusion to the poem *Máj* (May) by the Romantic poet Karel Hynek Mácha. *Jám* is a neologism combining the two Czech words *já* and *jáma* (I and pit), and at the same time it is *máj* in reverse.

Another of the youngest of the samizdat poets to win recognition besides Jáchym Topol (see p. 183) was J. H. KRCHOVSKÝ[17] whose collection of poems *Básně* (Poems) was published in 1998. By its obsession with death, the terror and the emptiness of life, erotica as pictures of sexual coupling, and perversion, Krchovský's poetry shocks. The author works with conventional stylistic forms wearing a mask of decadence and morbidity but he is also self-deprecating and intentionally embarrassing. There is no integrated vision of the world and the lyrical subject splits into two – the manuscript of one of his works from the eighties is entitled *Valčík s mým stínem* (Waltzing with My Shadow). Now and again, as an effective contrast with new Czech poetry, he uses regular dactylic verse.

Jenom já a můj stín . . . – Zbylí dva v arše
Gramofon vyhrává smuteční marše
A břehu nevidno, ani hor, natož měst . . .
poslední večeře (jednotné menu):

prsíčka holubic, obloha – ratolest
stylové prostředí, nelidské ceny[18]

Only me and my shadow . . . – Two remained in Noah's ark
A gramophone is playing a sad march
Nothing to be seen no river-bank, no mountains or towns . . .
the last supper (a single menu):
pigeon breast, the trimmings – sprigs
stylish surroundings, fiendish prices

(*Všechno je jako dřív* [Everything Is as Before], written between 1995 and 1996)

After 1989 the youngest generation of poets came on the scene. These were writers born in the sixties or at the beginning of the seventies. Most of them were active in unofficial circles or in the grey zone of youth clubs, the poetry-reading programme *Zelené peří* (Green Feathers, see p. 194) presented by Mirek Kovařík and others. The poets centred on the samizdat journal *Kvašňák* made up one such group. The name Kvašňák combines the words *kvas* and *kvasit* (ferment or turmoil and to ferment) but it is also an allusion to the former popular footballer Kvašňák. The journal was started by the brothers Tomáš and Štěpán Kafka, Jaroslav Pížl and the writers and actors from the theatre *Sklep* (The Cellar, see p. 192). The collection *Zlatí hadi – zlatě kadí* (Golden Serpents – Golden Crap) combines style, humour and irony. In his collection *Manévry* (Manoeuvres, 1992) and *Svět zvířat* (The World of Animals, 1996) JAROSLAV PÍŽL bases his poetry on the conventions of the late 19th century, using assimilation and inner rhyme like the decadent poet Karel Hlaváček. He does not use this merely as a parody but also in order to heap up styles and meaning.

The use of conventional forms is also an important element in the poetry of JAROMÍR TYPLT, the author of the passionate, energetic, imaginative *Koncerto grosso* (Concerto Grosso, 1990) inspired by rock music and surrealism. NORBERT HOLUB is a completely different type of writer. His works are keenly observed and are based on systematic rationalism. In the collection *Cizí sonety* (Other People's Sonnets, 1996) he paraphrases stories from the Bible and the works of different authors in their various styles. In his next book, *Úplně úzké úly* (Tiny Little Beehives, 1999) he continues to write sonnets experimenting with traditional forms, abandoning strong rhymes, transposing the order of quatrains and tercets, and adding a fifteenth or sixteenth line.

Another reaction to imagination run riot, and to the postmodern relativization of values in general, is the return to the spiritual tradition of Christianity. As the literary scholar Jaroslav Med writes in *Host*, "Poetry misses order and that is why there is a more or less explicitly expressed thirst for metaphysics [. . .] the desire to come alight again, to shed light on man's age-old religious experiences and rediscover their justification for the present day."[19]

Some poets formed groups with a spiritual orientation. Even before 1989, *Skupina XXVI* (Group XXVI) had become established. Within it there were poets, as well as prose and essay writers associated with the parish of Příchovice in the

Jizerské mountains in North Bohemia. Their spokesman was ROMAN SZPUK, the author of *Bludiště* (The Labyrinth, 1994), a collection of subjective lyric poems, litanies and prayers in verse.

Another group, *Portál* (Portal), and the samizdat journal of the same name were also associated with Christianity, and to a certain extent the Prague publishing house *Portál* continues that tradition. *Portál* included among its members the older Protestant clergyman Pavel Rejchrt, the younger poets PAVEL KOLMAČKA and EWALD MURRER. Murrer is the son of Ivan Wernisch, the influence of whose poetics can be seen in some of Murrer's texts. These poets tend to go back to countryside themes and, inspired by Reynek, they present the unexceptional countryside and apparently banal scenes in the guise of dreams, mysterious and eternal. In 1993 Murrer published *Vyznamenání za prohranou válku* (Award for a Lost War), a collection of poems and poetic prose. Kolmačka published his collection *Vlál za mnou směšný šos* (My Ridiculous Coat-tails Flapped behind Me) in 1994 though it had been written between 1984 and 1991. Family and family life are the themes of *Viděl jsi, že jsi* (You Saw That You Were, 1998), another collection by Kolmačka.

Mlčky jsme jedli chléb krajiny
dokola nastavený.
Otevřeným jak lekníny
srdcem, v němž pukly stěny.

A někdo řekl: Kameny se staňme,
ať toto teď víc nepomine.
Kéž anděl věčnosti nás zajme,
vítr a déšť ať brousí nás svým mlýnem.

Vzduch horký po poli se lil.
Bíle žhnul slunce ovál.
Po dlouhé době s přáteli.
Tiše a beze slova.[20]

In silence, we ate the bread of the coutryside
set out all round.
With our hearts, open
like waterlilies where the walls have burst.

And someone said: Let us become stones,
so that this now doesn't pass away.
Let the angel of eternity capture us,
let wind and rain grind us in their mill.

Scorching air blew across the field.
The oval sun glowed whitely.
Long after with friends.
Silently and without a word.

Other writers with similar tendencies are Pavel Petr from Zlín, who was inspired by the work of Kuběna, two authors writing for the periodical *Host* in Brno, Martin Josef Stöhr and Tomáš Reichel, and also Miloš Doležal, who comes from the Bohemian-Moravian Highlands. In *Obec* (The Parish, 1996) and other works, Doležal presents, in poetic form, stories of a traditional country community. However, as the critic Jan Wiendl pointed out in *Tvar*, "this is not the result of living in one's native countryside but from the very fact of being away from it". It is the result of the "remorseless tension [. . .] between one's birthplace and the place where one has chosen to live".[21]

Petr Borkovec is one of the writers associated with the periodical *Souvislosti* (see p. 201). In 1991 he published *Poustevna věštírna loutkárna* (Hermitage, Oracle, Puppet Theatre). These first poems resembled magic incantations based on inventive metaphor and invented words. In his later collections he also tends towards contemplation, symbolism and recurring images with a country background.[22] Bogdan Trojak, a Silesian now living in South Moravia, who was the chief editor of *Weles*, is a completely different type of writer. His precise, keenly observed poetry stands out by its terseness and concision. "Dvě věci ve tmě střetlé. / A kymácení stálé. // Bůh – // Červeným světlem / prosvícený palec."[23] (Two things clash in the dark. / And are still swaying. // God – // A thumb / with red light shining through.)

Two outstanding young women poets from the beginning of the 21st century are Věra Rosí and Kateřina Rudčenková. Rosí's *Holý bílý kmen* (Bare White Stem) was published in 1999 and Rudčenková's *Není nutné, abyste mě navštěvoval* (You Don't Have to Visit Me) in 2001. Rosí belongs to the previously mentioned contemplative movement in Czech poetry, whose verse is based on terse expressions punctuated by pauses. In Rosí, spirituality shows through her verses about life in Brno, in particular in the part of the town called Královo Pole. In Rudčenková, more than in any other poet, sensuality is reflected in her perceptive verses.

Těším se na spánek
Jako by bylo možné jím vycouvat
ze života

Večer je vyhrazen ženám
Přimknout se těsně, dusivě

Ještě to vydrž, slibují
Jako by bylo na co čekat[24]

I long for sleep
As if it were possible through it to retreat
from life

Night is reserved for women
To embrace tightly, suffocatingly

Just hold on, they promise
As if there were something to wait for

3. Prose

As the nineties had seen the return of the poets, so they also saw the return of prose writers whose works had been officially banned or distorted. Thus readers were able to get hold of the complete works of Jan Čep, Egon Hostovský and Jakub Deml, and the novels and essays of Jaroslav Durych. An important development was the publication in nineteen volumes of a critical edition of Bohumil Hrabal by the publishing house *Pražská imaginace* and the publication of works by the classic writers Richard Weiner, Karel Poláček, František Langer and Ladislav Klíma. The novelists Josef Škvorecký, Ivan Klíma, Arnošt Lustig, Ludvík Vaculík and Vladimír Körner lived to see the publication of their collected works. In contrast the works of Milan Kundera (see pp. 83, 170, → PROFILES) have been slow to appear, and even some of his books written in Czech, *Život je jinde* (Life Is Elsewhere), *Kniha smíchu a zapomnění* (The Book of Laughter and Forgetting), *Nesnesitelná lehkost bytí* (The Unbearable Lightness of Being) were, up to 2006, available only in editions published abroad.[25] This applies also to Kundera's later novels, written in French (with the exception of the novel *L'Identité*, an anonymous, unauthorized Czech translation of which appeared on the internet in 2006).

There are two general trends regarding the previous decade that we must note. On the one hand there is the attempt at authenticity, focusing on an individual, personal view of reality; on the other hand there is a more general, universal view aimed at embracing the world as a whole.[26] Sometimes the two trends merge; both use various literary techniques, unadorned accounts, unbridled imagination and irony. Bohumil Hrabal, according to Jiří Kratochvil, is the cult writer above all others of the period after November 1989: "If the nineties are indeed the first real period of freedom for Czech literature, and that, I think, is beyond doubt, then Bohumil Hrabal is their John the Baptist."[27] However, besides Hrabal, others like Ladislav Klíma, Jakub Deml, Richard Weiner and Josef Váchal were greatly influential. Váchal was a highly rated graphic artist and writer who was regarded by the younger generation as the pioneer of postmodernism.

Czech prose in the nineties is weighted towards contemplation and self-examination and is frequently concerned with art for art's sake. In contrast to this exclusive literature, there is of course the literature written with the reader in mind, which relies on a story told as a traditional narrative, sometimes with autobiographical elements, interesting plots in attractive settings or coming to terms with the past. Erotica and humour are an essential part of this type of writing. Such for example are the books of PETR ŠABACH. The story *Šakalí léta* (The Years of the Jackal), which originally appeared in the book *Jak potopit Austrálii* (How to Drown Australia, 1986), a collection of stories expanded in 1993 as *Šakalí léta*, and *Hovno hoří* (Shit Burning, 1994) were both the basis of popular films by Jan Hřebejk. MICHAL VIEWEGH'S (→ PROFILES) cleverly written books remain highly (on the list of books) popular with readers. His stories are well thought-out, ironical and filled with various allusions. He began with the remarkable topsy-turvy detective story *Názory na vraždu* (Thoughts on Murder, 1990) set in the "idyllic" small town of Sázava in Central Bohemia. He uses the mysterious death of a young woman, a teacher, to show how mass hysteria can develop and affect an entire community. His next book, *Báječná léta pod psa* (The Blissful Years of Lousy Living), was published in 1992 and filmed in 1997. In this book the author, barely thirty years old, wrote about the years of normalization with gentle humour, thereby presenting it in a different light, not as a time of rapid progress, nor on the other hand as a time of general moral decline. Although these years were wretched, "lousy", they cannot be dismissed out of hand because the narrator's youth and some never-to-return happy times are associated with them. So for one individual there was an artistic truth impossible to confirm or deny. Viewegh juggles "reality" and "fiction"; his stories are brilliant and very readable. However, as his next novels show, these qualities have been a stumbling block for the development of his talent. In places, they are merely witty and amusing or a record of an era. His next novel, *Výchova dívek v Čechách* (1994; published in English as *Bringing up Girls in Bohemia*, 1996), which was also made into a film in 1997, aroused sharp criticism which the author countered with, among other things, a diatribe in *Účastníci zájezdu* (Holiday-makers, 1996, filmed in 2006). However, neither in this nor in his other books is there evidence of any new artistic development, although it is true that some of his recent novels, *Vybíjená* (Knocking Out, 2004) and *Lekce tvůrčího psaní* (A Lesson in Creative Writing, 2005) deal with the serious topics of ageing and death.

Some young novelists like Bohuslav Vaněk-Úvalský in *Zabrisky* (1999) and Roman Ludva in *Jezdci pod slunečníkem* (Riders under a Sunshade, 1999) use the poetic techniques of the action film or the detective story to play sophisticated games with the reader. Ludva for example uses a puzzle both as a motif and as the principal basis of the story. The search for the murderer forms one line of the story, the other is a monologue by the murderer himself.

Some interesting books of memoirs and diaries were published, particularly in the early nineties. Besides those already mentioned, including works by Jan Zábrana and Ivan Diviš (see pp. 156, 173, → PROFILES), LUDVÍK VACULÍK'S (see pp. 82–3, 159, → PROFILES) lengthy text *Milí spolužáci!* (Dear Schoolfriends!, 1995) and the novel *Jak se dělá chlapec* (How a Boy Is Made, 1993) aroused great interest. Parts of *Milí spolužáci!* had already been published in samizdat in 1981 and 1986. In it he uses notes from a diary and correspondence from his childhood and youth. In his novel *Jak se dělá chlapec*, he frankly describes provocative erotic autobiographical scenes, but he also portrays the world of an ageing man and his vain attempts to mould the character of his son. *Památník* (The Memorial, 1994) by EVA KANTŮRKOVÁ is a personal account of life among the dissidents before November 1989 and in the first years after the revolution when the author engaged in politics.

Another kind of testimony was written by IVAN MATOUŠEK, a graphic artist, poet and author of a different type, who had published in samizdat. His novel *Ego* (Ego), completed during the eighties but not published till 1997, gives a different account of several months during normalization in an intricate web of inner reflections and imagination.

Václav Kahuda and Emil Hakl were members of the former group *Moderní analfabet* (The Modern Ignoramus). A journal and an anthology of the same name existed in the early nineties. Their novels were not based on impersonal reporting but on the personal experience of the narrator, the "I". VÁCLAV KAHUDA's long novel *Houština* (The Undergrowth, 1999) gives a picture of childhood and youth, above all focusing on the ugly side of life. Reflections and wild imagery are interspersed with keenly observed snippets of reality, the author not eschewing obscenities. His apparently static style gives rise to tension.[28] EMIL HAKL, who uses more traditional forms of narrative, is the author of *Intimní schránka Sabriny Black* (Sabrina Black's Intimate Mailbox, 2002), a novel set in the contemporary Czech Republic, and other works.

IVAN LANDSMANN's *Pestré vrstvy* (Colourful Layers), which was written in the eighties and published in 1999, belongs to the school of "confessional novels". The author, a self-taught writer, uses coarse language and a great many slang and dialect expressions to portray the life of a miner in Ostrava and his later life in the Netherlands as an immigrant. *Pestré vrstvy* refers to a geological formation that can be dangerous for miners and so is a metaphor for life itself. To quote Jiří Peňás, the author records "actions and situations not by noting emotions and thoughts but by drawing raw, authentic word pictures".[29]

Besides Landsmann, whose next works did not find favour with the critics, several other novelists reappeared from exile. These included the well-known authors Josef Škvorecký, Vlastimil Třešňák and Sylvie Richterová, Iva Pekárková (see pp. 168, 158, 164), Lubomír Martínek and the late beginner Jiří Drašnar. Škvorecký's *Nevysvětlitelný příběh* (1998; in English as *An Inexplicable Story*, 2000), in the spirit of Edgar Allan Poe, is outstanding among his later works. Iva Pekárková's novel *Dej mi ty prachy* about New York taxi drivers was published in 1996 (translated into English as *Gimme the Money*, 2000).

Emigration is "an excellent way of getting to know human nature" said LUBOMÍR MARTÍNEK. In the eighties he was one of the associates of Jiří Kolář (→ PROFILES) and editor of *Edice K*. Martínek is the very antithesis of the plebeian Landsmann. His novels are decidedly intellectual, with a complicated structure and no cohesive narrative. They go back to the theme of exile and home, of man's lack of ties, spiritual or physical, with any community. *Opilost z hloubky* (Intoxication from the Depths) was published in 2000.

JIŘÍ DRAŠNAR, who lives in California, aroused interest with his book *O revolucích, tajných společnostech a genetickém kódu* (On Revolutions, Secret Societies and the Genetic Code, 1996). In it he follows, with many digressions and episodes even going back to the distant past, the tangled history of two Czech-German families in the 20th century, the Švestkas and the Kerschners. The 20th century is shown as a time of terrible cruelty and repeated violence when man is governed by rage. Ever present are the themes of witchcraft and the devil.

JAN KŘESADLO, one of the older authors, is a special case. He published his first books in exile when he was over sixty. He also published in English (translating Seifert's *Věnec sonetů* [A Wreath of Sonnets, 1987] into English) and wrote poetry even in ancient Greek. By profession, the author was a psychologist dealing with sexual deviations. This is evident in his novels along with his long-standing interest in music and comparative, historical linguistics. In his novels, he creates weird, almost grotesque situations, which he sees as portraying the atrocity of a totalitarian regime. His novel *Mrchopěvci* (Carcass Singers), which was published in Toronto in 1984 and in Prague in 1990, is set in the days after the coup of February 1948. His novels also include erudite digressions and fictional essays, as for example in *La Calle Neruda* (Neruda Street, 1995), the study of a visual arts historian on "the arse as a principle of the Baroque". He also plays with various languages and styles, using for example the techniques of the adventure story. In the novel *Zámecký pán aneb Antikuro* (The Lord of the Castle or Anti-Dawn, 1992) he entered into a controversy with the serene spirituality of Viktor Fischl (see pp. 172–173) in *Kuropění* (Dawn). Křesadlo's works may be interpreted as postmodern farce, but also as a special kind of moralizing.

The historical novel was rather neglected in the nineties in comparison with the preceding decade. VLADIMÍR KÖRNER'S (see pp. 86, 144) novel *Smrt svatého Vojtěcha* (The Death of Saint Adalbert, 1993), set in the early Middle Ages, continues to show his sceptical view of man's place in history. Some historical novels have reintroduced the thorny subject of Czech–German coexistence. Besides the works of Drašnar already mentioned, other novels of this kind are *Cejch* (Branding, 1992) by Zdeněk Šmíd, previously better known as an author of humorous prose, and *Pátým pádem* (In the Vocative, 1996) by Václav Vokolek. The literary scholar VLADIMÍR MACURA wrote a tetralogy, *Ten, který bude* (He Who Will Be), set in the patriotic Czech society of the mid 19th century, comprising of *Informátor* (The Informer, 1992), *Komandant* (The Commander, 1994), *Guvernantka* (The Governess, 1998) and *Medikus* (The Doctor), which was first published with the other four books in 1999. Each part is written in the prose style of the era it describes: as a novella, "a living picture", an elegy, a memoir. The narrative includes historical fact, real people, such as the revolutionary and poet J. V. Frič, the poet and scholar F. L. Čelakovský, and complete fiction. As a result, there are demystifying views of the Czech nationalistic past, of history and man's place in it. In this way, his novels create a parallel view to his literary-historical study of the Czech National Revival (see p. 179) and the myths of more recent times.

At the opposite end of the scale from texts with facts or documentary evidence to support them are novels based on imagination and fantasy. These often aim at giving a more general, more universal picture of reality. Jiří Kratochvil's (see p. 189, → PROFILES) *Truchlivý Bůh* (The Mournful God, 2000), Daniela Hodrová's (see pp. 189–190, → PROFILES) *Perunův den* (Perun's Day, 1994)[30] and Michal Ajvaz's *Tyrkysový orel* (The Turquoise Eagle, 1997) fall into this category. After some narrative acrobatics, Kratochvil has returned, in the novella *Truchlivý Bůh*, to a more traditional form of fiction. It is an original continuation of Kundera's *Já, truchlivý bůh* (I, the Mournful God, see p. 83). VÁCLAV VOKOLEK, who has already been mentioned, the son of the poet and novelist Vladimír Vokolek, also wrote fantastic novels based on old legends and myths. He was unable to publish openly till after 1989; his *Triptych* (Triptych) was published in 1995.

Like some of Vokolek's novels, *Sud* (The Barrel) by KAREL MILOTA was a very long time in reaching the reading public. It had been written at the beginning of the seventies but was not published till 1993. It is an experimental work bringing together traditional romanticism and the French *nouveau roman.* There is no clear plot, the narrative branches out into several variations, the identity of the characters is unclear, the *sud* of the title changes into *osud* (fate) and the consciousness of death.

PAVEL ŘEZNÍČEK's prose was inspired by the poetics of surrealism. In the seventies and eighties he belonged to a group of Bohemians in Brno. His *Strop* (The Ceiling) was first published in French in 1983 with a foreword by Milan Kundera. It was published in Czech in 1991. *Alexandr v tramvaji* (Alexander on the Tram) was published in 1994. Both works are full of black and absurd humour, unfettered imagination and both had been written in the seventies.

The imaginative fiction of JÁCHYM TOPOL (see pp. 183, → PROFILES) is a product of his purely subjective views. His texts sometimes have almost the rhythm of rock music, that is, they are aggressive and at first sight chaotic. The novel *Anděl* (The Angel), published in 1995, and filmed in 2000, shows the same poetic techniques and a similar distinctive construction as *Sestra* (The Sister, in English *City Sister Silver,* see p. 184). Topol's strongly held views are connected with collective folk myth and its recurring motifs. His book *Trnová dívka* (Thorn Girl, 1997) reveals his interest in the legends and folk tales of the North American Indians. The element of water, standing for the initiation of the hero, and other mysteries of legend and myth, and the ever-present theme of danger, also appear in the novel *Noční práce* (Night Work, 2001). The setting, hitherto unusual for the author, is the Czech countryside in August 1968. In this novel a different kind of artistic technique seems to be taking shape. Repetitions and variations or snatches of conversation indicate different points of view. The next novel, with the bizarre title *Kloktat dehet* (To Gargle Tar, 2005), continues with this technique. The narrator is a man who grew up in the Communist era in a children's home somewhere in South Bohemia. His unconventional account culminates in a phantasmagoric picture of the Soviet invasion in August 1968 developing into a third world war.

The novel *Selský baroko* (Peasant Baroque, 2005), by Topol's contemporary JIŘÍ HÁJÍČEK, also goes back to the Communist past. It too is set in the countryside of South Bohemia. A scholar searching the archives while piecing together other people's family trees becomes interested in a story from the fifties about some farmers being denounced and imprisoned. In the novel questions are posed on guilt, revenge, forgiveness and to what extent we should return to the past.

VLADIMÍR BINAR, the literary historian and editor of the works of Jakub Deml, surprised readers with his remarkable work *Playback* (Playback, 2001). Yet it too had been written a quarter of a century earlier, between 1975 and 1976. Superficially it is a "taproom story" (→ see Bohumil Hrabal, p. 80); it is written as a confession in a single unending sentence. But, reminiscent of William Faulkner, imagination transports the narrator, not to a steady flow of memory, but, by skipping certain times and places, to a variety of different memories, ideas and visions which call up times of turbulence, dullness, mystery, anxiety and loneliness. There are repeated reminders of the search for home and the passage of time, "eternal time, which creates us and carries us away, but our knowledge is always out of date: we suffer and despair because we want to stop the flow [. . .] and most of us are completely unaware that death itself is always present within us".[31] Binar put at the heart of his historical narrative a small part of Prague: the area between the centre and the periphery; between Vyšehrad and Charles Square.

If the first half of the nineties was synonymous with the emergence of new poetry, new prose clearly took pride of place at the end of the decade. MILOŠ URBAN, originally a translator and editor in a publishing house, and others are proof of this. Under the name of Josef Urban, he began with the novella *Poslední tečka za Rukopisy* (The Final Full Stop to the Manuscripts, 1998), a light-hearted hoax defending the so-called Manuscripts, forged literary historic documents in Old Czech with which Czech patriots at the beginning of the 19th century, following the example of Ossian, intended to prove the value of the great age of Czech culture. The controversy was resolved scientifically more than a hundred years earlier but ever more defenders of the authenticity of the Manuscripts keep appearing. Behind Urban's novel there seems to lurk the Goethean concept that lies and fiction can also be beautiful and meaningful. In this and in other work the author combines popular fiction, elements of mystery, even horror, with actual events and the expression of his own thoughts. However, the irony he uses in so doing brings him very near to disparaging his own work. His best work is the novel *Sedmikostelí* (Seven Churches, 1999), with the subtitle "a Gothic Novel from Prague". It is set in the present day in the Prague upper New Town, the boundaries of which were marked in the Middle Ages by seven churches. A descendant of the knight Gmünd, builder of the churches, wants to restore not only the churches, but the way of life of the 14th century in the time of Charles IV. He hates the Enlightenment and the present day, which exploits everything in the name of profit. He drags his enemies to churches, sacred places, where he kills them. At last, amid modern-day Prague, he creates an oasis of a town of the Middle Ages . . .

> "Democracy is dynamic and swift, it counts on the growth of everything under the sun, it lives by the cult of the new. How monstrous! How wrong! Against the order of the universe! [. . .] Monarchy offers constant, slow progress, it honours what is old and loves tradition. Consistency. Order. Peace. Quiet. Time."[32]

The novel has a gripping plot and erotic scenes, but it also contains many allusions, for example, to Umberto Eco's *The Name of the Rose*, false clues, light-hearted hoaxes. The next novel, *Hastrman* (The Water Sprite, 2001), also brings together past and present. It has fantastic themes and an exciting plot. It is set in modern times, first in the 19th century and then in the present day. And its hero, a water sprite endowed with supernatural powers, in the end defends his conservationism, which is the preservation of the natural order in the face of the present day devastation, by means of terrorist acts. Other Urban novels, however, have not come up to the level of these works.

Conclusion: Lines of Development

Czech literature in the second half of the 20th century in general developed within two literary contexts. On the one hand, there was "pure" literature, when poetry, prose and drama continued or rejected important stages in development from the twenties and thirties. Thus postwar literature carried on from Jaroslav Hašek's *Švejk* and the novels and plays of Josef and Karel Čapek. They were the inspiration for those authors who portrayed the great "small events" of everyday life, sometimes with compassion for life in all its forms, sometimes with humour, parody, satire and imaginative exaggeration. Literature following this course reached its peak with the inimitable novels of Bohumil Hrabal and Josef Škvorecký and the absurd plays of Václav Havel. The avant-garde poetry of Vítězslav Nezval and Jaroslav Seifert from the times before the Second World War, like the highly imaginative novels of Vladislav Vančura, which played games with the narrative, were at one time seen as lively and up-to-date and at other times as *passé*. The novelist Milan Kundera and the poet Karel Šiktanc, who of course grew out of avant-garde idealism to adopt scepticism, may be regarded as their heirs. The other direction taken by Czech literature between the wars is represented by the Kafka-like, contemplative, dreamlike stories and poems of Richard Weiner and Jakub Deml, the sparse memoirs and visions of Jan Čep and the spiritual poems of Jan Zahradníček. In the twenties and thirties their work tended to be disregarded; however, it became of great importance in the postwar era. Existentialist questions appeared in the work of members of Group 42 (*Skupina 42*), who, like Jiří Kolář, also wrote in the form of a diary. Several generations of poets, such as Ivan Diviš, Ivan Slavík and the writers of the early years of the 21st century like Miloš Doležal and Pavel Kolmačka, were inspired by the kind of spirituality that does not consider faith as fixed but as dynamic, constantly lost and constantly rediscovered. After the war the poetry of František Halas, full of experimental language, motifs of futility and death, sceptical rather than hopeful or optimistic, came into prominence more and more. The younger poet Vladimír Holan was a friend of Halas and subscribed to his poetics. He was clearly the greatest of the postwar poets, but even more importantly he influenced the terse, concise poetry of Jan Skácel and a whole group of poets of the sixties.

In Czechoslovakia, as in other countries in the fifties, but especially in the sixties, modern avant-gardism was clearly in decline. Poetry and literature in general with a predominantly aesthetic function was losing prestige. In recent decades, because we have been living more obviously in a society dominated by it, the media has been a powerful influence on what we perceive and how we perceive it. It forms our ways of behaving and communicating, it shapes the way we remember things. The tradition of reading things slowly over and over again, which for many centuries was a factor in forming European society, is disappearing. Poetry representing artistic communication has lost its function and is being replaced by other types of art and culture based on the auditory and visual senses, chiefly on the visual. This is a culture mostly disseminated by the mass media, in which precedence is given to rapidly changing and exciting information. These new means of communication, however, do not offer literature any new opportunities to progress. Michal Viewegh is an example of a Czech author who uses this method of communication, building into his novels elements of popular culture. Jáchym Topol also does this but in a different way, as in his novel *Sestra* (in English translated as *City Sister Silver*, see p. 184), where he was inspired by the rhythm of rock music.

The second line of development of Czech literature grew out of social and political conditions. By the end of the thirties, when the Czech lands were occupied by the Nazis, strict state control of literature was introduced. Czech authors found themselves under siege. Some went into exile, others kept silent or attempted to speak in allegorical images or parables. Because free political and civic life was totally suppressed, a kind of cryptic literature came into being, which was nonetheless understandable as expressing resistance to the German occupiers.

This situation repeated itself twice in the course of the 20th century: first after the introduction of Stalinist totalitarianism at the end of the forties and then again at the beginning of the seventies after the suppression of the Prague Spring. Literature and cultural life once more came under strict control of the state and the party, this time not the Nazi party but the Communist. Writers in Czechoslovakia again found themselves under siege. Some, like the poets Vítězslav Nezval and the younger Josef Kainar, who had been a member of Group 42, adapted to the ruling ideology and were able to continue publishing their works. Some, like the novelists Egon Hostovský, Jan Čep, Milada Součková and the poet Ivan Blatný went to the West where the journals *Sklizeň* (The Harvest), *Svědectví* (Testimony), *Proměny* (Metamorphoses) and the exile publishing house *Křesťanská akademie* (Christian Academy) were founded. Others tried to continue writing freely at home. Among them may be included the poets Vladimír Holan, Jiří Kolář, another member of Group 42, and Josef Škvorecký and Josef Jedlička, who belonged to the younger generation of novelists. In the fifties they could work only at great risk to themselves and their manuscripts circulated within small groups of faithful friends. In the sixties, when censorship of the arts was gradually becoming less severe – it was completely abolished, but only for a short time in the spring and summer of 1968 – it was possible for a number of these works to be published and books previously printed in exile also began to appear. Czech literature revived and flourished for a time, writers became spokesmen for the nation and to a great extent replaced politicians and journalists. However, the

Soviet invasion in August 1968 led to further purges at the beginning of the seventies. Neo-Stalinism led once more to strict control of literature and the arts. Most of the well-known writers, including many former Communists, such as Pavel Kohout, Ivan Klíma and Ludvík Vaculík, distanced themselves from the new regime and started up a parallel system with the samizdat publishing houses *Petlice* (Padlock) and *Expedice* (Dispatch) and samizdat journals. A greater number of writers went into exile at the end of the sixties and the beginning of the seventies than in the late thirties and after 1948. The novelists Josef Škvorecký, Arnošt Lustig, Věra Linhartová, Milan Kundera, the poets Ivan Diviš and Antonín Brousek, the dramatist Vratislav Blažek and many journalists went to the West. New, much more influential exile publishing houses were founded: *Sixty-Eight Publishers* in Toronto, *Index* in Cologne and also such journals as *Listy* (Gazette). Unlike in the fifties these institutions retained contact with independent literature at home. Czech dissident writers like Václav Havel were supported in the West and free exile publications were occasionally successfully smuggled into Czechoslovakia.

All this meant that for a long time Czech literature functioned, often predominantly, in its non-aesthetic role, acting as a free press, replacing suppressed civic institutions. Czech writers were persecuted, their works were banned but all this simply elicited a greater response from readers. Queues could be expected at bookshops for books by authors who, like the poets Jaroslav Seifert, Oldřich Mikulášek, Jan Skácel and the novelist Bohumil Hrabal, had been unable to publish for several years and had returned to literature sanctioned by the state. "Banned" texts of such authors as Josef Škvorecký, Václav Havel and Ludvík Vaculík were eagerly read and copied.

However, this great interest in literature in the Czech lands came to an end several years after the "Velvet Revolution" in November 1989. The re-establishment of basic democratic institutions, freedom of the press, the introduction of a market economy and the freedom to travel abroad led to Czechs finding an outlet for their talents in different fields, as businessmen, politicians, journalists. Commercial art and entertainment value often force high-quality literature out of the culture market. The state does not have the resources, perhaps not even the interest, to support new literature and the arts. Paradoxically, at the beginning of the new millennium Czech writers again find themselves under siege, this time however by the mass media, commerce and the dictates of the market. The future will show how they come to terms with the reality of their position.

Profiles of the Most Important Czech Writers Since 1945

Blatný, Ivan

Poet. Born in 1919 in Brno, the largest city in Moravia. His father was the expressionist dramatist and poet Lev Blatný (1894–1930). Both parents died prematurely. He began his studies at Masaryk University in Brno. With the closure of the universities during the Nazi occupation he worked in the family optician's business. He was a friend of Jiří Orten, Josef Kainar and other contemporary poets and was a member of Group 42 (*Skupina 42*). After the Communist coup in February 1948 he remained in Britain on a scholarship. In exile he contributed for a short time to *Radio Free Europe*. Because of a phobia about being followed by Communist agents he spent practically four decades in psychiatric institutions in England. In the seventies he began writing again. Thanks to one of the nurses his writing survived. He died in 1990 in Colchester.

Frequently inspired by his native Brno he wrote Seifert-like, delicate, melodious, nostalgic lyric poetry: *Melancholické procházky* (Melancholy Walks, 1941). At the height of the war he turned to the poetics of Group 42, to the rawness and ordinariness of the life of the big city and in that spirit he wrote the cycle of poems *Tento večer* (This Evening, 1945). In the poem *Terrestris* (Terrestris) from *Hledání přítomného času* (The Search for the Present Time), which followed in 1947, the eponymous character, a cruel, ugly and at the same time beautiful woman, represents the appalling cruelty and seductiveness of life. The poetry of his last period, *Stará bydliště* (The Old Homesteads, edited by Antonín Brousek, Toronto, 1979; Brno, 1992) and *Pomocná škola Bixley* (Bixley Special School, samizdat, 1982, another version Toronto, 1987 [edited by Brousek], Prague, 1994), often hark back to childhood and youth. They are made up of diary entries, fragments, memoirs and visions. In addition to Czech the author uses English, German, French and other languages. A collection of poetry from 1933 to 1953 was published in 1995 by *Atlantis* in Brno (edited by Rudolf Havel, afterword by Jan Marius Tomeš). Also published in Brno in 1999 were the author's letters and other documents pertaining to his works between 1930 and 1948 (*Texty a dokumenty*, ed. and afterword by Jiří Trávníček). A critical edition of his manuscripts from the seventies and eighties is being prepared for publication.

Edition in English: "Poems" (translated by Edwin Morgan, postscript by Jan Čulík), *Scottish Slavonic Review*, 7 (1986), pp. 91–95.

Bibliography: Jiří Trávníček, "Básnický kontakt Ivana Blatného se Skupinou 42: Interpretace sbírky Tento večer," *Česká literatura*, 38 (1990), pp. 425–434. – Jiří Trávníček, "Ivan Blatný: Pomocná škola Bixley," in *Český Parnas: Literatura 1970–1990* (edited by Jiří Holý and Jiřina Táborská), Prague, 1993, pp. 258–263. – Julie Hansen, "Singing the Blues: Intertextuality in the Poetry of Ivan Blatný", in *Kosmas,* 16 (Fall 2002), pp. 21–36. – Julie Hansen, "A Python Can Have Up to Three Tongues. The Use of Multiple Languages in the Poetry of Ivan Blatný," in *Kosmas*, 16 (Spring 2003), pp. 44–58.

BRABCOVÁ, ZUZANA

Novelist. She was born in Prague in 1959, the daughter of the literary scholars Jiří Brabec (1929) and Zina Trochová (1924). After her final school examinations she worked as a cleaner. For a short time after 1989 she was employed in the Ministry of Foreign Affairs and then she joined the editorial staff of a publishing house.

Until the "Velvet Revolution" she published only in samizdat and abroad. To date she has brought out three works with long intervals between them: *Daleko od stromu* (Far from the Tree, samizdat,1984; Cologne, 1987; Prague, 1991); *Zlodějina* (Thieving, 1995); and *Rok perel* (The Year of the Jewel, 2000). Outstanding for a style refined to the point of sophistication, the stories are laid out in disconnected fragments, impressions, recurring themes and reflections. Věra, the narrator in *Daleko od stromu*, represents the young generation born in the seventies in the Husák era of "actually-existing socialism" (as the Soviet rulers defined it in the 1970s). On principle she refuses to conform to the moral code of the society of the day, attempts suicide and is confined in an asylum. From time to time she seeks salvation in friendly relationships with other people, and in writing, as evidence of the independence of her spirit. In the novel *Zlodějina* the two main characters, a young man beaten up by the police during the demonstrations of 1989 and a shopgirl (who becomes trapped in a lift), find their lives closely interlinked. The latest novel to date, *Rok perel*, which has autobiographical elements, draws attention to overt homosexuality; the chief character, the narrator, is openly lesbian.

Editions in English: "The Slaughtering" (trans. James Naughton), in *This Side of Reality* (edited by Alexandra Büchler), London, 1996, pp. 140–153. – "Far from the Tree" (translated by James Naughton), in *Allskin and Other Tales by Contemporary Czech Women* (ed. by Alexandra Büchler), Seattle, 1998, pp. 15–28.

Bibliography: Veronika Ambros, "Bohemia Lies in the Sea: The Quest for an Anchor in Far from the Tree," *Czechoslovak and Central European Journal*, 10, no. 1 (Summer 1991), pp. 73–82. – Jiří Zizler, "Zuzana Brabcová: Daleko od stromu," in *Český Parnas: Literatura 1970–1990* (edited by Jiří Holý and Jiřina Táborská), Prague, 1993, pp. 287–291. – Natascha Drubek-Meyer, "Zářezy v rámu dveří: Metafory písma v románu Zuzany Brabcové Daleko od stromu," *Česká literatura*, 43 (1995), pp. 215–224. – Zuzana Stolz-Hladká, "Hledání skutečnosti

90. let – nad prózami Daniely Hodrové, Zuzany Brabcové a Terezy Boučkové," in *Česká próza 90. let 20. století* (edited by Michal Bauer), České Budějovice, 2002, pp. 36–44. – Rajendra A. Chitnis, "Writing as Being: Jiří Kratochvil, Zuzana Brabcová, Daniela Hodrová, Michal Ajvaz, Jáchym Topol," in his *Literature in Post-Communist Russia and Eastern Europe*, London, 2005, pp. 80–114.

Černý, Václav

Literary scholar, critic, essayist and translator. Černý was born in Náchod in Eastern Bohemia in 1905 into a family of teachers. He attended the lycée in Dijon in France and studied Czech and Romance languages and literatures at Charles University in Prague. In 1929 he was awarded a doctorate. Between 1931 and 1934 he worked in the Institute of Slavonic Languages in Geneva. He was a secondary school teacher and university lecturer and a researcher for the Czech Academy of Sciences. Between 1945 and 1951 and 1968–1970 he was Professor of Comparative Literature at Charles University. In the Czech archives he discovered two hitherto unknown works by the Spanish dramatist Pedro Calderón. He founded and edited the journal *Kritický měsíčník* (Criticism Monthly, 1938–1942 and 1945–1948). During the German occupation he was imprisoned for taking part in the resistance against the Nazis. Between 1952 and 1953 he was held under arrest charged with "subversive activities". After 1970 he could neither lecture nor publish. He published his studies in samizdat and in exile and was a signatory of the human rights manifesto *Charter 77*. He died in Prague in 1987.

Václav Černý was an authority on Czech and Romance literatures, particularly the literature of the Middle Ages, see *Staročeská milostná lyrika* (Mediaeval Czech Love Poetry, 1948) and other works. He was also interested in the Baroque. His collection of studies, *Až do předsíně nebes* (To the Gates of Heaven), was completed in 1970 and published posthumously in 1996. The literature of the 19th and 20th centuries was another interest (*Essai sur le titanisme dans la poésie romantique occidentale* [An Essay on Titanism in Western Romantic Poetry], 1935). In his capacity as a critic he advocated the concept of literature based on moral responsibility and the freedom of the individual (see essays *Osobnost, tvorba a boj* [Character, Creativity and Struggle, 1947]). He became an interpreter of Jiří Orten's generation of war poets in *Druhý sešit o existencialismu* (Second Folio on Existentialism, banned in 1948, unpublished till 1992). Among his late works the outstanding but subjective three-volume *Paměti* (Recollections, Toronto, 1977–1983; Brno, 1992–1994) reconstructs not only the author's life but the entire period of Czech history from the Czechoslovak Republic between the wars to the seventies and affirms Černy's ideals of democracy and morality. A wide-ranging collection of his studies and criticism was published with the title *Tvorba a osobnost I–II* (Creativity and Character, edited by Jan Šulc, Prague, 1992–1993). His work as a scholar and critic went hand in hand with his work as a translator of Romance literatures (Miguel de Cervantes, Ortega y Gasset, Michel de Montaigne).

Edition in English: *Dostoevsky and His Devils* (translated by František William Galan), Ann Arbor, 1975.

Bibliography: *Václav Černý* (edited by Marie Langerová, introduction by Milan Jungmann), Prague, 1994. – *Václav Černý: Život a dílo* (edited by Věra Brožová), Prague 1996. – Július Vanovič, *Osobnosť Václava Černého*, Bratislava, 1999. – Michael Špirit, "Šaldův následník," *Česká literatura*, 49 (2001), pp. 451–481. – *Česká literární kritika 20. století. K 100. výročí narození Václava Černého* (edited by Marta Zahradníková and Jarmila Schreiberová), Prague, 2006.

Diviš, Ivan

Poet and essayist. He was born in Prague in 1924 and was imprisoned by the Gestapo during the war. He finished his studies of philosophy and aesthetics at Charles University in 1949. He was employed as a turner. From 1961 to 1968 he was an editor in the Prague publishing house *Mladá fronta* (Frontline Youth). In 1969 he left for the Federal Republic of Germany where he worked as a librarian in *Radio Free Europe* in Munich. He published his works through émigré publishing houses and in samizdat. After 1989 he divided his time between Germany and the Czech Republic. He died in Prague in 1999.

After the war he was a member of the group *Ohnice* (Charlock), a group of poets that espoused the work of the prematurely deceased Jewish poet Jiří Orten (Diviš's first collection was *První hudba bratřím* [First Music to the Brethren], 1947). A long silence ensued and it was not till the sixties that he began publishing a series of collections of poems that were characterized by the bleakness of his vision, deliberately violent language and the accumulation of metaphors. See *Chrlení krve* (Spitting Blood, 1964). The work of Vladimír Holan was a powerful influence on him as was the Catholic faith, to which he was drawn in the mid-sixties: the collection *Sursum* (1967, meaning "upwards", "in the heavens above"). The poem *Thanatea* (the female form of the ancient Greek god of death Thanatos; Thanatea, 1968) is an agonized, passionate dialogue of the poet with death, in which, characteristic of the author's style, vulgarity alternates with spirituality and the concrete with the abstract.

Diviš found exile hard to bear. For ten years he wrote no poetry. He returned to literature with the poetry *Beránek na sněhu* (The Lamb in the Snow, Munich, 1980; Prague 1990) and *Odchod z Čech* (Departure from Bohemia, Munich, 1981; Prague, 1990). In these and in other works his poetic vision is at its most extreme: on the one hand there is hatred aggressively directed at the present day, especially the spiritual emptiness and limitations of contemporary Czech society, while on the other hand regeneration in the name of God brings hope. Outstanding among Diviš's last works is *Teorie spolehlivosti* (Theory of Reliability, 1994, expanded 2002), a collection of meditations and diary-like entries from the years 1960–1999.

Edition in English: seven poems (translated by George Theiner), in *Modern Poetry in Translation: Czech* (edited by Ted Hughes and Daniel Weissbort), London, 1967; "From a Theory about Dependability" (translated by Jeanne Němcová), in *Universum: A Review of Czechoslovak Literature and Arts*, 3 (1968), no. 5, pp. 15, 21, 57; six poems in *New Writing in Czechoslovakia* (translated by George Theiner), Baltimore, 1969.

Bibliography: Josef Jedlička, "Poezie Ivana Diviše jako osobní riziko,"

Svědectví, 13 (1975/1976), no. 50, pp. 309–322. – Rio Preisner, "Pavana pro Ivana Diviše," *Proměny*, 17 (1980), no. 1, pp. 43–51. – Jiří Cieslar, "Možnosti hněvu aneb Jsoucno onemocnělo!" in his *Hlas deníku*, Prague, 2002, pp. 325–338. – Jaroslav Med, "'Pokleknouti trvám! Žádné rozumět!' Básnický apel Ivana Diviše," in his *Spisovatelé ve stínu* (2nd edition), Prague, 2004, pp. 131–139.

DRDA, JAN

Prose writer, dramatist, journalist. Born in Příbram in Central Bohemia in 1915. He completed his studies of philology at Charles University in Prague in 1938. From 1937 to 1942 he was arts editor at the daily paper *Lidové noviny* (The People's Paper). After the war he was enthusiastic about the changes advocated by the Communists and was an official representative of the party. From 1949 to 1956 he was president of the Union of Czechoslovak Writers, member of parliament and a member of the Central Committee of the Communist Party of Czechoslovakia. In August 1968 he opposed the Soviet invasion ("not even a drop of water for the invaders"). He died in Dobříš in 1970.

Drda wrote his best work early in his career. His columns (*Svět viděný zpomaloučka* [The World Viewed in Slow Motion], 1943) and his courtroom reports, published posthumously as *Milostenky nemilované* (Unloved Loves, 1995, edited by Petr Drda), are in the traditions of Karel Čapek and the liberal democratic daily *Lidové noviny*. The main features of his first novel, *Městečko na dlani* (Small Town Revealed, 1940), filmed by Václav Binovec, 1942, in which the little town of Rukapáň (The Hand of the Lord), with its miners, farmers and tradesmen, was inspired by his native Příbram, are benign humour, spontaneous narrative and sympathy for ordinary people. His next novels, *Živá voda* (Living Water, 1941) and *Putování Petra Sedmilháře* (The Peregrinations of Peter the Liar, 1943), have a psychological basis. During the Nazi occupation he wrote his successful comedy *Hrátky s čertem* (Chatting with the Devil) which could not be staged till after the war. It was premiered in 1945.

After the war he wrote stories about the German occupation and the insurrection *Němá barikáda* (The Silent Barricade, 1946), which highlighted the extreme passions current at the time. This black and white oversimplicity intensified in the works that followed. He sought a solution for his creative stalemate by returning to fairy-tales and stories in the style of folk tales: *České pohádky* (Czech Fairy Tales, 1958), *Posvícení v Tramtárii* (The Village Fair at Neverland, published posthumously in 1972) and *Nedaleko Rukapáně* (Near to the Hand of the Lord, edited by Jaroslava Janáčková and Milena Masáková, 1989). Drda himself took part in the production of numerous film adaptations of his work. Outstanding among them were *Němá barikáda* (directed by Otakar Vávra) in 1949, *Hrátky s čertem* (directed by Josef Mach) in 1956 and *Vyšší princip* (The Highest Principle [in English as *Old Morality*, 1962] directed by Jiří Krejčík) in 1960.

Editions in English: "The Silent Barricade" (translated by Iris Urwin), in *Four Czech Stories* (edited by Iris Urwin), Prague, 1957, pp. 13–31; "Old Morality" (translated by Edith Pargeter), in *The Linden Tree* (edited by Mojmír Otruba and Zdeněk Pešat), Prague, 1962, pp. 240–245; "The Village Story" (translated by

Jeanne W. Němcová), in *Czech and Slovak Short Stories* (edited by Jeanne W. Němcová), London and New York, 1967, pp. 149–159.

Bibliography: Jaromíra Nejedlá, *Dvě studie o stylu v próze Jana Drdy*, Prague, 1970. – Erik Gilk, "Trojí maloměsto před první světovou válkou," *Česká literatura*, 49 (2001), pp. 151–163. – Jiří Holý, "Vyšší princip a Vyšší princip po deseti letech," in his *Možnosti interpretace*, Olomouc, 2002, pp. 202–210.

FUKS, LADISLAV

Novelist and essayist. He was born in Prague in 1923 into the family of a highly ranked police officer. Some autobiographical elements appear in the novels *Variace pro temnou strunu* (Variations for a Dark String, 1966) and *Příběh kriminálního rady* (The Case of the Senior Police Investigator, 1971). Fuks wrote the first version of *Variace* as a secondary school student. He studied philosophy, psychology and history of art at Charles University in Prague and was awarded a doctorate in 1949. He worked in paper mills, in the Ancient Monuments Authority and in the Prague National Gallery and is the author of a study in art history, *Zámek Kynžvart* (Castle Kynžvart, 1958).

Following the success of his first novel, *Pan Theodor Mundstock* (1963; *Mr Theodore Mundstock*, translated by Iris Urwin, New York, 1968, London, 1969, and successively published in seventeen countries), he devoted himself entirely to literature. He travelled frequently, enjoying his stays in Vienna, but he lived in seclusion, mostly in his study in Prague which was crammed with bizarre objects and pictures. The author's homosexuality was a contributory factor in keeping him isolated from the normal world. He died in Prague in 1994.

His first published novel *Pan Theodor Mundstock* was an outstanding success. The subject, the fate of the Jews during the Nazi occupation, was still topical at the beginning of the 1960s. The story of a minor civil servant waiting to be transported to a concentration camp is told as an extraordinary narrative; reality subtly impinges on fantasy and there are many evocative allusions, symbolic appellations and variations. The author perfected this technique in the works that followed, for example, in *Variace pro temnou strunu* (Variations for a Dark String, 1966), the story, with some biographical elements, of an adolescent boy in Prague at the end of the thirties. The following novella *Spalovač mrtvol* (1967; *The Cremator*, translated by Eva M. Kandler, London and New York, 1984) verges on a horror story, in which the characters become more grotesque while the mystery and the symbolism of the imagery intensify. The novella, like other of the author's works, may be taken as a parable of the power and the evil latent in the human soul. A film version, with the collaboration of the author and directed by Juraj Herz, was made in 1968.

His next novels, usually based on crime themes, for example, *Myši Natálie Mooshabrové* (Natalie Mooshabrová's Mice, 1970) and *Příběh kriminálního rady* (The Case of the Senior Police Investigator, 1971) did not differ in approach and subject matter from his previous work. The artistic standard of *Pasáček z doliny* (The Shepherd Boy from the Valley, 1977) and Fuks's other work published officially during the seventies, deteriorated in an attempt to conform to the demands of the regime. Fuks's artistic ideas are to a certain extent restored in the novel *Obraz Martina Blaskowitze* (The Picture of Martin Blaskowitz, 1980) which is reminiscent of *Variace pro temnou strunu* through its chief character. In the extensive novel *Vévodkyně a kuchařka* (The Duchess and the Housekeeper, 1983), which evokes the atmosphere of Art Nouveau Vienna at the beginning of the 20th century and may be considered the first Czech post-modern novel, his ideas are fully restored. His autobiography *Moje zrcadlo* (My Mirror, 1995, edited by Jiří Tušl, introduction by Arnošt Lustig) was published posthumously. From 2003 to 2006 *Odeon* in Prague published the work of Ladislav Fuks (seven volumes, edited and with commentary by Miloš Pohorský).

Other editions in English: "The Candle-End" (translated by Iris Urwin), in *Universum: A Review of Czechoslovak Literature and Arts*, 1 (1966), no. 2, pp. 25–34; "The Picture of Martin Blaskowitz" (translated by Edith Pargeter), in *Panorama of Czech Literature*, 4 (1982), pp. 30–40; "The Duchess and the Housekeeper" (translated by Edith Pargeter), in *Panorama of Czech Literature*, 6 (1984), pp. 49–72; "Kchony Sees the World" (translated by Alex Zucker), in *This Side of Reality* (edited by Alexandra Büchler), London, 1996, pp. 1–17.

Bibliography: Aleš Haman, "Paradox života jako strukturní princip literárního tvaru," in *Příběhy pod mikroskopem* (edited by Radko Pytlík), Prague, 1966, pp. 85–103. – Thomas Winner, "Some Remarks on the Art of Ladislav Fuks," *Revista storica italiana*, 17–19 (1970–1972), pp. 587–599. – Thomas G. Winner, "Mythic and Modern Elements in the Art of Ladislav Fuks: Natalia Mooshaber's Mice," in *Fiction and Drama in Eastern and Southeastern Europe* (edited by Henrik Birnbaum and Thomas Eekman), Columbus, 1980, pp. 443–461. – Sonia Ivanovna Kanikova, "The Jews in the Works of Ladislav Fuks," in *Remembering for the Future* (edited by Yehuda Bauer et al.), vol. III, Oxford, 1989, pp. 2946–2957. – Luboš Merhaut, "Nelehká cesta za poznáním zla: Interpretace Fuksova románu Myši Natálie Mooshabrové," *Česká literatura*, 37 (1989), pp. 398–412. – Miloš Pohorský, *Zlomky analýzy*, Prague, 1990, pp. 77–109. – Jiřina Táborská, "Ladislav Fuks: Pan Theodor Mundstock," in *Česká literatura 1945–1970* (edited by Jiřina Táborská and Milan Zeman), Prague, 1992, pp. 279–288. – Bohumil Svozil, *Próza obrazná i věcná*, Prague, 1995, pp. 7–43. – Natascha Drubek-Meyer, "Der Leichenverbrenner von Ladislav Fuks und seine Verfilmung durch Juraj Herz im Kontext der tschechischen Nachkriegsprosa über den Holocaust," in *Juden und Judentum in Literatur und Film des slawischen Sprachraumes* (edited by Peter Kosta et al.), Wiesbaden, 2000, pp. 53–69. – *Tvar*, 14 (2003), no. 15 (several articles on the work of Ladislav Fuks). – Cythia A. Klíma, "Ladislav Fuks," "Mr Theodore Mundstock," in *Reference Guide to Holocaust Literature* (edited by Thomas Riggs), Detroit, 2002, pp. 101–102, 512–513. – David Mesher, "Ladislav Fuks," in *Holocaust Literature* (edited by S. Lillian Kremer), New York and London, 2003, pp. 396–398. – Robert B. Pynsent, "Ladislav Fuks," in *Dictionary of Literary Biography: Holocaust Novelists*, vol. 299 (edited by Efraim Sicher), Detroit, 2004, pp. 89–94. – Rajendra A. Chitnis, "Remaining on the Threshold: The Cunning of Ladislav Fuks," *Central Europe*, 2 (2005), no. 1, pp. 47–59. – Aleš Kovalčík, *Ladislav Fuks: Tvář a maska*, Prague, 2006.

GRUŠA, JIŘÍ

Poet, novelist, essayist and translator. He was born in Pardubice in Eastern Bohemia in 1938, completed his studies of philosophy and history at Charles University in Prague in 1962 and worked as an editor. After 1970, when he could not publish, he worked as a junior clerk and published abroad and in samizdat. He was a signatory of the human rights manifesto *Charter 77*. Between 1969 and 1970 and again in 1978 he was prosecuted for his literary works, once for "pornography" and a second time for "sedition". From 1981 he lived in the West, mostly in Germany. After 1990 he was in the Czechoslovak, later the Czech, diplomatic service as ambassador to Germany and Austria. He is now President of the International Pen Club.

In the sixties he was one of the writers connected with the reviews for the young generation *Tvář* (The Countenance) and *Sešity* (Notebooks). As a poet he began with *Torna* (Haversack, 1962) and *Světlá lhůta* (A Lucid Interval, 1964) and, as a journalist, in opposition to the official demands, he stressed the need for "clean hands", that is morality as a prerequisite for literature. From the end of the sixties he wrote mainly prose. His well-known works are the novels *Dotazník aneb Modlitba za jedno město a přítele* (samizdat, 1976; Toronto, 1978; Brno, 1990; published in English as *The Questionnaire, or, Prayer for a Town and a Friend,* translated by Peter Kussi, London and New York, 1982, Toronto and New York, 1983) and *Doktor Kokeš, Mistr Panny: Ackermann aus Böheim* (Doctor Cocker, Virgin Master: Ackermann aus Böheim; samizdat, 1980; Toronto, 1984, with the title *Mistr Panny aneb Ackermann aus Behaim* Prague, 1992; a chapter translated by Alex Zucker as "Honking Horns" in *This Side of Reality*, 1996). In 1984 the author wrote a version in German which he entitled *Janinka*. In the novel *Dotazník* the narrator Jan Chrysostom Kepka, in the Czechoslovakia of the seventies, has made sixteen unsuccessful applications for jobs and still has to fill in application forms with his CV. This is the starting point for reflections on his own life and the life of his ancestors going back to the distant past. It is a picture of man, half brutally realistic, half fantastic, bewildered by himself, his surroundings and the changing regimes of the 20th century. Gruša published poems in German, *Der Babylonwald* (The Babylonian Forest, 1991, with an afterword by Sarah Kirsch, translated into Czech by Tomáš Kafka, 1998), and essays *Das Gesicht – der Schriftsteller – der Fall* (The Countenance – the Author – the Case, 2000, preface by Utz Rachowski, afterword by Ludger Udolph, bibliography by Susanne Fritz; in Czech in Jiří Gruša, *Šťastný bezdomovec* [Happily Homeless], 2003). He translated into Czech poems by Paul Celan, Rainer Maria Rilke and others. He is the author of an unconventional guidebook in German to the Czech Republic, *Gebrauchsanweisung für Tschechien* (1999; in Czech *Česko – návod k použití* [The Czech Republic – Instructions for Use], 2001). In Germany he prepared several selections of Czech literature and in the seventies in Czechoslovakia he even collaborated in publishing *Slovník zakázaných autorů* (Dictionary of Banned Authors) with Jiří Brabec, Jan Lopatka, Petr Kabeš and Igor Hájek. It was originally published in samizdat in 1978, then in Toronto in 1982 and in Prague in 1991. In 2003 a collection of his poems, *Právo útrpné* (Subjecting to Torture), with an afterword by Vladimír Karfík was published by the Prague publishing house *Akropolis*. In 2004 a book form of a dialogue with Daniel Dobiáš entitled *Umění stárnout* (The Art of Growing Old) was published.

Other editions in English: "Song of a Sergeant's Death" (translated by Káča Poláčková), in *Modern Poetry in Translation: Czech* (edited by Ted Hughes and Daniel Weissbort), London, 1967; *Franz Kafka of Prague* (translated by Eric Mosbacher), New York, 1983; three texts (translated by Miroslav Rensky and Peter Kussi), in *The Writing on the Wall* (edited by Peter Kussi and Antonín Jaroslav Liehm), Princeton, 1983, pp. 34–58; "What's a Life Worth? An Interview with Jiří Gruša" (translated by Jan Čulík and Alan Mason), *Edinburgh Review*, 80 (1988), no. 1, pp. 112–122; "Honking Horns" (translated by Alex Zucker), in *This Side of Reality* (edited by Alexandra Büchler), London, 1996, pp. 77–93.

Bibliography: Jiří Lederer, *České rozhovory*, Prague, 1991, pp. 161–182 (originally samizdat 1977, and Cologne, 1979). – Daniel Dobiáš, "Zlo v Dotazníku," *Svět literatury*, 2000, no. 19, pp. 76–82. – Ludger Udolph, "Über Jiří Grušas Poetik," in Jiří Gruša, *Das Gesicht – der Schriftsteller – der Fall*, Dresden, 2000, pp. 59–76. – Alfrun Kliems, "Jiří Gruša und die 'weibliche anima'. Paradigmenwechsel in der Lyrik am Beispiel von Heimat, Sprache und Tod," in her *Im Stummland: Zum Exilwerk von Libuše Moníková, Jiří Gruša und Ota Filip*, Frankfurt a. M., 2002, pp. 145–194. – Vladimír Karfík, "Živý poeta doctus," in Jiří Gruša, *Právo útrpné* (edited by Jiří Tomáš), Prague, 2003, pp. 219–225. – Jiří Trávníček, "Komentář," in Jiří Gruša, *Dotazník aneb Modlitba za jedno město a přítele*, Prague, 2004, pp. 259–298.

HAVEL, VÁCLAV

Dramatist, essayist and journalist. He was born in Prague in 1936 into a cultured, entrepreneurial family. After the Communist coup of February 1948, as a "member of the bourgeoisie" he was not admitted to higher education. It was not till 1966 that, as an extramural student, he completed his studies of dramaturgy at the Theatre Faculty of the Academy of Performing Arts in Prague. He worked as a laboratory assistant, stagehand and technician. From 1963–1968 he was repertory adviser at the Prague *Divadlo Na zábradlí* (The Theatre on the Balustrade). He was involved with the production of the review *Tvář* (Countenance) and edited the anthologies *Podoby II* (Resemblances II, 1969) and *Pohledy I* (Views I, samizdat, 1976). After 1969, banned from publishing, he led or took part in many cultural and dissident political enterprises – the meetings of banned authors, the samizdat *Edice Expedice*, *Charter 77*, the samizdat reviews and journals *Obsah* (Contents), *O divadle* (About Theatre), *Lidové noviny* (The People's Paper). He was persecuted and imprisoned by the ruling Communist regime, for the longest time between 1979–1983. His letters to his wife in which he sums up his views on philosophy and culture date from that period. *Dopisy Olze* were published in samizdat in 1983, in Toronto in 1985, and in Brno in 1990.Translated by Paul Wilson as *Letters to Olga* they were published in New York and London in 1988. In November 1989 he led the "Velvet Revolution" and in December was elected President of Czechoslovakia; and after the partition of the two states, President of the Czech Republic. He became a famous figure world-wide, campaigning for democracy and a global view of political problems. His *Projevy* (Speeches) was published in 1990 and *Vážení občané* (Dear Fellow-Citizens) in 1992. Later on, he published his speeches in annual volumes *Václav Havel 1992 & 1993, 1994*, etc. They are all reprinted in volumes VI and VII of the Collected Works (*Spisy VI, VII*, 1999, edited by Jan Zelenka and Jan Šulc). Havel's speeches were translated by Paul Wilson and others as *Toward a Civil Society* and published in English in Prague in 1995. Further speeches by Havel, *The Art of the Impossible*, also translated by Paul Wilson et al., were published in New York in 1997.

Havel began as critic, essayist and poet. Later he published only typographical poetry. Some of his *Antikódy* (Anticodes) were published in Václav Havel, *Protokoly* (Protocols), 1966, and all came out in 1993. A collection of his poems and anticodes appears in volume I of his Collected Works, edited by Jan Šulc and Zuzana Dětáková (1999). *Divadlo Na zábradlí* in Prague became the regular stage for his plays in the sixties. He gained fame with his first independent play *Zahradní slavnost* (translated by Vera Blackwell, London, 1969, as *The Garden Party*). It had its premiere in 1963 and was inspired by the theatre of the absurd. It contains the key themes of his work: the abuse of language, which is also the abuse of power, and the dehumanization of people. The structure too is remarkable – alternating scenes present thesis and antithesis, individual speeches are repeated by different characters as mirror images in slightly changed form. Similar plays that followed are *Vyrozumění*, which was premiered in 1965, published in Václav Havel, *Protokoly*, in 1966 (translated by Vera Blackwell as *The Memorandum*, London and New York, 1967, 1981 with a introduction by Tom Stoppard), and *Ztížená možnost soustředění*, premiered in 1968, published in 1969 (translated by Vera Blackwell as *The Increased Difficulty of Concentration*, London, 1972; New York, 1976).

In the seventies and eighties the author could not stage his work. An exception was a single amateur production in 1975 of the play *Žebrácká opera* in Počernice near Prague. The play was first published in samizdat in 1974, translated into English as *The Beggar's Opera* by Paul Wilson, New York, 2001, and made into a film by Jiří Menzel in 1991. Those who took part in the 1975 production, both actors and spectators, were severely persecuted. As a result Havel the dramatist was overshadowed by Havel the essayist and dissident. The one-act plays, especially *Audience* and *Vernisáž*, with Vaněk, a writer, as the main character, are highly significant. They were both published in samizdat in 1975 and first performed in Vienna in 1976. An English version of *Audience* appeared in *Sorry . . . : Two Plays: Audience, Private View* (London, 1978, translated by Vera Blackwell); the first translation of *Audience* was made by George Theiner as *Conversation* (*Index on Censorship*, 1976, no. 3, also in *Selected Plays, 1963–1983*, London and Boston, 1992). A new translation was made by Jan Novák in *The Vaněk-Plays*, edited by Marketa Goetz-Stankiewicz, Vancouver, 1987. This anthology came out in Czech as *V hlavní roli Ferdinand Vaněk*, edited by Jan Šulc, epilogue by Lenka Jungmannová, Prague, Academia, 2006. The plays *Largo desolato* and *Pokoušení* are also important. *Largo desolato* appeared in samizdat in 1984 and had its premiere in Vienna in 1985. Translated into English by Tom Stoppard, 1987, the play is dedicated to the British playwright. *Pokoušení* was published in samizdat in 1985; it was premiered in Vienna in 1986 and translated as *Temptation* by George Theiner, London and Boston, 1988. Havel's poetics had not really changed since the 1960s. What was new was the use of personal experience – *Audience* was inspired by the author's work in a country brewery and *Largo desolato* is a self-mocking portrayal of the situation of a dissident. The outstanding example of his works of this period is *Pokoušení*, in which he makes original use of the theme of Faust's pact with the devil.

Besides his creative literary work Havel has from the beginning written essays and studies on the arts and public life, commentaries on his own work, etc. *O lidskou identitu* (On Human Identity, edited by Vilém Prečan and Alexandr Tomský) was published in London and Paris in 1984 and in Prague in 1990. *Do různých stran* (To Various Recipients, edited by Vilém Prečan) was published in samizdat and Scheinfeld in 1989 and in Prague in 1990. Now both are in volumes III and IV of Havel's Collected Works, 1999 (*Spisy III*, *IV*, edited by Jan Šulc and Jarmila Víšková). Texts translated into English are also: *The Power and the Powerless* (edited by John Keane and translated by Paul Wilson and A. G. Brain [Gerald and Alice Turner], London and New York, 1985); *Open Letters: Selected Writings, 1965–1990* (translated by Paul Wilson, edited by Paul Wilson et al., London and New York, 1991). The lengthy interview with Karel Hvížďala was published as *Dálkový výslech* (Distance Interrogation, samizdat and Purley, 1986; Prague, 1989), translated as *Disturbing the Peace* by Paul Wilson and published in New York in 1990.

Plays from the years 1970–1976 were first published in Czech in Toronto in 1977, and a collection of plays from 1963–1988 came out in Prague in 1992. The Prague publishing house *Torst* issued *Spisy Václava Havla* (Collected Works of Václav Havel) in seven volumes in 1999 (edited by Jan Šulc et al.). Published in English in London in 1992 was *Selected Plays, 1963–1983* (translated by Vera Blackwell et al. as *The Garden Party and Other Plays*, New York, 1993); also *Selected Plays, 1984–1987* (translated by Tom Stoppard et al.), was published in London and Boston in 1994.

Bibliography: Antonín Jaroslav Liehm, "Václav Havel" (interview), in his *The Politics of Culture*, New York, 1970, pp. 373–394 (in Czech Antonín Jaroslav Liehm, *Generace*, Prague, 1990, pp. 300–320). – Paul I. Trensky, "Václav Havel and the Language of the Absurd," *The Slavic and East European Journal*, 13 (1969), no. 1, pp. 42–65. – Paul I. Trensky, *Czech Drama since World War II*, New York, 1978. – Marketa Goetz-Stankiewicz, *The Silenced Theatre: Czech Playwrights without a Stage*, Toronto, 1979, pp. 43–88. – *Václav Havel, or Living in Truth* (edited by Jan Vladislav; six texts by Havel, texts by other authors are dedicated to Havel), Amsterdam, 1986, London, 1987. – Barbara Day, "Václav Havel in England," *Cross Currents*, 7 (1988), pp. 385–398. – Michael Simmons, *The Reluctant President: The Political Life of Václav Havel*, London, 1991 (in Czech 1993). – Eda Kriseová, *Václav Havel: The Authorized Biography*, New York, 1993 (in Czech 1991). – Robert B. Pynsent, "Questions of Identity and

Responsibility in Václav Havel," in his *Questions of Identity*, Budapest et al., 1994, pp. 1–42 (in Czech 1996). – Alfred Thomas, "Philosophy and Politics in Václav Havel's Largo Desolato," in his *The Labyrinth of the Word*, Munich, 1995, pp. 144–157. – Tamara Trojanowska, "Behind the Open Doors: Havel's *Largo Desolato*," *Canadian Slavonic Papers*, 38 (1996), nos. 3–4, pp. 419–427. – Marketa Goetz-Stankiewicz and Phyllis Carey (eds.), *Critical Essays on Václav Havel*, New York, 1999. – Hans Haider, *Václav Havel: Die Uraufführung der Stücke von Václav Havel im Wiener Burgtheater 1976 bis 1986: Mit einer Fortsetzung in Zürich*, Vienna, 1999. – John Keane, *Václav Havel: A Political Tragedy in Six Acts*, London, 1999 (in Czech 1999). – Klára Hůrková, *Mirror Images: A Comparison of the Early Plays of Václav Havel and Tom Stoppard with Special Reference to Their Political Aspects*, Frankfurt a. M., 2000. – Peter Steiner, "Cops or Robbers: The Beggar's Opera by Václav Havel," in his *The Deserts of Bohemia: Czech Fiction and Its Social Context*, Ithaca and London, 2000, pp. 218–240 (in Czech 2002). – Jan Čulík, "Václav Havel," in *Dictionary of Literary Biography: Twentieth-Century Eastern European Writers*, vol. 232 (edited by Steven Serafin et al.), Detroit, 2001, pp. 110–130. – James F. Pontuso, *Václav Havel: Civic Responsibility in the Postmodern Age*, Oxford and Lanham, 2004.

HODROVÁ, DANIELA

Prose-writer, literary theorist, essayist and translator. Born in Prague in 1946 into the family of an actor, she studied Russian, Czech and Romance languages and literatures at Charles University in Prague. On completion of her studies in 1972 she worked as an editor in the publishing house *Odeon*. From 1975 she was employed in the theoretical department of the Czech and World Literature Institute in the Academy of Sciences. Her first husband was the writer and translator Karel Milota (1937–2002).

Her trilogy of novels *Trýznivé město / Città dolente* (City in Torment) is outstanding. Written in the seventies and eighties, it could not be published till 1989. *Podobojí* (In Both Species) and *Kukly* (polysemic title: Pupae/Masks/Puppets) were both published in 1991 and *Théta* (Theta) came out in 1992. The setting of the trilogy, based on the plan of Dante's *Divine Comedy*, is the border area between the Prague districts of Vinohrady and Žižkov. The time scale extends from the Nazi occupation, with reminiscences of the 19th century and the Czech National Revival, to the present day. Real events and figures merge into fantasy; allusions and symbols pervade the narrative in which time and place are constantly changing. The main character goes through the work in search of herself and in the end becomes identified with the author. Her other novels, for example, *Perunův den* (Perun's Day, 1994) and *Ztracené děti* (Lost Children, 1997) are composed in similar fashion. Her studies and essays, *Hledání románu* (In Search of the Novel, 1989) and *Román zasvěcení* (A Novel of Initiation, 1993) give an inspirational view of the European and Czech novel and in them Hodrová uses her extensive knowledge to take an inventive look at literature. She investigated typology in literature in the publication *Místa s tajemstvím* (Places with Secrets, 1994) and in *Poetika míst* (The Poetics of Places, 1997) in which she was both collaborator and editor. She took part in a further series of literary-scientific team ventures, editing, for example, the collections *Proměny subjektu* I–II (Changes of Subject, 1993–1994), *... na okraji chaosu ...* (... on the Brink of Chaos ..., 2001) to which she was a prominent contributor. From the Russian she translated the studies of Mikhail Bakhtin.

Editions in English: "In Both Species" (translated by Tatiana Firkusny and Véronique Firkusny-Callegari), *Prairie Schooner*, 66 (1992), no. 44, pp. 36–45; "The Kingdom of Olšany" (translated by Tatiana Firkusny and Véronique Firkusny-Callegari), *The Prague Review*, 2 (1996), no. 2, pp. 67–91; "From Perun's Day" (translated by Tatiana Firkusny and Véronique Firkusny-Callegari), in *Daylight in Nightclub Inferno* (edited by Elena Lappin), North Haven, 1997, pp. 191–202; "Theta. Excerpts from a Novel" (translated by Tatiana Firkusny and Véronique Firkusny-Callegari), in *Allskin and Other Tales by Contemporary Czech Women* (edited by Alexandra Büchler), Seattle, 1998, pp. 50–71.

Bibliography: Jana Bartůňková and Alena Zachová, "Problém dvojnictví v trilogii Daniely Hodrové," *Česká literatura*, 42 (1994), pp. 522–532. – Robert Porter, "Daniela Hodrová, Michal Viewegh, Jáchym Topol: New Voices?" in his *An Introduction to Twentieth-Century Czech Fiction*, Brighton and Portland, 2001, pp. 162–171. – Jana Vrbová, "Koncepty prostoru v románových trilogiích Daniely Hodrové a Jiřího Kratochvila," *Tvar*, 12, suppl. vol. 2–3 (2001), pp. 1–64. – Anna Car, *O prozie Danieli Hodrovej*, Cracow, 2003. – Rajendra A. Chitnis, "Writing as Being: Jiří Kratochvil, Zuzana Brabcová, Daniela Hodrová, Michal Ajvaz, Jáchym Topol," in his *Literature in Post-Communist Russia and Eastern Europe*, London, 2004, pp. 80–114. – Helena Kosková, "Romány Daniely Hodrové jako hledání tajemství bytí," in *Ztěžklá křídla snů: Ženy v české literatuře*, Prague, 2004, pp. 231–249. – Pavlína Krupová, "Daniela Hodrová: Théta," *Česká literatura*, 53 (2005), pp. 395–406. – Milan Suchomel, "Komůrka obscura," in *Víra a výraz* (edited by Tomáš Kubíček and Jan Wiendl), Brno, 2005, pp. 326–333.

HOLAN, VLADIMÍR

Poet, prose-writer and translator. He was born in Prague in 1905. His father was a factory manager and from him he inherited his intense, melancholic nature. In contrast his mother's temperament was equable and cheerful. She appears frequently in his poems. While still at secondary school he published verses, and after his final school examinations he worked for a short time in an office. In 1935 he chose the precarious life of a freelance writer. He became friends with the poets František Halas, Jaroslav Seifert and other artists. After the Second World War he tended to favour Communism but soon became disillusioned. For many years from the end of the forties he could publish practically nothing but translations. He lived a strange reclusive life and after 1948 seldom left his flat in Prague beside the Vltava river; "for fifteen years I talked / to the walls". His only daughter's incurable mental disease caused him great distress. In the sixties his poetry was again published regularly and had an influence on the whole of Czech culture. He died in Prague in 1980.

In Holan's poetry the dark and tragic side of existence predominates – his friend Jaroslav Seifert called him "the black angel". His poems are based on the breaking down of convention in language and life. They are full of twists and sudden pauses (two voices in dialogue, question marks, unfinished sentences). He takes language to extremes, using bookish expressions, neologisms, symbolic language, colloquial Czech and vulgarisms. Metaphors, abstract and concrete expressions are closely interlinked, for example, "na kovadlině vody" (on the anvil of the water), "talíře lůny nad městem" (the dish of the moon above the house). Holan's work went through several phases. In the thirties, he wrote complex poetry, constructing a world of his own, sometimes based on nothing but imagination and language: *Oblouk* (The Arch, 1934, revised 1941 and 1948), *Kameni, přicházíš...* (You Are Coming, Stone . . ., 1937, revised 1948). But, unexpectedly, at the time of the Munich Agreement he spoke out clearly against capitulating to Hitler. He expressed outrage and despair at the capitulation and betrayal by Western allies and, especially in the compositions *Září 1938* (September 1938, 1938) and *Odpověď Francii* (The Answer to France, banned by the censor, published in 1946), he expressed the determination of the nation to defend the homeland.

For a short time after the war he continued writing social and political poetry. While his vision and ideals remained exalted to the highest degree, his style became simpler (see *Rudoarmějci* [Red Army Soldiers, 1947]). The positive values in life, childhood, nature, the countryside and pure love, exist beside the tragic, incomprehensible world. The tension between tragic situations and short bright spells of happiness is brought out chiefly by the non-traditional epic poetry written in regular verse form. After the long poem *První testament* (1940, translated as *The First Testament* by Josef Tomáš, Prague, Arima Publishing, 2005), which is still very abstract, *Terezka Planetová* (Terezka Planetová, 1943) in particular tells the story of a young life ruined and a compelling but unspoken love, loosely inspired by one of the essays by the composer Leoš Janáček. The ruination of a life, the lot of man at the mercy of a cruel fate, is a powerful theme running through the collection of epic poems in free verse *Příběhy* (Tales), written between the end of the forties and the beginning of the fifties, but not published till 1963. This collection was composed at the most difficult period in Holan's life. Lonely and in torment he nevertheless produced other supreme works including the collection of lyric poems *Bolest* (Pain, 1949–1955, published in 1965, expanded 1966) and the composition *Noc s Hamletem* (written 1949–1956, published 1964 and translated as *A Night with Hamlet* by Jarmila and Ian Milner, London, 1980; new translation by Clayton Eshleman, New York, 1988). The public reading of this poem in the Prague wine-cellar *Viola*, which was frequented by poets, was a cultural landmark; this performance was in the repertory of *Viola* for twenty-five years. Again we find the theme of walls and chasms, the crushing burden of existence, but also the magic moments of *Poézie* (Poetry), when man is aware of the hidden meaning of life. Love can be both animal carnality and the promise of tenderness and selfless emotion. The poet in his nocturnal conversation with Hamlet, his alter ego, wonders whether we are or are not lost souls and comes to the conclusion that we have to accept the precariousness of our fate. The final creative period in Holan's life embraces the sixties and seventies. The main features of his vision and style remained unchanged. The former richness of metaphor has gone, however. More often things are named unambiguously and the construction is concise, as for example in *Sbohem?* (Goodbye?), published posthumously in 1982.

Outstanding among Holan's translations in the wide selection edited by Oldřich Králík entitled *Cestou* (En Route, 1962), are the translations of Luis de Góngora, Nikolaus Lenau, Rainer Maria Rilke and others. A critical edition of the works of Vladimír Holan, edited by Vladimír Justl, was published in eleven volumes between 1965 and 1988 by *Odeon* in Prague. The final volume also includes a detailed biography of Holan by Vladimír Justl (1988). From 1999 the Prague publishing house *Paseka* has been publishing a new collected edition of Vladimír Holan's works, including translations (edited by Vladimír Justl and Pavel Chalupa). In Germany in 2003 the publishing house *Mutabene* in Cologne began issuing a German translation of the Collected Works of Vladimír Holan, edited by Urs Heftrich and Michael Špirit (so far, two volumes have come out, 2003 and 2005).

Other editions in English: three poems (translated by Edith Pargeter), in *The Linden Tree* (edited by Mojmír Otruba and Zdeněk Pešat), Prague, 1962, pp. 251–255; nine poems (translated by Káča Poláčková), in *Universum: A Review of Czechoslovak Literature and Arts*, 1 (1966), no. 1, pp. 34–41; seven poems (translated by George Theiner), in *New Writing in Czechoslovakia* (edited by George Theiner), Harmondsworth, 1969, pp. 251–255; *Selected Poems* (translated by Jarmila and Ian Milner), Harmondsworth, 1971; *Mirroring* (translated by C. G. Hanzlicek and Dana Hábová), Middletown, 1985; *Conductors of the Pit: Major Works by Rimbaud, Vallejo, Césaire, Artaud and Holan* (edited, translated and introduction by Clayton Eshleman), New York, 1988; *Rhymes Be Traded for Bread* (translated by Irma Charvátová, illustrated by Josef Istler), Brno, 1993.

Bibliography: Ian Milner, "Introduction," in Vladimír Holan, *Selected Poems*, Harmondsworth, 1971, pp. 9–15. – Eva Nitsch, *Thema und Anweisungsstruktur im Text: Mit einer Analyse des ersten Abschnittes aus Noc s Hamletem von Vladimír Holan*, Munich, 1979. – Verena Flick, *Die Möglichkeit der Gestaltung des Tragisches in der Lyrik: Dargestellt am Beispiel des tschechischen Dichters Vladimír Holan*, Giessen, 1982. – *Úderem tepny* (edited by Vladimír Justl), Prague, 1986. – Přemysl Blažíček, *Sebeuvědomění poezie*, Prague, 1991. – Miroslav Červenka, "Vědomí strasti" and "Žánrové souvislosti Holanových Příběhů," in his *Styl a význam*, Prague, 1991, pp. 107–134. – *La Revue de Belles-Lettres*, 114 (1991), no. 1–2 (special issue dedicated to Vladimír Holan). – Charles S. Kraszewski, "Vladimír Holan: Noc s Hamletem," in his *The Romantic Hero and Contemporary anti-Hero in Polish and Czech Literature*, New York, 1998, pp. 289–300. – Jiří Holý, "Vladimír Holan," in *Dictionary of Literary Biography: Twentieth-Century Eastern European Writers*, vol. 215 (edited by Steven Serafin et al.), Detroit, 1999, pp. 107–112. – Urs Heftrich, "Nachwort," in Vladimír Holan, *Epische Dichtungen* III, Cologne, 2003, pp. 225–238. – Jiří Opelík, *Holanovské nápovědi*, Prague, 2004.

HOLUB, MIROSLAV

Poet, prose-writer, essayist and translator. Holub was born in Plzeň in Western Bohemia in 1923 and finished his studies of medicine at Charles University in 1953. He worked in the Institute of Microbiology at the Academy of Sciences and edited the popular scientific magazine *Vesmír* (The Universe). After 1970 he worked in the Institute of Clinical and Special Medicine doing research in immunology (*Struktura imunitního systému*, 1979; *Immunology of Nude Mice*, 1989). He was one of a group of poets connected with the review *Květen* (May). Following a study tour of the USA he wrote the travel books *Anděl na kolečkách* (An Angel on Wheels, 1963, expanded 1964) and *Žít v New Yorku* (To Live in New York, 1969) and a collection of poems, *Beton* (Concrete, 1970). In 1973 a statement was published in his name in which Holub seemed to revoke his previously held "incorrect" views and which contradicted the ethos of all his work to date. After the fall of Communism, Holub argued that the statement came out without his knowledge and that no one would publish his protest at the time. From 1973, Holub could publish and travel in the West, but his new books did not come out in Czechoslovakia till 1982. He was very well known abroad, especially in the English-speaking world. He was vice-president of the *British Poetry Society* and was awarded the George Theiner Prize. He died in Prague in 1998 and his obituary appeared in the important American and English newspapers, *The New York Times*, *The Guardian*, *The Independent* and *The Times*.

The first collections *Denní služba* (Day Duty, 1958) and *Achilles a želva* (Achilles and the Tortoise, 1960) may be classed as "the poetry of the everyday". He made hospitals and laboratories the background for poetry, his heroes are obscure working people fulfilling the notion of man as a creative being. Holub gives intellect the leading role in these and his later work, using free verse without metaphor or any form of decoration, and plain stark expressions. At the end of the sixties this optimistic outlook is questioned, as can be seen in his outstanding collection of poems and aphorisms *Ačkoli* (1969; in English *Although*, in English, the selection of poems is not identical with the Czech original, translated by Jarmila and Ian Milner, London, 1971). For instance, see the poem *Tramvaj v půl šesté večer* (The Five-Thirty Tram in the Evening), the corresponding poem to *Tramvaj v půl šesté ráno* (The Five-Thirty Tram in the Morning) from the first book. The world appears as chaos from which all meaning has been lost, the poem is an attempt to contrast "existence with emptiness". And later collections continue in this sceptical vein: *Naopak* (1970–1981, published 1982, translated as *On the Contrary* by Ewald Osers, foreword by Alfred Alvarez, Newcastle upon Tyne 1984; the English translation is not identical with the Czech original, it also includes poems from the collection *Interferon*); *Interferon čili O divadle* (translated by David Young and Dana Hábová as *Interferon, or, On Theater*, introduction by David Young, Oberlin, 1982; not published in Czech in Prague until 1986); and *Syndrom mizející plíce* (1990, translated as *Vanishing Lung Syndrome* by David Young and Dana Hábová, London and Oberlin, 1990). Besides poetry Holub wrote informed essays on the meaning of poetry, the sciences and contemporary civilization (*K principu rolničky*, 1987, translated by

James Naughton as *The Jingle Bell Principle*, illustrated by Vladimír Renčín, photographs by Vojtěch Písařík, Newcastle upon Tyne, 1992; travel books from the USA (see above) and he was also a journalist. He translated poems from the Polish of Zbigniew Herbert and from other languages, and scientific works especially from English. He arranged collections of his poems, *Anamnéza* (Case History, 1964) and *Sagitální řez*, which was first published in English as *Sagittal Section* in a translation by Stuart Friebert and Dana Hábová, foreword by Lewis Thomas, Oberlin, 1980. It was not published in Czech until 1988, illustrated by Ota Janeček. The Moravian publishing house *Carpe diem* is publishing the collected works of Miroslav Holub: volume I as *Básně* (Poems, 2003), volume II as *Cestopisné prózy* (Travel Notes, 2003), volume III as *Eseje a sloupky* (Essays and Columns, 2005) all edited by Michal Huvar.

Other editions in English: *Selected Poems* (translated by Ian Milner and George Theiner, introduction by Alfred Alvarez), Harmondsworth and Baltimore, 1967; *From Notes of a Clay Pigeon* ([Holub means pigeon in Czech] translated by Jarmila and Ian Milner), London, 1977; *The Fly* (translated by Ewald Osers, George Theiner, Ian and Jarmila Milner), Newcastle upon Tyne, 1987; *The Dimension of the Present Moment and Other Essays* (edited by David Young), London and Boston, 1990; *Poems Before and After: Collected English Translations* (translated by Ian and Jarmila Milner, Ewald Osers and George Theiner, foreword by Ian Milner), Newcastle upon Tyne, 1990; *Intensive Care: Selected and New Poems* (translated by George Theiner, Dana Hábová, Stuart Friebert et al.), Oberlin, 1996; *The Rampage* (translated by Miroslav Holub, David Young, Dana Hábová and Rebekah Bloyd), London, 1997; *Shedding Life: Disease, Politics and Other Human Conditions* (translated by David Young et al.), Minneapolis, 1997.

Bibliography: P. Lewis, "In the Macroscope. The Poetry of Miroslav Holub," *Stand. Quarterly of the Arts*, 10 (1969), no. 2, pp. 11–19. – Bohumil Svozil, *Vůle k intelektuální poezii. O básnické tvorbě Miroslava Holuba*, Prague, 1971. – Amy Link, "The Uni(que)verse of Miroslav Holub," *Books Abroad*, 48 (1974), no. 3, pp. 506–511. In this article, Holub's poems "Křídla", "Polonius" and "Les" are reprinted from the volume *Selected Poems* (1967, translated by Ian Milner and George Theiner), the poem "Z mikrokosmu" has been translated by Jaroslav Tusek, Jr. – Jan Čulík and Jiří Holý, "Miroslav Holub," in *Dictionary of Literary Biography: Twentieth-Century Eastern European Writers*, vol. 232 (edited by Steven Serafin et al.), Detroit, 2001, pp. 139–145. – Michal Huvar, "Ediční poznámka," in Miroslav Holub, *Básně*, Brumovice, 2003, pp. 995–1014 (including epilogues by Jiří Brabec, Bohumil Svozil, Ewald Osers and Vladimír Justl to volumes of Miroslav Holub's poetry).

Hostovský, Egon

Prose-writer and journalist. He was born in 1908 in Hronov in Eastern Bohemia into a Czech Jewish family; he was related to the German-Austrian writer Stefan Zweig. After taking his final school examinations in 1927 he studied at Charles University, but after publishing his first books he gave up his studies and worked as a reader for a publishing house. From 1937 he was employed in the Foreign Office. He spent the years from 1939 to 1946 in exile in France, Portugal and the USA. As a writer abroad he won the approbation of Graham Greene. From 1948 to 1949 he was in the diplomatic service in Norway, after which he spent a second exile in the USA and, from 1964 to 1966, in Denmark. He worked as a teacher of Czech, as an editor in *Radio Free Europe* and as a writer. His work was published in the West in Czech and in translations, but it was not till the end of the sixties that he was published in Czechoslovakia. He died in 1973 in the USA, in Montclair, New Jersey.

Egon Hostovský is above all a writer of psychological novels whose heroes, usually portrayed from an inner perspective, seek an escape from loneliness, anxiety and chaos. They are often in stressful situations, such as having a deadly disease, as in the novel *Případ profesora Körnera* (The Case of Professor Körner, 1932), or emigration and war as in *Listy z vyhanství* (Chicago, 1941; Prague, 1946, translated by Ann Krtil as *Letters from Exile*, London, 1942). They are vulnerable or immature people, living more in imagination than in reality, for example, the adolescent hero in *Žhář* (The Arsonist, 1935), the children in the novel *Černá tlupa* (The Black Gang, 1933; both novels translated as *Hide and Seek* by Fern Long, Jindra Brumlíková and Isabella Athey, London, 1950). Positive values in Hostovský's novels mean a return to childhood, to spontaneity and living in a friendly society. Thus it is in the novel *Dům bez pána* (A House without a Master, 1937), the story of four siblings who meet in the family home after the death of their father. In this novel the author's interest in Judaism becomes apparent.

The precariousness of human existence is the theme of Hostovský's writing from the first and second periods of exile. At the same time he often introduces a thriller-like plot, as in *Sedmkrát v hlavní úloze* (New York, 1942, Prague, 1946, translated by Fern Long as *Seven Times the Leading Man*, London and New York, 1945), *Půlnoční pacient* (translated as *The Midnight Patient* by Philip H. Smith, New York, 1954, London, 1955; in Czech New York, 1959). In 1957 Henri-Georges Clouzot made a film version entitled *Les Espions* (The Spies). Typical of the novels also is the tragicomedy of the life of exiles, for example, in *Dobročinný večírek* (translated as *The Charity Ball* by Philip H. Smith, London, 1957; New York, 1958; published in Czech, New York, 1958). Symbolism has a greater place than before in the picture of the dehumanized world of New York in *Cizinec hledá byt* (A Foreigner Looks for a Flat, 1947). Outstanding in Hostovský's postwar work is *Všeobecné spiknutí* (A General Conspiracy, translated as *The Plot* by Alice Backer and Bernard Wolfe, London and New York, 1961, and published in Czech in Prague in 1969). It is a novel with autobiographical elements, about responsibility and relationships with others, about trying to find oneself. A book of memoirs was published in Toronto in 1966 entitled *Literární dobrodružství českého spisovatele v cizině* (The Literary Adventures of a Czech Writer Abroad). The Collected Works of Egon Hostovský, edited by Olga Hostovská, were published in twelve volumes between 1994 and 2002 in Prague by the publishing houses *ERM*, *Akropolis* and *Nakladatelství Franze Kafky*.

Other editions in English: *The Lonely Rebels* (translated by J. W. Bechyně and Willa Muir), New York, 1951; *Missing* (translated by Ewald Osers), New York and London, 1952.

Bibliography: *Padesát let Egona Hostovského* (edited by Jiří Pistorius), New York, 1958. – *Egon Hostovský: Vzpomínky, studie a dokumenty o jeho díle a osudu* (multilingual, edited by Rudolf Šturm, including as in the previous collection, the memoirs of Graham Greene in English), Toronto, 1974. – Vladimír Peška, "Deux types d´ecrivains en exil: Jan Čep et Egon Hostovský," in *Emigration et exil dans les cultures tchèque et polonaise* (edited by Hana Jechova and Hélène Wladarczyk), Paris, 1987, pp. 217–229. – Miloš Pohorský, "Úniky a návraty Egona Hostovského," in his *Zlomky analýzy*, Prague, 1990, pp. 25–44. – František Kautman, *Polarita našeho věku v díle Egona Hostovského*, Prague, 1993. – Vladimír Papoušek, *Egon Hostovský: Člověk v uzavřeném prostoru*, Jinočany, 1996. – Vladimír Papoušek, "Egon Hostovský," in *Dictionary of Literary Biography: Twentieth-Century Eastern European Writers*, vol. 215 (edited by Steven Serafin et al.), Detroit, 1999, pp. 120–128. – Jiří Holý, "Egon Hostovský und sein Romanwerk," in Egon Hostovský, *Siebenmal in der Hauptrolle*, Munich, 2004, pp. 293–305.

HRABAL, BOHUMIL

Novelist, essayist and poet. He was an illegitimate child, born in Brno in 1914. After his mother's marriage the family lived in Nymburk in Central Bohemia, where his adoptive father was the manager of a brewery. In 1924 uncle Pepin moved in with them and became the inspiration for and the hero of the author's later works. Hrabal describes the Nymburk years uninhibitedly in *Postřižiny* (Cutting It Short) and nostalgically in *Městečko, kde se zastavil čas* (The Little Town Where Time Stood Still). He studied law at Charles University in Prague, gaining his doctorate in 1946 but he held many other jobs: he was an office worker, tracklayer and train despatcher, insurance agent, labourer in the steelworks in Kladno from 1949–1952, packer of old paper from 1954 to 1959, and scene-shifter in a theatre. Most of these professions appear in his work. He lived in Libeň, a working-class quarter of Prague, and became a friend of the underground author Egon Bondy and the nonconformist artist Vladimír Boudník, who inspired *Něžný barbar* (The Gentle Barbarian). In the novels *Svatby v domě* (Weddings in the House) and *Vita nuova* (Vita nuova) he portrayed the Bohemian fifties. It was not till 1963 that he began to publish regularly. He became famous as a writer and travelled through Europe and the USA. After 1970 he was not allowed to publish and became "an author in liquidation". After expressing loyalty to the regime in the journal *Tvorba* (Creations) in 1975, new titles flowed from him, of course with alterations by the censor; at the same time he was publishing in samizdat and in exile (from now on we shall mention only the first editions). He died in Prague in 1997, probably by suicide.

It was not until the sixties that Hrabal became known to the public. He had, however, many years of literary work behind him. At first he was inspired by surrealism, then by *Skupina 42* (Group 42). His original poetic principles came into being at the end of the forties and the beginning of the fifties in the poems *Bambino di Praga* (The Baby Jesus of Prague), in *Krásná Poldi* (The Beautiful Poldi), the collage *Mrtvomat* (Death Dispenser) and the short story *Jarmilka* (Jarmilka) – in the original version they were not published till volumes II and III of his Collected Works (1991–1992). The basis of Hrabal's work is the plebeian view "from below"; he manages to reflect the way the people really speak; at the same time touches of harsh reality alternate with poetism, unconventional eroticism, reflections and reportage.

In rapid succession in the sixties he published older works altered in various ways: *Perlička na dně* (The Pearl in the Deep, 1963), *Pábitelé* (Palaverers, 1964). From these two books a film called *Perličky na dně* was made by the young film directors of the then Czech "New Wave": Jiří Menzel, Jan Němec, Evald Schorm, Věra Chytilová and Jaromil Jireš. There followed *Taneční hodiny pro starší a pokročilé* (1964, translated by Michael Henry Heim as *Dancing Lessons for the Advanced in Age*, New York, 1995) and *Ostře sledované vlaky* (1965, translated by Edith Pargeter as *A Close Watch on Trains*, London, 1968, in New York in 1968 as *Closely Watched Trains*, with an introduction by Josef Škvorecký). The 1966 film by Jiří Menzel entitled in English *Closely Observed Trains* won an Oscar, the American Film Academy Prize. The script, translated by Josef Holzbecher as *Closely Watched Trains*, was published in New York and London in 1971. In this period Hrabal's work portrayed imaginatively zany, "screwball", "palaverering" characters (*pábitelé*). Other aspects of his work appear in the more austere works, *Inzerát na dům, ve kterém už nechci bydlet* (Advertisement for a House I Don´t Want to Live in Anymore), which was filmed as *Skřivánci na niti* (Larks on a String), directed by Jiří Menzel in 1969. It was banned and was not shown till 1990 when it received the Golden Bear Prize at the Berlin festival. The collection *Morytáty a legendy* (Legends and Broadside Ballads of Murder, 1968) is a collage of admiring and scurrilous letters of readers, ingenuous diaries, court records, lives of saints, street talk and so on.

After his spell of top creative writing in the fifties, a second spell followed at the beginning of the seventies, paradoxically again at a time when he could not publish. That spell produced the prose works *Postřižiny* (translated by James Naughton as *Cutting It Short*, London and New York, 1993, filmed by Jiří Menzel in 1980), *Obsluhoval jsem anglického krále* (translated by Paul Wilson as *I Served the King of England*, London and San Diego, 1989, filmed by Jiří Menzel in 2006), *Městečko, kde zastavil čas* (translated as *The Little Town Where Time Stood Still* by James Naughton [also contains *Cutting It Short*], introduction by Josef Škvorecký, afterword by Bohumil Hrabal, London and New York, 1993), *Něžný barbar* (The Gentle Barbarian), all in Czech in samizdat, 1971–1974, *Příliš hlučná samota* (samizdat, 1977, translated as *Too Loud a Solitude* by Michael Henry Heim, San Diego, 1990; first published in 1986 in *Cross Currents*). A fairly unsuccessful film version was made by Věra Caisová in 1994. To a certain extent Hrabal had simplified his style, concentrating on existential aspects, symbols and ciphers, for example "hlučná samota" (loud solitude). *Příliš hlučná samota*, which appeared in parts in three versions, is the story of an old packer of paper called Haňťa, who for years has been reading books meant to be destroyed and has become "educated against his will". It is a tragic and at the same time poetic parable of a world from which all sense has been lost.

At the beginning of the eighties Hrabal wrote his most extensive work, the autobiographical trilogy *Svatby v domě* (Weddings in the House), *Vita nuova* (Vita nuova), *Proluky* (Vacant Lots), published in samizdat between 1986 and 1987. He presents himself in a particular way, through the eyes of his wife. Here the style is restrained, typical of his later work, which from the end of the eighties included short prose works such as fictional letters to the young American woman April (re-named by Hrabal in Czech "Dubenka") he met in his favourite pub, *U Zlatého tygra* (The Golden Tiger), translated as *Total Fears: Letters to Dubenka* by James Naughton (Prague, 1998), and "vnitřní hovory" (conversations with oneself) etc., for example, *Ponorné říčky* (Underground Streams, 1991). In the short work *Kouzelná flétna* (samizdat, 1989, translated as *The Magic Flute* by Lesley and Jan Čulík, with a postscript by Jan Čulík in *The Scottish Slavonic Revue*, 16 (1991), pp. 7–17; new translation by Peter Kussi in *Good-bye, Samizdat*, 1992, pp. 130–134) Hrabal, inspired by the demonstrations that led to the "Velvet Revolution", took up a position directly opposed to the totalitarian Communist regime.

Hrabal devoted many essays and meditations to literature, his own works and the visual arts. These texts are included in the two volumes of the Collected Works, *Kdo jsem* (Who I Am) and *Domácí úkoly* (Homework), both 1995. Hrabal's works have been translated into twenty-three languages in more than two hundred editions. The Collected Works of Bohumil Hrabal (*Sebrané spisy Bohumila Hrabala*) were published between 1991 and 1997 by the Prague publishing house *Pražská imaginace*, edited by Václav Kadlec, Karel Dostál et al.

Other edition in English: "The Legend of the Lovely Julinka" (translated by Jeanne Němcová), in *Universum: A Review of Czechoslovak Literature and Arts*, 4 (1969), no. 7, pp. 6–19; *The Death of Mr Baltisberger* (translated by Michael Henry Heim), New York, 1975, republished London, 1990.

Bibliography: George Gibian, "The Haircutting and I Served the King of England. Two Recent Works of Bohumil Hrabal," in *Czech Literature Since 1956* (edited by William E. Harkins and Paul I. Trensky), New York, 1980, pp. 74–90. – Josef Škvorecký, "American Motifs in the Work of Bohumil Hrabal," *Cross Currents*, 1 (1982), pp. 207–218. – Susanna Roth, *Laute Einsamkeit und bitteres Glück*, Bern and New York, 1986 (in Czech in 1993). – Miloslava Slavíčková, "Bohumil Hrabal and the Legacy of the Czech Avant-Garde," in *The Slavic Literatures and Modernism* (edited by Nils Äke Nilsson), Stockholm, 1987. – *Hommage à Hrabal* (edited by Susanna Roth), Frankfurt a. M., 1989. – *Hrabaliana* (edited by Milan Jankovič and Josef Zumr), Prague, 1990. – Susanna Roth, "The Reception of Bohumil Hrabal in Czechoslovakia and in the 'West'," *Czechoslovak and Central European Journal*, 11 (Summer 1992), pp. 66–72. – Jaroslav Kladiva, *Literatura Bohumila Hrabala*, Prague, 1994. – Milan Jankovič, *Kapitoly z poetiky Bohumila Hrabala*, Prague, 1996. – Karen Gammelgaard, *Spoken Czech in Literature: The Case of Bondy, Hrabal, Placák and Topol*, Oslo,

1997. – Radko Pytlík, *The Sad King of Czech Literature Bohumil Hrabal*, Prague, 2000 (in Czech in 1990). – L. S. Urbaszewski, "Rethinking the Grotesque in Hrabal's Fiction. Carnival as a Model for Closely Watched Trains," in *Modern Czech Studies* (edited by Alexander Levitsky and Masako U. Fidler), Providence, 2000, pp. 34–46. – Václav Kadlec, "Bohumil Hrabal," in *Dictionary of Literary Biography: Twentieth-Century Eastern European Writers*, vol. 232 (edited by Steven Serafin et al.), Detroit, 2001, pp. 146–157. – Robert Porter, "Bohumil Hrabal: Small People and Tall Tales," in his *An Introduction to Twentieth-Century Czech Fiction*, Brighton and Portland, 2001, pp. 52–86. – *Bohumil Hrabal, palabres et existence* (edited by Xavier Galmiche), Paris, 2002. – *Bohumil Hrabal: Papers from a Symposium* (edited by David Short), London, 2004. – Aleksander Kaczorowski, *Gra w życie: Opowieść o Bohumilu Hrabalu*, Wołowiec, 2004. – Tomáš Mazal, *Spisovatel Bohumil Hrabal*, Prague, 2004. – *Intorno a Bohumil Hrabal: Atti del Convegno internazionale di studi, Udine, 27–29 ottobre 2005* (edited by Annalisa Cosentino), Udine 2006 (in Czech as *Hrabaliana rediviva*, Prague, 2006).

HRUBÍN, FRANTIŠEK

Poet, dramatist, prose-writer and translator. He was born in Prague in 1910 and spent his childhood in Lešany in Central Bohemia. Recollections of that time are to be found in *U stolu* (At Table, 1958) and in the poem *Romance pro křídlovku* (Romance for a Flugelhorn, 1962). While still at secondary school he published poems and became friends with the poets František Halas, Jaroslav Seifert and Josef Hora. On leaving school in 1932 he studied for a short time; between 1934 and in 1945 he worked in the Prague Municipal Library, and subsequently he made his living from literature. From 1945–1950 he was editor of the children's magazine *Mateřídouška* (Thyme). At the beginning of the fifties all he could publish were translations and poems for children. From 1950 he made frequent stays in Chlum near Třeboň in South Bohemia; the collection of poems *Můj zpěv* (My Song, 1956) and the play *Srpnová neděle* (A Sunday in August, 1958) date from that time. In the sixties he helped in the establishment and work of the publication *Klub přátel poezie* (The Friends of Poetry Club) by the Prague publishing house *Československý spisovatel* (Czechoslovak Writers´ Publishing House). He died in 1971 in České Budějovice.

Poetry is the core of Hrubín's work. From his first collections *Zpíváno z dálky* (Distant Singing, 1933, expanded 1947) and *Krásná po chudobě* (Beauty in Poverty, 1935, revised 1947) he emerged as a lyrical poet of love and nature. Characteristic of his poetry is iambic rhythm, regular rhyme and melody. From the end of the thirties the poetry becomes less personal, the scenery around Lešany now becomes the ancestral country and traditional spiritual values tend to become certainties (see *Země po polednách* [A Country in the Afternoon, 1937]); *Včelí plást* [Honeycomb, 1940]). From the poems written in the later years of the war and immediately after, however, the symbolism becomes less abstract and acquires social elements – "the war of the poor" is the struggle for a new social order (*Jobova noc* [The Night of Job], 1945, revised 1948).

A new creative period began after the war. Hrubín expresses the horror and precariousness of human existence. The versification has now become more irregular and melody has disappeared. In the collections *Hirošima* (Hiroshima, 1948) and *Proměna* (Metamorphosis, 1957, illustrated by Josef Šíma), both revised in 1960 and again in 1964, various alternating themes are employed. *Proměna* was inspired by the Greek legend of Daedalus and Icarus alternating with the picture of a normal summer Sunday in Prague and with the news of the testing of the atom bomb. The prose work *Zlatá reneta* (The Golden Apple, 1964) and above all his greatest poem *Romance pro křídlovku* (Romance for Flugelhorn, 1962) are based on the principle that events in one age affect what happens in other ages. *Zlatá reneta* was made into a film by Otakar Vávra in 1965, who also made a film version of *Romance pro křídlovku* in 1966. In it the central motifs of Hrubín's work, one's first love, the death of a young girl, family reminiscences in the person of a grandfather, come into conflict, the countryside around Lešany and the river Sázava hold up a mirror to human destiny and the universal life cycle.

With a complete reversal of style Hrubín turned to children's literature. He had written his first verses for children, *Říkejte si se mnou* (Let's Say It Together, 1943), during the war. After it he wrote a great many more nursery rhymes, fairy-tales, etc., collected in one volume, *Špalíček pohádek* (Book of Fairy Tales), first illustrated by Jiří Trnka in 1957. With his spontaneous, light-hearted, easily comprehensible texts he created a new chapter in this genre of Czech literature. In English *Blue Sky* (translated by Iris Urwin, illustrated by Josef Čapek), *Butterfly Moments* (translated by Daphne Rusbridge, illustrated by Max Švabinský) and *The Enchanted Forest* (translated by Daphne Rusbridge), *Let's Tell a Tale Together* (translated by Daphne Rusbridge) were all published in Prague in 1954. *Primrose and the Winter Witch* (translated by James Reeves, illustrated by Jiří Trnka) was published in London and Prague in 1964.

Hrubín was also outstanding as a translator, especially of the French lyric poetry of Verlaine and Rimbaud and of ancient Chinese poetry. His memoirs of poets, *Lásky* (Loves), rather like essays, are invaluable. The stage play *Srpnová neděle* (A Sunday in August) was first performed and published in 1958, and a film version was made in 1960 by Otakar Vávra. His poetic work, including his translations of French lyric poetry, was published between 1966 and 1976 in six volumes by the publishing house *Československý spisovatel*, edited and with notes by Jiří Brabec, one volume by Miloš Pohorský.

Other editions in English: two poems (translated by Edith Pargeter), in *The Linden Tree* (edited by Mojmír Otruba and Zdeněk Pešat), Prague, 1962, pp. 257–260; nine poems in *Contemporary East European Poetry* (translated by Don Mager), Ann Arbor, 1983; one poem (translated by Alfred French), in *The Czech Avantgardists* (edited by Alfred French), Rockville, 1995, p. 87.

Bibliography: Věra Karfíková, "Hrubín," in *Jak číst poezii* (edited by Jiří Opelík, 2nd edition), Prague, 1969, pp. 194–207. – Josef Strnadel, *František Hrubín*, Prague, 1980. – Marie Mravcová, "František Hrubín, Romance pro křídlovku," in *Česká literatura 1945–1970* (edited by Jiřina Táborská and Milan

was published in a German translation in 1979 and in Czech in samizdat in 1980. It was revised in 1985, published in Purley in 1986 and in Prague in 1991. Translated as *Judge on Trial* by A. G. Brain (i.e. Alice and Gerald Turner), it came out in London, 1990, and in New York in 1993. The stories *Milostné léto* and *Láska a smetí* are more concerned with personal relationships and erotic problems. *Milostné léto* (samizdat, 1972; Toronto, 1979; Prague, 1992; translated as *A Summer Affair* by Ewald Osers, London, 1987), has human loneliness as its theme. *Láska a smetí* (samizdat, 1986; Purley, 1988; Prague, 1990; translated as *Love and Garbage* by Ewald Osers, London, 1990; New York, 1991) is a love story with a ravaged Prague as background. The story of *Poslední stupeň důvěrnosti* (1996, translated as *The Ultimate Intimacy* by A. G. Brain [i.e. Alice and Gerald Turner], London and New York, 1997) takes place just after the democratic revolution of 1989 and features a Protestant minister who finds himself in a crisis. *Ani svatí, ani andělé* (1999, translated as *No Saints or Angels* by Gerald Turner, London, 2001), is about the relationship of an older woman with a younger man.

Klíma's plays were parables about power and manipulation. *Zámek* (The Castle) was published and first staged in 1964 and *Porota* (The Jury) was published in 1968 and first performed in 1969. At the same time he was inspired by the theatre of the absurd and by Franz Kafka, for example, in *Klára a dva páni* (in English *Klára and the Two Men*, translated by Peter Sternberg and Marketa Goetz-Stankiewicz, *Prism International*, 24 [1983], no. 4), which was published in 1968 and first staged in New York in 1969. His interest in Kafka led him with Pavel Kohout to adapt Kafka's novel *America*, which was published in German in 1970 and in Prague in 1991, and to write the essays *Už se blíží meče* (The Sword Is About to Fall; samizdat 1984; expanded Prague, 1990, translated in part as *Kafka and Felice*, translated by Jan Drábek, *Cross Currents*, 5 [1986], pp. 337–381, introduction by Marketa Goetz-Stankiewicz). Since 1995 the Prague publishing house *Hynek* has been publishing the complete works of Ivan Klíma. *Lásky a řemesla Ivana Klímy* (The Loves and Trades of Ivan Klíma), a literary conversation with Miloš Čermák, was published in Prague in 1995.

Other editions in English: *A Ship Named Hope: Two Novels* (translated by Edith Pargeter), London, 1970; "A Christmas Conspiracy" (from *Má veselá jitra*, translated by Peter Kussi), in *The Writing on the Wall* (edited by Peter Kussi and Antonín Jaroslav Liehm), Princeton, 1983, pp. 87–104; "Games" (translated by Jan Drábek), in *Drama Contemporary: Czechoslovakia* (edited by Marketa Goetz-Stankiewicz), New York, 1985, pp. 177–222; "The Eyeglasses" (translated by Michal Pomichalek and Anna Mozga), in *Good-bye, Samizdat* (edited Marketa Goetz-Stankiewicz), Evanston, 1992, pp. 20–26; *The Spirit of Prague and Other Essays* (translated by Paul Wilson), London, 1994; New York, 1995; *Waiting for the Dark, Waiting for the Light* (translated by Paul Wilson), London, 1994.

Bibliography: Antonín Jaroslav Liehm, "Ivan Klíma" (interview), in his *The Politics of Culture*, New York, 1972, p. 355–370 (in Czech Antonín Jaroslav Liehm, *Generace*, Prague, 1990, pp. 284–299). – Philip Roth, "A Conversation in Prague," *New York Review of Books*, 37, 12 April 1990, pp. 14–22. – Marketa Goetz-Stankiewicz, *The Silenced Theatre: Czech Playwrights without a Stage*,

Toronto, 1979, pp. 116–145. – John Banville, "Judge on Trial by Ivan Klíma," *New York Review of Books*, 40, 15 July 1993. – Ian Ward, "Ivan Klíma. Judge on Trial," *Scottish Slavonic Review*, 20 (1993), pp. 23–44. – Gabriele Annan, "Waiting for the Light, Waiting for the Dark by Ivan Klíma," *New York Review of Books*, 42, 20 April 1995, pp. 15–16. – Jan Čulík and Jiří Holý, "Ivan Klíma," in *Dictionary of Literary Biography: Twentieth-Century Eastern European Writers*, vol. 232 (edited by Steven Serafin et al.), Detroit, 2001, pp. 173–179. – Robert Porter, "Ivan Klíma, Conscience and Moral Conundrum," in his *An Introduction to Twentieth-Century Czech Fiction*, Brighton and Portland, 2001, pp. 136–161.

KOHOUT, PAVEL

Dramatist, novelist, scriptwriter, poet and journalist, born in Prague in 1928. He left school in 1947 but even as a pupil in secondary school he was active in Communist youth organizations and in music ensemble groups with which he visited many countries. He was chief editor of the satirical magazine *Dikobraz* (The Porcupine) from 1951 to 1952 and edited the weekly *Československý voják* (The Czechoslovak Soldier) from 1953 to 1955. He was a professional writer and from 1963 to 1966 he was repertory adviser in the Prague *Divadlo Na Vinohradech* (The Vinohrady Theatre). At the 4th Congress of the Union of Czechoslovak Writers in June 1967 he critized the Communist regime. As a reformist he was famous during the Prague Spring. The book *Briefe über die Grenze* (Letters across the Frontier), containing the correspondence with the German writer Günter Grass discussing socialism and culture, was published in Hamburg in 1968. In the seventies he was persecuted. He writes about it in his fictionalized memoirs *Kde je zakopán pes* (Where the Dog Is Buried), published in Cologne in 1987 and Brno in 1990. His works were published in samizdat, in exile and in translation. He organized "house theatre" in which performances of plays by banned authors, for example his *Play Makbeth* (Play Macbeth), based on Shakespeare, were given in the flats of private individuals. He was also a dissident and a signatory of the human rights manifesto *Charter 77*. From 1979 he lived in exile, mainly in Austria. After 1989 he divided his time between Vienna and Prague. His third wife is the author and scriptwriter Jelena Mašínová (1941), his daughter is the prose-writer Tereza Boučková (1957). Jelena Mašínová was the co-author of several of his works.

A characteristic common throughout Kohout's extensive work is the ability to heighten dramatic effect and the ready reaction to contemporary problems. He was first known for plays that naïvely promoted socialism, for example *Dobrá píseň* (The Good Song), first staged and published in 1952 and revised in 1955 and for the script for the film *Zítra se bude tančit všude* (Tomorrow There Will Be Dancing Everywhere, 1952). Gradually he viewed things more critically, as in the play *Zářijové noci* (September Nights), which had its premiere in 1955 and was published in 1956, filmed by Vojtěch Jasný in 1957. The play *Taková láska* (Such Great Love), first performed and published in 1957, about the death of a young woman, already shows a tendency towards an ambiguous view of the world. It was revised in 1958 and 1959, filmed by Jiří Weiss in 1959 and published in 1967 with a selection of reviews and comments made by Alena Urbanová. In the sixties he worked in films. In 1965 he directed the film *Svatba s podmínkou* (The Conditional Wedding) made with his own script. In the plays *Válka s Mloky* and *August August, august* he used film techniques with added music, fantasy and absurd elements. *Válka s Mloky* (War with the Newts), very freely adapted from the novel by Karel Čapek, was first performed and published in 1963. *August August, august* had its first performance in 1967. It was published that same year, revised as *Klaun* (The Clown) and staged in 1994.

In the seventies and eighties Kohout's work, successful abroad, continued chiefly with drama, for example with an adaptation from the Russian writer Leonid Andreyev, *Ubohý vrah* (translated by Herbert Berghof and Laurence Luckinbill as *Poor Murderer*, New York and Harmondsworth, 1977). It was first performed in West Germany in 1973 and in Prague in 1990. He also wrote *"Ecce Constantia!"* ("Ecce Constantia!", Rome, 1989, Prague, 1990, television production by Luboš Pistorius, 1992), which abandoned tradition in writing about the Council of Constance at the beginning of the 15th century, which sentenced the Czech religious reformer Jan Hus to death. Kohout's plays *Atest* (samizdat, 1979; Prague, 1990; premiered in Vienna in 1979; translated into English by Jan Drábek as *Permit*), *Marast* (first performed in Germany in 1982; Prague, 1990; translated by Vera Pech as *Morass*) and *Safari* (written in German, in Czech in *Šest & Sex*, 1998; translated by Anna Mozga as *Safari*), take up the story of Vaněk, the intellectual and dissident in Václav Havel's plays. All were published in English in *The Vaněk Plays* (edited by Marketa Goetz-Stankiewicz, Vancouver, 1987) and in Czech as *V hlavní roli Ferdinand Vaněk* (edited by Jan Šulc, epilogue by Lenka Jungmannová, Prague, Academia, 2006). Then Kohout started writing fiction. In a change of direction, he produced the documentary novel *Z deníku kontrarevolucionáře*. It was published as *From the Diary of a Counter-revolutionary* in a translation by George Theiner in New York in 1972 and in a German translation in 1969. The Czech original did not come out until 1997. His bizarre, fantastic novel *Bílá kniha* came out in a German translation in 1970, in Czech in samizdat in 1975, in Toronto in 1978 and in Prague in 1991. The English translation as *White Book* by Alex Page was published in New York in 1977, and the the translation of the morbidly fantastic novel *Katyně* by Káča Poláčková came out as *The Hangwoman* in New York in 1981. *Katyně*, a major achievement of Kohout's, is a novel about a lovely young girl called Lízinka who is studying for the job of hangman. In the nineties Kohout has published other novels highlighting dramatic conflicts and moral problems, the relations between the Czechs and the Germans, the Nazi occupation and the postwar deportation of Germans from Czechoslovakia (see *Hvězdná hodina vrahů*, 1995, translated by Neil Bermel as *The Widow Killer*, New York, 1995). His autobiography came out in two volumes as *To byl můj život??* (This Has Been My Life??, Prague, 2005–2006.)

Other editions in English: "Fire in the Basement" (translated by Peter Sternberg and Marketa Goetz-Stankiewicz), in *Drama Contemporary: Czechoslovakia* (edited by Marketa Goetz-Stankiewicz), New York, 1985, pp.

91–126; *I am Snowing. The Confession of a Woman of Prague* (translated by Neil Bermel), New York, 1994.

Bibliography: Marketa Goetz-Stankiewicz, *The Silenced Theatre: Czech Playwrights without a Stage*, Toronto, 1979, pp. 89–115. – Siegfried Lenz, *Über Phantasie: Gespräche mit Heinrich Böll, Günter Grass, Walter Kempowski, Pavel Kohout* (edited by Alfred Mensak), Hamburg, 1982. – Robert B. Pynsent, "Kohout and the Banalisation of Brutality," *Bohemia*, 31 (1990), pp. 130–136. – Veronika Ambros, *Pavel Kohout und die Metamorphosen des Sozialistischen Realismus*, New York, 1993. – Marie Mravcová, "Pavel Kohout: Katyně," in *Český Parnas: Literatura 1970–1990* (edited by Jiří Holý and Jiřina Táborská), Prague, 1993, pp. 167–177. – Pavel Kosatík, *Fenomén Kohout*, Prague and Litomyšl, 2001. – Václav Maidl, "Pavel Kohout: Deusche, Sudentendeutsche und die Vertreibung in seinem Werk," in *Vertreibung. Aussiedlung. Transfer: Vyhnání. Odsun* (edited by Gertraude Zand and Jiří Holý), Brno, 2004, pp. 125–139.

KOLÁŘ, JIŘÍ

Graphic artist, poet, essayist and translator. He was born in 1914 in Protivín in South Bohemia into a family of bakers. He became a joiner in the industrial town of Kladno and held various manual jobs. From 1945 to 1950 he was an editor in a publishing house, and thereafter he devoted himself entirely to literature and the graphic arts. A member of *Skupina 42* (Group 42) from 1949 to 1957 he could not publish and from 1952 to 1953 he spent nine months in prison for the "subversive" manuscript of *Prométheova játra* (Prometheus´ Guts). He initiated the meetings of his artist friends the writers Josef Hiršal, Zdeněk Urbánek, the painter Kamil Lhoták, the musician Jan Rychlík and others in the coffeehouse *Slavia* and in their flats. From the end of the fifties he composed mainly visual poetry and collages which gradually won him world fame with dozens of exhibitions. His entire work was exhibited in the Guggenheim Museum in New York in 1975 and in other major Western museums of modern art. In the seventies and eighties again he could not publish except in samizdat and in exile. He was a signatory of the human rights manifesto *Charter 77*. Between 1974 and 1978 he, in a private capacity, gave a literary prize for unofficial authors. He studied for a year from 1978 to 1979 on a grant in West Berlin; from 1980 he lived in Paris where from 1981 he published the journal *Revue K* (Review K) dedicated to modern Czech art. His wife Běla Kolářová was an art photographer. He died in Prague in 2002.

His poems were written mostly in the forties and fifties; however, he could publish them only occasionally, and often belatedly. He continued from his first work *Křestný list* (Birth Certificate, 1941) to take his inspiration from the city streets, the spoken language and slang. His free verse is the very antithesis of poetic melody. It is made up of endless details and fragments of speech embracing different themes based on conversation, for example, *Ódy a variace* (Odes and Variations, 1946). Anti-poeticism increases in the harsh monologues of his characters, in the reflections and in the author's journals *Dny v roce* (Days in the Year, 1948) and in *Roky v dnech* (Years in Days, 1949), which was banned in 1949 and again in 1970, published in samizdat in 1975, and in volume I of the Complete Works of Jiří Kolář (1992). His outstanding works date from the years 1949 to 1950: *Očitý svědek* (Eyewitness) was published in samizdat in 1975, in Munich in 1983 with an afterword by Jan Vladislav, and in volume II of the Complete Works in 1997; *Prométheova játra* (Prometheus´ Guts) was published in samizdat in 1979, in Toronto in 1985, in Prague in 1990 with an afterword by Emanuel Frynta, and in volume IX of the Complete Works of Jiří Kolář, 2000. They are diaries, dreams and poems that reveal the horror of the times and the banality and pathos of human lives. In addition he composed a kind of poetic journal in verse, *Mistr Sun o básnickém umění* (Master Sun on the Art of Poetry, 1957). These poems have been collected in volume IV of the Complete Works (1995).

In the book *Prométheova játra* Kolář used texts of the Czech writer Ladislav Klíma and the Polish writer Zofia Nałkowska which he "cut up" and rearranged to form a new whole, as he later did with his famous pictures and photographs in his collages. Similarly, in the poetic cycle *Černá lyra* (The Black Lyre) he quoted from reports of human villainy throughout history retrospectively from concentration camps to ancient times, and in the cycle *Česká svita* (A Czech Suite) he quoted from letters of Czech artists. Both appear in *Vršovický Ezop* (Aesop from Vršovice, 1966) and in volume III of the Complete Works (1993). Visual poetry experimenting with extracts from texts and their special arrangement on the page, all collected in volume VI of the Complete Works (1994), introduced another phase. This was the forerunner of various types of collage, "crumplages", "confrontages", "rapportages" and other graphic art works. In relation to this, see the catalogues for the exhibitions and publications for the year abroad, especially the wide-ranging volumes in Czech, *Jiří Kolář* (1993), notes by Jindřich Chalupecký on the poetry and on his graphic art work; see also *Slovník metod* (Dictionary of Method, 1999, edited by Vladimír Karfík, notes by Gilbert Lascaut; in French in Paris, 1991).

As a translator he tended to look to authors whose poetics were similar to his own, for example, Sandburg, Masters, Whitman and Beckett. He worked mostly in collaboration with others. He wrote verse and stories for children, *Nápady pana Apríla* (Mr April's Ideas, 1961), and plays. The work of Jiří Kolář was published in stages between 1992 and 2000 by the Prague publishing houses *Odeon*, *Český spisovatel*, *Mladá fronta* and *Paseka* in eleven volumes edited by Vladimír Karfík.

Editions in English: four poems (translated by George Theiner), in *Modern Poetry in Translation: Czech* (edited by Ted Hughes and David Weissbort), London, 1967; five poems (translated by George Theiner), in *Universum: A Review of Czechoslovak Literature and Arts* 4 (1969), no. 6, pp. 12–15; two poems (translated by George Theiner), in *New Writing in Czechoslovakia* (edited by George Theiner), Harmondsworth, 1969, pp. 81–83; *Transformations* (essay by Charlotta Kotik), Buffalo, 1978; *Diary 1968*, Oxford 1984; "Selected Poems" (translated by John Carpenter), *Cross Currents*, 8 (1989), pp. 229–232.

Bibliography: Miroslav Lamač and Dietrich Mahlow, *Jiří Kolář*, Cologne, 1968. – Angelo Maria Ripellino, *Jiří Kolář*, Torino, 1976. – Michel Butor, Jindřich Chalupecký and Jiří Padrta, *Jiří Kolář*, Zirndorf, 1979. – Jindřich Chalupecký, *Jiří*

Kolář: Monographie mit einem Lexikon der Techniken, Nürnberg, 1979. – Meda Mládek, "Jiří Kolář Crumplages," in Jaroslav Seifert, *Morový sloup / The Plague Monument*, Silver Spring, 1980, pp. XI–XIV. – Emanuel Frynta, "Bytostný básník Jiří Kolář," in Jiří Kolář, *Prométheova játra*, Toronto, 1985, pp. 203–221 (2nd edition, Prague, 1990, pp. 203–216). – John Carpenter, "Jiří Kolář. Visual Poetry and Verbal Art," *Cross Currents*, 8 (1989), pp. 209–228. – Miroslav Červenka, "První sbírky Jiřího Koláře," in his *Styl a význam*, Prague, 1991, pp. 135–191. – Jan Grossman, "Horečná bdělost Jiřího Koláře," in his *Analýzy* (edited by Jiří Holý and Terezie Pokorná), Prague, 1991, pp. 364–376. – Sylvie Richterová, "Ticho, smích a proměna v díle Jiřího Koláře," in her *Ticho a smích*, Prague, 1997, pp. 165–190. – Vladimír Karfík, *Jiří Kolář*, Prague, 1994. – Eva Petrová et al., *Skupina 42*, Prague, 1998. – *Příběhy Jiřího Koláře*, Prague, 1999.

KRATOCHVIL, JIŘÍ

Novelist, essayist and dramatist. He was born in 1940 in Brno, the largest city in Moravia. His father was an ornithologist and the author of children's books, his uncle was a journalist; both went into exile in the West. He studied Czech and Russian at the university in Brno, finishing in 1965, and worked as a teacher and librarian. In the seventies and eighties he could not publish except in samizdat; at that time he had manual jobs as a crane-driver and a night watchman. From 1983 to 1991 he worked in the conservation office, later from 1991 to 1995 as a journalist for Brno radio, then he became a professional writer.

In the sixties Kratochvil began writing for the Brno review *Host do domu* (A Guest in the House) and other reviews. His first collection of short stories *Případ s Chatnoirem* (The Chatnoir Case) was banned in 1971. A new version was published in samizdat in 1978. A trilogy of novels, *Medvědí román* (Bear Novel, 1990), written in the eighties but the original version not published till 1999, *Uprostřed nocí zpěv* (Singing in the Middle of the Night, 1992) and *Avion* (Avion, 1995), are outstanding. In these works metaphor, Brno slang and a complicated structure of composition and narrative are salient features, and horrific reality alternates with fantasy. The setting of the novels *Uprostřed nocí zpěv* and *Avion* is Brno, which is described in accurate detail and at the same time presented as a magical place where reality spills over into fiction. This approach also enlivens other works, for example *Orfeus z Kénigu* (The Orpheus from Kenig, 1994) and other stories. Kratochvil is also the author of plays for radio and the theatre and essays on literature, including Borges and Kundera, in which he formulates his notion of "the novel as an open system" (*Příběhy příběhů* [Stories of Stories], 1995).

Editions in English: "The Orpheus from Kenig" (translated by Alexandra Büchler), in *This Side of Reality* (edited by Alexandra Büchler), London, 1996, pp. 129–139; "The Story of King Kandaules" (translated by Jonathan Bolton), in *Daylight in Nightclub Inferno* (edited by Elena Lappin), North Haven, 1997, pp. 103–146.

Bibliography: Marek Nekula, "Jiří Kratochvil: Uprostřed nocí zpěv," in *Český Parnas: Literatura 1970–1990* (edited by Jiří Holý and Jiřina Táborská), Prague,

1993, pp. 370–376. – Milan Jungmann, *V obklíčení příběhů*, Brno, 1997, pp. 135–140, 217–221. – Jana Vrbová, "Koncepty prostoru v románových trilogiích Daniely Hodrové a Jiřího Kratochvila," *Tvar*, 13 (2001), suppl. vol. 2–3. pp. 1–64. – Klára Lukavská, "Navrať se do domu svého . . . aneb Jiří Kratochvil – 'postmoderní literatura'," *Tvar*, 12, suppl. vol. 3 (2002), pp. 1–32. – Rajendra A. Chitnis, "Writing as Being: Jiří Kratochvil, Zuzana Brabcová, Daniela Hodrová, Michal Ajvaz, Jáchym Topol," in his *Literature in Post-Communist Russia and Eastern Europe*, London, 2004, pp. 80–114. – Květoslav Chvatík, *Od avantgardy k druhé moderně*, Prague, 2004, pp. 298–332.

KUNDERA, MILAN

Novelist, dramatist, essayist and poet. He was born in 1929 in Brno; his father was a musicologist, a pupil and interpreter of Leoš Janáček; his cousin Ludvík Kundera (1920) is a poet, essayist and translator. He studied composition, then literature and aesthetics at Charles University. He had to leave when in 1950 he, Jan Trefulka and another friend were expelled from the Communist Party after a student rag. Trefulka worked this episode into his short story *Pršelo jim štěstí* (Happiness Rained on Them, 1962); Kundera did the same in the novel *Žert* (The Joke, see below). He studied film production and scriptwriting at the Film Academy in Prague finishing in 1958. He then lectured in world literature in Prague becoming a senior lecturer in 1964. In the sixties he represented the school of thought that criticized and attempted to reform Communism. After 1970 he could not publish, his books appearing only in translation. In 1975 he went to France where he lectured in the universities of Rennes and Paris. From the beginning of his stay in France, he often came to the notice of the public, taking up the cause of Czech and Central European democratic culture. Deprived of his Czech citizenship in 1978 he became a French citizen in 1981. Since the eighties he has retreated more and more into his private world, disgusted with sensationalist journalists, the superficial film version of his novel *Nesnesitelná lehkost bytí* (The Unbearable Lightness of Being, see below) and offended by the critical reception of his works in his native land. From the mid-eighties his books have been written and published in French.

Kundera began as a poet, his best-known work is *Monology* (Monologues, 1957; revised in 1964 and 1965), a collection of bitter erotica, and from the mid-1950s he was also an essayist, defending modern art in articles and in a book about the avant-garde writer Vladislav Vančura, *Umění románu* (The Art of the Novel, 1960). From the end of the fifties he wrote plays, for example *Majitelé klíčů* (The Owners of the Keys), premiered in 1962 and published in 1963, an involved piece set in the time of the Nazi occupation. A free adaptation of Denis Diderot's *Jacques le Fataliste et son maître*, premiered in 1975 in Czechoslovakia under an assumed name, was published in Czech in 1992. The translation as *Jacques and His Master* by Michael Henry Heim came out in New York in 1985, in London in 1986, and also in *Drama Contemporary: Czechoslovakia* (edited by Marketa Goetz-Stankiewicz), New York, 1985, pp. 21–68. A new translation by Simon Callow was published in Boston in 1986. However, Kundera's main work is in prose, especially the novels with which he became internationally famous, and he has become the most published Czech writer.

Stories are the basis of Kundera's novels, but the ego and the reactions of the hero or the authorial narrator are fully explored. The characters often plan their actions precisely but come to grief in the trap that awaits them. In the short stories *Směšné lásky* ruin results from erotic motivation. *Směšné lásky* was published in three volumes between 1963 and 1968, and film versions of the stories *Nikdo se nebude smát* (Nobody Will Laugh), *Já, truchlivý bůh* (I, the Mournful God) and *Eduard a Bůh* (Eduard and God) were made in 1965 and 1969. Hynek Bočan directed *Nikdo se nebude smát* (1965), Antonín Kachlík directed *Já, truchlivý bůh* (1969) and Jan David *Eduard a Bůh* (1969). The definitive version of *Směšné lásky* came out in Czech in 1991 as part of his Complete Works. Translated as *Laughable Loves* by Suzanne Rappaport with an introduction by Philip Roth, it was published in New York in 1974 and in London in 1975. In the novel *Žert* (1967) all four narrators believe in their own version of truth and become disillusioned. The main hero Ludvík is even disillusioned twice, firstly with his faith in Communism and secondly when he seeks revenge for his ruined life. A film version directed by Jaromil Jireš was made in 1968 with the collaboration of the author. The translation, *The Joke*, by David Hamblyn and Oliver Stallybrass, was published in New York in 1969 and in Harmondsworth in 1970. The first English translation was truncated by the publishers and is no longer regarded as acceptable. A new translation by Michael Henry Heim came out in New York in 1982 and in London in 1983. The definitive version by Aaron Asher came out in New York in 1992. The next novel, *Život je jinde*, is composed of seven parts, as is often the case in Kundera, where every part is made up of short chapters in which the story is told from different points of view. It appeared in a French translation in 1973 and was published in Czech in Toronto in 1979. Translated from Czech as *Life Is Elsewhere* by Peter Kussi, it was published in New York in 1974, in New York and London in 1986 with a preface by the author. A new translation from the French by Aaron Asher came out in London in 2000. It is an account of the life of a poet called Jaromil, who substitutes "lyricism" for his lack of courage, at first by means of his poetry and finally by his admiration for Stalinism. Criticism of "the age of lyricism" represents criticism of impotent romanticism, and it expressed scepticism in the face of seductive ideological dogma. The last novel that Kundera wrote in his native land is *Valčík na rozloučenou*. It was published in a French translation in 1976, in Czech in Toronto in 1979 and in Brno in 1997. The English translation from the Czech by Peter Kussi, *The Farewell Party*, was published in New York in 1976 and in London in 1977. A new translation from the French by Aaron Asher, as *The Farewell Waltz*, came out in London 1998. It is a straightforward story about responsibility, banality and fate and includes a murder mystery.

Prose works written in France but still in Czech began with *Kniha smíchu a zapomnění*, published in a French translation in 1979 and in Toronto in Czech in 1981. It was translated from Czech as *The Book of Laughter and Forgetting* by Michael Henry Heim and published in New York in 1980 and in Harmondsworth in 1981. A new translation from the French by Aaron Asher came out in New York and London in 1996. *Nesnesitelná lehkost bytí*, published in a French translation in 1984 and in Czech in Toronto in 1985, and in Brno in 2006 (afterword by Květoslav Chvatík in both editions), is probably Kundera's best work from this period. Translated by Michael Henry Heim as *The Unbearable Lightness of Being*, it was published in New York, Toronto and London in 1984. Kundera dismissed the film version of 1987, directed by Philip Kaufman, as superficial. It is set partly in the Czechoslovakia of the Husák era of the seventies where the spirit of forgetting which turned people into callous, cruel creatures was prevalent. However, it equally called into question the myths of the Western world, for example, the naïve illusions of left-wing intellectuals. Kundera had already published essays written in French in the books *L'art du roman* (1986, The Art of the Novel – no connection with the 1960 treatise on Vladislav Vančura, which has the same title) and *Les testaments trahis* (1993). *The Art of the Novel* was translated by Linda Asher and published in New York and London in 1988. The translation, *Testaments Betrayed*, by Linda Asher was published in New York and London in 1995. Besides literature both books are concerned with music and the composers Igor Stravinsky and Leoš Janáček. Like his previous novels, *Nesmrtelnost* is also predominantly essay-like in style. As *L'immortalité* (1990) it was written almost simultaneously in French with Eva Bloch helping Kundera with the language. The English translation *Immortality* was by Peter Kussi and published in London and New York in 1991; it was published in Czech in 1993. Incorporated into this story, set in modern France, are the story of J. W. Goethe and reflections on the "imagology" that dominates the Western world. The works that followed are written in French, the most noteworthy being *L'Identité* (1997, translated as *Identity* by Linda Asher, London and New York, 1998), which is a story with the typical Kundera themes of love, manipulation and misunderstanding. *L'Ignorance* (2000, translated as *Ignorance* by Linda Asher, London, 2002) is a novel dealing with the issue of changed identity and experience in people who have lived outside their native country for many years with the impossibility of reintegration into their native community.

From the nineties the Brno publishing house *Atlantis* has been publishing the works of Milan Kundera in the exact form in which the author has gradually been releasing them.

Bibliography: Antonín Jaroslav Liehm, "Milan Kundera" (interview), in his *The Politics of Culture*, New York, 1972, pp. 131–150 (in Czech Antonín Jaroslav Liehm, *Generace*, Prague, 1990, pp. 48–65). – Antonín Jaroslav Liehm, " Milan Kundera: Czech Writer," in *Czech Literature Since 1956* (edited by William E. Harkins and Paul I. Trensky), New York, 1980, pp. 62–73. – Robert C. Porter, *Milan Kundera: A Voice from Central Europe*, Aarhus, 1981. – Alain Finkielkraut, "Milan Kundera: Interview," *Cross Currents*, 1 (1982), pp. 15–29. – Ian McEwan, "An Interview with Milan Kundera," *Granta*, 11 (1984), pp. 21–37. – Maria Němcová Banerjee, *Terminal Paradox: The Novels of Milan Kundera*. London and Boston, 1990. – *Milan Kundera and the Art of Fiction* (edited by Aron Aji), London and New York, 1992. – Fred Misurella, *Understanding Milan Kundera*, Columbia, 1993. – Květoslav Chvatík, *Die Fallen der Welt*, Munich and Vienna,

1994 (in Czech in 1994, in French in 1995). – Eva Le Grand, *Kundera ou la mémoire du désir*, Montreal, 1995 (in Czech in 1998). – John O'Brien, *Dangerous Intersection: Milan Kundera and Feminism*, New York, 1995. – Alfred Thomas, "Fiction and Non-Fiction in Milan Kundera's Kniha smíchu a zapomnění," in his *The Labyrinth of the Word*, Munich, 1995, pp. 132–143. – Sylvie Richterová, "Otázka Boha ve světě bez Boha," in her *Ticho a smích*, Prague, 1997, pp. 132–150. – Helena Kosková, *Milan Kundera*, Prague, 1998. – *Critical Essays on Milan Kundera* (edited by Peter Petro), New York, 1999. – Peter Steiner, "Ironies of History. The Joke by Milan Kundera," in his *The Deserts of Bohemia: Czech Fiction and Its Social Context*, Ithaca and London, 2000, pp. 196–217 (in Czech in 2002). – Tomáš Kubíček, *Vyprávět příběh*, Brno, 2001. – Jan Čulík, "Milan Kundera," in *Dictionary of Literary Biography: Twentieth-Century Eastern European Writers*, vol. 232 (edited by Steven Serafin et al.), Detroit, 2001, pp. 208–226. – Hana Píchová, *The Art of Memory in Exile: Vladimir Nabokov and Milan Kundera*, Southern Illinois University, 2002. – François Ricard, *Agnes' Final Afternoon*, New York, 2003 (in French in 2003). – *Milan Kundera* (edited and introduction by Harold Bloom), Broomall, 2003. – Michelle Woods, "A Very British Bohemia? The Reception of Milan Kundera and his Work in Great Britain", *Kosmas*, 16, no. 2 (Spring 2003), pp. 27-43 – Jakub Češka, *Království motivů: Motivická analýza románů Milana Kundery*, Prague, 2005. – Doris Boden, *Irritation als naratives Prinzip: Untersuchungen zur Rezeptionssteuerung in den Romanen Milan Kunderas*, Hildesheim et al., 2006.

LINHARTOVÁ, VĚRA

Prose-writer, essayist, art historian and poet. She was born in 1938 in Brno, studied history of art at the university in Brno and aesthetics at Charles University in Prague. She worked in the art gallery in the castle of Hluboká in South Bohemia and set up important exhibitions of avant-garde art (for instance, exhibitions of Jindřich Štyrský's and Toyen's work in 1966). After 1966 she devoted herself entirely to literature. Between 1962 and 1966 she took part in the unofficial activities of surrealist groups and contributed to the collections put out by the circle of writers connected with the journal *Tvář* (Countenance). Since 1968 she has lived in Paris where she studied Japanese. She spent the year 1989–1990 in Tokyo on a research fellowship. Her chief interest is Japanese and Chinese painting. She edited, translated and annotated *Dada et surréalisme au Japon* (Dadaism and Surrealism in Japan, 1987). Since the early seventies she has been writing in French. In the seventies and eighties her works could not be published in Czechoslovakia.

Linhartová's literary output consists mainly of prose works, beginning as early as 1957 but not published till the mid-sixties. The collections of short stories *Meziprůzkum nejblíž uplynulého* (Intersurvey of the Nearest Past) and *Prostor k rozlišení* (Space for Differentiation) were published in 1964, the prose work *Rozprava o zdviži* (Discourse about a Lift) in 1965 and the collection of short stories *Přestořeč* (Despitespeech) in 1966. As a result of her method of presentation, intentionally disrupting "credibility", and the illusion of the narrative and by her style, using specialist technical devices, essays, numerous allusions and quotations, these texts do not conform to the usual idea of literature and, as it were, do not react to contemporary stimuli. It is not the story but its validity that is highlighted, and language itself, its basis and capability, is also called into question. In her next works and her poetry, and also in texts written in French, the departure from narrative is even more radical. Gradually, even grammar and syntax are thrown into confusion and the texts change into ambiguous, freely associated fragments. *Dům daleko* (A House in the Distance), written between 1963 and 1965, published in 1968), and *Chiméra neboli průřez cibulí* (Chimera, or a Cross Section of Onions), completed by 1967 but not published till 1993, the poems in the book *Ianus tří tváří* (The Three Faces of Janus) and *Twor* (1974), originally written in French but in also in Czech in the bilingual edition of 1992, are all structured in this way.

Linhartová researched the work of the Czech writer and poet Richard Weiner, the surrealist Jindřich Heisler and published *Vysoká hra / Le Grand Jeu* (The Great Game, 1993), a volume of articles and translations of poems into Czech by a group of French parasurrealists of the same name. She edited and annotated Richard Weiner's *Hra doopravdy* (Really a Play, 1967) and Jindřich Heisler's poems, *Aniž by nastal viditelný pohyb* (Without Visible Movement, Toronto, 1977). She concentrated her interest in Czech painters chiefly on Josef Šíma, publishing a monograph in French in 1974 in Brussels.

Editions in English: "The Room" (translated by Jeanne W. Němcová), in *Czech and Slovak Short Stories* (edited by Jeanne W. Němcová), London and New York, 1967, pp. 284–296; "The Road to the Mountains" (translated by Ewald Osers), in *This Side of Reality* (edited by Alexandra Büchler), London, 1996, pp. 18–24; "A Barbarian Woman in Captivity" (translated from French original by Keith Waldrop), in *Allskin and Other Tales by Contemporary Czech Women* (edited by Alexandra Büchler), Seattle, 1998, pp. 202–208.

Bibliography: Vera Blackwell, "Věra Linhartová: Mirrors and Masks," in *Tri-Quarterly*, 9 (Spring 1967), pp. 209–213 (also in *New Writing of East Europe*, edited by George Gömöri and Charles Newman, Chicago, 1968, pp. 233–237). – Bronislav Pražan and Oleg Sus, "Proměny kontextu a významotvorného principu v próze Věry Linhartové," *Česká literatura*, 18 (1970), pp. 60–80. – Sylvie Richterová, "Ritratto dellautrice," in Věra Linhartová, *Ritratti carnivori*, Rome, 1987, pp. 55–76 (in Czech S. Richterová, *Místo domova*, Brno, 2004, pp. 144–152). – Daniela Hodrová, "Věra Linhartová: Meziprůzkum nejblíž uplynulého," in *Česká literatura 1945–1970* (edited by Jiřina Táborská and Milan Zeman), Prague, 1992, pp. 304–312. – Zuzana Stolz-Hladká, "Human Existence as Strangeness and Writing as Estrangement: Aspects of Exile in the Texts of Věra Linhartová," *Canadian-American Slavic Studies*, 33 (1999), no. 2–4, pp. 153–177. – Milan Suchomel, "Překročit práh nemožného," in *Zlatá šedesátá* (edited by Radka Denemarková), Prague, 2000, pp. 153–157.

Lustig, Arnošt

Novelist, scriptwriter and journalist. He was born in 1926 in Prague into a family of tradesmen. In 1941 as a Jew he was expelled from secondary school, and in 1942 he was deported to the concentration camp at Theresienstadt (Terezín). He spent the year 1944–1945 in the concentration camps at Auschwitz and Buchenwald. In April 1945 he was being deported to a death camp when he escaped. This experience inspired the story *Tma nemá stín* (Darkness Casts No Shadow) in the book *Démanty noci* (Diamonds in the Night, 1958). *Tma nemá stín* was expanded and translated by Jeanne Němcová, Washington, 1977, London, 1989; in Czech in 1991. After 1945 he studied journalism in Prague, completing his studies in 1950 and then working as a journalist. From 1961 to 1968 he was a scriptwriter for the state film industry. In 1968 he went into exile, first to Israel, then from 1970 he lived in the USA where he lectured, mostly in Washington, on creative writing, film and literature. He was appointed professor in 1978. He now divides his time between the USA and the Czech Republic. In 1995–1997 he was chief editor of the Czech version of *Playboy*.

More or less the sole topic to which Lustig keeps returning in his writing is the Holocaust: "Of the fifteen thousand children in the ghetto in Theresienstadt not quite a hundred got back . . . I was one of the children who survived." His first works are among his best. They included the short stories *Noc a naděje* (1958, translated as *Night and Hope* by George Theiner, published in New York and London in 1962 and republished in 1985 with an introduction by Jonathan Brent). In 1962, freely adapted, it was made into a film by Zbyněk Brynych called *Transport z ráje* (Transport from Paradise). *Démanty noci* (1958) was translated as *Diamonds in the Night* by Iris Urwin-Levit in Prague in 1962. A new translation as *Diamonds of the Night* was made by Jeanne Němcová and published in Washington in 1977. An excellent film version of the story *Tma nemá stín* with the title *Démanty noci* (Diamonds of the Night) was made by Jan Němec in 1964. Arnošt Lustig collaborated in the production of both films. The constrained situation in the Nazi camps is treated with restraint and objectivity, the main characters being children, the young, and old people.

Outstanding among his next works are the novella *Modlitba pro Kateřinu Horovitzovou* (1964), which was translated as *A Prayer for Katerina Horovitzova* by Jeanne Němcová (published in New York in 1973, in London in 1990, and made into a film for Czechoslovak Television in 1965 by Antonín Moskalyk), and the short novel *Nemilovaná,* which was published in Toronto in 1979 and in Prague in 1991. It was translated as *The Unloved* and published in New York in 1985 and in London in 1986. It was subtitled "Z deníku sedmnáctileté Perly Sch." (the English subtitle was "From the Diary of Perla S."). The stories are shocking tales of beautiful Jewish girls in prison camps who finally take their revenge on cynical guards – it is possible to see in them parallels with the story of the biblical Judith. Fear, horror and brutality are present but there is also the struggle for morality and human dignity. The fate of a girl who survived the concentration camp but could not come to terms with life after the war is the subject of *Dita Saxová* (1962, revised in 1997). It was translated as *Dita Sax* by George Theiner and published in London in 1966. A new translation by Jeanne W. Němcová, was published New York in 1979 and in London in 1994 with an afterword by Byron L. Sherwin. The author collaborated with Antonín Moskalyk in making a film version in 1967. Some parts of Lustig's extensive and as yet unfinished work *Král promluvil, neřekl nic* (The King Spoke – and Said Nothing) have been published separately, for example, *Colette: Dívka z Antverp* (Colette. The Girl from Antwerp), *Tanga: Dívka z Hamburku* (Tanga. The Girl from Hamburg). Both were published in Czech in 1992, *Colette* translated by Tim Whipple in *Kenyon Review*, Spring 1991, and *Tanga* translated by Káča Poláčková in *Formations*, 1988. *Král promluvil, neřekl nic* is based on the frequently revised and expanded story *Můj známý Vili Feld* (My Friend Vili Feld), which originally appeared in the 1959 collection *Ulice ztracených bratří* (The Street of Lost Brothers). It was revised in 1996 as *Street of Lost Brothers* and translated by Jeanne W. Němcová with a foreword by Jonathan Brent, Evanston, 1990. It is typical of Lustig's later work that the author adapted and expanded his earlier texts, their original introspective and laconic character changing to a contemplative, verbose style. For example, from the collection of short stories *Nikoho neponížíš* (Nobody Is Humiliated, 1963) emerged a new version, *Neslušné sny* (1995), translated as *Indecent Dreams* by Iris Urwin-Levit, Vera Borkovec and Paul Wilson with an afterword by Josef Škvorecký, Evanston, 1988. The novel *Krásné zelené oči,* written in 2000, expanded in 2003 and translated as *Lovely Green Eyes* by Ewald Osers, London, 2001, is another of Lustig's stories about Jewish girls in Auschwitz. It was developed in similar fashion. Lustig and his son Josef wrote *Film and Holocaust* (Chicago, 1978). Some of his many essays and interviews were issued in Czech, *Eseje* in 2001, with an afterword by Michal Bauer, *Interview* (2002), *Interview II* in 2004. All were edited by Jan Suk. In 1991 the publishing house *Odeon* began publishing the works of Arnošt Lustig. One volume has been published. Since 1995 the Prague publishing house *Hynek* has been arranging a new edition of his works.

Other editions in English: three volumes of *Children of the Holocaust: The Collected Works of Arnošt Lustig* (*Night and Hope*, *Diamonds of the Night*, *Darkness Casts No Shadow*, Washington, 1976–1978, republished Evanston, 1995); "Night" (translated Lesley Keen and Jan Čulík), *Argo*, 7 (1988), no. 3, pp. 26–39; "The River Where the Milky Way Flows" (translated by Josef Lustig), in *This Side of Reality* (edited by Alexandra Büchler), London, 1996, pp. 94–110; *Waiting for Lea,* translation of *Lea z Leeuwardenu*, made by Ewald Osers, London, 2004; "Lea of Leeuwarden" (no translator is given), *Partisan Review*, 67 (Spring 2000), pp. 296–318; *The House of Returned Echoes* (translated by Josef Lustig), Evanston, 2001. – "From Leah" (translated by Ewald Osers), *Kosmas*, 17, no. 1 (Fall 2003), pp. 80-103.

Bibliography: Byron L. Sherwin, "The Holocaust Universe of Arnošt Lustig," *Midstream*, 25 (1979), no. 7, pp. 44–48. – Sidra DeKoven Ezrahi, *By Words Alone: The Holocaust in Literature* (foreword by Alfred Kazin), Chicago, 1980. – Aleš Haman, "Man in a Violent World," *Czechoslovak and Central European Journal*, 11, no. 1 (Summer 1992), pp. 73–80. – David H. Lynn, "The Lost Brother," *Kenyon Review*, 14, no. 3 (Summer 1992), pp. 161–165. – Milan Suchomel, *Literatura z času krize*, Brno, 1992, pp. 19–36. – Aleš Haman, *Arnošt Lustig*, Prague, 1995. – Josef Vohryzek, *Literární kritiky* (edited by Jan Lopatka and Michael Špirit),

Prague, 1995, pp. 81–84, 126–130, 143–146. – Byron L. Sherwin, "Moral Implications of the Holocaust in Holocaust Literature: Levi, Lustig, Kosinski," in *The Holocaust* (edited by Franklin H. Littell et al.), London, 1996, pp. 112–148. – Rob Trucks, "A Conversation with Arnošt Lustig," *New England Review*, 20, no. 14 (Spring 1999), pp. 68–77. – Aleš Haman, "Arnošt Lustig," in *Dictionary of Literary Biography: Twentieth-Century Eastern European Writers*, vol. 232 (edited by Steven Serafin et al.), Detroit, 2001, pp. 233–242. – Cythia A. Klíma, "Arnošt Lustig," "Darkness Casts No Shadow," "Diamonds of the Night," "Night and Hope," "A Prayer for Katarina Horovitzova" and "The Unloved" in *Reference Guide to Holocaust Literature* (edited by Thomas Riggs), Detroit, 2002, pp. 202–203, 402–403, 408, 524, 550, 609–610. – Michal Bauer, "Ani zapomenout, ani odpustit," in Arnošt Lustig, *Modlitba pro Kateřinu Horovitzovou*, Prague, 2003, pp. 131–155. – Joshua L. Charlson, "Arnost Lustig," in *Holocaust Literature* (edited by S. Lillian Kremer), London and New York, 2003, pp. 779–784. – Robert B. Pynsent, "Arnošt Lustig," in *Dictionary of Literary Biography: Holocaust Novelists*, vol. 299 (edited by Efraim Sicher), Detroit, 2004, pp. 220–226.

Mikulášek, Oldřich

Poet and journalist. He was born in 1910 in the Moravian town of Přerov into a family of railwaymen. After leaving school and commercial college, from 1927 he held various odd jobs. From 1937 he lived in Brno where from 1937 to 1945 and from 1948 to 1952 he worked in the editorial office of the daily paper *Lidové noviny* (The People's Paper), which changed its name after the war to *Svobodné noviny* (The Liberated Newspaper). He also worked for *Rovnost* (Equality), in radio and between 1956 and 1964 for the review *Host do domu* (A Guest in the House). Thereafter he devoted himself entirely to literature. He was a friend of the authors in *Skupina 42* (Group 42) and of Jan Skácel. At Easter 1967 he had a serious accident and as a result could walk only with the help of crutches. In the seventies he could not publish, and his collection *Agogh* was issued in samizdat and in exile. His new poetry was not published officially till 1981. He died in Brno in 1985.

Mikulášek's work was formed by his lifelong association with Brno and South Moravia. Unlike most of his contemporaries he only gradually gained recognition as a poet. His first important work is the 1947 collection *Pulsy* (Pulses), the title poem typically dedicated to František Halas, the poet who extolled the drama of human existence. In this collection the world is seen as the struggle of bitter opposites, life is a drama with constant reversals. Indifference and calm are rejected; against them are placed *puls* (pulse) and *krev* (blood) – the tension and slippery slope of life, perhaps even its destructiveness.

After a period of publishing poetry aimed at harmonizing the opposite poles of life, Mikulášek, continuing from *Pulsy*, wrote his key work, the lyric collection *Ortely a milosti* (Judgment and Mercy). It was published in 1958. The tragic, existentialist, agonizing situations in the poems *Vyvolavač* (The Town Crier) and *Výčitky* (Reproaches) invade times of rapture and happiness (*Pokušení na Špilberku*, Temptation on Špilberg). Only through pain and death can the most exalted moments in life be experienced: "ó bože, hromů tři sta / do tebe, / když není proč se chvět, / když kotle dovřely / a naše duše, které přešel var, / jsou zase k snědku, jako byly dříve, / tak trochu kližka . . ." (oh God, let three hundred thunderclaps / strike you / when there is no reason to tremble, / when the boiler closed / and our seething souls, / are again about to be consumed as before, / like a morsel of gristle . . .) Here we have the author's poetics in a nutshell. His poetry is based on antithesis, parallelism and variation, paradox and irony. The spoken word is the basis of the language but there are also quotations from folk song, literary expressions and neologisms.

The collections of the sixties, *Svlékání hadů* (Sloughing of Snakes, 1963), introduced by Jan Skácel and illustrated by Arnošt Paderlík, and *Šokovaná růže* (The Shattered Rose, 1969), extend Mikulášek's poetic vision. Typically they give pictures of wine, nature, the nature of man, above all of love, that dangerous passion that tears body and soul apart. In the poem *Utrpení starého Werthera* (The Sufferings of Old Werther), which came out in a special limited edition in 1974, there is, in addition to irony, a greater degree of self-mockery and bitterness. *Utrpení starého Werthera* has been included in the collection *Žebro Adamovo* (Adam's Rib, 1981) although it had been written between 1971 and 1973. The poetry is sometimes harsh and sometimes more like free verse. One collection in particular stands out among his later works. *Agogh* (Agogh) was published in samizdat in 1972, in Munich in 1980, and in Prague in 1989. The Prague edition was illustrated by František Burant and the afterword is by Josef Peterka. The title and some of the themes, poetry, love, the drama of the battle of the sexes, suggest the mysterious atmosphere of the Orient. There are even brief references to the most up-to-date creations, such as James Bond and electric guitars. The language is also complex and ambiguous, ranging from vulgarisms to magic incantations. Oldřich Mikulášek's poetry was collected in four volumes and published between 1997 and 2000 by the Prague publishing house *Ivo Železný* (*Verše I–IV*), edited by Jiří Kudrnáč and Zdeněk Drahoš.

Editions in English: four poems (translation and commentary by Jessie Kocmanová), in *Universum: A Review of Czechoslovak Literature and Arts*, 4 (1970), no. 8, pp. 1–3; two poems (Devastated by Love, Mutenesses, translated by Bronislava Volková and James Felak), in *The Boundaries of Twilight: Czecho-Slovak Writing from the New World* (edited by C. J. Hribal), Minneapolis, 1991, pp. 211–212.

Bibliography: Jiří Opelík, "Mikulášek," in *Jak číst poezii* (edited by Jiří Opelík, 2nd edition), Prague, 1969, pp. 178–193. – Miroslav Petříček, *Oldřich Mikulášek*, Prague, 1970. – Zdeněk Kožmín, *Umění básně*, Brno, 1990, pp. 45–69. – *Pět na jednoho: Interpretační symposium nad Mikuláškovým Vyvolavačem* (edited by Jiří Trávníček), Prague, 1995. – Oldřich Mikulášek, *Královské léto* (edited by Zdeněk Drahoš, including Mikulášek's poems, memories, letters and essays of his friends), Brno, 1995. – Jiří Trávníček, "Král černý nicoty a sebezmaru. Oldřich Mikulášek, Agogh," in his *Poezie poslední možnosti*, Prague, 1996, pp. 150–165. – Jiří Opelík, "Strmý úděl," in his *Milované řemeslo*, Prague, 2000, pp. 271–295.

NEZVAL, VÍTĚZSLAV

Poet, essayist, novelist and dramatist. He was born in 1900 in the little village of Biskoupky near Brno in Moravia into a family of teachers. The family soon moved to the village Šamikovice near Třebíč in the Czech-Moravian Highlands where Nezval spent his childhood. This was the inspiration for many of his poems and for the 1931 novel *Dolce far niente*. On leaving school in Třebíč he studied law for a short time at the university in Brno; from 1920 to 1924 he studied literature at Charles University but did not complete his studies. He lived in Prague and supported himself by working chiefly as a freelance writer. His poetry mentor was the Brno writer Jiří Mahen. Nezval was a friend of Karel Teige, Vladislav Vančura, Konstantin Biebl and other writers. He was a Communist by conviction, a foremost member of the avant-garde group *Devětsil* (Butterbur/Nine Powers). Later he was a member of *Surrealistická skupina* (Surrealist Group) until 1938 when he came into conflict with the other surrealists because of his defence of Stalinism. He travelled abroad and his visit to France and Italy in 1933 was the inspiration for the 1934 collection *Sbohem a šáteček* (A Farewell with a Scarf). Between 1945 and 1950 he was in charge of the film department of the Ministry of Information. He became an important political and cultural activist, promoting Communism but also defending important persecuted writers, such as Jakub Deml, Jaroslav Seifert and František Langer. He died in Prague in 1958.

Nezval's work is founded on lyric poetry, based on concrete, sensual vision and metaphorical images created by free association. The lesser, light-hearted fantasy poems, such as *Abeceda* (1926, translated as *Alphabet* by Jindřich Toman and Matthew S. Witkowsky, Ann Arbor, 2001) and *Básně na pohlednice* (Poems on a Postcard, 1926) belong to Nezval's first poetistic period (poetism was a Czech avant-garde movement of the 1920s). The poems modelled on Apollinaire's *Zone*, especially *Podivuhodný kouzelník* (The Magic Magician), *Akrobat* (The Acrobat, 1927) and *Edison* (1928), all appear in the volume *Básně noci* (Poems of the Night, 1930). *Podivuhodný kouzelník* was first published in the 1922 collection *Devětsil* (Butterbur/Nine Powers) and also in Nezval's 1924 book *Pantomima* (Pantomime). The original graphic design was by Karel Teige. *Pantomime* was republished in its original 1924 graphic design by Teige in 2004. The sublime composition *Edison* (translated by Ewald Osers, Pelhřimov, 2003) in particular, based on a rhythmical musical plan and only freely inspired by the famous inventor, expresses the idea of liberation through living with poetry. In the thirties the joyful light-heartedness of Nezval's work was lost, replaced on the one hand by "anti-lyricism", that is, poetry with socialist themes, and on the other hand by surrealist texts. Socialist poems appear in the book *Skleněný havelok* (The Glass Cloak, 1932) and in *52 hořkých balad věčného studenta Roberta Davida* (52 Bitter Ballads of the Eternal Student Robert David), originally published anonymously in 1936. The surrealist texts *Žena v množném čísle* (Woman in the Plural, 1936, graphic design by Karel Teige) and *Absolutní hrobař* (The Absolute Gravedigger, 1937) draw on bizarre ideas, the subconscious, eroticism and infantility. The novel *Valérie a týden divů*, inspired by the French Roman Noir, is also almost surreal. It was written in 1935, published in 1945 and illustrated by Kamil

Lhoták. Translated into English as *Valerie and Her Week of Wonders*, it came out in Prague in 2005. A remarkable film version was made by Jaromil Jireš in 1970. Nezval's later works are more like traditional poetry, for example *Pět minut za městem* (Five Minutes Past the Town, 1940). In his postwar collections, praise of socialism is a dominant theme. This is true of the 1949 poem *Stalin* and the book *Zpěv míru* (1950). The translation as *Song of Peace* by Jack Lindsay and Stephen Jolly was published in London in 1951. In his last years the author occasionally returned to some of the themes and techniques of his avant-garde poetry, for example in *Chrpy a města* (Cornflowers and Cities, 1955) and *Nedokončená* (Unfinished, edited by Vlastimil Fiala, 1960).

Lyricism also permeates Nezval's prose including the incomplete memoirs *Z mého života* (From My Life, edited by Vlastimil Fiala, 1959), his plays for the theatre, *Milenci z kiosku* (Lovers in a Kiosk), which was first performed and published in 1932, *Manon Lescaut*, based on Prévost's novel and first performed and published in 1940, poetic manifestos and essays (included in the Collected Works *Dílo*, volumes 24–26, edited by Milan Blahynka in 1967, 1974 and 1976), and also his imaginative stories for children, like *Anička skřítek a Slaměný Hubert* (The Brownie Anička, and Hubert, the Straw Man, 1936), a book reminiscent of Lewis Carroll, republished with illustrations by Jiří Trnka in 1963. Nezval also prepared and annotated the anthology of poetry *Moderní básnické směry* (Modern Trends in Poetry, 1937). His outstanding translations of E. A. Poe, Arthur Rimbaud and other authors are in the Collected Works *Dílo*, volumes 35–36 (edited by Milan Blahynka, Kateřina Blahynková and Václav Kubín, 1982 and 1984). *Dílo Vítězslava Nezvala* (The Work of Vítězslav Nezval) was published between 1950 and 1990 by the publishers *Československý spisovatel* in 36 volumes, most of them edited by Milan Blahynka. The volumes published during the author's lifetime were censored by the author himself.

Other editions in English: five poems (translated by Ewald Osers), in *Modern Czech Poetry* (edited by Ewald Osers and J. K. Montgomery), London, 1945, pp. 53–58; *Antonín Slavíček: A Great Czech Painter* (translated by Ilse Gottheiner), Prague, 1955; three poems (translated by Edith Pargeter), in *The Linden Tree* (edited by Mojmír Otruba and Zdeněk Pešat), Prague, 1962, pp. 157–163; twenty-one poems (translated by Ewald Osers), in *Three Czech Poets: Vítězslav Nezval, Antonín Bartušek, Josef Hanzlík* (introduction by Graham Martin), Harmondsworth, 1971, pp. 25–63; "Two Poems for Roman Jakobson," *Cross Currents*, 2 (1983), pp. 203–204; seven poems (translated by Alfred French), in *The Czech Avantgardists* (edited by Alfred French), Rockville, 1995, pp. 40–44, 46, 51–59, 62–66, 71–72.

Bibliography: Antonín Jelínek, *Vítězslav Nezval,* Prague, 1961. – Milan Kundera, in Vítězslav Nezval, *Podivuhodný kouzelník* (edited by Milan Kundera), Prague, 1963, pp. 7–30. – Liudmila Norairovna Budagova, *Vitezslav Nezval,* Moscow, 1967. – Alfred French, "The Czech Lyric Poet Vítězslav Nezval," *Melbourne Slavonic Studies*, 2 (1968), pp. 21–38. – Alfred French, *The Poets of Prague*, London and New York, 1969. – Mojmír Grygar, "Nezval," in *Jak číst poezii* (edited by Jiří Opelík, 2nd edition), Prague, 1969, pp. 83–113. – Alfred

French, "Nezval's Amazing Magician," *Slavic Review*, 32 (1973), pp. 358–370. – Arne Novák, *Czech Literature* (edited by William E. Harkins, translated by Peter Kussi), Ann Arbor, 1976, pp. 319–331. – Maria Němcová Banerjee, "Nezval's Prague with Fingers of Rain. A Surrealistic Image," *Slavic and East European Journal*, 23 (1979), pp. 505–514. – Milan Blahynka, *Vítězslav Nezval*, Prague, 1981. – Marie Kubínová, "Vítězslav Nezval – představitel poetismu," in her *Proměny české poezie dvacátých let*, Prague, 1984, pp. 37–80. – *Vítězslav Nezval: Spolutvůrce pokrokové kulturní politiky* (edited by Jaroslav Kabíček), Brno, 1986. – Igor Vladimirovič Inov, *Sudba i muzy Vitezslava Nezvala*, Moscow, 1990. – Zdeněk Pešat, "Vítězslav Nezval: Chrpy a města," in *Česká literatura 1945–1970* (edited by Jiřina Táborská and Milan Zeman), Prague, 1992, pp. 88–96. – Lilly Hodáčová, *Zpěv Orfeův*, Prague, 1995. – Jiří Holý, "Vítězslav Nezval," in *Dictionary of Literary Biography: Twentieth Century Eastern European Writers*, vol. 215 (edited by Steven Serafin et al.), Detroit, 1999, pp. 289–294. – *Hra v kostky. Vítězslav Nezval a výtvarné umění* (edited by David Voda), Olomouc and Brno, 2004.

PÁRAL, VLADIMÍR

Novelist. He was born in 1932 in Prague into a military family. He spent his childhood in Brno, studied chemistry in Pardubice, graduating in 1954. He worked as a chemist and scientific officer, especially in Ústí nad Labem in Northern Bohemia. From 1967 he earned his living as a writer and editor. He travelled widely, visiting India in 1968, Central Asia in 1978 and China in 1988.

In the sixties Páral began writing novels set in the industrial region of Northern Bohemia. His characters are stereotypes in their lives, work and erotic experiences. For a short time they become free of their stereotypical image but eventually degenerate into new stereotypes. This mechanical view of life is reinforced by the writer's style, based on repetition and variation, abbreviations and ellipses, sentences with no verb and so on. The novella *Veletrh splněných přání* (The Fair of Dreams Fulfilled, 1964) and the novels *Soukromá vichřice* (A Private Gale, 1966) and *Katapult* (1967) fall into this category. The translation as *Catapult*, with an introduction by William E. Harkins, was published in Highland Park in 1989. The film version was made by Jaromil Jireš in 1983. A film version of *Soukromá vichřice* was made by Hynek Bočan in 1967. The lengthy novel *Milenci a vrazi* (1969, translated as *Lovers and Murderers* by Craig Cravens, North Haven, 2001), postulates on this basis that even history is a struggle between "The Reds", that is, "The Conquerors", who seek power, possessions and sex, and "The Blues" in other words "The Besieged"; in the course of history the two groups exchange positions. In 2004, the novel was made into a film by Viktor Polesný. The following novel, *Profesionální žena* (A Woman by Profession, 1971), was adapted for the theatre by Milan Uhde in 1974 and by Evald Schorm in 1975. The translation by William Harkins, *The Four Sonyas*, was published in North Haven in 1993. It is a parody of adventure stories and stories for girls but at the same time it makes use of their conventions.

In the seventies and eighties Páral remained one of the few important writers officially recognized. In accordance with the demands of the time and using the same techniques as before, he tried to create positive heroes whom he grafted on to his previous themes, as for example in *Mladý muž a bílá velryba* (The Young Man and the White Whale, 1973). It was adapted for the theatre by Zdenek Potužil in 1976 and filmed in 1978 by Jaromil Jireš. Later he turned from contemporary subjects to science fiction. *Pokušení A–ZZ* (Temptation A–ZZ, 1982) dealt with an encounter with an extraterrestrial civilization, but could be understood as a parable of enslavement by Communism; in the novel *Válka s mnohozvířetem* (War with the Multibeast, 1983), which is a variation on Čapek's novel *Válka s Mloky* (War with the Newts), the subject is ecological and moral devastation. In work from his latest period including the partly autobiographical novel *Kniha rozkoší, smíchu a radosti* (The Book of Delight, Laughter and Joy, 1992), his style is even more openly erotic. With the collaboration of Heda Bartíková he wrote the memoir *Profesionální muž* (A Man by Profession, 1995).

Bibliography: Josef Škvorecký, "Páralovo permanentní posvícení," in Josef Škvorecký and Antonín Brousek, *Na brigádě*, Toronto, 1979, pp. 213–231. – William E. Harkins, "Vladimír Páral's Novel Catapult," in *Czech Literature Since 1956* (edited by William E. Harkins and Paul I. Trensky), New York, 1980, pp. 62–73. – Jan Čulík, "Integrity, Creativity and Death," *Irish Slavonic Studies*, 6 (1985), pp. 133–141. – David Short, "Páralův Veletrh splněných přání – učebnicový vzor překladatelské problematiky," *Proměny*, 19 (1988), no. 1, pp. 35–41. – Pavel Janoušek, "Vladimír Páral: Katapult," in *Česká literatura 1945–1970* (edited by Jiřina Táborská and Milan Zeman), Prague, 1992, pp. 374–383. – Robert B. Pynsent, *Sex under Socialism: An Essay on the Works of Vladimír Páral*, London, 1994. – Pavel Janoušek, "Vladimír Páral," in *Dictionary of Literary Biography: Twentieth-Century Eastern European Writers*, vol. 232 (edited by Steven Serafin et al.), Detroit, 2001, pp. 290–295.

PATOČKA, JAN

Philosopher and historian of philosophy and civilization, aesthetitian, translator. He was born in 1907 in the town of Turnov in Eastern Bohemia. His father was a secondary school teacher. He studied philosophy, Czech language and French at Charles University in Prague, in France and in Germany, also with Edmund Husserl and Martin Heidegger, gaining his doctorate in 1932. First he taught in a secondary school, then from 1945 he taught philosophy at the Arts Faculty in Prague, but after the Communist coup of 1948 he was dismissed. He worked as a librarian and in the Educational Institute and from 1958 to 1968 in the Institute of Philosophy. At the end of the sixties he returned for a short time to the faculty as a professor. He held seminars in private flats, published in samizdat and was a signatory of the human rights manifesto *Charter 77*. He was also one of their first three spokesmen. After lengthy questioning by the police he had to be taken to hospital where he succumbed to a stroke in 1977.

Besides his purely philosophical works, which were based on phenomenology and embraced the entire spectrum of philosophical problems, Patočka was always concerned with other problems. *Česká vzdělanost v Evropě* (Czech Civilization in Europe, 1939) and *Co jsou Češi?* (What Are the Czechs?) deal with the question of what it means to be Czech and with the vocation of an intellectual who in Patočka's view was supposed to develop the ideas of morality. *Co jsou Češi?* was translated from a manuscript written in German in the seventies, published in samizdat in 1989 and in Prague in 1992. Patočka was also interested in art and especially in literature as a peculiarly spiritual manifestation. He kept going back to one Czech pedagogue, the Protestant theologist and philosopher Comenius (J. A. Komenský), and also to the first Czechoslovak president T. G. Masaryk. The collection *Masaryk* was published in samizdat 1979 and *Tři studie o Masarykovi* (Three Studies on Masaryk), which was edited by Ivan Chvatík and Pavel Kouba, came out in Prague in 1991. Between 1997 and 1999 Věra Schifferová edited Patočka's *Komeniologické studie I–III* (Comenius Studies), in the Complete Works of Jan Patočka, vols. IX–XI. Patočka's articles on art were published together in *Umění a čas* I–II (Art and Time) as vols. IV–V of the complete works, edited by Daniel Vojtěch and Ivan Chvatík in 2004. The works of Jan Patočka based on samizdat editions have been in the process of being published since 1996 by the Prague publishing house *Oikúmené* (edited by Ivan Chvatík and Pavel Kouba).

Editions in English: *An Introduction to Husserl's Phenomenology* (translated by Erazim Kohák, edited and introduction by James Dodd), Chicago, 1996; *Heretical Essays in the Philosophy of History* (translated by Erazim Kohák, preface by Paul Ricoeur), Chicago, 1996; *Body, Community, Language, World* (translated by Erazim Kohák, edited and introduction by James Dodd), Chicago, 1998; *Plato and Europe* (translated by Petr Lom), Stanford, 2002.

Bibliography: *Die Welt des Menschen, die Welt der Philosophie: Festschrift für Jan Patočka* (edited by Walter Biemel et al.), The Hague, 1976. – Milan Walter, *Jan Patočka, sein Leben und sein Werk*, Munich, 1985. – *Jan Patočka: Ästhetik, Phänomenologie, Pädagogik, Geschichts- und Politiktheorie* (edited by Matthias Gatzemeier), Aachen, 1994. – *Jan Patočka: Bibliographie* (edited by Jiří Němec and David Souček), Prague, 1997. – Ivan Blecha, *Jan Patočka*, Olomouc, 1997. – Edward F. Findlay, *Caring for the Soul in a Postmodern Age: Politics and Phenomenology in the Thought of Jan Patočka*, Albany, 2002.

PEROUTKA, FERDINAND

Journalist and essayist, novelist, dramatist. He was born in 1895 in Prague into a Czech-German family. His father was a civil servant. Peroutka did not complete his studies but worked as a critic and journalist. In 1919 he became chief editor of the daily paper *Tribuna* (Forum), and later from 1924–1939 of the weekly *Přítomnost* (The Present) which promoted liberal democratic views. He also wrote articles for the daily *Lidové noviny* (The People's Paper). He belonged to the circle of friends of the brothers Čapek. In 1939 he was arrested and held in concentration camps till 1945. His stay in Buchenwald inspired the novel *Oblak a valčík* (A Cloud and a Waltz). After the war for a short time he was a member of parliament, then he became editor in chief of *Svobodné noviny* (The Liberated Newspaper, formerly *Lidové noviny*) and of the review *Dnešek* (Today, formerly *Přítomnost*).

Shortly after the Communist coup of 1948 he went into exile. From 1950 he lived in New York and was in charge of Czechoslovak broadcasting on *Radio Free Europe* from 1951 to 1961, to which he sent weekly reports till 1977. These reports were collected under the title *Budeme pokračovat* (We Shall Continue), which was introduced by Jiří Kovtun and published in Toronto in 1984, and *Úděl svobody* (The Fate of Freedom, Prague, 1995). *Demokratický manifest* was published in New York in 1959 and in Prague in 1991. The English translation *Democratic Manifesto*, introduced by Adolf A. Berle, came out in New York in 1959. It was also translated into nine other languages. Peroutka died in New York in 1978.

Peroutka was first and foremost a political and cultural journalist. He never stopped defending, controversially and with wit, the principles of liberalism and democracy, especially in the four volumes of *Budování státu* (The Building of a State). Written between 1933 and 1938, unfinished but republished in 1991, it is the detailed description of the rise of Czechoslovakia and its first years. However, he was also a literary critic and essayist who took his criteria from J. W. Goethe, the Russian realists, and from the Czech authors he held in high regard, Karel Havlíček Borovský and his own friends Karel Poláček and Karel Čapek. The collections *Ano a ne* (Yes and No, 1932), *Osobnost, chaos a zlozvyky* (Personality, Chaos and Bad Habits, 1939) and the posthumous volume *Sluší-li se býti realistou?* (Is It Fitting to Be a Realist?, 1993, edited by Daniel Bohdan with an introduction by Petr Fidelius), show Peroutka to be highly critical of the symbolist Otokar Březina and the avant-gardists Vítězslav Nezval and Vladislav Vančura. It was not until after the Second World War that Peroutka began writing belles lettres. He started by writing plays, notably *Oblak a valčík* (A Cloud and a Waltz), which was first staged in 1947 and published in 1948. An adaptation by Antonín Přidal was put on and published in Prague in 1991. Surprisingly, in his later years Peroutka turned to writing novels. In 1976 *Oblak a valčík*, a novel about World War Two, was published in Toronto. It came out in Prague in 1991. Based on the earlier play and written in a laconic style, it offers a panoramic view of the war. *Pozdější život Panny* (The Later Life of the Virgin) was issued posthumously, in 1980 in Toronto and in 1991 in Prague. This is a piece of historical fiction about Joan of Arc but it includes autobiographical elements. Peroutka allows Joan of Arc to be saved from burning and removes all the grandiloquent heroism. A collection of Peroutka's journalism from the years 1920–1947 was published in Prague in 1991 entitled *O věcech obecných I–II* (On Common Matters I–II) and edited by Daniel Bohdan. Since 2003 the Prague publishing house *Argo* has been publishing an extensive collection of radio talks given on *Radio Free Europe*, entitled *Mluví k vám Ferdinand Peroutka* (Ferdinand Peroutka Speaking). Edited by Zuzana Fialová they have an afterword by Jiří Pernes. Three volumes have already appeared.

Bibliography: Jiří Opelík, "Ferdinand Peroutka: Oblak a valčík," in *Český Parnas: Literatura 1970–1990* (edited by Jiří Holý and Jiřina Táborská), Prague, 1993, pp. 127–133. – Jiří Opelík, "Literárnost Peroutkova Budování státu," in his *Milované řemeslo*, Prague, 2000, pp. 182–220. – Pavel Kosatík, *Ferdinand Peroutka: Pozdější život. 1938–1978*, Prague, 2000. – Jiří Cieslar, "Horské chvíle

Ferdinanda Peroutky" and "Americké deníky Ferdinanda Peroutky," in his *Hlas deníku*, Prague, 2002, pp. 228–248. – Pavel Kosatík, *Ferdinand Peroutka: Život v novinách 1895–1938*, Prague, 2003.

RICHTEROVÁ, SYLVIE

Prose-writer, literary scholar, essayist, poet and translator. She was born in 1945 in Brno, the largest city in Moravia. Her father was also a scholar. She studied French and Russian in Prague, gaining her doctorate in 1971. She married an authority on Czech language and literature, Sergio Corduas, and since 1971 she has lived in Italy where she has worked as a literary researcher and teacher of Czech. In 1987 she became a Professor of Czech Studies at the University of Padua, moving to Viterbo in 1990 and later to Rome. She published abroad, in exile and in samizdat. Since 1989 her prose works and studies have been published in Czechoslovakia/the Czech Republic.

As a prose-writer, Richterová has become known for five titles so far, three of them in the volume *Slabikář otcovského jazyka* (Father's Language Primer, 1991), which came out in samizdat in 1978, 1981 and 1985, in Toronto in 1978 and in Cologne in 1983. The other titles are *Rozptýlené podoby* (Vanished Images), which came out in samizdat in 1979 and in Prague in 1993, and the latest to date *Druhé loučení* (The Second Parting, 1994). In these pieces there are quotations, diary entries, etc. and fictional stories alternating with reminiscences that are very close to being autobiographical. The structure is deliberately fragmented with the subject matter and narrators constantly changing. Through these changes the narrative becomes ambiguous and is continually being reviewed. As a literary scholar Richterová is influenced by Prague structuralism and semiology but she also seeks out the essential, existentialist meaning of a work. She is particularly interested in Jaroslav Hašek, Vladimír Holan, Věra Linhartová, Milan Kundera and Jan Skácel. Her collection of literary studies, *Slova a ticho* (Words and Silence), was published in Munich in 1986 and in 1991 in Prague with an afterword by Květoslav Chvatík. *Ticho a smích* (Silence and Laughter) came out in 1997 and *Místo domova* (Where the Home Is) in 2004. Among her translations into Italian are the poems of Jan Skácel and Jiří Kolář.

Editions in English: "Fear Trip" (translated by Michael Henry Heim), in *This Side of Reality* (edited by Alexandra Büchler), London, 1996, pp. 94–110; "Fragments and Likeness" (translated by Alexandra Büchler), in *Allskin and Other Tales by Contemporary Czech Women* (edited by Alexandra Büchler), Seattle, 1998, pp. 209–223.

Bibliography: Zuzana Stolz-Hladká, "Vzdálení od sebe sama aneb Lov na slepého Narcise," in *Světová literárněvědná bohemistika II* (edited by Luboš Merhaut), Prague, 1996, pp. 709–723. – Nathalie Zanellová, "Motiv návratu u Sylvie Richterové," *Česká literatura*, 44 (1996), pp. 66–78. (Originally in *Le roman tchèque dans le contexte international*, edited by Hana Voisine-Jechová, Paris, 1992). – Alice Jedličková, "Heterogenní kód současné prózy: Vícejazyčnost textů Sylvie Richterové," *Česká literatura*, 44 (1996), pp. 480–497. – Sylvie Richterová, "O otázkách, které zůstávají otázkami," interview with Karel Hvížďala, in his

Dialogy, Prague, 1999, pp. 169–196. – Irina Wutsdorffová, "Dialogičnost v prozaické trilogii Sylvie Richterové," *Česká literatura*, 47 (1999), pp. 364–386.

SEIFERT, JAROSLAV

Poet, translator, essayist and journalist. He was born in 1901 in Žižkov, a suburb of Prague. His family were locksmiths and art dealers. He left school early and became a journalist. He worked for the magazine *Reflektor* (Spotlight), a Communist journal. He was a member of the avant-garde group *Devětsil* (Butterbur/Nine Powers), and was co-editor of the 1922 collection *Devětsil* and of the reviews *Disk* (Discus) and *Pásmo* (Zone). In 1924 he went to France and Italy with Karel Teige, a trip that led to the collection *Na vlnách TSF* (On the Waves of TSF). Among his friends he numbered S. K. Neumann, František Halas, Vladislav Vančura, Vladimír Holan and other writers. He signed a letter of protest against the new Stalinist leadership of the Communist party in 1929 and then worked for the social democratic press. After 1945 he was employed at the daily paper *Práce* (Labour) and also edited the periodical *Kytice* (The Garland). From 1949 he earned his living from literature. After the war he lived in a house he owned in Břevnov, a district of Prague. He campaigned on several occasions for freedom and for the abolition of doctrinairism; first in a speech to the 1956 Congress of Czechoslovak Writers´ Union, then during his chairmanship of the rehabilitation committee of the Writers´ Union in 1968–1969, and again in 1977 when he signed the human rights manifesto *Charter 77*. In the seventies he published in samizdat and abroad. His new poems were not published by the state publishing house till the end of the seventies. In 1984 Seifert was awarded the Nobel Prize for literature. He died in Prague in 1986.

Seifert's literary career of more than sixty years, in which lyric poetry played the greatest part, went through several stages. The first stage was marked by *Město v slzách* (1921), which was translated by Dana Loewy as *City in Tears*, in *The Early Poetry of Jaroslav Seifert*, published in Evanston in 1997. The introduction was written by Vladislav Vančura but signed U. S. Devětsil. This was proletarian poetry with free verse and naïve revolutionary romanticism. After that he showed a tendency towards avant-garde poetism, fantasy, intoxication by the beauty and delights of the world and the use of surprising associations and plays on words. *Na vlnách TSF* (1925, with the original graphic design by Karel Teige) was revised in 1938 as *Svatební cesta* (The Honeymoon Trip); it was translated by Dana Loewy as *On the Waves of TSF* (first edited 1995). In Prague in 2004 a bilingual edition in its original form was published. The collection *Slavík zpívá špatně* (1926), illustrated by Josef Šíma, was translated by Dana Loewy as *The Nightingale Sings Poorly* and published as part of *The Early Poetry of Jaroslav Seifert* in Evanston in 1997. The work reflects the poet's experience of World War One. The end of the twenties was the beginning of another period when his poetry became consistently harmonious, melodic, with regular stanzas and colloquial language. It revealed an emotional, trusting relationship with the world, which was at times ironic. In *Jablko z klína* (An Apple from the Lap, 1933), illustrated by Josef Šíma, and *Ruce Venušiny* (The

Hands of Venus, 1936), the predominant themes are the magic of love, the passing of time and nostalgic memories. These same themes appeared also earlier, in some of the poems of *Slavík zpívá špatně.* At the same time *Zpíváno do rotačky* (Singing in the Press, 1936), poems on topical themes, often including social criticism, were printed in the daily papers. Seifert's literary principles remained unchanged even in the poetry he wrote in reaction to the threat to Czechoslovakia at the end of the thirties and to the German occupation. This poetry includes *Osm dní* (1937, translated by Paul Jagasich and Tom O´Grady as *Eight Days*, and published in Iowa City in 1983), the cycle of poems about the death and burial of T. G. Masaryk and the second part of the collection *Zhasněte světla* (Put Out the Lights, 1938). Both *Osm dní* and *Zhasněte světla* appear in the postwar collection *Přilba hlíny* (A Helmetful of Earth, 1945). *Světlem oděná* (Arrayed in Light, 1940), a celebration of home and Prague, and *Kamenný most* (The Stone Bridge), illustrated by Karel Svolinský in 1944, are reactions to the Nazi occupation as is *Vějíř Boženy Němcové* (Božena Němcová's Fan), also illustrated by Karel Svolinský, in 1940, which celebrates the "mother tongue" of the 19th-century author. Seifert returned to one of Božena Němcová's characters in the postwar collection *Píseň o Viktorce* (The Story of Viktorka, 1950) in which the loveliness and tragic fate of her heroine Viktorka became a picture of the fate of the artist herself. In *Maminka* (Mummy, 1954) and other works Seifert developed his motifs of love, his native Prague and home. After several years of silence caused by a serious illness, a new creative phase began in the mid-sixties. The poet had radically changed his style, rejecting poetic metaphors and rhyme, using harsher, more everyday expressions. There is now obvious scepticism. Although *Koncert na ostrově* (The Concert on the Island, 1965) is a variation on known themes, nevertheless everything is seen through the "dark mirror" of death, with which the author had come face to face. Other collections continuing in the same vein are *Odlévání zvonů* (1967), *Morový sloup* and *Deštník z Piccadilly. Odlévání zvonů* was translated by Paul Jagasich and Tom O´Grady as *The Casting of Bells* and was published in Iowa City in 1983. *Morový sloup* was published in samizdat in 1973, in Cologne in 1977, and in Prague in 1981. The translation by Ewald Osers as *The Plague Column,* with an introduction by Cecil Parrott, illustrations and photographs by Gilman Parsons, came out in London and Boston in 1979. A new translation by Lyn Coffin as *The Plague Monument*, with illustrations by Jiří Kolář and a preface by William E. Harkins, was published in Silver Spring in 1980 in a bilingual edition and republished in *Cross Currents*, 3 (1984). *Deštník z Piccadilly* was published in samizdat in 1978, in Munich and Prague in 1979. It was translated as *An Umbrella from Piccadilly* by Ewald Osers, who also wrote an introduction, and was published in London in 1983. Outstanding among his later works are the essay-like memoirs *Všecky krásy světa* (All the Beauties of the World), parts of which were translated into English (see below). They came out in samizdat in 1979, were published in Toronto and Cologne in 1981, and in Prague in 1982 but the complete edition did not appear till 1992. Seifert's translations of poetry consist chiefly of lyric poetry, especially that of

Guillaume Apollinaire and Paul Verlaine. With the help of the Hebrew scholar Stanislav Segert, in 1958 he translated *The Song of Songs* from the Bible. A revised translation dates from 1964. He prepared several anthologies, particularly of authors like the 19th-century poets Jan Neruda and Jaroslav Vrchlický, whose work was similar to his own. Since 2000 the Prague publishing house *Akropolis* has been issuing the work of Jaroslav Seifert – sixteen volumes are planned.

Other editions in English: "Enough of Wolker!" (translated by Ruth Leadbetter), *Scottish Slavonic Review*, 3 (1984), pp. 119–126; "Skating with Lenin" (translated by J. R. Dorrel), *Granta*, 14 (Winter 1984), pp. 218–228; "Paradise Lost," *Cross Currents*, 4 (1985), pp. 291–293; all these are chapters from *Všecky krásy světa*; *Mozart in Prague: Thirteen Rondels* (translated by Paul Jagasich and Tom O´Grady), Iowa City, 1985 (bilingual edition); *The Selected Poetry of Jaroslav Seifert* (edited by George Gibian, translated by Ewald Osers), New York, 1986; *A Wreath of Sonnets* (translated and introduction by J. K. Klement [= Jan Křesadlo] and Eva Stucke), Toronto, 1987 (bilingual edition); seven poems (translated by Alfred French), in *The Czech Avantgardists* (edited by Alfred French), Rockville, 1995, pp. 35, 38–39, 44–46, 51, 86; *The Early Poetry of Jaroslav Seifert* (translated by Dana Loewy), Evanston, 1997; *The Poetry of Jaroslav Seifert* (edited by George Gibian, translated by Ewald Osers, introduction by George Gibian), London, New York and Toronto, 1998.

Bibliography: Alfred French, *The Poets of Prague*. London and New York, 1969. – Arne Novák, *Czech Literature* (edited by William E. Harkins, translated by Peter Kussi), Ann Arbor, 1976, pp. 322–344. – William E. Harkins, "On Jaroslav Seifert's Morový sloup," *Cross Currents*, 3 (1984), pp. 131–135. – Josef Škvorecký, "Jaroslav Seifert – the Good Old Drinking Poet," *Cross Currents*, 4 (1985), pp. 283–290. – Zdeněk Pešat, "Jaroslav Seifert," in his *Dialogy s poezií*, Prague, 1985, pp. 101–124. – Pavel Pešta, "Jaroslav Seifert," in *Literatur in der CSSR 1945–1980: Einzeldarstellungen* (edited by Štěpán Vlašín and Stanislav Šmatlák), Berlin, 1985, pp. 200–216. – *Atta vara poet – Jaroslav Seifert mellan poesi och politik* (edited by František Janouch and Miloslava Slavíčková), Stockholm, 1986. – Bohuslava R. Bradbrook, "A True Nationalist Poet," *Culture, Education and Society*, 40 (1986), no. 2, pp. 100-104. – Marie Kubínová, "Seifertova poezie plynoucího času," *Česká literatura*, 35 (1987), pp. 306–319. – Antonín Brousek, "Jaroslav Seifert," in *Zur tschechischen Literatur 1945–1985* (edited by Wolfgang Kassack), Berlin, 1990, pp. 63–80. – Zdeněk Pešat, *Jaroslav Seifert*, Prague, 1991. – Václav Černý, "Jaroslav Seifert," in his *Tvorba a osobnost I* (edited by Jan Šulc), Prague, 1992, pp. 810–815. – Alena Štěrbová and Zdeněk Vaníček, "Ewald Osers o Jaroslavu Seifertovi," *Česká literatura*, 44 (1996), pp. 622–624. – Alexandr Stich, *Seifertova Světlem oděná*, Prague, 1998. – *S Jaroslavem Seifertem časem i nečasem* (edited by Marie Jirásková and Hana Klínková), Prague, 2001.

Šiktanc, Karel

Poet and prose-writer. He was born in 1928 in Hřebeč near Kladno in Central Bohemia. His father was a cabinet maker. He was a student at the Teachers´

Training College in Prague but did not complete his studies. He worked as an editor in radio and in the publishing house *Mladá fronta* (Frontline Youth) where from 1961 to 1970 he was editor in chief. He was one of the circle of authors connected with the periodicals *Květen* (May) and *Orientace* (The Way to Go). In 1971 he was dismissed and in the seventies and eighties he took whatever jobs he could find, for example as tennis court groundsman. He published only in samizdat and in exile. After 1989 he was the first chairman of the newly founded *Obec spisovalelů* (Council of Writers).

As a poet he began with naïvely committed Communist poetry which was no different from the average at the time, moving on to poetry "of the everyday". *Heinovské noci* (Heine's Nights, 1960), a collection of poems with an accompaniment of pictures by children from Lidice, is outstanding. It was inspired by the Nazi extermination of the village of Lidice – Šiktanc came from a nearby village. In this for the first time there were signs of his later authoritative poetics: metaphor, drama, the merging of several time phases, the use of different levels of vocabulary. Since the sixties the most outstanding feature of Šiktanc's work has been epic poetry with elements of drama and lyricism, in which the theme of memory, individual, ancestral, national and mythical, predominates. Typical examples are *Adam a Eva* (Adam and Eve, 1968) and *Mariášky* (Card Games) dating from 1970, the whole edition of which was destroyed. *Český orloj* (The Czech Clock), published in samizdat in 1974, in Munich in two volumes in 1980 and 1981, in Prague in 1990 illustrated by Jaroslav Šerých, is a collection of twelve poems from January to December, which are conceived as a fictional dialogue between father and son, linking personal and ancestral memory. In the course of the text there are many recurring features, personal memories, folklore, Christian ideas, archaic language, neologisms and even vulgarisms. The length of the verses, rhythm and rhyme all change. Šiktanc went on to write his next collections, *Jak se trhá srdce* (Heartbreak) and *Tanec smrti aneb Ještě Pámbu neumřel* (The Dance of Death or God Is Not Dead Yet), in a similar kind of polythematic poetry, drawing on the reality of traditional country life but based on metaphor and phonetic composition and with an emphasis on the individual. *Jak se trhá srdce*, which was completed as early as 1970, appeared in samizdat in 1978, was published in Munich in 1983, and the Prague edition of 1991 was illustrated by Aleš Krejča. *Tanec smrti aneb Ještě Pámbu neumřel*, illustrated by Bohdan Kopecký, was published in samizdat in 1979, and in Prague in 1992. It is an unusual variation on Baroque "dances of death" and popular theatre. Since the end of the eighties there have been changes in the author's poetics. Šiktanc has abandoned lengthy works and returned to collections based on shorter poems and economy of expression. In *Hrad Kost* (Castle Bone, 1995) and *Šarlat* (Scarlet, 1999) his poetry features a different area. The scenery of Central Bohemia native to him is now replaced by the mountainous region České středohoří, the countryside of the Czech Romantic poet Karel Hynek Mácha. Šiktanc is also the author of *Královské pohádky* (Royal Fairy Tales, 1994, illustrated by František Skála). Since 2000 the Prague publishing house *Karolinum*, where the editor is Jiří Brabec, has been publishing the works of Karel Šiktanc including the collections of poems from the end of the fifties.

Editions in English: "From Dance of Death" (translated by Daniela Dražanová and Karel Dražan), *Prairie Schooner*, 66 (1992), no. 44, p. 171–172; "Nightfall" (translated by Randall Lyman), in *Czech Writers on Tolerance*, Prague, 1994, pp. 231–232.

Bibliography: Miloš Pohorský, "Šiktancovo tažení proti smrti," in his *Zlomky analýzy*, Prague, 1990, pp. 383–390. – Miroslav Červenka, "Verš a řádek: Experiment Karla Šiktance s básnickým rytmem," in his *Styl a význam*, Prague, 1991, pp. 214–245. – Vladimír Macura, "Karel Šiktanc: Heinovské noci," in *Česká literatura 1945–1970* (edited by Jiřina Táborská and Milan Zeman), Prague, 1992, pp. 204–215. – *Hebenon*, 11–12 (2006), no. 7–8, Numero speciale per Karel Šiktanc (special issue of Karel Šiktanc).

Skácel, Jan

Poet, essayist and journalist. He was born in 1922 in the village of Vnorovy in South Moravia. His father was a teacher and his brother, Petr Skácel, was a painter. He passed his final school examinations in 1941, then he was *im Totaleinsatz,* that is, sent to work in German industry; he had to spend three years of his punishment in a labour camp. His poetic mentor and friend was Oldřich Mikulášek. After the war he studied Czech and Russian at Masaryk University in Brno but did not complete his studies. He worked as an editor on the daily paper *Rovnost* (Equality) from 1948 to 1952, then he was forced to work repairing tractors. From 1963 to 1969 he was editor in chief of the Brno journal *Host do domu* (A Guest in the House). In the seventies he could not publish except in samizdat and in exile. It was not till 1981 that his new collections were published without attracting the authorities´ attention. He became a member of the Bavarian Academy of Fine Art, and in 1989 was awarded the Italian Petrarch Prize and the Slovenian Vilenica Prize for literature. He died in Brno in 1989.

In his poetry Skácel does not portray the world in dazzling terms, his language is restrained. In comparison with Oldřich Mikulášek, for example, his poetry is more conservative, holding on rather to the traditional values of country life which take precedence over the individual. In 1957, at the age of thirty-five, he published his first work *Kolik příležitostí má růže* (The Many Occasions of a Rose) in which there are themes typical of his entire poetic output: nature, the countryside, home, childhood. The poet does not use rhyme, he does not overwhelm the reader with imagery. Instead, he goes deeper, challenging the reader to think. The best works of his first period are the collections *Smuténka* (Little Sadness, 1965) and *Metličky* (Gentle Scourges, 1968). The style is rather terse with frequent pauses, phrases left uncompleted and oblique allusions. Rivers, waters, pain, purity and death are recurring themes. Associations are implied; permeating everything is the awareness of a higher order, anchored in nature and the earth, a picture of "smuténka", a neologism created by Skácel and intentionally veiled in mystery.

Characteristic of Skácel's poetry of the seventies and eighties are the four-lined poems *Naděje s bukovými křídly* (Hope with Beechwood Wings, 1983, epilogue by Vilém Závada), the four-liners in part of the collection *Kdo pije potmě víno* (Who Drinks Wine in the Dark, 1988) and the sonnets in for example *Dávné proso*

(Ancient Millet, 1981). The two parts of *Naděje s bukovými křídly* were first published in samizdat in 1975 and 1976, then in Toronto in 1978, and in Hamburg in 1980. *Kdo pije potmě víno*, illustrated by Bohdan Kopecký, was published in 1988, and the collection *Dávné proso*, illustrated by Oleg Toman, was published in 1981. Regular structure, rhyme and rhythm, dactyls with occasional iambuses, now replace the earlier free verse. The poems are reminiscent of oriental poetry, especially Japanese haiku and the Chinese lyric. They are tightly constructed, with no superfluous words, and are mysterious and magical. Typically, anxiety and the threat of death are evident, at the same time however the "ego" gives way and is replaced by collective memory in which the natural and human worlds are blended. Home and childhood clearly represent positive values.

Skácel's collections of poems for children, *Uspávanky* (Lullabies, 1983), illustrated by Ota Janeček, and *Kam odešly laně* (Where the Gazelles Went, 1985, inspired by the pictures of Josef Čapek) bear witness to the closeness of the world of childhood, naïvety and poetic nonsense. Skácel is also the author of interesting newspaper articles. He became known for these "short reviews" expressing his thoughts on a variety of subjects from spring to writings on lavatory walls. A collection of these prose works was published in 1964 entitled *Jedenáctý bílý kůň* (The Eleventh White Horse), expanded in 1966 and illustrated by Jan Steklík. It was not till after his death that the collection was completed by the publication in 1993 of *Třináctý černý kůň* (The Thirteenth Black Horse), edited by Jiří Opelík. The Brno publishing house *Blok* published in 1995–1996 *Básně I–II*, books of unabridged Jan Skácel's poems. Also in 1996 they issued the collections for children, all edited by Jiří Opelík. His correspondence with the writer and editor Jiří Fried came out in 2001, edited also by Jiří Opelík.

Editions in English: "The Last Time I Saw Gary Cooper" (translated by Jeanne Němcová), in *Universum: A Review of Czechoslovak Literature and Arts*, 1 (1966), no. 1, pp. 31–32; four poems (translated by Jessie Kocmanová), in *Universum: A Review of Czechoslovak Literature and Arts*, 1 (1966), no. 2, pp. 40–41; three poems (translated by Káča Poláčková), in *Modern Poetry in Translation: Czech* (edited by Ted Hughes and David Weissbort), London, 1967; five poems (translated by George Theiner), in *New Writing in Czechoslovakia* (edited by George Theiner), Harmondsworth, 1969, pp. 168–170; "A Selection from Jan Skácel's Poetry" (translated by Lyn Coffin, introduction by Zdenka Brodská), *Cross Currents*, 2 (1983), pp. 365–368; two poems (translated by Edward Joseph Czerwinski and Stana Dolezal), in *Shifting Borders: East European Poetries of the Eighties* (edited by Walter Cummins), Rutherford, 1993, pp. 204–205; *Banned Man: Selected poems* (translated by Ewald Osers, introduction by Ivan Klíma), Mississauga, 2001.

Bibliography: Oleg Sus, "Od moudrosti k ironickému humoru," in *Cesty k dnešku* (edited by Oleg Sus), Brno, 1964, pp. 167–194. – Jiří Opelík, "Třeskuté ticho poezie," in his *Nenáviděné řemeslo*, Prague, 1969, pp. 66–69. – Zdeněk Kožmín, *Umění básně*, Brno, 1990, pp. 17–42. – Sylvie Richterová, "Krajina proměn a tvary ticha," in her *Slova a ticho*, Prague, 1991, pp. 94–106 (originally in Italian in Jan Skácel, *Il diffeto delle pesche*, Rome, 1981). – Jiří Trávníček, "Jan

Skácel, Smuténka," in *Česká literatura 1945–1970* (edited by Jiřina Táborská and Milan Zeman), Prague, 1992, pp. 320–330. – *Bílá žízeň* (edited by Emanuel Ranný), Třebíč, 1993. – Zdeněk Kožmín, *Skácel*, Brno, 1994. – Jiří Opelík, "Skácelovo erbenovství," in his *Milované řemeslo*, Prague, 2000, pp. 296–318. – Jiří Trávníček, "Jan Skácel," in *Dictionary of Literary Biography: Twentieth Century Eastern European Writers*, vol. 232 (edited by Steven Serafin et al.), Detroit, 2001, pp. 330–335.

ŠKVORECKÝ, JOSEF

Novelist, essayist, translator and poet. He was born in 1924 in the town of Náchod in Eastern Bohemia. His was a conservative, patriotic family. When he left school in 1943 he worked as a labourer. From his youth he was an enthusiastic jazz musician, first playing the saxophone in his native town, later promoting jazz with his friend and jazz theorist Lubomír Dorůžka. Together they prepared the anthologies *Tvář jazzu* (The Countenance of Jazz, 1964), *Jazzová inspirace* (The Inspiration of Jazz, 1966) and other works. Jazz, which, as an expression of free individualism and love of things American, was suppressed both by the Nazi and Stalinist regimes, became an important source of inspiration for many of Škvorecký's works including *Eine kleine Jazzmusik* (Eine kleine Jazzmusik, for English translation see below), *Bassaxofon* (The Bass Saxophone, see below) and the novel *Zbabělci* (The Cowards, see below). After the war he studied English and philosophy at Charles University in Prague, gaining his degree in 1951. After army service from 1951 to 1953, which became the subject of the humorous satirical novel *Tankový prapor* (The Tank Battalion, see below), he worked as an editor of English and American literature at the publishing house *SNKLHU* (Státní nakladatelství krásné literatury, hudby a umění – State Publishing House for Literature, Music and Art) and the review *Světová literatura* (World Literature). He was severely criticized by the authorities after the publication of his novel *Zbabělci* and had to leave the review but was allowed to remain at the publishing house in an inferior position. From 1963 when he could publish again he became a professional writer. In 1968 he went to the USA and since the autumn of 1969 he has lived in Toronto where he lectured in English and American literature at Toronto University. There he and his wife Zdena Salivarová founded and managed *Sixty-Eight Publishers*, the most important Czech publishing house in exile in the West, which brought out 227 titles. From 1973 to 1990 he collaborated with Czech broadcasters working for the radio station *The Voice of America*. When Josef Škvorecký and Zdena Salivarová returned to Czechoslovakia for the first time in 1990 they were awarded the Order of the White Lion by President Václav Havel. Škvorecký's work was acclaimed particularly in North America.

His first novel *Zbabělci,* written between 1948 and 1949 and published in 1958, has all the characteristics of the author's writing. An English translation by Jeanne W. Němcová, *The Cowards*, came out in New York and London in 1970. It is the story of twenty-year-old Danny Smiřický, who lives in the Czech provincial town of Kostelec, modelled on the author's native town of Náchod. He experienced the last days of the German occupation and the revolutionary coup in 1945. He is however more interested in jazz and girls than in these historic events and great ideas, of which he is highly sceptical. The novel suggests an affinity with American writing, especially that of Ernest Hemingway and Jerome David Salinger. Danny Smiřický has certain autobiographical features, and appears also in several other of Škvorecký's books. Danny is portrayed progressively during and after the war in *Prima sezona*, *Tankový prapor*, *Mirákl*, *Příběh inženýra lidských duší* and *Obyčejné životy*. *Prima sezona* was published in Toronto in 1975 (Prague, 1990) and was serialized on television in 1994, directed by Karel Kachyňa. It was translated by Paul Wilson as *The Swell Season*, published in Toronto in 1982; London, 1983; New York, 1986. *Tankový prapor* describes his service in the Communist army. In 1971, it came out in Czech in Toronto, but it was 1990 before it came out in Prague. There was a film version by Vít Olmer in 1991. Translated as *The Republic of Whores* by Paul Wilson it was published in Toronto in 1993 and in Hopewell, New Jersey, and in London in 1994. *Mirákl* was published in Czech in Toronto in 1972 and in Brno in 1991. The translation by Paul Wilson, *The Miracle Game*, was published in Toronto in 1990 and in New York and London in 1991. It portrays life in Czechoslovakia in the fifties and sixties. *Příběh inženýra lidských duší* was published in Toronto in 1977 and in Brno in 1992. Translated by Paul Wilson as *The Engineer of Human Souls*, it was published in New York and Toronto in 1984 and in London in 1985. It relates the fortunes of Danny as a lecturer in the University of Toronto and his reminiscences about the past. The last book to date of this series is *Obyčejné životy* (Ordinary Lives, 2004), bringing the stories of Danny and his friends up to the present day. In this series the author brings his characters face to face with Nazi and Communist totalitarianism and with their experiences in exile. He makes frequent use of humour and satire, especially in style and language, using the language of ideological propaganda, the Czech of Czech-Americans, slang and so on. Besides this series Škvorecký is also the author of many other prose writings, for example, the detective stories *Smutek poručíka Borůvky* (1966), translated as *The Mournful Demeanour of Lieutenant Boruvka* by Rosemary Kavan, Káča Poláčková and George Theiner and published in London in 1973. He is also the author of essays and articles on literature and films. *All the Bright Young Men and Women* is a translation by Michael Schonberg of *Všichni ti bystří mladí muži a ženy: osobní historie českého filmu.* It came out in English in Toronto in 1971 and in Czech in Prague in 1991. The work deals with the "New Wave" in Czech film in the sixties. One of his most important novellas is *Bassaxofon* (1967), which appears in *Babylonský příběh a jiné povídky*. The translation by Káča Poláčková in *The Bass Saxophone. Two Novellas* (pp. 107–186) was published in Toronto in 1977, in London in 1978, and in New York in 1979. This was the most successful of Škvorecký's works in the Anglo-American world. John Robby wrote a jazz opera based on it. The narrator, an enthusiastic Czech jazzman, plays with German musicians during the occupation and the musical experience triumphs over national hatred. Another important work is *Legenda Emöke* (1963). The translation by Káča Poláčková, *Emöke*, was published in *The Bass Saxophone* (pp. 35–103), in Toronto in 1977, London in 1978, New York in 1979. It is the story of frustrated love and the conflict between truly living and merely keeping a low profile. In the sixties Škvorecký collaborated in the making of several films with his own scripts or based on his books. One was *Farářův konec* (The End of the Priest, 1968), directed by Evald Schorm. Another was *Zločin v šantánu* (A Nightclub Crime, 1968) directed by Jiří Menzel. In 1969, Václav Gajer made the film *Flirt se slečnou Stříbrnou* (Flirting with Miss Stříbrná), based on Škvorecký's novel *Lvíče* (1969), in English as *Miss Silver's Past*, translated by Peter Kussi, New York, 1974, London, 1976.

In exile Škvorecký wrote two lengthy novels about the fortunes of Czechs in the United States. *Scherzo capriccioso* came out in Toronto in 1984, and in Prague in 1991. About the composer Antonín Dvořák's stay in America, it was translated by Paul Wilson as *Dvorak in Love* and published in Toronto and in London in 1986, and in New York in 1987. *Nevěsta z Texasu* was translated by Káča Poláčková as *The Bride of Texas* and was published in Czech in Toronto in 1995, and in English in London and Boston in 1996. From the English Škvorecký has translated works by Ernest Hemingway, William Faulkner and Henry Miller. The Prague publishing house *Ivo Železný* has been publishing Škvorecký's work since 1994. The first volume, edited by Vladimír Justl and Michael Špirit, came out in *Odeon* in 1991.

Other editions in English: *Oh, My Papa!* (edited by Itaru Iijima and Minoru Miyata), Tokyo, 1972; "Eine Kleine Jazzmusik" (translated by Alice Denesová), in *White Stones and Fir Trees* (edited by Vasa D. Mihailovich), Lewisburg, 1977, pp. 351–364; *Jiří Menzel and the History of the Closely Watched Trains*, Boulder, 1982; *Sins for Father Knox* (translated by Káča Poláčková), Toronto, 1988; London and New York, 1989; *Talkin´ Moscow Blues: Essays about Literature, Politics, Movies, and Jazz* (edited and introduction by Sam Solecki), Toronto, 1988; London and New York, 1990; *The End of Lieutenant Boruvka* (translated by Paul Wilson), Toronto, 1989; London and New York, 1990; *The Return of Lieutenant Boruvka* (translated and adapted by Paul Wilson), Toronto and London, 1990; New York, 1991; *Leading a Literary Double Life in Prague*, Toronto, 1991; *Headed for the Blues* (translated by Káča Poláčková, Celeb Crain and Peter Kussi), Hopewell, 1996; Toronto, 1997; London, 1998; *In the Lonesome October*, Toronto, 1993; *The Tenor Saxophonist's Story* (translated by Celeb Crain, Káča Poláčková and Peter Kussi), Hopewell, 1997; *Two Murders in My Double Life*, Toronto, 1999; New York, 2001; *When Eve Was Naked*, Toronto, 2000; New York, 2002; *An Inexplicable Story* (translated by Káča Poláčková), Toronto, 2000.

Bibliography: Erazim V. Kohák, "The Cowards," *Dissent*, 17 (1970), pp. 543–556. – Antonín Jaroslav Liehm, "Josef Škvorecký" (interview), in his *The Politics of Culture*, New York, 1970, pp. 153–180 (in Czech Antonín Jaroslav Liehm, *Generace*, Prague, 1990, pp. 66–87). – *World Literature Today* (Homage to Josef Škvorecký), 54 (Autumn 1980), no. 4. – Václav Pletánek, "The Language and Style of Škvorecký's Cowards," *Canadian Slavonic Papers*, 23 (1981), pp. 384–393. – Alfred French, *Czech Writers and Politics*, New York, 1982, pp. 129–132. – Květoslav Chvatík, "Švejk and Danny Smiřický," *Scottish Slavonic Review*, 3 (1985), no. 4, pp. 69–80. – Jana Kalish, *Josef Škvorecký: A Checklist (bibliography)*, Toronto, 1986. – Sam Solecki, *Prague Blues: The Fiction of Josef*

Škvorecký, Toronto, 1990. – Paul Trensky, *The Fiction of Josef Škvorecký*, London and New York, 1991 (in Czech in 1995). – Přemysl Blažíček, *Škvoreckého Zbabělci*, Prague, 1992. – Karel Hvížďala, *Opustíš-li mne, nezahyneš* (interview with Josef Škvorecký and Zdena Salivarová), Prague, 1993. – Milan Jungmann, *O Josefu Škvoreckém*, Prague, 1993. – *The Achievement of Josef Škvorecký* (edited by Sam Solecki), Toronto, 1994. – *Review of Contemporary Fiction* (special issue of Mario Vargas Llosa and Josef Škvorecký), 17 (Spring 1997), no. 1. – Edward L. Galligan, *The Truth of Uncertainty*, Columbia, 1998, pp. 84–107. – Michael Špirit, "Komentář," in Josef Škvorecký, *Zbabělci*, Prague, 1998, pp. 447–518. – Martin Pilař and Jan Čulík, "Josef Škvorecký," in *Dictionary of Literary Biography: Twentieth-Century Eastern European Writers*, vol. 232 (edited by Steven Serafin et al.), Detroit, 2001, pp. 336–351. – Robert Porter, "Josef Škvorecký, Fascism, Communism and all that Jazz," in his *An Introduction to Twentieth-Century Czech Fiction*, Brighton and Portland, 2001, pp. 87–122. – *Bibliografie Josefa Škvoreckého I–II* (edited by Michal Přibáň), Prague, 2004 and 2005. – Helena Kosková, *Škvorecký*, Prague, 2004. – *Škvorecký 80. Sborník z mezinárodní konference o životě a díle Josefa Škvoreckého* (edited by Michal Přibáň), Prague, 2005.

SOUČKOVÁ, MILADA

Writer, poet, essayist and literary historian. She was born in Prague in 1899. Her father was the owner a firm of builders. She studied in Prague at Charles University in the Natural Philosophy Faculty, gaining her degree in 1923. She married the painter and writer Zdenek Rykr (1900–1940). Her approach to literature was very close to that of *Skupina 42* (Group 42). She was influenced by the Prague Linguistic Circle and collaborated in the writing of Chapter 1 of the historical novel by Vladislav Vančura, *Obrazy z dějin národa českého* (Pictures from the History of the Czech Nation, 1939). In 1945 after World War Two she was in New York as Czechoslovak cultural attaché. After 1948 she resigned and remained in the USA lecturing at the universities of Harvard, Chicago and Berkeley. In exile her work was published in periodicals and by publishing houses abroad. She died in Boston in 1983.

Součková became known in literary circles in the thirties chiefly through her prose works. The short stories *První písmena* (First Letters, 1934) and the novel *Amor a Psyché* (Amor and Psyche, 1937) clearly indicate the influence of surrealism. In *Amor a Psyché* she used an experimental style of composition and narration. These techniques, the interplay of fact and fiction, the unfolding of the narrative from different points of view and from different times, prevents *Odkaz* (The Legacy) and *Zakladatelé* (The Progenitors, both 1940) from being traditional novels about the decline of a bourgeois family. In these novels she drew, as she did in other works, on autobiographical material. The following novel, *Bel canto* (1944), the story of an ambitious but untalented woman and singer, was composed in the same way.

Her poetry is also predominantly intellectual. The short piece *Kaladý, aneb: útočiště řeči* (Kaladý, or: Havens for Speech), came out in a bibliophile edition in

1938 with drawings by Zdenek Rykr. Set in the time of the Munich crisis, it calls for "the words of my mother tongue". Poetry forms the bulk of her postwar work which in many ways retains the artistic principles of her earlier prose; for example *Sešity Josephiny Rykrové* (Josephine Rykrová's Notebooks, Toronto, 1981), with a postscript by Roman Jakobson. Expanded as *Sešity Josefíny Rykrové* and edited by Kristián Suda, it was published in Prague in 1993. Her collected poetry was published in volume 10 of the works of Milada Součková. In the literary studies and essays written in English, *The Czech Romantics* (1958) and *Baroque in Bohemia* (1980, with a postscript by Roman Jakobson), Součková deals with important periods and personages in Czech literature. Since 1995 the work of Milada Součková has been published in Prague, first by the publishing house *ERM*, then by *Prostor*, edited by Kristián Suda with 13 volumes planned.

Other editions in English: *A Literature in Crisis: Czech Literature 1938–1950*, New York, 1954; *The Parnassian Jaroslav Vrchlický*, The Hague and London, 1964; *A Literary Satellite: Czechoslovak–Russian Literary Relations*, Chicago and London, 1970; "The Prague Structuralist Circle. A Collage," in *Sound, Sign, and Meaning* (edited by Ladislav Matějka), Ann Arbor, 1976, pp. 1–5.

Bibliography: *Neznámý člověk Milada Součková* (edited by Michal Bauer), Prague, 2001. – Vladimír Papoušek, *Trojí samota ve velké zemi: Česká literatura v americkém exilu v letech 1938–1968*, Prague, 2001, pp. 127–165.

TOPOL, JÁCHYM

Novelist and poet. He was born in Prague in 1962, the son of the dramatist and poet Josef Topol (b. 1935) and the grandson of the writer Karel Schulz (1899–1943). His brother Filip Topol (b. 1964) is a musician and writer. Jáchym Topol left school in 1981 but could not go to university till after November 1989 when he studied ethnology at Charles University. He signed the human rights manifesto *Charter 77*, worked as a storeman, stoker, etc. Since 1991 he has been a writer by profession. He was one of the group connected with the review *Revolver Revue* and after it was legalized, he was its editor in chief from 1990 to 1993. He wrote texts for the rock groups *Psí vojáci* (Dog Soldiers) and *Národní třída* (National Avenue), with which he also played.

Topol began as a poet; his poetry, originally in samizdat, was published in two books, *Miluju tě k bláznění* (I'm Madly in Love with You, 1991) and *V úterý bude válka* (On Tuesday There Will Be War, 1992). The world here is seen as chaotic, almost apocalyptic. The author portrays it piecemeal, using spoken and vulgar language. He also applies these techniques in his prose, of which *Sestra* (Sister, 1994), about the fortunes of a group of young people in Prague after 1989, is outstanding. The English translation, *City Sister Silver*, by Alex Zucker was published in 2000 in North Haven and in London. The author's style is highly lyrical, and sometimes the text is more like a lamentation or an incantation. This kind of subject and artistic treatment is continued in the novella *Anděl* (Angel, 1995), parts of which have been translated by Alex Zucker in *Daylight in Nightclub Inferno* (pp.190–202), edited by Elena Lappin, and published in North Haven, 1997. A film version, *Anděl Exit*, by Vladimír Michálek was made in 2000.

Topol's interest in events and concerns beyond Europe, particularly in ancient American civilizations, is evident in the book *Trnová dívka* (Thorn Girl, 1997) in which he retells Red Indian fairy-tales and legends. His conversation with Tomáš Weiss has been published in the book *Nemůžu se zastavit* (I Can´t Stop, 2000). The subsequent novels, *Noční práce* (Night Work, 2001) and *Kloktat dehet* (To Gargle Tar, 2005), still use phantasmagoric motifs, but their style is changed; the narration is fragmentary and unclear. In both of these novels, the main protagonist, a child, experiences bizarre situations: in *Noční práce* during 1968 and in *Kloktat dehet* in the 1960s and again during 1968.

Other editions in English: "A Trip to the Railway Station" (translated by Alex Zucker), in *This Side of Reality* (edited by Alexandra Büchler), London, 1996, pp. 204–222.

Bibliography: Karen Gammelgaard, *Spoken Czech in Literature: The Case of Bondy, Hrabal, Placák and Topol*, Oslo, 1997. – Jaroslaw Anders, "City, Sister, Silver," *The New Republic*, 19 June 2000, pp. 45–49. – Robert Porter, "Daniela Hodrová, Michal Viewegh, Jáchym Topol: New Voices?" in his *An Introduction to Twentieth-Century Czech Fiction*, Brighton and Portland, 2001, pp. 177–183. – Rajendra A. Chitnis, "Writing as Being: Jiří Kratochvil, Zuzana Brabcová, Daniela Hodrová, Michal Ajvaz, Jáchym Topol," in his *Literature in Post-Communist Russia and Eastern Europe*, London, 2004, pp. 80–114.

VACULÍK, LUDVÍK

Novelist and journalist. He was born in 1926 in Brumov in East Moravia. His father was a carpenter. After school, from 1941 to 1946, he worked and studied in the world-famous Bata shoemaking factory in Zlín. After the war he studied journalism in Prague till 1950. He was a warden in a children's home and this became the inspiration for the 1963 novel *Rušný dům* (A Busy House). From 1953 to 1965 he was an editor in a publishing house and for radio, where he reported on the life of young people. However, his criticisms brought him into conflict with officialdom. From 1965 he was an editor and reporter for the weekly *Literární noviny* (Literary News) and he won great acclaim for his bitterly critical speech at the congress of writers in 1967, published in book form, in English, as *The Relations between [the] Citizen and Power* (London, 1968) and in Czech in *Protokol IV. sjezdu svazu československých spisovatelů* (The Fourth Congress of Czechoslovak Writers´ Union, Prague, 1968), anticipating the Prague Spring of 1968. In June 1968 he wrote the manifesto *Dva tisíce slov, které patří dělníkům, zemědělcům, úředníkům, vědcům, umělcům a všem* (Two Thousand Words to Workers, Farmers, Officials, Scientists, Artists and Everyone) demanding more far-reaching reforms, which had soon more than 100,000 signatures. After the Soviet invasion in August 1968, Vaculík was designated one of the main agents of "counter-revolution"; in the seventies and eighties he could neither publish nor hold any public office. He founded and became the chief editor of the most important samizdat publication *Petlice* (Padlock), which from 1973 to 1989 circulated 410 volumes of texts by banned authors; he signed the human rights manifesto *Charter 77*, took an important part in editing other samizdat publications, including regular collections of articles, and the almanac *Hodina naděje* (The Hour of Hope) which was published in samizdat in 1978, in Toronto in 1980 and in a German translation in Frankfurt am Main in 1978. After 1989 he again worked with the resurrected *Literární noviny* and in radio. He also took part in the documentary television series *Dějiny samizdatu* (The History of Samizdat, 2002).

Vaculík's novels are closely connected with, and generally inspired by, his personal experiences. This is true of his first and probably most important novel *Sekyra* (1966), which was translated by Marian Šling as *The Axe* and published in London and New York in 1973. It is the story of a man comparing himself to his father, who for him is the embodiment of the limitations of Communist ideology, but who also embodies the true values of home and tradition. It has clearly autobiographical features and is set in the author's native Moravian Wallachia. The novel is remarkable for its style, using several different levels of language, Wallachian East Moravian dialect, common Czech especially as spoken in Prague, etc. The action moves from the narrator's childhood to contemporary times. Different eras are fused together, thus upsetting the traditional chronological narrative. Vaculík retained these distinctive stylistic features in other works, for example, in many original short, witty, essayistic texts starting in the sixties. He published a number of collections of these articles. A book of selections *Stará dáma se baví* (The Old Lady Is Enjoying Herself, 1991), dates from the sixties and *Jaro je tady* (Spring Is Here) from the eighties. *Jaro je tady* was published in samizdat in 1981, in Cologne in 1988, and in Prague in 1990. Parts of it were translated in *The Writing on the Wall* (1983, see below) and in Vaculík's volume *A Cup of Coffee with My Interrogator*, translated by George Theiner, with an introduction by Václav Havel, and published in London in 1987. Vaculík's second novel *Morčata*, was published in samizdat in 1973, in Toronto in 1977, and in Prague in 1991. The translation by Káča Poláčková as *The Guinea Pigs* came out in New York in 1973 and in London in 1974. It is a parable of totalitarian society, differing from his other works by the absurdity of the situations and its enigmatic, Kafkaesque qualities. In a contrast *Český snář* is based on the author's actual diaries. It came out in samizdat in 1981, was published in Toronto in 1983, and in Brno in 1990. Excerpts as *A Czech Dreambook*, translated and introduced by Michael Henry Heim, were published in *Cross Currents* in 1984 (pp. 71–86). With shocking frankness it described life in the "dissident ghetto", samizdat publishing, persecution by the police and the author's love affairs. Vaculík went even further in suggestive and openly licentious descriptions of eroticism that were again based on personal experience. In his next novels, *Jak se dělá chlapec* (How A Boy Is Made, 1993), parts translated and edited by Alexandra Büchler in *This Side of Reality*, London, 1996, pp. 190–203, and *Loučení k Panně* (A Farewell to the Virgin, 2002).

Other editions in English: "The Hatchet" (translated by Jean Layton), in *Universum: A Review of Czechoslovak Literature and Arts*, 4 (1969), no. 6, pp. 16–23; eight feuilletons (translated by Káča Poláčková and William E. Harkins), in *The Writing on the Wall* (edited by Peter Kussi and Antonín Jaroslav Liehm), Princeton, 1983, pp. 220–252; "A Recreational River-Boat," *Cross Currents*, 4

(1985), pp. 279–281; five feuilletons (translated by A. G. Brain [i.e. Alice and Gerald Turner], Michal Pomichalek and Anna Mozga), in *Good-bye, Samizdat* (edited Marketa Goetz-Stankiewicz), Evanston, 1992, pp. 114–129.

Bibliography: Antonín Jaroslav Liehm, "Ludvík Vaculík " (interview), in his *The Politics of Culture*, New York, 1970, pp. 91–108 (in Czech Antonín Jaroslav Liehm, *Generace*, Prague, 1990, pp. 88–104). – Herbert Eagle, "Ludvík Vaculík: The Axe: A Quest for Human Dignity," *Books Abroad Today*, 45 (1975), no. 2, pp. 7–12. – Antonín Jaroslav Liehm, "Ludvík Vaculík and His Novel The Axe," in *Czech Literature Since 1956* (edited by William E. Harkins and Paul Trensky), New York, 1980, pp. 91–102. – Kees Mercks, "The Semantic Gesture in The Guinea Pigs," in *Vosmi na radosť. To Honour Jean von der Eng-Liedmeier*, Amsterdam, 1980, pp. 309–322. – Bronislava Volek, "The Guinea Pigs by LudvíkVaculík," *Slavic Review*, 43 (1984), pp. 17–37. – *Hlasy nad rukopisem Vaculíkova Českého snáře*, Prague, 1991 (originally samizdat, 1981). – Michael Špirit, "Postscript: A Discussion with Ludvík Vaculík," *Trafika. An International Literary Review*, no. 3 (Summer 1994), pp. 71–75 (in Czech *Kritická Příloha Revolver Revue* 1 [1995], pp. 44–50). – Jan Čulík, "Ludvík Vaculík," in *Dictionary of Literary Biography: Twentieth-Century Eastern European Writers*, vol. 232 (edited by Steven Serafin et al.), Detroit, 2001, pp. 386–392. – Vladimír Karfík, "Deník jako román," in his *Literatura je čitelná: K moderní české próze a poezii*, Prague, 2002, pp. 71–92.

VIEWEGH, MICHAL

Novelist and journalist. He was born in Prague in 1962. His father was a chemist, his mother a lawyer. On leaving school in 1980 he studied economics for a time, then he took various casual jobs. From 1983 to 1988 he studied Czech and pedagogy at Charles University. He has been a teacher, an editor in a publishing house and from 1995 a professional writer. He is one of the most successful Czech authors and is frequently translated.

Viewegh's first two novels are probably his most significant. His first one, *Názory na vraždu* (Thoughts on Murder, 1990), describes, in the guise of a detective story, an apparently idyllic small town in Bohemia where mass hysteria takes hold. The next novel, *Báječná léta pod psa* (The Blissful Years of Lousy Living, 1992), has autobiographical elements and portrays the seventies and eighties in Bohemia from the point of view of a family that did not belong either to the ruling party or to the dissidents. Parts of the English translation by O. T. Chalkstone appear on pp. 154–164 of *This Side of Reality*, edited by Alexandra Büchler and published in London in 1996. A film version was made by Petr Nikolajev in 1997. Already evident in these novels is the author's humour, his gentle irony and self-deprecation, and the ability to write attractive, readable prose. This is repeated in various forms in other novels, for example *Výchova dívek v Čechách* (1994), a film version of which was made in 1997 by Petr Koliha. It was translated as *Bringing up Girls in Bohemia* by A. G. Brain (Alice and Gerald Turner) and published in London in 1996. Viewegh displays the same skills in the literary parodies *Nápady laskavého čtenáře* (Your Ideas, Dear Reader, 1993) and *Nové nápady laskavého čtenáře* (Your New Ideas, Dear Reader, 2000). Viewegh is often accused of writing, for commercial reasons, "purely entertainment" literature, mostly dealing with sexual relationships, but in his latest novels, *Vybíjená* (Knocking Out, 2004), *Lekce tvůrčího psaní* (A Lesson in Creative Writing, 2005), and *Báječný rok (deník 2005)* (A Wonderful Year [A Diary for 2005], 2006), serious themes appear. *Vybíjená* follows the life story of a group of characters who had been pupils together at secondary school. Thus the work is overshadowed by feelings of a middle-age crisis, awareness of growing old and fear of death.

Other editions in English: "Sightseers" (translated by Alex Zucker), in *Daylight in Nightclub Inferno* (edited by Elena Lappin), North Haven, 1997, pp. 20–28, 229–237.

Bibliography: Robert Porter, "Daniela Hodrová, Michal Viewegh, Jáchym Topol: New Voices?" in his *An Introduction to Twentieth-Century Czech Fiction*. Brighton and Portland, 2001, pp. 171–177.

WEIL, JIŘÍ

Novelist and translator. He was born in 1900 into a Czech Jewish family in Praskolesy in Central Bohemia. He studied Slavonic philology and comparative history at Charles University, finishing in 1928. He was an editor for Communist cultural journals and a translator from Russian. From 1933 he worked in Moscow as a translator. In 1935 he was expelled from the Communist party and sent to Soviet Central Asia for re-education, returning to Czechoslovakia in 1936. During the German occupation he escaped persecution, first because of a "mixed marriage" and then by feigning suicide. At the end of the war, he was in hiding. After the war he became an editor in a publishing house but after 1949 he could not publish and worked in the Jewish Museum. He died in Prague in 1959.

Weil is the author of two novels that caused him to be bitterly criticized by the Communist party and after 1948 brought him into disfavour with the regime. The first of them, *Moskva-hranice* (Moscow-Frontier, 1937), is the story, with many biographical features, of Fischer, a Czech intellectual in Moscow, who, during the Stalinist trials, is expelled from the Communist party and persecuted. It is one of the first true pictures of what life was like during Stalinism in the Soviet Union. The sequel, *Dřevěná lžíce* (The Wooden Spoon), was written between 1937 and 1938 and is set partly in Kazakhstan. Weil did not publish it during his lifetime. It came out first in Italian in 1970, in Czech in samizdat in 1978, and in Prague in 1992. The second controversial novel is *Život s hvězdou* (1949). It was translated as *Life with a Star* by Rita Klímová and Roslyn Schloss, with a preface by Philip Roth, and published in London in 1988. It describes the life of an obscure Jewish clerk in Prague during the German occupation. This work is completely devoid of pathos, heroism and the black and white values which until then had been characteristic of portrayals of the occupation. Like *Moskva-hranice*, *Život s hvězdou* is a dispassionate description of everyday life and tragi-comic situations that are almost Kafkaesque in their absurdity. With these works Weil anticipated the Czech novels of the sixties on the subject of the Holocaust, for example those of

Ladislav Fuks and Hana Bělohradská. The fate of Czech Jews was the subject of other works including the collection *Žalozpěv za 77 297 obětí* (Lament for 77,297 Victims, 1958) where the author introduces documents relating to the Holocaust alongside his own poetic commentary and quotations from the Old Testament. It was also the subject of his last work, *Na střeše je Mendelssohn* (1960), translated by Marie Winn as *Mendelssohn Is on the Roof*, with a preface by Philip Roth, published in New York in 1991, and in London in 1992.

Other editions in English: *I Never Saw Another Butterfly: Children's Drawings from Terezín Concentration Camp* (translated by Jeanne Němcová), New York, 1962; "The Prisoner of Chillon" (translated by Jean Layton), in *Universum: A Review of Czechoslovak Literature and Arts*, 3 (1968), no. 5, pp. 16–21; "Two Stories about Nazis and Jews" (translated by Káča Poláčková), *American Poetry Review*, 3 (1974), no. 4, pp. 22–24; *Colors* (translated by Rachel Harell), Ann Arbor, 2002.

Bibliography: Egon Hostovský, "Participation in Modern Czech literature," in *The Jews of Czechoslovakia: Historical Studies and Surveys*, vol. I, Philadelphia, 1968, pp. 439–453. – Josef Škvorecký, "The Art of Survival," *New Republic*, 209 (1989), no. 10, pp. 30–34. – Jan Grossman, "Weilův Život s hvězdou," in his *Analýzy* (edited by Jiří Holý and Terezie Pokorná), Prague, 1992, pp. 259–363. – Alice Jedličková, "Jiří Weil: Život s hvězdou," in *Česká literatura 1945–1970* (edited by Jiřina Táborská and Milan Zeman), Prague, 1992, pp. 61-69. – Růžena Grebeníčková, *Literatura a fiktivní světy (I)* (edited by Michael Špirit), Prague, 1995, pp. 389–447. – Jiří Holý, "Komentář," in Jiří Weil, *Život s hvězdou, Na střeše je Mendelssohn, Žalozpěv za 77 297 obětí*, Prague, 1999, pp. 481–505. – A. G. Mayor, "Czech-Jewish Identity after the Holocaust. The Case of Jiří Weil, the Pinkas Synagogue and Weil's Elegy for 77,297," in *Modern Czech Studies* (edited by Alexander Levitsky and Masako U. Fidler), Providence, 2000, pp. 141–148. – David Scrase, "Jiří Weil" and "Life with a Star," in *Reference Guide to Holocaust Literature* (edited by Thomas Riggs), Detroit, 2002, pp. 332–333, 499. – David Mesher, "Jiří Weil," in *Holocaust Literature* (edited by S. Lillian Kremer), London and New York, 2003, pp. 1296–1299. – Jindřich Toman, "Jiří Weil," in *Dictionary of Literary Biography: Holocaust Novelists*, vol. 299 (edited by Efraim Sicher), Detroit, 2004, pp. 89–94.

WERNISCH, IVAN

Poet and translator. He was born in 1942 in Prague. Wernisch comes from a German-Czech family of civil servants. His grandmother was a Tartar. At secondary school he studied ceramics, gaining his leaving certificate in 1959. For a short time he worked as a potter, then he had a succession of different jobs, builder, cleaner, nightwatchman. In the seventies and eighties he could publish nothing but translations. He published his poems in samizdat and abroad. In the nineties he was editor of the weekly *Literární noviny* (Literary News). His son Michal Wernisch born in 1964 is the poet Ewald Murrer.

Wernisch belongs to the generation that began writing in the early sixties. His first work was the poetically naïve *Kam letí nebe* (Whither Are the Heavens

Flying, 1961) but he soon discovered his own domain in the bizarre, dreamy and often grotesque visions of the collection *Zimohrádek* (Wintercastle, 1965). The language of Wernisch's poetry is taken from colloquial speech, fragments of monologue or dialogue. He often uses nursery rhymes and paraphrases of folk tales and well-known stories. His poems in samizdat from the seventies and eighties were published complete in the lengthy book *Blbecká poezie* (Daft Poetry, 2002), edited by Jan Šulc and Milena Vojtková. Characteristic of Wernisch's technique is the use of deliberate deception. Sometimes he publishes his own poetry as translations from foreign poets, for example *Frc: Překlady a překrady* (Pawnbroker. Translations and Plagiarisms, 1991). At other times, as in *Doupě latinářů* (The Lair of the Latinists, 1992), he concocts fictitious lives for his contemporaries and for well-known historical personages, such as Jan Neruda and Karolina Světlá, placing them in strange, unaccustomed situations. He published selections of the work of forgotten Czech poets in the volumes *Zapadlo slunce za dnem, který nebyl* (The Sun Has Gone Down on a Day That Never Was, 2000) and *Píseň o nosu* (Sing of the Nose, 2005).

Editions in English: two poems (translated by George Theiner), in *New Writing in Czechoslovakia* (edited by George Theiner), Harmondsworth et al., 1969, pp. 34–39; *In the Puppet Gardens: Selected Poetry 1963–2003* (edited and translated by Jonathan Bolton), Ann Arbor, 2006.

Bibliography: Karel Milota, "Ivan Wernisch: Včerejší den," in *Český Parnas: Literatura 1970–1990* (edited by Jiří Holý and Jiřina Táborská), Prague, 1993, pp. 377–382. – Jiří Trávníček, "Krajina bezčasí. Ivan Wernisch: Zimohrádek," in his *Poezie poslední možnosti*, Prague, 1996, pp. 117–131.

ZAHRADNÍČEK, JAN

Poet, translator and journalist. He was born in 1905 into a family of farmers in the village of Mastník in the Czech-Moravian Highlands. He was born with a disability, and an injury he sustained in childhood when he fell from a hayloft made his physical handicap worse. He studied German language and literature at Charles University in Prague but did not complete the course and earned his living as a reader in a publishing house, and as a translator and journalist. Among his close friends were František Halas and the Catholic authors Jan Čep, Bedřich Fučík and other literary figures. From 1940 to 1944 and from 1945 to 1948 he was in charge of the literary review *Akord* (The Chord). In June 1951 he was arrested, and in July 1952, in a show trial with an artificially set up "subversive group", he was sentenced to thirteen years in prison. In 1956 he was allowed to visit his wife and children who were in hospital suffering from mushroom poisoning. His wife and son were saved but his two daughters died. In spite of a promise that the remainder of his sentence would be quashed, Zahradníček had to go back to prison. He was not freed till the amnesty of 1960, and several months later, in October 1960, he died in Uhřínov in the Czech-Moravian Highlands.

Zahradníček is an outstanding representative of modern Catholic, spiritual poetry. His first collections in the early thirties are dominated by grief, worship of pain, and images of death pictured as symbols of destruction. In the subsequent collections *Jeřáby* (Rowans, 1933), *Žíznivé léto* (Arid Summer, 1935) and *Pozdravení slunci* (Greetings to the Sun, 1937) his personal pain and melancholy change to a feeling of being part of the life of others and of his native region. The meaning of life is determined by God's mysterious purpose. The author's verse, previously irregular, becomes much more harmonious, using, for example, sonnet forms. During the war and the German occupation Zahradníček turned to the Czech patron saints, especially Saint Wenceslas. His view of the nation as a metaphysical society of the dead and the living is confirmed by the passionate lines in the collection *Korouhve* (The Banners, 1940) and in the poem *Svatý Václav* (Saint Wenceslas, 1946). From this point of view he argued against liberalism and against Masaryk's idea of democracy with its Protestant concept of the Czech nation. Zahradníček became the subject of attacks by the Communist Party for his staunch Catholicism. His poetry is dominated by invocation, prophecy and a dark vision of the world of the future, which, without God, will be given over to the powers of evil; such are the long poems *La Saletta* (1947) and *Znamení moci* (The Sign of Power), which was finished in 1951, published in book form in Rome in 1968, and in Prague in 1990. Zahradníček's last poems, *Dům Strach* (House of Fear), dating from 1951 to 1955, published in Toronto in 1981 and in Prague in 1990, and *Čtyři léta* (Four Years) date from 1956 to 1960. Published in Prague in 1969 they are reflections on his personal situation and on the death of children. They are the expression of a deep, inner Christian faith. They also bear witness to life in Communist prisons. As a translator, Zahradníček turned to poets who were closest to him, such as Friedrich Hölderlin, Rainer Maria Rilke and Paul Claudel. Zahradníček helped Otto František Babler with his translation of Dante's *Divine Comedy*. His work, including his journalism and translations, appeared in six volumes in samizdat in 1984 and 1985, edited by Bedřich Fučík, Mojmír Trávníček and Radovan Zejda. His correspondence with Jan Čep was published in two volumes in Prague in 1995 and 2000, edited by Mojmír Trávníček, and his correspondence with František Halas was published in 2003, edited by Jan Wiendl and Jan Komárek. A complete critical edition of all his poetry came out in Prague in 2001, edited and with a 200-page critical commentary by Jitka Bednářová and Mojmír Trávníček.

Edition in English: one poem (translated by Alfred French), in *The Czech Avantgardists* (edited by Alfred French), Rockville, 1995, pp. 87; "Sign of Power" (translated by Charles S. Kraszewski), *Kosmas*, 19 (2005), no. 1, pp. 37–63.

Bibliography: Zdeněk Kalista, *Vzpomínání na Jana Zahradníčka* (afterword by Jaromír Hořec), Munich, 1988. – Bedřich Fučík, "Bujará chudoba," in his *Čtrnáctero zastavení* (edited by Vladimír Binar and Mojmír Trávníček), Prague, 1992, pp. 237–258. – Bedřich Fučík, *Píseň o zemi* (edited by Vladimír Binar and Mojmír Trávníček), Prague, 1994, pp. 59–69, 87–96. – Jan Wiendl, "Rané básnické sbírky Jana Zahradníčka," *Česká literatura*, 45 (1997), pp. 258–276. – Charles S. Kraszewski, "Jan Zahradníček: Znamení moci," in his *The Romantic Hero and Contemporary Anti-Hero in Polish and Czech Literature*, New York, 1998, pp. 273–288. – Urs Heftrich, "Nachwort," in Jan Zahradníček, *Vogelbeeren*, Furth im Wald, 2000, pp. 77–80. – Aleksandra Pająková, "Zahradníček a Polsko," *Česká literatura*, 48 (2000), pp. 537–552. – Jan Wiendl, "Krajina, člověk, víra: Ideologický aspekt v Zahradníčkově poezii druhé poloviny třicátých let," *Česká literatura*, 48 (2000), pp. 476–482. – Radovan Zejda, *Byl básníkem! Život a dílo Jana Zahradníčka*, Tišnov, 2004. – *Víra a výraz* (edited by Tomáš Kubíček and Jan Wiendl), Brno, 2005.

Anthologies of Czech Postwar Literature in English

Four Czech Stories. Edited, introduced and translated by Iris Urwin. Prague, Orbis, 1957. 130 pp. (Jan Drda, Ludvík Aškenazy, Jan Weiss, Jiří Marek.)

Back to Life: Poems from Behind the Iron Curtain. Edited by Robert Conquest. London, Hutchinson, 1958. 108 pp. (Jiří Filip, Jaromír Hořec, Jiří Robert Pick, Miloš Macourek.)

A Handful of Linden Leaves: An Anthology of Czech Poetry. Edited by Jaroslav Janů, translated and introduced by Edith Pargeter. Prague, Artia, 1958. 52 pp. (Josef Václav Sládek, Josef Hora, Jaroslav Seifert, Konstantin Biebl, Jaroslav Vrchlický, Julius Zeyer, S. K. Neumann, Jiří Wolker, Fráňa Šrámek, Karel Toman, Vítězslav Nezval, František Halas, František Branislav, František Hrubín, Svatopluk Čech, Jan Neruda.)

The Linden Tree: An Anthology of Czech and Slovak Literature 1890–1960. Edited by Mojmír Otruba and Zdeněk Pešat, introduced by František Buriánek, translated by Edith Pargeter. Prague, Artia, 1962. 404 pp. (Julius Fučík, Václav Řezáč, Jan Drda, Ludvík Aškenazy, Jan Otčenášek, Arnošt Lustig, Vítězslav Nezval, Konstantin Biebl, Jaroslav Seifert, František Halas, Vilém Závada, Vladimír Holan, František Hrubín, Josef Kainar, Ivan Skála et al.)

Universum: A Review of Czechoslovak Literature and Arts. Vols. I–V. Edited by Jiří Hájek et al. Prague, Artia, 1966–1970.

Czech and Slovak Short Stories. Edited, introduced and translated by Jeanne W. Němcová. London and New York, Oxford University Press, 1967. 296 pp. (Jan Drda, Ludvík Aškenazy, Josef Škvorecký, Arnošt Lustig, Josef Nesvadba, Ivan Klíma, Jan Beneš, Bohumil Hrabal, Věra Linhartová et. al.)

Seven Short Stories. Edited by Oldřich Beneš, introduction by Jiří Hájek, translated by George Theiner, Rosemary Kavanová and Marian Wilbraham. Prague,

Orbis, 1965. 142 pp. 2nd edition 1967. (Bohumil Hrabal, Ivan Vyskočil, Josef Škvorecký, Vladimír Vondra et al.)

New Writing of East Europe. Edited by George Gömöri and Charles Newman. Chicago, Quadrangle Books, 1968. 266 pp. (Bohumil Hrabal, Miroslav Holub, Vera Blackwell on Linhartová et al.)

Modern Poetry in Translation: Czech. Edited by Ted Hughes and Daniel Weissbort, translated by George Theiner, Edith Pargeter, Káča Poláčková et al. London, Cape Goliard, 1969. (Jiří Kolář, Josef Kainar, Antonín Bartušek, Jan Skácel, Miroslav Holub, Jiří Šotola, Ivan Diviš, Miroslav Florian, Josef Hanzlík, Antonín Brousek, Ivan Wernisch, Ludvík Kundera, Oldřich Wenzl, Ladislav Novák, Jan Zábrana, Jiří Gold, Petr Kabeš.)

New Writing from Czechoslovakia. Edited by Jon Silkin et al., translated by Jarmila and Ian Milner, Vera Blackwell et al. In: *Stand: Quarterly of the Arts* 10 (1969), no. 2. (Miroslav Holub, Josef Hanzlík, Josef Škvorecký, Václav Havel, Jaroslav Seifert, Antonín Bartušek, Vladimír Holan.)

New Writing in Czechoslovakia. Edited and introduced by George Theiner. Baltimore and Harmondsworth, Penguin, 1969. 248 pp. (Jiří Brdečka, Ivan Wernisch, Arnošt Lustig, Josef Hanzlík, Miloš Macourek, Josef Škvorecký, Jiří Kolář, Miroslav Florian, Jiří Suchý, Vladimír Holan, Jaroslav Seifert, Karel Pecka, Miroslav Holub, Karel Michal, Josef Nesvadba, Jan Skácel, Ivan Diviš, Milan Kundera, Antonín Brousek, Alexandr Kliment, Antonín Bartušek, Ivan Vyskočil.)

Three Czech Poets. Vítězslav Nezval (translated by Ewald Osers), Antonín Bartušek (translated by Ewald Osers and George Theiner), Josef Hanzlík (translated by Ewald Osers). Introduction by Graham Martin. Harmondsworth, Penguin, 1971. 160 pp.

White Stones and Fir Trees: An Anthology of Contemporary Slavic Literature. Edited by Vasa D. Mihailovich. Lewisburg, Bucknell University Press, 1977. 604 pp. (Ivan Diviš, Vladimír Holan, Václav Havel, Miloš Macourek, Miroslav Florian, Jiří Šotola, Vladimír Vondra, Jan Skácel, Josef Škvorecký, Ivan Vyskočil, Miroslav Holub, Bohumil Hrabal et al.)

New Czech Prose. Translated by Norah Hronková and Joy Moss-Kohoutová. Prague, Orbis, 1980. 156 pp. (Bohumil Říha, Pavel Francouz, Josef Kadlec, Jan Kostrhun, Jan Kozák, Jana Moravcová, Miloslav Nohejl, Josef Rybák, Jiří Stano, Eduard Petiška.)

Panorama of Czech Literature. Vol. I–X. Edited by Josef Rybák et al. Prague, Panorama, 1980–1988.

Contemporary East European Poetry: An Anthology. Edited by Emery George. Ann Arbor, Ardis, 1983. 456 pp. New York and Oxford, Oxford University Press, 1993. 490 pp. (Jaroslav Seifert, Vladimír Holan, František Hrubín, Antonín Bartušek, Miroslav Holub, Josef Hanzlík, Antonín Brousek et al.)

The Writing on the Wall: An Anthology of Contemporary Czech Literature. Edited by Antonín Liehm and Peter Kussi, foreword by Antonín Liehm, introduced by Ludvík Vaculík. Princeton and New York, Karz-Cohl Publishing, 1983. 254 pp. (Lumír Čivrný, Ladislav Dvořák, Jiří Gruša, Jiří Hájek, Václav Havel, Jiří Hochman, Jaroslav Hutka, Eva Kantůrková, Ivan Klíma, Alexandr Kliment, Pavel Kohout, Eda Kriseová, Pavel Landovský, Sergej Machonin, Milan Šimečka, Jan Trefulka, Vlastimil Třešňák, Ludvík Vaculík.)

Drama Contemporary: Czechoslovakia. Edited and introduced by Marketa Goetz-Stankiewicz, translated by Vera Blackwell, Jan Drábek et al. New York, Performing Arts Journal Publications, 1985. 224 pp. (Milan Kundera, Václav Havel, Pavel Kohout, Milan Uhde, Pavel Landovský, Ivan Klíma.)

The Power of the Powerless: Citizens against the State in Central-Eastern Europe. Edited by John Keane, introduced by Steven Lukes. London, Hutchinson and Armonk, Sharpe, 1985. 228 pp. 2nd edition 1990. (Václav Havel, Rudolf Battěk, Václav Benda, Václav Černý, Jiří Hájek, Ladislav Hejdánek, Miroslav Kusý, Jan Ruml, Petr Uhl, Josef Vohryzek, Josef Zvěřina.)

The Poets' Lamp: A Czech Anthology. Edited by Alfred French, translated by Alfred French et al. Canberra, Leros Press, 1986. 146 pp. Parallel English and Czech text. (Vítězslav Nezval, Konstantin Biebl, Jaroslav Seifert, Jiřina Hauková, Vladimír Holan, Kamil Bednář, Miroslav Holub, František Hrubín, Josef Kainar, Josef Hanzlík.)

The Vaněk Plays: Four Authors, One Character. Edited by Marketa Goetz-Stankiewicz, translated by Jan Novák. Vancouver, University of British Columbia Press, 1987. 258 pp. London, Faber & Faber, 1990. (Václav Havel, Pavel Kohout, Pavel Landovský, Jiří Dienstbier.) In Czech as *V hlavní roli Ferdinand Vaněk*, edited by Jan Šulc, epilogue by Lenka Jungmannová. Prague, Academia, 2006.

The New Czech Poetry. Jaroslav Čejka, Michal Černík, Karel Sýs. Translated and introduced by Ewald Osers. Newcastle upon Tyne, Bloodaxe Books, 1988. 62 pp.

Child of Europe: A New Anthology of East European Poetry. Edited by Michael March, translated by Jarmila and Ian Milner et al. London and New York, Penguin, 1990. 254 pp. (Sylva Fischerová, Ivo Šmoldas, Ewald Murrer, Jana Štroblová et al.)

The Boundaries of Twilight: Czecho-Slovak Writing from the New World. Edited and introduced by C. J. Hribal. Minneapolis, New Rivers Press, 1991. 356 pp. (Josef Škvorecký, Zdena Salivarová, Oldřich Mikulášek, Jan Skácel, Jiřina Fuchsová, Vladimír Holan, Erazim Kohák, Iva Pekárková, Jan Ulč, Bronislava Volková, Jaroslav Seifert, Eva Kantůrková et al.)

Good-bye, Samizdat: Twenty Years of Czechoslovak Underground Writing. Edited by Marketa Goetz-Stankiewicz, foreword by Timothy Garton Ash, translated by A. G. Brain (Alice and Gerald Turner) et al. Evanston, Northwestern University Press, 1992. 310 pp. (Igor Hájek, Alexandr Kliment, Ivan Klíma, Pavel Kohout, Jan Trefulka, Jiří Gruša, Karel Pecka, Erazim Kohák, Václav Havel et al.)

Interference: The Story of Czechoslovakia in the Words of Its Writers. Edited by Peter Spafford, foreword by Miroslav Holub. Cheltenham, New Clarion Press, 1992. 170 pp. (Antonín Bartušek, Konstantin Biebl, Sylva Fischerová, Josef Hanzlík, Václav Havel, Vladimír Holan, Miroslav Holub, Bohumil Hrabal, Eva Kantůrková, Ivan Klíma, Heda Kovályová, Milan Kundera, Jiří Mucha, Vítězslav Nezval, Jan Pelc, Jaroslav Seifert, Milan Šimečka, Josef Škvorecký, Zdena Tominová, Ludvík Vaculík, Jiří Weil.)

Shifting Borders: East European Poetries of the Eighties. Edited by Walter Cummins. Rutherford, Fairleigh Dickinson University Press, 1993. 482 pp.

Czech Plays: Modern Czech Drama. Edited and introduction by Barbara Day. London, Nick Hern Books, 1994. 224 pp. (Václav Havel, Ivan Klíma, Josef Topol, Daniela Fischerová).

Czech Writers on Tolerance. Foreword by Jiří Stránský, translated by Anna Bryson, Louis Charbouneau et al. Prague, Readers International, 1994. 238 pp. (Václav Havel, Lumír Čivrný, Miroslav Červenka, Daniela Fischerová, Miroslav Holub, Jaroslav Vejvoda, Eva Kantůrková, Pavel Šrut, Jan Trefulka, Miroslav Huptych, Alexandr Kliment, Jana Štroblová, Alexandra Berková, Zdeněk Rotrekl, Ivan Klíma, Josef Škvorecký, Karel Šiktanc, Milan Uhde et al.)

Description of a Struggle. The Picador Book of Contemporary East European Prose. Edited by Michael March, translated by James Naughton et al. London, Picador, 1994. 404 pp. (Bohumil Hrabal, Eda Kriseová, Alexandra Berková, Ondřej Neff et al.)

Prague: Traveller's Literary Companion. Edited by Paul Wilson. San Franscisco, Whereabouts Press, 1995. 242 pp.

The Czech Avantgardists. Edited and translated by Alfred French. Introduction by René Wellek. A study by Zdeněk Pešat. Afterword by Zdeněk Kalista. Rockville, Kabel Publishers, 1995. 104 pp. (F. X. Šalda, S. K. Neumann,

Fráňa Šrámek, Jakub Deml, Otakar Theer, Jaroslav Durych, Richard Weiner, Josef Hora, Josef Palivec, Konstantin Biebl, Jiří Wolker, Vítězslav Nezval, Jaroslav Seifert, František Halas, Jan Zahradníček, Vilém Závada, Vladimír Holan, František Hrubín, Jiří Orten, Jiřina Hauková, Josef Kainar.)

This Side of Reality: Czech Short Stories. Edited and introduced by Alexandra Büchler. London, Serpent's Tail and New York, 1996. 230 pp. (Ladislav Fuks, Věra Linhartová, Arnošt Lustig, Ewald Murrer, Ota Filip, Bohumil Hrabal, Josef Škvorecký, Jiří Gruša, Sylvie Richterová, Ivan Klíma, Jiří Kratochvil, Zuzana Brabcová, Michal Viewegh, Alexandra Berková, Michal Ajvaz, Ludvík Vaculík, Jáchym Topol.)

Daylight in Nightclub Inferno: Czech Fiction from the post-Kundera Generation. Edited by Elena Lappin, translated by Jonathan Bolton, Alex Zucker et al. North Haven, Catbird Press, 1997. 306 pp. (Jáchym Topol, Michal Viewegh, Daniela Fischerová, Václav Koubek, Tereza Boučková, Ewald Murrer, Michal Ajvaz, Jiří Kratochvil, Alexandra Berková, Daniela Hodrová, Pavel Řezníček, Alexandr Kliment et al.)

Allskin and Other Tales by Contemporary Czech Women. Edited and introduced by Alexandra Büchler. Seattle, Women in Translation, 1998. 234 pp. (Daniela Fischerová, Zuzana Brabcová, Tereza Boučková, Daniela Hodrová, Alexandra Berková, Jana Červenková, Iva Pekárková, Eda Kriseová, Lenka Procházková, Zdena Salivarová, Věra Linhartová, Sylvie Richterová et al.)

A Handbook of Czech Prose Writing, 1940–2005. Edited by Bohuslava Bradbrook. Brighton & Portland, Sussex Academic Press, 2007. 156 pp.

Notes

The Forties and Fifties

1. Dodatek k nenapsaným dějinám české literatury. *Rozmluvy*, 5 (1987), no. 7, p. 138.
2. *Poesie za mřížemi*. Ed. by Karel Josef Beneš. Prague, Melantrich, 1946, p. 163.
3. This excerpt, and all the others (unless otherwise stated) have been translated by Elizabeth Morrison.
4. Filmed by Jaroslav Balík, 1961.
5. *Reportáž, psaná na oprátce*. První úplné, kritické a komentované vydání. Ed. by František Janáček et al. Comm. Alena Hájková, afterword Vladimír Macura. Prague, Torst, 1995. In English, *Report from the Gallows*, Prague, Orego, 2000. See also Peter Steiner, The Past Perfect Hero: Julius Fučík and Reportage: Written from the Gallows, in his *The Deserts of Bohemia: Czech Fiction and Its Social Context*. Ithaca, NY, Cornell University Press, 2000, pp. 94–150.
6. Several short stories from this collection were filmed by Otakar Vávra, 1949, Jiří Krejčík, 1960 and others.
7. On *Němá barikáda* see *Malá knížka o Němé barikádě*. Ed. by Jaroslava Janáčková. Prague, Albatros, 1988.
8. In English Mucha's novel *Spálená setba* (1948) also came out as *Scorched Crop* (translated by E. Osers), London, Hogarth, 1949.
9. Jan Zahradníček, *Knihy básní*. Ed. by Jitka Bednářová and Mojmír Trávníček. Prague, NLN, 2001, pp. 550–1.
10. Vladimír Vokolek, *Ke komu mluvím dnes*. Brno, Atlantis, 1998, p. 11.
11. Václav Černý, *Skutečnost svoboda*. Ed. by Jan Šulc and Jaroslav Kabíček. Prague, Český spisovatel, 1995, p. 31. Also Milada Součková, Marxist Theory in Czech Literature. *Harvard Slavic Studies* I (ed. by Horace G. Lunt). Cambridge, MA, Harvard University Press, 1953, pp. 335–61, in particular pp. 340–8.
12. Cf. the anthology *Z dějin českého myšlení o literatuře I*. 1945–1948. Ed. by Michal Přibáň. Prague, ÚČL AVČR, 2001, pp. 217–48.
13. František Kovárna, O kulturní autonomii. *Svobodné slovo*, 23 June 1946.
14. *Účtování a výhledy*. Sborník prvního sjezdu Syndikátu českých spisovatelů. Ed. by Jan Kopecký. Prague, Syndikát českých spisovatelů, 1948, p. 22.
15. Miloš Dvořák, Duch svobody. *Akord*, 14 (1947–1948), no. 6, p. 204.
16. Ladislav Fikar, *Samotín*. Prague, Mladá fronta, 1992, p. 42.
17. Jindřich Chalupecký, *Obhajoba umění*. Ed. by Miroslav Červenka and Vladimír Karfík. Prague, Československý spisovatel, 1991, pp. 111–12.
18. Ivan Blatný, *Verše 1933–1955*. Ed. by Rudolf Havel. Brno, Atlantis, 1995, p. 129.
19. About Group 42, cf. *Skupina 42: Antologie*. Ed. by Zdeněk Pešat and Eva Petrová. Brno, Atlantis, 2000. Přemysl Blažíček, Skupina 42 – nové směřování poezie. In his *Kritika a interpretace*. Ed. and afterword by Michael Špirit. Prague, Triáda, 2002, pp.

105–25. Leszek Engelking, *Codzienność i mit: Poetyka, programy i historia Grupy 42 w kontekstach dwudziestowiecznej awangardy i postawangardy*. Łodź, Wydawnictwo Uniwersytetu Łódzkiego, 2005.

20. "Kafka's works enable us to experience the physical malaise of being an outsider experienced by every Prague inhabitant, of being a foreigner in one's own city and the victim of abuse by unapproachable authorities, the swift yet evasive inquisition that hunts, scrutinizes and manipulates." (Angelo Maria Ripellino, *Magic Prague*. Ed. by Michael Henry Heim, translated by David Newton Marinelli. London, Picador, 1995, p. 48.)
21. *Egon Hostovský: Vzpomínky, studie a dokumenty o jeho díle a osudu*. Ed. by Rudolf Šturm. Toronto, Sixty-Eight Publishers, 1974, pp. 31–3.
22. František Hrubín, *Můj zpěv*. Ed. by Jiří Brabec. Prague, Československý spisovatel, 1969, p. 11.
23. Cf. D. E. Viney, Czech Culture and the "New Spirit", 1948–1952. *Slavonic and East European Review*, 31, no. 77 (June 1953), pp. 466–94. Michal Bauer, *Ideologie a paměť: Literatura a instituce na přelomu 40. a 50. let 20. století.* Jinočany, H+H, 2003. Jiří Knapík, *Únor a kultura: Sovětizace české kultury 1948–1950*. Prague, Libri, 2004. Jiří Knapík, *V zajetí moci: Kulturní politika, její systém a aktéři 1948–1956*. Prague, Libri, 2006.
24. Jiřina Hauková, *Básně*. Ed. by Michael Špirit. Prague, Torst, 2000, p. 834.
25. *Jak hromady pobitých ptáků*. Ed. by Robert Krumphanzl. Prague, Torst, 1998, p. 277.
26. *Od slov k činům: Sjezd československých spisovatelů 4.-6. března 1949*. Ed. by Oldřich Kryštofek and Jan Noha. Prague, Orbis, 1949, pp. 31, 63.
27. The pivotal show trial was held in Prague in 1952. Fourteen leading Czech Communists, including Rudolf Slánský, the second-highest ranking state official, were imprisoned and tortured into confessing to acts of treason which they had not committed. Eleven of them were executed. Cf. Artur Gerard London, *On Trial* (translated by Alastair Hamilton). London, Macdonald, 1970 (as *The Confession*, New York, Morrow, 1970); filmed by Constantin Costa-Gavras (1970). See also the documentary *A Trial in Prague* (2000), directed by Zuzanna Justman.
28. *Žaluji II: Vrátit slovo umlčeným*. Ed. by Antonín Kratochvil. Prague, Česká expedice, 1991, p. 57.
29. Milan Kundera, *The Unbearable Lightness of Being*. Translated by Michael Henry Heim. London, Faber and Faber, 1999, pp. 171–2.
30. See Heinrich Kunstmann, *Tschechische Erzählkunst im 20. Jahrhundert*. Köln, Böhlau, 1974, pp. 69–71.
31. Vlastimil Školaudy, *Hlas doby*. Prague, Československý spisovatel, 1950, p. 41.
32. Josef Kainar, *Vybrané spisy II*. Ed. by Miloš Pohorský. Prague, Československý spisovatel, 1989, pp. 16–17. See also the anthology *Podivuhodní kouzelníci: Čítanka českého stalinismu v řeči vázané z let 1945–1955*. Ed. and afterword by Antonín Brousek. Purley, Rozmluvy, 1987. Přemysl Blažíček, Poezie 1948–1958 jako výraz oficiální ideologie. In his *Kritika a interpretace*. Ed. and afterword by Michael Špirit. Prague, Triáda, 2002, pp. 146–65.
33. Filmed by Otakar Vávra as *Jan Hus*, 1954.
34. See Přemysl Blažíček, Básníci avantgardy v poúnorových letech. In his *Kritika a interpretace*. Ed. and afterword by Michael Špirit. Prague, Triáda, 2002, pp. 126–45.
35. Filmed by Jiří Sequens in 1973.
36. About Zdeněk Němeček see Beatrice M. Nosko, Zdeněk Němeček. Poet of Czech Emigrants. *The Slavic and East European Journal*, 17 (New Series 3), no. 1 (Spring

1959), pp. 43–6. *Zdeněk Němeček.* Ed. by Ivan Herben. New York, NY, Moravian Library, 1958. Also Vladimír Papoušek, *Trojí samota ve velké zemi: Česká literatura v americkém exilu v letech 1938–1968.* Jinočany, H+H, 2001, pp. 85–126. *Legionář, diplomat a spisovatel Zdeněk Němeček.* Jaroměř, Městské muzeum, 2002.

37. Petr Den, Země bez dialogů. *Sklizeň* (Hamburg), 6 (1958), no. 5, p. 11.
38. Zdeněk Rotrekl, *Spisy I: Nezděné město.* Ed. by Jana Uhdeová. Brno, Atlantis, 2001, pp. 139–79.
39. Vladimír Holan, *Lamento.* Ed. by Vladimír Justl. Prague, Odeon, 1970, p. 81.
40. Vladimír Holan, *Selected Poems.* Translated by Jarmila and Ian Milner. Harmondsworth, Penguin Books, 1971, p. 55.
41. Bohuslav Reynek, *Podzimní motýli, Sníh na zápraží, Mráz v okně.* Ed. by Ivan Diviš. Afterword by Jaroslav Med. Hradec Králové, Kruh, 1969. Reynek's last collection, *Odlet vlaštovek* (The Migration of Swallows), written at the end of the 1960s, was published in samizdat in 1975 and in Munich in 1980. A complete edition of Reynek's poetry, prepared for publication by Josef Hradec (Josef Mlejnek), was brought out in Purley in 1985 and 1986. A critical edition *Básnické spisy* (Poetical Works) was edited by Milada Chlíbcová, afterword by Mojmír Trávníček. Zlín, Archa, 1995. In English *Fish Scales.* Translated by Kelly Miller and Zdenka Brodska. Ann Arbor, Michigan Slavic Publications, 2001. Some poems were also translated by Alfred Thomas in *Scottish Slavonic Review*, 11 (Autumn 1988), pp. 118–21.
42. Jiří Kolář, *Prométheova játra.* Ed. by Vladimír Karfík. Prague, Paseka, 2000, p. 57.
43. Vladimír Vokolek, *Tak pravil Švejk.* Prague, Mladá fronta, 1995, pp. 21–2.
44. Egon Bondy's poems appeared in nine volumes. Bondy, Egon, *Básnické dílo I–IX.* Ed. by Martin Machovec. Prague, Pražská imaginace, 1990–1993. Excerpts from Bondy's novels appeared in English in *Yazzyk Magazine*, 1 (Prague 1992) and *Yazzyk Magazine*, 4 (Prague 1995).
45. See Gertraude Zand, *Totaler Realismus und Peinliche Poesie: Tschechische Untergrund-Literatur 1948–1953.* Frankfurt a. M., Peter Lang, 1998. In Czech *Totální realismus a trapná poezie: Česká neoficiální literatura 1948–1953.* Brno, Host, 2002. Also Egon Bondy, The Roots of the Czech Literary Underground in 1949–1953. In *Views from the Inside: Czech Underground Literature and Culture.* Ed. by Martin Machovec. Prague, Ústav české literatury a literární vědy, 2006, pp. 49–58.
46. Bohumil Hrabal, *Jarmilka.* Ed. by Karel Dostál and Václav Kadlec. Prague, Pražská imaginace, 1992, p. 88.
47. Bohumil Hrabal, *Pábitelé.* Prague, Mladá fronta, 1964, p. 7.
48. *Život je všude: Almanach z roku 1956.* Ed. by Kateřina Ondřejová and Stanislav Wimmer. Afterword by Michael Špirit. Prague and Litomyšl, Paseka, 2005.
49. Cf. *Český surrealismus: 1929–1953.* Ed. by Lenka Bydžovská and Karel Srp. Prague, Argo, 1996.
50. Karel Hynek, *S vyloučením veřejnosti.* Preface by Vratislav Effenberger (pp. 9–77). Ed. by Jan Šulc and Alena Nádvorníková. Prague, Torst, 1998.
51. Zbyněk Havlíček, *Otevřít po mé smrti.* Ed. and afterword by Jiří Brabec. Prague, Český spisovatel, 1994. The essays and articles of Zbyněk Havlíček were published in *Skutečnost snu.* Ed. and afterword by Stanislav Dvorský. Prague, Torst, 2003.
52. His studies came out in Vratislav Effenberger, *Realita a poesie: K vývojové dialektice moderního umění.* Afterword by Květoslav Chvatík. Prague, Mladá fronta, 1969.
53. Pavel Kohout, *Čas lásky a boje.* Prague, Mladá fronta, 1954, p. 87.
54. See *Z dějin českého myšlení o literatuře II: 1948–1958.* Ed. by Michal Přibáň. Prague, ÚČL AVČR, 2002, pp. 177–215.

55. *Měsíc nad řekou* (1953), *Stříbrný vítr* (filmed 1954, premiere 1956).
56. *Literární noviny*, 5 (1956), no. 18, p. 10.
57. See the anthology *Z dějin českého myšlení o literatuře II: 1948–1958*. Ed. by Michal Přibáň. Prague, ÚČL AVČR, 2002, pp. 417–68.
58. Dominik Tatarka, *Démon súhlasu*. Bratislava, Slovenský spisovateľ, 1963, p. 68. Excerpts from Tatarka's fiction were published as *The Demon of Conformism* (translated by Peter Petro) in *Cross Currents*, 6 (1987), pp. 285–97.
59. Jan Grossman, *Analýzy*. Ed. by Jiří Holý and Terezie Pokorná. Prague, Československý spisovatel, 1991, pp. 14–15.
60. Ivan Sviták, Filosofie a život. *Literární noviny*, 5 (1956), no. 52, p. 3.
61. Karel Kosík, Přeludy socialismu. *Literární noviny*, 5 (1956), no. 11, p. 6.
62. Ladislav Štoll, *Literatura a kulturní revoluce*. Prague, Československý spisovatel, 1959. Also in part in *Z dějin českého myšlení o literatuře III: 1958–1969*. Ed. by Michal Přibáň. Prague, ÚČL AVČR, 2003, pp. 7–39.
63. On *Laterna magika*, cf. Jarka M. Burian, Laterna magika as a Synthesis of Theatre and Film. *Theatre History Studies*, 17 (1997), pp. 33–62.
64. The following texts have been published in English: *Blue Sky* (illustrated by Josef Čapek, translated by Iris Urwin), *Butterfly Moments* (illustrated by Max Švabinský, translated by Daphne Rusbridge), *The Enchanted Forest* (illustrated by Jiří Trnka, translated by Daphne Rusbridge), *Let's Tell a Fairy Tale* (illustrated by Jiří Trnka, translated by Daphne Rusbridge), *Let's Tell a Tale Together* (illustrated by Jiří Trnka, translated by Daphne Rusbridge) – all in Prague in 1954. *Primrose and the Winter Witch* (illustrated by Jiří Trnka, translated by James Reeves) was published in London and Prague in 1964.
65. On this poem, cf. *Pět na jednoho: Interpretační symposion nad Mikuláškovým Vyvolavačem*. Ed. by Jiří Trávníček. Jinočany, H+H, 1995.
66. Jan Skácel, *Básně I*. Ed. by Jiří Opelík. Brno, Blok, 1995, p. 51.
67. Jan Skácel, *Banned Man: Selected Poems*. Ed. by Peter Milcak. Translated by Ewald Osers. Mississauga (Canada), Modry Peter Publishers, p. 7.
68. Jan Skácel, *Básně I*. Ed. by Jiří Opelík. Brno, Blok, 1995, p. 67.
69. František Halas, *Básně*. Ed. by Jan Grossman and Vladimír Justl. Preface by Jan Grossman (pp. 7–52).
70. See also in the anthology *Z dějin českého myšlení o literatuře II:* 1948–1958. Ed. by Michal Přibáň. Prague, ÚČL AVČR, 2002, pp. 537–81. See Paul I. Trensky, The Květen Generation in Perspective. *The Slavic and East European Journal*, 16 (1972), no. 4, pp. 414–26. *Časopis Květen a jeho doba* (ed. by Bohumil Svozil). Prague and Opava, ÚČL, 1994. Přemysl Blažíček, Poezie všedního dne, skupina Května 1956–1958. In his *Kritika a interpretace*. Ed. and afterword by Michael Špirit. Prague, Triáda, 2002, pp. 166–83.
71. Miroslav Holub, *Spisy I: Básně*. Ed. by Michal Huvar. Brumovice, Carpe diem, 2003, p. 42.
72. Miroslav Holub, *Selected Poems*. Translated by Ian Milner and George Theiner. Harmondsworth and Baltimore, MD, Penguin Books, 1967, p. 25.
73. Jiří Šotola, *Svět náš vezdejší*. Prague, Mladá fronta, 1957, p. 55.
74. Josef Vohryzek, *Literární kritiky*. Ed. by Jan Lopatka and Michael Špirit. Prague, Torst, 1995, p. 72.
75. Filmed by Jiří Weiss, 1959.
76. František Langer, *Tři hry o spravedlnosti: Periferie, Andělé mezi námi,*

Dvaasedmdesátka. Preface by Vítězslav Nezval. Prague, Československý spisovatel, 1957.

77. About the Czech theatre of these times see Jarka M. Burian, The Dark Era of Modern Czech Theatre, 1948–1958. *Theatre History Studies*, 15 (1995), pp. 44–53. Also his *Modern Czech Theatre*, University of Iowa City, Iowa City, IO, 2000.
78. Vratislav Blažek, *Příliš štědrý večer*. Prague, Orbis, 1961, p. 60. On Vratislav Blažek, cf. Marie Valtrová, *Vratislav Blažek: Hráč před Bohem a lidmi*. Prague, Achát, 1998.
79. On Alfréd Radok, cf. Antonín J. Liehm, Alfred Radok. *International Journal of Politics*, 3, no. 1–2 (Spring–Summer 1973), pp. 23–38. Zdeněk Hedvábný, *Alfréd Radok: Zpráva o jednom osudu*. Prague, Divadelní ústav, 1994. Jarka M. Burian, *Leading Creators of Twentieth-Century Czech Theatre*. London and New York, Routledge, 2002, pp. 59–76.
80. Josef Hiršal and Bohumila Grögerová, *Let let II*. Prague, Mladá fronta, 1994, pp. 13–14.
81. Filmed by Otakar Vávra, 1958; another version was made by Ladislav Helge in 1961.
82. Josef Škvorecký, *The Cowards*. Translated by Jeanne Němcová. London, Victor Gollancz, and New York, NY, Grove Press, 1970, p. 413.
83. See Michael Špirit, Komentář. In: Josef Škvorecký, *Zbabělci*. Prague, NLN, 1998, pp. 452–68. Also in *Z dějin českého myšlení o literatuře III: 1958–1969*. Ed. by Michal Přibáň. Prague, ÚČL AVČR, 2003, pp. 41–64.
84. On Czech historical fiction of the 1940s and 1950s, cf. Walter Schamschula, The Contemporary Czech Historical Novel and Its Political Inspiration. In: *East European Literature*, ed. by Evelyn Bristol, Berkeley, CA, Berkeley Slavic Specialities, 1982, pp. 57–68. Also Walter Schamschula, *Geschichte der tschechischen Literatur III*. Köln et al., Böhlau, 2004, pp. 360–7.
85. Valja Stýblová's later novel *Skalpel, prosím* (1981), filmed by Jiří Svoboda, 1985, was published in English as *Scalpel, Please*. Translated by John Newton. Prague, Orbis, 1985.
86. See also a volume of Aškenazy's work, *One Round World*, 1963.
87. See a volume of Nesvadba's work in English, *In the Footsteps of the Abominable Snowman*, 1970.
88. Filmed by Václav Vorlíček, 1964.
89. Alexandr Kliment, *Marie*. Prague, Československý spisovatel, 1963, p. 106.
90. Aleš Haman, *Arnošt Lustig*. Jinočany, H+H, 1995, p. 10.

The Sixties

1. S Jiřím Voskovcem o čemkoliv. Zaznamenal Antonín Jaroslav Liehm. *Listy* (Roma), 5 (1975), no. 5, p. 7. Also in *Když se řekne Werich a když se řekne Voskovec*. Ed. by Jiří Lederer. Prague, Orbis, 1990, p. 221.
2. On the sixties in Czech literature cf. *Zlatá šedesátá: Česká literatura a společnost v letech tání, kolotání a . . . zklamání*. Ed. by Radka Denemarková. Prague, ÚČL AV, 2000.
3. See *Slovník českých literárních časopisů, periodických literárních sborníků a almanachů 1945–2000*. Ed. by Blahoslav Dokoupil. Brno, Votobia, 2002.
4. http//www.hutka.cz/new/html/ge01.htm (accessed on 24 May 2007).
5. *Rezoluce XIII. sjezdu KSČ k naléhavým otázkám dalšího rozvoje socialistické kultury*. Prague, ÚV KSČ, 1967, pp. 9, 11.
6. Jiří Trnka's illustrations of classical fairy-tales came out also in Britain: Hans Christian

Andersen, *Fairy Tales*. London, Hamlyn, 1959. Jakob Grimm and Wilhelm Grimm, *Grimm's Fairy Tales*. London, Hamlyn, 1961.

7. There is an English language publication *A Midsummer Night's Dream*. Photographs show scenes from Jiří Trnka's puppet film version of Shakespeare's play. Retold for children by Eduard Petiška. Translated into English by Jean Layton. Prague, Artia, 1960.
8. Pavel Tigrid et al., Československo a jeho lid. *Svědectví* (Paris), 4 (1961), no. 13, p. 65.
9. See also the papers of Ladislav Novomeský and Ladislav Mňačko and the reply of Ladislav Štoll at the 3rd Congress of Czechoslovak Writers' Union in the spring of 1963. *Třetí sjezd Svazu československých spisovatelů: Protokol.* Prague, Československý spisovatel, 1963, pp. 119, 138, 185–8. The arguments concerning František Halas are presented in Michael Bauer, *Tíseň tmy aneb Halasovské interpretace po roce 1948*. Prague, Akropolis, 2005.
10. *Třetí sjezd Svazu československých spisovatelů: Protokol.* Prague, Československý spisovatel, 1963, pp. 6, 115.
11. Cf. the review Some Recent Czech Memoirs by Bohuslava R. Bradbrook. *Slavonic and East European Review*, 44 (1966), no. 103, pp. 486–90.
12. Milan Kundera disowns the work today; he has tried to negate its existence by publishing a new volume of literary essays *L'art du roman* (1986; published in English as *The Art of the Novel*, 1988).
13. The collection of studies on the Czech avant-garde by Oleg Sus, *Estetické problémy pod napětím: Meziválečná avantgarda, surrealismus, levice*, was banned in 1970 and was only published posthumously in 1992.
14. Květoslav Chvatík, K diskusi o vývoji naší socialistické literatury. *Česká literatura*, 11 (1963), no. 6, p. 490. Cf. also Květoslav Chvatík, *Strukturalismus a avantgarda*. Prague, Československý spisovatel, 1970. In German *Strukturalismus und Avantgarde*. München, C. Hanser, 1970.
15. Karel Teige, *Výbor z díla I: Svět stavby a básně.* Preface by Robert Kalivoda. Ed. and comm. by Jiří Brabec and Vratislav Effenberger. Afterword by Vratislav Effenberger. Prague, Československý spisovatel, 1966. Karel Teige, *Výbor z díla II: Zápasy o smysl moderní tvorby*. Ed. and comm. by Jiří Brabec and Vratislav Effenberger. Afterword by Vratislav Effenberger. Prague, Československý spisovatel, 1969. Volume III, *Osvobozování života a poezie*, had to wait till 1994 (Prague, Aurora).
16. *Surrealistické východisko 1938–1968.* Ed. and intr. by Stanislav Dvorský, Vratislav Effenberger and Petr Král. Prague, Československý spisovatel, 1969.
17. Zbyněk Hejda, K tématu avantgarda a ideologie. *Podoby II*. Ed. by Václav Havel. Prague, Československý spisovatel, 1969, p. 143. Also in *Tvář: Výbor z časopisu* (ed. and afterword by Michael Špirit). Prague, Torst, 1995, p. 208.
18. *Franz Kafka: Liblická vědecká konference.* Prague, ČSAV, 1963. In German *Franz Kafka aus Prager Sicht 1963.* Ed. by Eduard Goldstücker, František Kautman and Paul Reiman. Afterword by Paul Reiman. Prague, Academia, and Berlin, Voltaire Verlag, 1965. Alfred Kurella, Eduard Goldstücker and Roger Garaudy, Kafka a pražské jaro. In: *Pro a proti: Kritická ročenka 63.* Ed. by Jaroslav Opavský, Zdeněk Pešat and Milan Suchomel. Prague, Československý spisovatel, 1964, pp. 180–96. See also Alexej Kusák, *Tance kolem Kafky: Liblická konference 1963.* Prague, Akropolis, 2003.
19. Ladislav Radimský, Kafka opět v Praze. *Perspektivy* (New York), 6 (1963), p. 1.
20. Přemysl Blažíček, Katedrová věda. *Tvář*, 1 (1965), no. 5, pp. 6–9. Also in Přemysl

Blažíček, *Kritika a interpretace.* Ed. and afterword by Michael Špirit. Prague, Triáda, 2002, pp. 291–300.

21. See *Z dějin českého myšlení o literatuře III: 1958–1969.* Ed. by Michal Přibáň. Prague, ÚČL AVČR, 2003, pp. 65–101.
22. Josef Jedlička, Neschopnost ke svobodě. *Host do domu*, 11 (1964), no. 2, p. 24.
23. Antonín Jaroslav Liehm, *The Politics of Culture.* Translated by Peter Kussi. Intr. by Jean-Paul Sartre. New York, NY, Grove Press, 1970, p. 399.
24. *České slovo* (Munich), 11 (1965), no. 9, p. 1.
25. Ladislav Štoll, Literatura a kulturní revoluce. In: *Z dějin českého myšlení o literatuře III: 1958–1969.* Ed. by Michal Přibáň. Prague, ÚČL AVČR, 2003, p. 35.
26. Oldřich Mikulášek, *Verše III.* Ed. by Jiří Kudrnáč and Zdeněk Drahoš. Prague, Ivo Železný, 1999, p. 24.
27. Vladimír Holan, *Nokturnál.* Ed. by V. Justl. Prague, Odeon, 1980, p. 157.
28. Wine harvest.
29. Vladimír Holan, *A Night with Hamlet.* Translated by Jarmila and Ian Milner. Prague, Academia, 1999, p. 46.
30. Holan, *A Night with Hamlet*, p. 11.
31. See catalogues of exhibitions as *Jiří Kolář: The Visual Images of a Poet*, London, 1963; *Jiří Kolář: Tranformations*, Buffalo, 1978, and others.
32. For an outline of Czech poetry of the 1960s, see Vladimír Karfík, The Face of Contemporary Czech Poetry. *Books Abroad*, 44 (1970), no. 3, pp. 411–15.
33. František Hrubín, *Můj zpěv.* Ed. by Jiří Brabec. Prague, Československý spisovatel, 1969, p. 178.
34. František Hrubín, *Černá denice, Lešanské jesličky.* Prague, Ivo Železný, 1998, p. 49.
35. Cf. Přemysl Blažíček, Generace Května v šedesátých letech. In his *Kritika a interpretace.* Ed. and afterword by Michael Špirit. Prague, Triáda, 2002, pp. 184–96.
36. Miroslav Holub, *Spisy I: Básně.* Ed. by Michal Huvar. Brumovice, Carpe diem, 2003, p. 349.
37. Miroslav Holub, *Poems Before and After.* Translated by Ian and Jarmila Milner, Ewald Osers and George Theiner. Newcastle upon Tyne, Bloodaxe Books, 1990, p. 129.
38. Jaroslav Seifert, *Koncert na ostrově, Halleyova kometa, Odlévání zvonů.* Ed. by Jiří Flaišman. Prague, Akropolis, 2004, p. 78.
39. Seifert, *Koncert na ostrově*, p. 104.
40. On Christian poets, cf. Jaroslav Med, *Spisovatelé ve stínu.* 2nd ed. Prague, Portál, 2004.
41. Ivan Slavík, *Básnické dílo II.* Brno, Host, 1999, p. 21.
42. On Fried see Robert B. Pynsent, Uncertainty and Jiří Fried. *Cambridge Review*, 89A (1968), pp. 402–5.
43. Filmed by Antonín Kachlík, 1963.
44. Excerpts from *Svatá noc* appeared in English in *Universum: A Review of Czechoslovak Literature and Arts*, 4 (1969), no. 7, pp. 62–71.
45. Milan Suchomel, *Literatura z času krize.* Brno, Atlantis, 1992, p. 12.
46. See Avigdor Dagan (Viktor Fischl), Jewish Themes in Czech Literature. In: *The Jews of Czechoslovakia.* Vol. II. Philadelphia, Jewish Publication Society of America and New York, NY, Society for History of Czechoslovak Jews, 1971, pp. 456–67.
47. Excerpts from *Obchod na korze* were published in English in *Universum: A Review of Czechoslovak Literature and Arts*, 2 (1967), no. 3, pp. 11–21.

48. "... an endless monologue, an entertaining, bubbly chat, a web of memories from the time of the Dual Monarchy, bombastic phrases, wild references to pious parables and dream books, erotic anecdotes, tall tales and tittle-tattle – a stream of chatter constantly shifting between subtle deceit and simplemindedness on parade" (Angelo Maria Ripellino, *Magic Prague*. Ed. by Michael Henry Heim, translated by David Newton Marinelli. London, Picador, 1995, p. 219).
49. Bohumil Hrabal, *Dancing Lessons for the Advanced in Age*. Translated by Michael Henry Heim. London, Harvill, 1998, p. 17.
50. Bohumil Hrabal, *Kafkárna*. Ed. by Karel Dostál, Claudio Poeta and Václav Kadlec. Prague, Pražská imaginace, 1994, pp. 155, 169.
51. For an outline of Czech prose writing of the second half of the sixties see Vladimír Karfík, Recent Czech Prose. *Books Abroad*, 43 (1969), no. 3, pp. 224–33. Thomas G. Winner, Czech Avant-garde Prose of the Sixties. *Mosaic: A Journal for the Comparative Study of Literature and Ideas*, 6, no. 4 (Summer 1973), pp. 107–19.
52. František Hrubín, *Zlatá reneta*. Prague, Československý spisovatel, 1964, p. 9.
53. Excerpts from *Smrtelná neděle* appeared in English in *Universum: A Review of Czechoslovak Literature and Arts*, 4 (1969), no. 7, pp. 20–30.
54. Ludvík Vaculík, *Sekyra*. Ed. by Jitka Uhdeová. Brno, Atlantis, 2003, pp. 7, 70. Ludvík Vaculík, *The Axe*. Translated by Marian Sling. Evanston, IL, Northwestern University Press, 1994, pp. 10, 91.
55. Milan Kundera, *Laughable Loves*. Translated by Suzanne Rappaport. London, Faber & Faber, 1991, p. 25.
56. Milan Kundera, *Směšné lásky*. Prague, Československý spisovatel, 1963, pp. 21–2.
57. Filmed by Josef Mach, 1976.
58. Excerpts in English from *Tovaryšstvo Ježíšovo* appeared in *Universum: A Review of Czechoslovak Literature and Arts*, 5 (1970), no. 8, pp. 4–17.
59. Jiří Šotola, *Tovaryšstvo Ježíšovo*. Prague, Československý spisovatel, 1990, p. 313.
60. Ludvík Vaculík, Doslov. In: Ota Filip, *Cesta k hřbitovu*. Ostrava, Profil, 1990, p. 355.
61. Excerpts from *Trampoty pana Humbla* appeared in English in *Universum: A Review of Czechoslovak Literature and Arts*, 4 (1969), no. 6, pp. 47–63.
62. Vladimír Neff, *Trampoty pana Humbla*. Prague, Československý spisovatel, 1967, p. 325.
63. On this literature see Jan Lukeš, *Stalinské spirituály: Zkušenost politických vězňů 50. let v české próze*. Prague, Český spisovatel, 1995.
64. On Pecka see Irena Zítková, Karel Pecka. Review and Excerpts, in *Universum: A Review of Czechoslovak Literature and Arts*, 5 (1970), no. 8, pp. 51–61. A conversation of Karel Pecka and Jan Lukeš was published in book form as *Hry doopravdy: Rozhovor se spisovatelem Karlem Peckou*. Prague and Litomyšl, Paseka, 1998.
65. Studies dedicated to the memory of Felix Vodička came out in the volume entitled *The Structure of the Literary Process*. Ed. by Peter Steiner, Miroslav Červenka and Ronald Vroon. Amsterdam, J. Benjamins, 1982.
66. Roman Jakobson, *Poetická funkce*. Ed. by Miroslav Červenka. Jinočany, H+H, 1995, p. 17.
67. On Czech structuralism cf. *Semiotics of Art: Prague School Contributions*. Ed. by Ladislav Matejka and Irwin R. Titunic. Cambridge, MA, and London, MIT, 1976. *The Prague School: Selected Writings*. Ed. by Peter Steiner. Austin, University of Texas Press, 1982. *Jan Mukařovský and the Prague School/Jan Mukařovský und die Prager Schule*. Ed. by Vladimír Macura and Herta Schmid. Prague, ÚČL, 1999.

68. Miroslav Červenka, Zdroje tvořivosti. *Orientace*, 1 (1966), no. 1, p. 19. Also in his *Obléhání zevnitř*. Prague, Torst, 1996, p. 328.
69. Jan Patočka, *Umění a čas I*. Ed. by Daniel Vojtěch and Ivan Chvatík. Prague, Oikoymenh, 2004, p. 314.
70. On the New Wave of Czech and Slovak cinema cf. Josef Škvorecký, *All the Bright Young Men and Women: A Personal History of the Czech Cinema*. Translated by Michael Schonberg. Toronto, Peter P. Martin Associates, 1971. Antonín J. Liehm, *Closely Watched Films: The Czechoslovak Experience*. White Plains, NY, International Arts and Sciences Press, 1974. Peter Hames, *The Czechoslovak New Wave*. Berkeley, University of California Press, 1985.
71. *Generace 1935–1945*. Ed. by Karel Hvížďala. Munich, Arkýř, 1986, p. 22.
72. Petr Kabeš, *Čáry na dlani*. Prague, Mladá fronta, 1961, p. 8.
73. Jiří Gruša, Realismus jako mravnost. In: *Z dějin českého myšlení o literatuře III: 1958–1969*. Ed. by Michal Přibáň. Prague, ÚČL AVČR, 2003, pp. 273–6.
74. *Z dějin českého myšlení o literatuře III: 1958–1969*. Ed. by Michal Přibáň. Prague, ÚČL AVČR, 2003, pp. 194–205.
75. Tvář Tváře. *Tvář*, 1 (1964), no. 1, p. 3.
76. Examples of these essays have been published in English in *Universum: A Review of Czechoslovak Literature and Arts*, 4 (1969) no. 6, pp. 47–63.
77. See *Tvář: Výbor z časopisu*. Ed. by Michael Špirit. Prague, Torst, 1995.
78. Josef Hanzlík, *Lampa*. Prague, Československý spisovatel, 1988, pp. 86–7. In English see the collection of Hanzlík's work, *Selected Poems*. Translated by Ewald Osers, Jarmila Milner and Ian Milner. Foreword by Graham Martin. Newcastle upon Tyne, Bloodaxe Books, 1993.
79. Ivan Wernisch, *Dutý břeh*. Prague, Mladá fronta, 1967, p. 16.
80. Jiří Gruša, *Právo útrpné*. Ed. by Jiří Tomáš. Prague, Akropolis, 2003, p. 134.
81. Antonín Brousek, *Netrpělivost*. 2nd edition. Prague, Československý spisovatel, 1968, p. 33.
82. Zbyněk Hejda, *Básně*. Ed. by Vratislav Färber and Antonín Petruželka. Prague, Torst, 1996, p. 85.
83. In English see the collection of Hejda's work, *A Stay in a Sanatorium and Other Poems*. Translated by Bernard O'Donoghue. Cork, Southword Edition, 2005.
84. Zbyněk Hejda, *Básně*. Ed. by Vratislav Färber and Antonín Petruželka. Prague, Torst, 1996, p. 198.
85. Special shops with Western luxury goods for the privileged under Communism.
86. Václav Hrabě, *Blues*. Ed. by Jan Miškovský. Prague, Labyrint, 1995, p. 29.
87. See Jindřich Černý, Czech Drama in the Sixties. *Universum: A Review of Czechoslovak Literature and Arts*, 5 (1970), no. 8, pp. 76–80. Jarka M. Burian, Art and Relevance. The Small Theatres of Prague 1958–1970. *Educational Theatre Journal*, 23 (1971), no. 3, pp. 229–57. Also his *Modern Czech Theatre*. Iowa City, IO, University of Iowa City, 2000, pp. 117–36.
88. Ivan Vyskočil, Meziřeči. *Divadlo*, 17 (1966), no. 8, pp. 82–3.
89. A complete edition of Suchý's work, prepared for publication by Václav Kadlec, came out as *Encyklopedie Jiřího Suchého* in Prague, Pražská imaginace and Karolinum, *Básně* (1999), *Povídky* (1999), *Písničky* (5 volumes, 2000–2001), *Divadlo* (8 volumes, 2001–2004), *Film* (2 volumes, 2004), *Rozhlas* (2005), *Úvahy* (2005), *Televize* (2005).
90. Milan Uhde, *Desítka her*. Brno, Atlantis, 1995, p. 31.
91. On absurd drama see Martin Esslin, *Theatre of the Absurd*. 3rd edition, London,

Methuen, 1974. Petr Den (Ladislav Radimský), Notes on Czechoslovakia's Young Theatre of the Absurd. *Books Abroad*, 41 (1967), no. 2, pp. 157–63. Marketa Goetz-Stankiewicz, A Revealing Encounter. The Theatre of the Absurd in Czechoslovakia. *A Journal of the East and West Studies*, 21 (1975), no. 1–2, pp. 85–100.

92. Václav Havel, *Selected Plays, 1963–1983*. Translated by Vera Blackwell, Jan Novak and George Theiner. London, Faber & Faber, 1992, pp. 50–1.
93. On Otomar Krejča, cf. Jarka M. Burian, *Leading Creators of Twentieth-Century Czech Theatre*. London and New York, NY, Routledge, 2002, pp. 77–96.
94. Published in English as *Cat on the Rails*. Translated by George and Christine Voskovec. In *Czech Plays*. Ed. by Barbara Day. London, Nick Hern Books, 1994, pp. 95–138.
95. The short story *Kokeš* was translated by George Theiner as *Purvis* in *New Writing in Czechoslovakia*. Ed. by George Theiner. Harmondsworth, Penguin, 1969, pp. 145–57.
96. Karel Michal, *Soubor díla*. Ed. by Milena Masáková. Prague, Nakladatelství Lidové noviny, 2001, p. 193.
97. Michal, *Soubor díla*, p. 189.
98. Karol Sidon, *Sen o mém otci, Sen o mně*. Prague, Mladá fronta, 1992, p. 283.
99. Vladimír Merta, *Narozen v Čechách . . .* Ed. by Stanislav Zárybnický-Houla. Prague, ARTeM, 1992, p. 80.
100. Effenberger's essay The Raw Cruelty of Life and the Cynicism of Fantasy was published in *Cross Currents*, 6 (1987), pp. 437–44.
101. Emanuel Frynta, *Písničky bez muziky*. Prague, Albatros, 1988, p. 70.
102. Frynta's short story Paradoxical Twins was published in an English translation by Jean Layton in *Universum: A Review of Czechoslovak Literature and Arts*, 1 (1966), no. 2, pp. 37–53.
103. Emanuel Frynta, *Zastřená tvář poezie*. Ed. by Jiří Honzík. Afterword by Ivan Vyskočil. Prague, Nakladatelství Franze Kafky, 1993, p. 133.
104. Miroslav Topinka, *Krysí hnízdo*. Prague, Mladá fronta, 1991, p. 80.
105. Věra Linhartová, *Ianus tří tváří*. Prague, Český spisovatel, 1993, p. 6.
106. Jiří Stanislav Guth-Jarkovský, author of Czech handbooks on polite deportment.
107. Jan Hanč, *Události*. Ed. by Jan Lopatka and Michael Špirit. Prague, Torst, 1995, pp. 240–1.
108. Vladimír Páral, *Catapult*. Translated by William Harkins. North Haven, CT, Catbird Press, 1992, pp. 7, 166.
109. Věra Linhartová, *Meziprůzkum nejblíž uplynulého*. České Budějovice, Krajské nakladatelství, 1964, p. 59.
110. Ivan Vyskočil, *Kosti*. Prague, Mladá fronta, 1993, pp. 12–13. The following works by Ivan Vyskočil have been published in English: Why, It's Easy to Fly! in *Universum: A Review of Czechoslovak Literature and Arts*, 2 (1967), no. 3, pp. 27–38; Jakob's Well (translated by Růžena Kavanová) in *Stand*, 10 (1969), no. 2, pp. 54–6; The Incredible Rise of Albert Uruk (translated by George Theiner) in *New Writing in Czechoslovakia* (ed. by George Theiner). Baltimore and Harmondsworth, Penguin, 1969, pp. 223–39. The Vyskočil book interview with Přemysl Rut came out as *Vždyť přece létat je o hubu*. Prague, Portál, 2000.
111. Wide-ranging literature on the "Prague Spring" in English → see BIBLIOGRAPHY.
112. *Vyznání příběhovosti*. Brno, Petrov, 2000, p. 51.
113. *Mluví k vám Ferdinand Peroutka: Rozhlasové komentáře, Rádio Svobodná Evropa*

II. Ed. by Zuzana Fialová. Epilogue by Milan Schulz. Prague, Argo, 2005, page 347.

114. Cf. Dušan Hamšík, *Spisovatelé a moc*. Prague, Československý spisovatel, 1969. In English *Writers against Rulers*. Translated by D. Orpington. Intro. by William Leslie Webb. London, Hutchinson, and New York, NY, Vintage Books, 1971. Also Karel Kaplan, *"Všechno jste prohráli!"* Prague, Ivo Železný, 1997.
115. *Protokol IV. sjezdu Svazu československých spisovatelů*. Prague, Dilia, 1968, p. 16.
116. *Protokol IV. sjezdu Svazu československých spisovatelů*, pp. 16–17.
117. *Protokol IV. sjezdu Svazu československých spisovatelů*, p. 184.
118. See The Action Programme of the Communist Party of Czechoslovakia, 5 April 1968. *Spokesman Pamphlet*, 1 (Nottingham 1970), no. 8.
119. Ivan Sviták left Czechoslovakia for the USA after the Warsaw Pact invasion of 1968. His articles on art and film came out in English as *Man and His World*. New York, NY, 1970. Art *in the Manipulated World: Essays from Prague, 1963–1967*. Chico, CA, 1977. *Film in the Manipulated World. Reviews from Prague, 1963–1967*. Chico, CA, 1977.
120. Ladislav Hejdánek, Kultura tváří v tvář politice. *Tvář*, 3 (1968), no. 2, p. 12. Also in *Tvář: Výbor z časopisu*. Ed. by Michael Špirit. Prague, Torst, 1995, pp. 320–1.
121. Petr Pithart, *Osmašedesátý*. Prague, Rozmluvy 1990, p. 292.
122. Karel Kryl, *Texty písní*. Ed. by Jan Šulc and Jana Jiskrová. Prague, Torst, 1998, p. 112.
123. A high hill where there is a TV transmitter.
124. Václav Havel, *Disturbing the Peace: A Conversation with Karel Hvížďala*. Translated by Paul Wilson. London, Faber & Faber, 1990, pp. 106–8.
125. Josef Kainar, *Vybrané spisy III*. Ed. by Miloš Pohorský. Prague, Československý spisovatel, 1990, p. 249.
126. On Palach see Jiří Lederer, *Jan Palach*. Prague, Novinář, 1990 (in German *Jan Palach*. Zürich, Unionsverlag, 1982).
127. Milan Kundera, Český úděl. *Listy*, 1 (1968), no. 7–8, pp. 1, 5.
128. Václav Havel, Český úděl? *Tvář*, 4 (1969), no. 2, pp. 30–3. Also in his *Eseje a jiné texty z let 1951–1969*. Ed. by Jan Šulc. Prague, Torst, 1999, pp. 888–97.
129. *Ustavující sjezd Svazu českých spisovatelů*. Prague, Svoboda, 1972, p. 36.

The Seventies and Eighties

1. Čehona is the protagonist of the story *Můj přítel Čehona* (1926) by Viktor Dyk, an early 20th-century poet of irony and disillusionment. The name comes from altering a line in the Czech version of the Austrian national anthem "Čeho nabyl občan pilný" (What a diligent citizen has acquired) to "Čehona byl občan pilný" (Čehona was a diligent citizen).
2. *Magic Prague*. Ed. by Michael Henry Heim, translated by David Newton Marinelli. London, Picador, 1995, p. 279.
3. See Ivan Binar, On the Usefulness of Literature in Maintaining Mental Health. In *Literatura, vězení, exil / Literature, Prison, Exile*. Ed. by Miloš Vacík and Libuše Ludvíková. Prague, České centrum Mezinárodního PEN klubu, 1997, p. 75 ff.
4. Bohumil Hrabal, *Too Loud a Solitude*. Translated by Michael Henry Heim. London, Abacus, 2001, p. 22.
5. Milan Šimečka, *Obnovení pořádku*. Brno, Atlantis, p. 71. (In English *The Restoration of Order*. Translated by A. G. Brain [Alice and Gerald Turner]. Preface by Zdeněk Mlynář. London, Verso, 1984.)

6. http//www.hutka.cz/new/html/texty2.html (accessed on 24 May 2007).
7. Václav Havel, *Temptation*. Translated by Marie Winn. New York, Grove Weidenfeld, 1989, p. 59.
8. See *Československo roku 1968 II: Počátky normalizace*. Ed. by Vojtěch Mencl. Prague, Parta, 1993, p. 68.
9. *Ustavující sjezd Svazu českých spisovatelů*. Prague, Svoboda, 1972, p. 21.
10. Cf. Igor Hájek, Precarious Survival. *Formations*, 1, no. 1 (Spring 1984), pp. 114–21.
11. Milan Šimečka, *The Restoration of Order: The Normalization of Czechoslovakia*. Translated by A. G. Brain (Alice and Gerald Turner). London, Verso, 1984, p. 14. Šimečka's *Letters from Prison* was also published in English. Selected and translated by Gerald Turner. Prague, Twisted Spoon Press, 2001.
12. Václav Havel, *Disturbing the Peace: A Conversation with Karel Hvížďala*. Translated by Paul Wilson. London, Faber & Faber, 1990, pp. 183–4.
13. Kozák's short stories *Bílý hřebec* (1975) were published English in Prague in 1980 as *The White Stallion* (translated by Ruth Shepherd and Norah Hronková).
14. Filmed by Jaromil Jireš, 1978.
15. Jan Lopatka, *Předpoklady tvorby*. Prague, Československý spisovatel, 1991, pp. 41–2.
16. Filmed by Jaroslav Papoušek, 1984.
17. Filmed by Magdalena Pivoňková, 1987.
18. Stanislav Vodička, *Tam, kde usínají motýlové*. Afterword by Vladimír Binar. Prague, Vyšehrad, 1978, p. 28.
19. A new edition, prepared by Jan Šulc, came out in Prague 2005 (afterword by Petr Král).
20. On Czech fiction of the 1970s, cf. Igor Hájek, The Rule of the Average. Czech Official Literature in the 1970s. *International Journal*, 33 (1978), no. 33, pp. 702–19. In Czech in: I. H., *Prokletá i požehnaná*. Ed. by Martin Pilař. Praha, Dokořán, 2007, pp. 46–61. Robert B. Pynsent, Assimilation, Childhood and Death, New Czech Fiction Writers of the 1970s. *The Slavonic and East European Review*, 59 (1981), no. 3, pp. 370–84. *Normy normalizace*. Ed. by Jan Wiendl. Prague and Opava, ÚČL AVČR and Slezská univerzita, 1996.
21. Cf. the anthology *The New Czech Poetry (Jaroslav Čejka, Michal Černík, Karel Sýs)*. Translated and intr. by Ewald Osers. Newcastle upon Tyne, Bloodaxe, 1988.
22. The officially published works of Czech literature, especially those by members of the Writers' Union, came out in English in the annual publication *Panorama of Czech Literature* (1980–1988), which was published in Prague.
23. Jiří Šotola, *Vaganten, Puppen und Soldaten*. Luzern and Frankfurt a. M., Bucher, 1972.
24. A 15th-century post-Hussite.
25. A battle in which the mainstream branch of Hussites (the Utraquists) allied themselves with the Catholics and defeated the radical Hussites, led by priest Prokop Holý (1434).
26. Filmed by Jiří Menzel in 2006.
27. Filmed by Jiří Menzel in 1980.
28. Filmed by Věra Caisová in 1994.
29. Bohumil Hrabal, *Kluby poezie*. Afterword by Jaromíra Nejedlá. Prague, Mladá fronta, 1981.
30. Filmed by Karel Kachyňa in 1986.
31. On Ota Pavel see Hana Svobodová, The Death of Beautiful Fish. *Cross Currents*, 2

(1983), pp. 285–90. Bohumil Svozil, *Krajiny života a tvorby Oty Pavla*. Prague, Akropolis, 2003.

32. Oldřich Mikulášek, *Verše IV*. Ed. by Jiří Kudrnáč and Zdeněk Drahoš. Prague, Ivo Železný, 2000, p. 225.
33. Jan Skácel, *Básně II*. Ed. by Jiří Opelík. Brno, Blok, 1996, p. 122.
34. Jan Skácel, *Banned Man: Selected Poems*. Ed. by Peter Milcak. Translated by Ewald Osers. Mississauga, Ontario (Canada), Modry Peter Publishers, p. 66.
35. The publishing houses *Prostor* (Prachatice) and in particular *Atlantis* (Brno) issue *Spisy Ludvíka Kundery* (Collected Works of L. K.), to date 11 volumes. Kundera's poems came out as *Bez názvu: Poezie 1939–1945* (Prachatice, 1994), *Úhledná džungle: Texty 1973–1993* (Prachatice, 1995), *Meandry: Poezie 1945–1969* (Brno, 2000), *Mrznoucí mrholení: Básně 1969–1980* (Brno, 2004).
36. On samizdat see Harold Gordon Skilling, *Samizdat and an Independent Society in Central and Eastern Europe*. Basingstoke, Macmillan, and Columbus, OH, Ohio State University Press, 1989. – *Good-bye, Samizdat: Twenty Years of Czechoslovak Underground Writing*. Ed. by Marketa Goetz-Stankiewicz. Foreword by Timothy Garton Ash. Evanston, IL, Northwestern University Press, 1992. *Piśmiennictwo – systemy kontroli – obiegi alternatywne I–II*. Ed. by Janusz Kostecki and Alina Brodzka. Warszawa, Biblioteka narodowa, 1992. *Im Dissens zur Macht: Samizdat- und Exilliteratur der Länder Ostmittel- und Südosteuropas*. Ed. by Ludwig Richter and Heinrich Olschowsky. Berlin, Akademieverlag, 1995.
37. Ludvík Vaculík, *Český snář*. Brno, Atlantis, 1990, p. 10.
38. Cf. Bronislava Volek and Emil Volek, *Guinea Pigs* and the Czech Novel 'Under Padlock' in the 1970s. *Rocky Mountain: Review of Language and Literature*, 37 (1983), no. 1–2, pp. 20–52.
39. *Charta 77: Od morální k demokratické revoluci*. Ed. by Vilém Prečan. Scheinfeld and Bratislava, Čs. středisko nezávislé literatury, 1990, p. 42. Cf. Harold Gordon Skilling, *Charter 77 and Human Rights in Czechoslovakia*. London, Allen & Unwin, 1981.
40. *Charta 77: Od morální k demokratické revoluci*. Ed. by Vilém Prečan. Scheinfeld and Bratislava, Čs. středisko nezávislé literatury, 1990, p. 75.
41. Texts on "parallel polis" by Václav Benda, Jiří Dienstbier, Václav Havel, Ladislav Hejdánek, Ivan Martin Jirous, Eva Kantůrková, Jan Šimsa, Josef Zvěřina et al., see in *Civic Freedom in Central Europe*. Ed. by Harold Gordon Skilling and Paul Wilson. New York, St. Martin's Press, 1991.
42. Jiří Gruntorád, Edice Popelnice. *Kritický sborník*, 12 (1992), no. 2, p. 67.
43. *Stunde namens Hoffnung: Almanach tschechischer Literatur, 1968–1978*. Ed. by Jiří Gruša et al. Collages by Jiří Kolář. Frankfurt a. M., Fischer Verlag, 1978. *Hodina naděje: Almanach české literatury, 1968–1978*. Ed. by Jiří Gruša et al. Foreword by Ludvík Vaculík. Toronto, Sixty-Eight Publishers, 1980.
44. In English see the volume *About Theatre*. Translated by A. G. Brain (Alice and Gerald Turner). Stockholm, Charta 77 Foundation, 1989. In Czech *O divadle*. Ed. by Přemysl Rut. Prague, Lidové noviny, 1990.
45. On the Jazz Section trial see protests by major British and US writers and artists (Edward Albee, Joan Baez, E. L. Doctorow et al.) in *Cross Currents*, 6 (1987), pp. 53–66.
46. Jiří Gruša, *Cenzura a literární život mimo masmédia*. Prague, Ústav pro soudobé dějiny, 1992, p. 23.
47. Jiří Lederer, *České rozhovory*. Prague, Československý spisovatel, 1991, pp. 300–1.

48. *Pařížský zápisník*. Prague, Orbis, 1991, pp. 152–3.
49. *Proglas* is a rhymed preface to a 9th-century Church Slavonic translation of the gospels. It was written in Moravia, possibly by St Constantine. *Proglas* is a celebration of literacy which leads to one's knowledge of God. It is an appeal to the Slavonic nation to cultivate literacy in its own language.
50. See Milan Kundera, The Tragedy of Central Europe. *New York Review of Books*, 26 April 1984, pp. 33–8. Timothy Garton Ash, Does Central Europe Exist? *The New York Review*, 9 October 1986. Ladislav Matejka, Milan Kundera's Central Europe. *Cross Currents*, 9 (1990), pp. 127–34. Václav Bělohradský, Mitteleuropa. Rakouská říše jako metafora. In his *Přirozený svět jako politický problém*. Prague, Československý spisovatel, 1991, pp. 39–60. Karel Kosík, Co je střední Evropa. In his *Století Markéty Samsové*. Prague, Český spisovatel, 1993, pp. 63–99. Petr A. Bílek, The East, West, and the Center of Europe as Cultural Concepts. In *Brown Slavic Contributions*. Vol. 13. Ed. by Alexander Levitsky and Masako U. Fidler. Providence, Brown University, 2000, pp. 78–101.
51. Zdeněk Rotrekl's collected poems came out as *Nezděné město*. Ed. by Jana Uhdeová. Brno, Atlantis, 2001. His collected essays on literature came out as *Skryté tváře*. Ed. by Jana Uhdeová. Brno, Atlantis, 2005.
52. His essays and articles came out in seven volumes in Prague, 1992–2007 (Melantrich and Triáda). Ed. by Vladimír Binar and Mojmír Trávníček. See also Robert Sak, *"Život na vidrholci": Příběh Bedřicha Fučíka*. Prague and Litomyšl, Paseka, 2004.
53. Jiří Melantrich of Aventinum was a well-known Czech 16th-century printer and publisher.
54. Josef Florian initiated the revival of cultural Catholicism at the beginning of the 20th century. He lived in the Czech-Moravian Highlands in Stará Říše and published dozens of titles, especially translations of theological, philosophical and literary works, as well as works from the natural sciences (for instance Léon Bloy, Franz Kafka, Georg Trakl, Gilbert Keith Chesterton). Florian's associates and collaborators were also Jakub Deml, Jaroslav Durych, Bohuslav Reynek, Josef Čapek, Jan Čep et al.
55. Bedřich Fučík, *Čtrnáctero zastavení*. Ed. by Vladimír Binar and Mojmír Trávníček. Prague, Melantrich and Arkýř, 1992, p. 341.
56. Ivan Martin Jirous, *Magorova suma*. Ed. by Martin Machovec. Prague, Torst, 1998, pp. 318, 333. On Czech underground literature cf. Martin Machovec, Czech Underground Literature, 1969–1989, in *Voice, Text, Hypertext*. Ed. by Raimonda Modiano et al. Seattle and London, University of Washington Press, 2004. Also *Views from the Inside*. Ed. by Martin Machovec. Prague, Ústav české literatury a literární vědy, 2006. Martin Pilař, *Underground*. 2nd edition. Brno, Host, 2002.
57. On Romanies in Czechoslovakia see the memoires by Elena Lacková *Narodila jsem se pod šťastnou hvězdou* (translated from the Romany language and ed. by Milena Hübschmannová). Prague, Torst, 1997. In English *A False Dawn*. Translated by Carleton Bulkin. Paris, Centre de recherches tsiganes, and Hatfield, University of Hertfordshire Press, 1999. Třešňák's short stories from the seventies came out as *U jídla se nemluví*. Prague, Torst, 1996.
58. Also her short novel *Nebe, peklo, ráj* (Toronto, 1976) came out in English as *Ashes, Ashes, All Fall Down* (translated by Jan Drábek, Toronto, Sixty-Eight Publishers 1987).
59. English excerpts *A Czech Dreambook* (translated by Michael Henry Heim) in *Cross Currents*, 3 (1984).

60. Cf. *Hlasy nad rukopisem Českého snáře*. Ed. by Ludvík Vaculík. Samizdat 1981. As *Hlasy nad rukopisem Vaculíkova Českého snáře*. Prague, Torst, 1991.
61. Karel Šiktanc, *Zaříkávání živých, Adam a Eva, Jak se trhá srdce*. Ed. by Jiří Brabec. Prague, Karolinum, 2001, p. 64.
62. Karel Šiktanc, *Český orloj, Tanec smrti*. Ed. by Jiří Brabec. Prague, Karolinum, 2000, p. 162.
63. Karel Šiktanc, From Dance of Death. Translated Daniela Dražanová and Karel Dražan. *Prairie Schooner*, 66 (1992), no. 44, p. 171.
64. Cf. Miroslav Červenka, Verš a řádek. Experiment Karla Šiktance s básnickým rytmem. In his *Styl a význam*. Prague, Československý spisovatel, 1991, pp. 214–45.
65. Karel Šiktanc, *Pro pět ran blázna krále, Sakramenty, Srdce svého nejez, Ostrov Štvanice*. Ed. by Jiří Brabec. Prague, Karolinum, 2002, p. 87.
66. Jiřina Hauková, *Básně*. Ed. by Michael Špirit. Prague, Torst, 2000, p. 679.
67. Emil Juliš, *Blížíme se ohni*. Ústí n. L., Severočeské nakladatelství, 1988, p. 23.
68. Ivan Wernisch's collected samizdat poems came out as *Blbecká poezie*. Ed. by Milena Vojtková and Jan Šulc. Brno, Petrov, 2002. In English his poems have been published as *In the Puppet Gardens: Selected Poetry 1963–2003*. Translated by Jonathan Bolton, Ann Arbor, MI, University of Michigan, 2006.
69. Václav Černý, *Eseje o české a slovenské próze*. Ed. by Eva Červinková and Jan Šulc. Prague, Torst, 1994, p. 137.
70. *Ackermann aus Böhmen* is a work written in German on the territory of Bohemia at the beginning of the 15th century. It features a dispute between the poet (ploughman) and Death who took away his wife at childbirth.
71. Originally published in samizdat in 1980 and in Toronto (1984) entitled *Doktor Kokeš, Mistr Panny* (Dr Cocker, Master of the Virgin).
72. Karol Sidon, *Dvě povídky o utopencích*. Munich, Index, 1988, p. 139.
73. On exile literature from East-Central Europe (Poland, Rumania, Slovakia, Czech Republic, Hungary) see the exhaustive publication *Grundbegriffe und Autoren ostmitteleuropäischer Exilliteraturen 1945–1989*. Ed. by Eva Behring, Alfrun Kliems and Hans-Christian Trepte. Stuttgart, Franz Steiner Verlag, 2004.
74. Filmed by Vít Olmer in 1991.
75. See Josef Škvorecký, At Home in Exile. Czech Writers in the West. *Books Abroad*, 50, no. 2 (Spring 1976), pp. 308–13. *Literatura, vězení, exil / Literature, Prison, Exil*. Ed. by Miloš Vacík and Libuše Ludvíková. Prague, České centrum Mezinárodního PEN klubu, 1997. *Jak reflektujeme českou literaturu vzniklou v zahraničí*. Ed. by Pavlína Kubíková. Prague, Obec spisovatelů, 2000.
76. Milan Kundera, Frankofobie existuje. *Akord*, 21 (1996), no. 2, pp. 75.
77. Věra Linhartová, Pour une onthologie de l'exil. *L'Atelier du roman*, 2 (1994), May, pp. 127–32. In English and in Czech in *Literatura, vězení, exil / Literature, Prison, Exile*. Ed. by Miloš Vacík and Libuše Ludvíková. Prague, České centrum Mezinárodního PEN klubu, 1997, p. 138 ff.
78. On the review *Studie* cf. Tomáš Halík, *Víra a kultura: Pokoncilní vývoj českého katolicismu v reflexi časopisu Studie*. Preface by Karel Skalický. Afterword by Karel Vrána. Prague, Zvon, 1995.
79. Filmed by Philip Kaufman in 1987.
80. About Vejvoda's work see Helena Kosek, The Work of Jaroslav Vejvoda. In: *Aspects of Modern Russian and Czech Literature*. Ed. by Arnold McMillin. Columbus, OH, Slavica Publishers, 1989, pp. 224–37.

81. Novák wrote in English the novel *The Willy's Dream Kit*. San Diego, Harcourt Brace Jovanovich, 1985. In Czech as *Milionový jeep* (translated by Jaroslav Kořán, afterword by Václav Havel). Toronto, Sixty-Eight Publishers, 1989.
82. Josef Škvorecký, *The Engineer of Human Souls*. Translated by Paul Wilson. London, Vintage, pp. 11, 478–9.
83. Cf. Ladislav Matejka, Milan Kundera's Central Europe. *Cross Currents*, 9 (1990), pp. 127–34. Petr A. Bílek, The East, West, and the Center of Europe as Cultural Concepts, Emblems, and Vehicles of Creative Misunderstandings. In *Modern Czech Studies, Brown Slavic Contributions*. Vol. 13. Ed. by Alexander Levitsky and Masako U. Fidler. Providence, Brown University, 2000, pp. 78–101.
84. Milan Kundera, *The Unbearable Lightness of Being*. Translated by Michael Henry Heim. London, Faber & Faber, 1999, pp. 248–9.
85. Milada Součková, *Sešity Josefíny Rykrové*. Ed. by Kristián Suda. Afterword by Roman Jakobson. Prague, Prostor, 1993, p. 117.
86. On the shifting of languages in Czech literature see Petr Mareš, *"Also: Nazdar!": Aspekty textové vícejazyčnosti*. Prague, Karolinum, 2003.
87. Ivan Blatný, *Tento večer*. Ed. by Jan Marius Tomeš. Prague, Československý spisovatel, 1991, p. 156.
88. Karel Brušák, František Listopad, Jaroslav Dresler – Czech exile writers and journalists.
89. Ivan Jelínek, *V sobě letohrad*. Ed. by Jiří Trávníček. Brno, Host, 1998, p. 92.
90. Psalm 92, verse 15.
91. Ivan Diviš, *Obrať koně!* Prague, Československý spisovatel, 1992, p. 96.
92. Jiří Lederer, *České rozhovory*. Prague, Československý spisovatel, 1991, pp. 259–60.
93. Translated by George Theiner. Also as *Audience* in Václav Havel, *Selected Plays, 1963–1983*. London, Faber & Faber, 1992 (new edition as *The Garden Party and Other Plays*. New York, NY, Grove Press, 1993); newly translated as *Audience* by Vera Blackwell in Václav Havel, *Sorry . . . : Two Plays*. London, Eyre Methuen and BBC, 1978; translated again by Jan Novák in *The Vaněk-Plays: Four Authors, One Character*. Ed. by Marketa Goetz-Stankiewicz. Vancouver, University of British Columbia Press, 1987.
94. Václav Havel, *Audience*. Translated by Jan Novak. In *The Vaněk-Plays: Four Authors, One Character*. Ed. and intro. by Marketa Goetz-Stankiewicz. Playwright's comments by Václav Havel, Pavel Kohout, Pavel Landovský and Jiří Dienstbier. Vancouver, University of British Columbia Press, 1987, pp. 6–7.
95. In Czech as *V hlavní roli Ferdinand Vaněk*. Edited by Jan Šulc, epilogue by Lenka Jungmannová. Prague, Academia, 2006. On Vaněk plays see Igor Hájek, The Cloning of Ferdinand Vaněk. In *Aspekte kultureller Integration*. Ed. by Karel Mácha and Peter Drews. Munich, Saur Verlag, 1991, pp. 163–74. In Czech Igor Hájek, *Prokletá a požehnaná*. Ed. by Martin Pilař. Prague, Dokořán, 2007, pp. 104–13.
96. In English in *Index on Censorship*, April 1989 (translated by Jitka Martin and Barbara Day).
97. Vladimír Just, *Proměny malých scén*. Prague, Mladá fronta, 1984, p. 153.
98. It is the former name of his well-known *The Labyrinth of the World and the Paradise of the Heart* (written 1623, in English 1901, newly translated 1972, and again in 1997).
99. In Czech 1932, in English *Nikola Suhaj Robber*, 1954, newly translated as *Nikola Suhaj the Outlaw*, 2001.
100. Ivo Šmoldas, *Zimní srst*. Prague, Československý spisovatel, 1988, p. 12.

101. Zuzana Brabcová, *Daleko od stromu.* Prague, Československý spisovatel, 1991, p. 14.
102. Josef Vohryzek, Topolova křižovatka. *Respekt*, 7 (1996), no. 8, p. 18.
103. Jáchym Topol, *City Sister Silver.* Translated by Alex Zucker. North Haven, CT, Catbird Press, 2000, p. 17. Jiří Peňás wrote, "City Sister Silver marks a turning point in Czech prose, the one that comes after all the tiring twists and turns and subtle detours, when finally there is a break in literary evolution and it strikes out in a new direction" (quoted on the cover of the English edition).
104. Petr Placák, *Medorek.* Prague, Lidové noviny, 1990, pp. 6–7.
105. Rajendra Anand Chitnis has analyzed the works *Daleko od stromu, Medorek* and *Lodní deník* in his *Literature in Post-Communist Russia and Eastern Europe: The Russian, Slovak and Czech Fiction of the Changes, 1988–1998.* London, Routledge Curzon, 2005, pp. 39 ff.
106. See Jan Čulík, Breaking the Rule of the Average. A Review of Recent Czech Fiction. *Irish Slavonic Studies*, 4 (1983), pp. 123–35. Robert B. Pynsent, Adolescence, Ideology and Society. The Young Hero in Contemporary Czech Fiction. In: *The Adolescent Hero.* Ed. by Ian Wallace. Dundee, GDR Monitor, 1984, pp. 65–84. Robert B. Pynsent, Social Criticism in Czech Literature of 1970s and 1980s Czechoslovakia. *Bohemia*, 27, no. 1 (1986), pp. 1–36. Igor Hájek, Changing Attitudes in Recent Czech Fiction, Towards a Typology of Actually Existing Socialism. In: *Aspects of Modern Russian and Czech Literature.* Ed. by Arnold McMillin. Columbus, OH, Slavica Publishers, 1989, pp. 214–24.
107. Cf. *Panorama of Czech Literature*, 8 (1986). Ed. by Josef Nesvadba. The issue devoted to Czech contemporary science-fiction authors (Josef Nesvadba, Ludvík Souček, Zdeněk Volný, Ondřej Neff, Vladimír Páral, Jaroslav Veis).
108. See *Z dějin českého myšlení o literatuře IV: 1970–1989.* Ed. by Michal Přibáň. Prague, ÚČL AVČR, 2005, pp. 421–60.
109. Excerpt in English (translated by Tatiana Firkusny and Véronique Firkusny-Callegari) in *Allskin and Other Tales by Contemporary Czech Women.* Ed. by Alexandra Büchler. Seattle, WA, Women in Translation, 1998, pp. 50–71.
110. Rajendra Anand Chitnis has been writing on Jiří Kratochvil and Daniela Hodrová in his *Literature in Post-Communist Russia and Eastern Europe: The Russian, Slovak and Czech Fiction of the Changes, 1988–1998.* London, Routledge Courzon, 2005, pp. 80–114. Cf. also Anna Car, *O prozie Danieli Hodrovej.* Kraków, Wydawnictwo Uniwersytetu Jagiellonskiego, 2003.
111. In English two short stories translated by James Naughton in *Storm*, 1991, no. 3, and one in *Description of a Struggle:The Picador Book of Contemporary East European Prose* (ed. by Michael March, London, Picador, 1994).
112. Josef Škvorecký, *The Cowards.* Translated by Jeanne Němcová. London, Victor Gollancz, and New York, NY, Grove Press, 1970, p. 415.
113. Alexandra Berková, *Knížka s červeným obalem.* Prague, Práce, 1988, p. 52.
114. See also Jarka M. Burian, *Modern Czech Theatre.* Iowa City, IO, University of Iowa City, 2000, pp. 153 ff.
115. Fischerová's stories came out in English as *Fingers Pointing Somewhere Else* (translated by Neil Bermel), North Haven, CT, Catbird Press, 2000. On her work cf. Veronika Ambros, Daniela Fischerová's New Palimpsest between "Living in Truth" and "The Battle for an Island of Trust", *Canadian Slavonic Papers*, 36 (1994), no. 34, pp. 363–76.
116. About Steigerwald see Štěpán S. Šimek, Theater as a "Temple of the Mind" and the

Remarkable Moralist Karel Steigerwald. *Slavic and East European Performance*, 23, no. 3 (Fall 2003) / 24, no. 1 (Winter 2004), pp. 42–55. Štěpán S. Šimek together with Roger Downey translated Steigerwald's later play *Hoře, hoře, strach, oprátka a jáma* (premiere 1991) as *Sorrow, Sorrow, Fear, the Rope, and the Pit* (Seattle, 1997).

117. *Lidové noviny 1989.* Reprint. Prague, Lidové noviny, 1990. October 1989, p. 22.
118. *Most* (Bonn), 1 (1989), no. 1, p. 7.
119. See *Z dějin českého myšlení o literatuře IV: 1970–1989.* Ed. by Michal Přibáň. Prague, ÚČL AVČR, 2005, pp. 484–8.
120. Excerpt in English (translated by Tatiana Firkusny and Véronique Firkusny-Callegari) in *Daylight in Nightclub Inferno: Czech Fiction from the post-Kundera Generation.* Ed. by Elena Lappin. North Haven, CT, Catbird, 1997, pp. 87–97.
121. Petr A. Bílek, "*Generace*" *osamělých běžců.* Prague, Československý spisovatel, 1991.
122. A collection of Sylva Fischerová's poems was published in English as *The Tremor of Race Horses.* Translated by Jarmila and Ian Milner. Intro. by Ian Milner. Newcastle upon Tyne, Bloodaxe Books, 1990.
123. Lubor Kasal, *Dosudby*. Prague, Mladá fronta, 1989, p. 36.
124. Cf. *Den bude dlouhý: Antologie textů českých písničkářů.* Ed. by Jan Šulc and Jaroslav Riedel. Prague and Litomyšl, Paseka, 2004.
125. Jiří Dědeček, *Blues pro slušný lidi.* Prague, Academia, 2002, p. 127.
126. On the independent religious movement in Czechoslovakia see Václav Benda, Catholicism and Politics. In: Václav Havel et al., *The Power of the Powerless.* London, Hutchinson, 1985, pp. 110–24. Jiřina Šiklová, Young People and Religion in Czechoslovakia. *East European Reporter* 2 (1987), no. 1, pp. 9–12. Paul Wilson, Religious Movement in Czechoslovakia. Faith or Fashion? *Cross Currents* 7 (1988), pp. 109–19. Joseph N. Rostinsky, Czech Catholic Writers under Communist Normalization. *Kosmas*, 20 (2006), no. 1.
127. This is when, after student demonstrations, the Nazis closed down Czech universities, deporting many Czech students to concentration camps and executing some of them.
128. Cf. also a documentary *The Artists' Revolution* (1995), directed by Daniel Moore.

The Nineties and the Early Twenty-first Century

1. Česká próza v pohybu. *Tvar*, 7 (1996), no. 17, p. 4.
2. *Petrov* closed down in December 2005 and its owner Martin Pluháček-Reiner founded a new publishing house *Druhé město* (The Second City).
3. *Paseka* (Clearing) is the name of an engraver who appears in Josef Váchal's novel *Krvavý román* (A Novel Drenched in Blood, 1924). The name is the literary image of the author itself. Váchal's paintings and literary texts became popular since the 1980s.
4. Josef Jungmann (1773–1847), an important figure of the Czech National Revival, translated Milton's *Paradise Lost*, Chateaubriand's *Atala* and other works into Czech. Thus he made an important contribution to the development of the modern Czech language.
5. The novel *The Façade* also came out in English (translated by John E. Woods). New York, Knopf, 1991. London, Chatto & Windus, 1992.
6. Cf. Margarete Buber-Neumann, *Mistress to Kafka: The Life and Death of Milena* (intro. by Arthur Koestler), London, Secker & Warburg, 1966. As *Milena.* New York,

Seaver Books, 1988. London, Collins, 1989. Jana Černá, *Kafka's Milena*. Translated from the Czech by A. G. Brain (Alice and Gerald Turner). London, Souvenir Press, 1988. Evanston, IL, Northwestern University Press, 1993 (intro. by George Gibian). Mary Hockaday, *Kafka, Love and Courage: The Life of Milena Jesenská*. London, Deutsch, 1995. Woodstock, NY, Overlook Press, 1997.

7. *Host*, 17 (2001), no. 9, p. 41.
8. Jolana Poláková, Řeč pronesená u příležitosti udělení Ceny Toma Stopparda. *Tvar*, 8 (1997), no. 12, p. 1.
9. Pavel Janoušek, *Time-out: Mé kritické pokusy, bláboly a omyly z let 1987–1999*. Brno, Host, 2001, p. 75.
10. "When I was first in Czechoslovakia, it occurred to me that I work in a society where, for writers, everything goes and nothing matters, while for the Czech writers I met in Prague nothing goes and everything matters." Philip Roth, The Romance of Oppression. In: *Besieged Culture* (ed. by A. Heneka et al.). Stockholm and Vienna, The Charta 77 Foundation et al., 1985, p. 52.
11. Jiří Kratochvil, *Vyznání příběhovosti*. Brno, Petrov, 2000, p. 75.
12. Zdeněk Kožmín and Jiří Trávníček, *Na tvrdém loži z psího vína: Česká poezie od 40. let do současnosti*. Brno, Jota, 1998, p. 247.
13. This castle really exists in Eastern Bohemia.
14. Viola Fischerová, *Zádušní básně za Pavla Buksu*. Brno, Petrov, 1993, p. 11.
15. Wacht am Rhein is a German nationalist song and the name for the German counteroffensive in the Ardennes in December 1944.
16. Pavel Šrut, *Zlá milá*. Prague, Torst, 1997, pp. 102–3.
17. His pseudonym is derived from the colloquial expression *krchov* (cemetery).
18. J. H. Krchovský, *Básně*. Brno, Host, 1998, p. 150. In English seven poems (translated by Justin Quinn) came out in *METRE (Magazine of International Poetry)*, Hull, Prague and Dublin, Autumn 2001.
19. Jaroslav Med, Všechno začalo v Petrkově . . . *Host*, 20 (2002), no. 4, p. 7.
20. Pavel Kolmačka, *Vlál za mnou směšný šos*. 2nd edition. Prague, Kalich, 1996, p. 23.
21. Jan Wiendl, Podél podivických mezí. *Tvar*, 6 (1995), no. 21, p. 22.
22. Some poems were translated into English by Justin Quinn. See *Prague Literary Review*, 1 (2003), no. 3, and *A Fine Line: New Poetry from Eastern and Central Europe*. Ed. by Jean Boase-Beier et al., intro. by Fiona Sampson. Todmorden, Arc Publications, pp. 116–27.
23. Bogdan Trojak, *Pan Twardowski*. Brno, Host, 1998, p. 27.
24. Kateřina Rudčenková, *Není nutné, abyste mě navštěvoval*. Prague, Klokočí, 2001, p. 11.
25. *Nesnesitelná lehkost bytí* was finally published by Atlantis, Brno, in 2006.
26. Cf. articles by Aleš Haman and Petr A. Bílek. Also *Česká próza 90. let 20. století*. Ed. Michal Bauer. České Budějovice, Jihočeská univerzita, 2002.
27. Jiří Kratochvil, *Vyznání příběhovosti*. Brno, Petrov, 2000, p. 83.
28. About Kahuda see Rajendra A. Chitnis, *Literature in Post-Communist Russia and Eastern Europe*. London, Routledge Curzon, 2005, pp. 136ff.
29. Jiří Peňás, Zázrak z hlubin. *Respekt*, 10 (1999), 23 August 1999.
30. An extract from Hodrová's *Perunův den* appeared in English (translated by Tatiana Firkusny and Véronique Firkusny-Callegari) in the anthology *Daylight in Nightclub Inferno: Czech Fiction from the post-Kundera Generation* (ed. by Elena Lappin). North Haven, Catbird, 1997, pp. 191–202.

31. Vladimír Binar, *Playback*. Prague, Triáda, p. 58.
32. Miloš Urban, *Sedmikostelí*. Prague, Argo, 1999, pp. 300–1.

Bibliography

Handbooks and Dictionaries in Czech

Ivan Adamovič, *Slovník české literární fantastiky a science fiction*. Introduction by Ondřej Neff. Prague, R3, 1995. 352 pp.

Milan Blahynka (ed.), *Čeští spisovatelé 20. století: Slovníková příručka*. Prague, Československý spisovatel, 1985. 832 pp.

Jiří Brabec [et al.], *Slovník zakázaných autorů*. Prague, SPN, 1991. 542 pp. (Orig. in samizdat in 1978, and in Toronto in 1982.)

Jan Čulík, *Knihy za ohradou. Česká literatura v exilových nakladatelstvích 1971–1991*. Introduction by Igor Hájek. Prague, Trizonia, 1991. 420 pp.

Blahoslav Dokoupil (ed.), *Slovník českých literárních časopisů, periodických literárních sborníků a almanachů*. Brno, Host and Votobia, 2002. 336 pp.

Blahoslav Dokoupil and Miroslav Zelinský (eds.), *Slovník české prózy 1945–1994*. Ostrava, Sfinga, 1994. 492 pp.

Vladimír Forst (ed.), *Slovník české literatury 1970–1981*. Prague, Československý spisovatel, 1985. 504 pp.

Josef Galík [et al.], *Panorama české literatury*. Olomouc, Rubico, 1994. 550 pp.

Rudolf Havel and Jiří Opelík (eds.), *Slovník českých spisovatelů*. Prague, Československý spisovatel, 1964. 628 pp.

Jiří Holý [et al.], *Český Parnas: Literatura 1970–1990*. Prague, Galaxie, 1993. 406 pp.

Pavel Janoušek [et al.] (eds.), *Slovník českých spisovatelů od roku 1945*. I–II. Prague, Brána. Vol. 1, 1995, 552 pp. Vol. 2, 1998, 792 pp.

Vladimír Just [et al.], *Česká divadelní kultura 1945–1989 v datech a v souvislostech*. Prague, Divadelní ústav, 1995. 470 pp.

František Knopp, *Česká literatura v exilu 1948–1989. Bibliografie*. Prague, Makropulos, 1996. 634 pp.

Zdeněk Kožmín and Jiří Trávníček, *Na tvrdém loži z psího vína: Česká poezie od 40. let do současnosti*. Brno, Books, 1998. 320 pp.

Jan Lehár [et al.], *Česká literatura od počátků k dnešku*. Prague, NLN, 1998. Suppl. 2nd edition, 2002. 1080 pp. (Includes a detailed bibliography of Czech literature.)

Věra Menclová [et al.], *Slovník českých spisovatelů*. Prague, Libri, 2000. Suppl. 2nd edition, 2005. 822 pp.

Antonín Měšťan, *Česká literatura 1785–1985*. Toronto, Sixty-Eight Publishers, 1987. 454 pp. (Originally in German: *Geschichte der tschechischen Literatur im 19. und 20. Jahrhundert*, Cologne, 1984.)

Jiřina Táborská [et al.], *Česká literatura 1945–1970: Interpretace vybraných děl*. Prague, SPN, 1992. 428 pp.

History of Czech Literature since 1945 in Other Languages

Ludmilla B. Hankó and Veronika Heé, *A cseh irodalom története*. Budapest, Magyarországi Eszperantó Szövetség, 2003. 968 pp. (The work concentrates on portraits of the most significant authors.)

Jiří Holý, *Geschichte der tschechischen Literatur des 20. Jahrhunderts*. Wien, Edition Praesens, 2003. 436 pp. (Deals with literary trends and developments, includes literature written in German in Bohemia.)

Arne Novák, *Czech Literature*. Edited and suppl. by William E. Harkins. Translated by Peter Kussi. Ann Arbor, Michigan Slavic Publications, 1976, 376 pp. A new edition, 1986, 382 pp. (A history of Czech literature until the end of 1930s, including an outline of later literature.)

Walter Schamschula, *Geschichte der tschechischen Literatur III: Von der Gründung der Republik bis zur Gegenwart*. Cologne et al., Böhlau Verlag, 2004. 674 pp. (Deals with literature until 1970 and contains portraits of individual authors.)

Hana Voisine-Jechova, *Histoire de la litterature tchèque*. Paris, Fayard, 2001. 794 pp. (Published in Czech 2005. The work concentrates on old Czech and 19th century literature.)

Bibliography in English

Georg J. Kovtun, *Czech and Slovak Literature in English: A Bibliography*. Washington, Library of Congress, 1984. Suppl. 2nd edition, 1988, 152 pp.

George J. Kovtun, *Czech and Slovak History. An American Bibliography*. Introduction by Stanley B. Winters. Washington, Library of Congress, 1996. 482 pp.

David Short, *Czechoslovakia*. Oxford and Santa Barbara, Clio Press, 1986. 409 pp. 2nd, revised edition: Vlaďka Edmonson and David Short, *Czech Republic*. Oxford et al., Clio Press, 1999. 432 pp. (For a chapter dealing with literature see pp. 253–297.)

Literature in English

Veronika Ambros, Czech Women Writers after 1945. In: Celia Hawkesworth (ed.), *A History of Central European Women's Writing*. Houndmills, Palgrave, 2001. pp. 201–219.

Henrik Birnbaum and Thomas Eekman (eds.), *Fiction and Drama in Eastern and Southeastern Europe: Evolution and Experiment in the Postwar Period*. Columbus, Slavica Publishers, 1980. 464 pp. (Entries on Ladislav Fuks, Václav Havel, Bohumil Hrabal.)

Jarka M. Burian, *Modern Czech Theatre: Reflector and Conscience of a Nation*. Iowa City, University of Iowa Press, 2000. 266 pp.

Jarka M. Burian, *Leading Creators of Twentieth-Century Czech Theatre*. London and New York, Routledge, 2002. 226 pp.

Richard Burton, *Prague: A Cultural and Literary Companion*. Oxford, Signal, 2003. 256 pp.

Otakar Chaloupka, *Czech Literature for Children*. Prague, Dilia, 1980. 222 pp.

Rajendra A. Chitnis, *Literature in Post-Communist Russia and Eastern Europe. The Russian, Czech and Slovak Fiction of the Changes 1988–1998*. London, Routledge, 2005. 208 pp.

Robert G. Collins and Kenneth McRobbie (eds.), *The Eastern European Imagination in Literature*. Winnipeg, University of Manitoba Press, 1973. 238 pp.

Lubomír Doležel, *Narrative Modes in Czech Literature.* Toronto, University of Toronto Press, 1973. 152 pp. (Published in Czech 1993.)

Alfred French, *The Poets of Prague: Czech Poetry between the Wars.* London and New York, Oxford University Press, 1969. 130 pp.

Alfred French, *Czech Writers and Politics, 1945–1969.* Canberra, Australian National University Press and Boulder, and New York, Columbia University Press, 1982. 436 pp.

Karen Gammelgaard, *Spoken Czech in Literature: The Case of Bondy, Hrabal, Placák and Topol.* Oslo, Scandinavian University Press, 1997. 272 pp.

Marketa Goetz-Stankiewicz, *The Silenced Theatre: Czech Playwrights without a Stage.* Toronto et al., University of Toronto Press, 1979. 320 pp.

Marketa Goetz-Stankiewicz (ed.), *Good-bye, Samizdat: Twenty Years of Czechoslovak Underground Writing.* Translated by A. G. Brain (Alice and Gerald Turner) et al. Foreword by Timothy Garton Ash. Evanston, Northwestern University Press, 1992. 310 pp.

Elizabeth Gray, *The Fiction of Freedom, the Development of the Czechoslovak Literary Reform Movement, 1956–1968.* Clayton, Monach University, 1991. 74 pp.

Mojmír Grygar (ed.), *Czech Studies. Literature. Language. Culture. / České studie. Literatura. Jazyk. Kultura.* Amsterdam and Atlanta, Rodopi, 1990. 336 pp.

Igor Hájek (ed.), Czechoslovak Literature. In: Vasa D. Mihailovich [et al.] (eds.), *Modern Slavic Literatures.* Vol. 2. New York, Ungar, 1976, pp. 38–230.

Peter Hames, *The Czechoslovak New Wave.* Berkeley and London, University of California Press, 1985. 322 pp. London, Wallflower Press, 2005. (Czech cinematography.)

Dušan Hamšík, *Writers against Rulers.* Translated by D. Orpington. Introduction by W. L. Webb. London, Hutchinson and New York, Random House, 1971. 208 pp. (Orig. published in Czech as *Spisovatelé a moc*, Prague, 1969.)

William Edward Harkins and Paul I. Trensky (eds.), *Czech Literature since 1956. A Symposium.* New York, Bohemica, 1980. 162 pp.

Peter Hruby, *Daydreams and Nightmares: Czech Communist and Ex-Communist Literature 1917–1987.* New York, Columbia University Press, 1990. 362 pp. (Published in Czech as *Osudné iluze*, Rychnov, 2000.)

Charles S. Kraszewski, *The Romantic Hero and Contemporary anti-Hero in Polish and Czech Literature: Great Souls and Grey Men.* New York and Lampeter, Edwin Mellen Press, 1998. 326 pp. (Studies on Jan Zahradníček, Vladimír Holan, Václav Havel etc.)

S. Lillian Kremer (ed.): *Holocaust Literature: An Encyclopedia of Writers and Their Work. I–II.* London and New York, Routledge, 2003. 1500 pp. (Entries on Ladislav Fuks, Arnošt Lustig, Jiří Weil.)

Alexander Levitsky and Masako U. Fidler (eds.), *Modern Czech Studies: Brown Slavic Contributions.* Vol. 13. Providence, Brown University, 2000. 166 pp.

Antonín J. Liehm, *The Politics of Culture.* Translated by Peter Kussi. Introduction by Jean Paul Sartre. New York, Grove Press, 1970. 412 pp. (Published in Czech as *Generace*, 1969 banned, in Cologne in 1988, Prague, 1990.)

Martin Machovec (ed.), *Views from the Inside: Czech Underground Literature and Culture (1948–1989).* Translated by Tomáš Liška, Gerald Turner and Paul Wilson. Prague, Ústav české literatury a literární vědy, 2006. 96 pp. (Contributions by Ivan Martin Jirous, Paul Wilson, Egon Bondy, Jáchym Topol.)

Vladimír Macura and Herta Schmid (eds.), *Jan Mukařovský and the Prague School / und die Prager Schule*. Potsdam, Universität Potsdam and Ústav pro českou literaturu, 1999. 332 pp.

Arnold McMillin (ed.), *Aspects of Modern Russian and Czech Literature*. Columbus, Slavica Publishers, 1989. 240 pp. (3 entries on Czech literature.)

Jane Eldridge Miller (ed.), *Who's Who in Contemporary Women's Writing*. London and New York, Routledge, 2001. 386 pp. (Entries on Alexandra Berková, Tereza Boučková, Daniela Fischerová, Sylva Fischerová, Daniela Hodrová, Eva Kantůrková, Eda Kriseová, Libuše Moníková, Iva Pekárková, Lenka Procházková, Sylvie Richterová, Zdena Salivarová.)

Leslie Miller [et al.] (eds.), *Literature and Politics in Central Europe: Studies in Honour of Markéta Goetz-Stankiewicz*. Columbia, Camden House, 1993. 148 pp.

James Naughton (ed.), *Traveller's Literary Companion to Eastern and Central Europe*. Brighton, In Print, 1995. 440 pp. (For a chapter dealing with the Czech literature see pp. 50–135.)

Arne Novák, *Czech Literature*. Edited and complemented by William E. Harkins. Translated by Peter Kussi. Ann Arbor, Michigan Slavic Publications, 1976. 376 pp. 1986. 382 pp.

Robert Porter, *An Introduction to Twentieth-Century Czech Fiction: Comedies of Defiance*. Brighton and Portland, Sussex Academic Press, 2001. 210 pp.

Robert B. Pynsent [et al.] (eds.), *The Everyman Companion to East European Literature*. Introduction by Martyn Rady. London, J. M. Dent, and New York, HarperCollins, 1993. 606 pp.

Robert B. Pynsent, *Questions of Identity: Czech and Slovak Ideas of Nationality and Personality*. London and New York et al., Central European University Press, 1994. 244 pp. (Published in Czech in 1996.)

Angelo Maria Ripellino, *Magic Prague*. Translated by David Newton Marinelli. Edited by Michael Henry Heim. Basingstoke, Macmillan, and Berkeley, University of California Press, 1994. London, Picador, 1995. 334 pp. (Published in Czech in Cologne in 1978, in Prague in 1992.)

Steven Serafin [et al.] (eds.), *Dictionary of Literary Biography: Twentieth-Century Eastern European Writers*. Vol. 232. Third Series. Detroit et al., Gale, 2001. 484 pp. (Entries on Václav Havel, Miroslav Holub, Bohumil Hrabal, Ivan Klíma, Milan Kundera, Arnošt Lustig, Vladimír Páral, Jan Skácel, Josef Škvorecký, Ludvík Vaculík.)

David Short, *Essays in Czech and Slovak Language and Literature*. London, University of London, 1996. 216 pp.

Efraim Sicher (ed.), *Dictionary of Literary Biography: Holocaust Novelists*. Vol. 299. Detroit et al., Gale, 2004. 502 pp. (Entries on Josef Bor, Ladislav Fuks, Arnošt Lustig, Jiří Weil.)

Josef Škvorecký, *Talkin' Moscow Blues*. Edited by Sam Solecki. Toronto, Lester & Orpen Dennys, 1988. 368 pp. London, Faber & Faber, 1989.

Milada Součková, *A Literature in Crisis: Czech Literature 1938–1950*. New York, National Committee for a Free Europe, 1954. 158 pp.

Milada Součková, *A Literary Satellite: Czechoslovak-Russian Literary Relations*. Chicago, University of Chicago Press, 1970. 180 pp.

Peter Steiner [et al.] (eds.), *The Structure of the Literary Process: Studies Dedicated to the Memory of Felix Vodička*. Amsterdam and Philadephia, J. Benjamins, 1982. 614 pp.

Peter Steiner, *The Deserts of Bohemia: Czech Fiction and Its Social Context*. Ithaca, Cornell University Press, 2000. 244 pp. (Published in Czech as *Lustrování literatury*, Prague, 2002.)

Alfred Thomas, *The Labyrinth of the Word: Truth and Representation in Czech Literature*. München, Oldenbourg, 1995. 174 pp.

Paul I. Trensky, *Czech Drama since World War II*. Introduction by William E. Harkins. White Plains, Sharpe, 1978. 250 pp.

Miloš Vacík and Libuše Ludvíková (eds.), *Literatura, vězení, exil / Literature, Prison, Exile*. Prague, Readers International and České centrum Mezinárodního PEN klubu, 1997. 222 pp.

Jan Vladislav (ed.), *Living in Truth: Twenty-two Essays Published on the Occasion of the Award of the Erasmus Prize to Václav Havel*. Amsterdam, 1986. London, Faber & Faber, 1987. The Hague, Pax Christi, 1989. 316 pp. (Six texts by Václav Havel and sixteen texts for Václav Havel.)

Bronislava Volková, *A Feminist's Semiotic Odyssey through Czech Literature*. Lewiston et al., Edwin Mellen Press, 1997. 196 pp.

René Wellek, *Essays on Czech Literature*. Introduction by Peter Demetz. The Hague, Mouton, 1963. 214 pp.

Political and Historical Literature in English

Bradley F. Abrams, *The Struggle for the Soul of a Nation: Czech Culture and the Rise of Communism*. Lanham, Rowman & Littlefield, 2004. 363 pp.

René Allio [et al.] (eds.), *White Paper on Czechoslovakia*. Paris, International Committee for the Support of Charter 77 in Czechoslovakia, 1977. 270 pp.

Timothy Garton Ash, *The Uses of Adversity: Essays on the Fate of Central Europe*. Cambridge, Granta, 1989. 306 pp. New York, Random House, 1989. 336 pp. New York, Vintage, 1990. Cambridge, Granta and Penguin, 1991. London, Penguin, 1999.

Timothy Garton Ash, *We the People: The Revolution of '89 Witnessed in Warsaw, Budapest, Berlin and Prague*. Cambridge et al., Granta, 1990, and New York, Penguin. 156 pp. London, Penguin, 1999. (In Czech as *Rok zázraků* in Prague in 1991.)

Philip Bergmann, *Self-Determination: The Case of Czechoslovakia, 1968–1969*. Foreword by John N. Hazard. Lugano, Grassi, 1972. 160 pp.

Jon Bloomfield, *Passive Revolution: Politics and the Czechoslovak Working Class, 1945–1948*. London, Allison & Busby, 1979. 290 pp.

Yorick Blumenfeld, *Seesaw: Cultural Life in Eastern Europe*. New York, Harcourt, 1968. 276 pp.

John Francis N. Bradley, *Politics in Czechoslovakia, 1945–1990*. Boulder, Columbia University Press, 1991. 138 pp.

John Francis N. Bradley, *Czechoslovakia's Velvet Revolution: A Political Analysis*. Boulder, Columbia University Press, 1992. 140 pp. (Including Annex 1 – Annex 23.)

Jaroslav Brodský, *Solution Gamma*. Translated by Káča Poláčková. Toronto, Gamma Print, 1971. 256 pp. (Published in Czech in Toronto in 1970.)

Vratislav Busek and Nicolas Spulber (eds.), *Czechoslovakia*. New York, Praeger, and London, Stevens, 1956. 520 pp. New York, Atlantic, 1957. Facsimile Ann Arbor, University of Michigan, 1971.

Vlastislav Chalupa, *Rise and Development of a Totalitarian State*. Leiden, Kroese, 1959. 294 pp.

Colin Chapman, *August 21st: The Rape of Czechoslovakia*. With on the Spot Reports from Prague by Murray Sayle. London, Cassell, 1968. 124 pp.

Edward Joseph Czerwiński and Jaroslaw Piekalkiewicz (eds.), *The Soviet Invasion of Czechoslovakia: Its Effects on Eastern Europe*. London and New York, Praeger, 1972. 210 pp.

Avigdor Dagan (= Viktor Fischl) et al. (eds.), *The Jews of Czechoslovakia: Historical Studies and Surveys*. I–III. Philadelphia, Jewish Publication Society of America and New York, Society for the History of Czechoslovak Jews, 1968, 1971, 1984. Vol. 1: 583 pp. Vol. 2: 708 pp. Vol. 3: 700 pp.

Barbara Day, *The Velvet Philosophers*. London, Claridge Press, 1999. 344 pp. (Published in Czech as *Sametoví filozofové*, Brno, 1999.)

Tamara Deutscher [et al.] (eds.), *Voices of Czechoslovak Socialists*. Kent, Merlin Press, 1976. 134 pp. (Jiří Müller, Michal Reiman, Karel Kaplan, Zdeněk Mlynář, Václav Havel.)

Alexander Dubček, *Hope Dies Last. The Authobiography of Alexander Dubček*. Edited and translated by Jiří Hochman. London, HarperCollins, and New York, Kodansha, 1993. 354 pp. (In Slovak and in Czech in 1993.)

Fred H. Eidlin, *The Logic of "Normalization": The Soviet Intervention in Czechoslovakia of 21 August 1968 and the Czechoslovak Response*. Boulder and New York, Columbia University Press, 1980. 278 pp.

Zdeněk Eliáš and Jaromír Netík, Czechoslovakia. In: William E. Griffith (ed.), *Communism in Europe*. Vol. 2. Cambridge, MIT Press, 1966, pp. 157–276.

Paul Ello (ed.), *Czechoslovakia's Blueprint for "Freedom": Dubček's Unity "Socialism and Humanity": The Original and Official Documents Leading to the Conflict of August, 1968*. Introduction and comm. by Paul Ello. Washington, Acropolis, 1968. 304 pp.

Adam Fagan, *Environment and Democracy in the Czech Republic: The Environmental Movement in the Transition Process*. Cheltenham and Northhampton, Edward Elgar, 2004. 196 pp.

Rick Fawn, *The Czech Republic: A Nation of Velvet*. Amsterdam, Harwood Academic, 2000. 176 pp.

Ján Filípek, *Reflections and Perspectives: Czechoslovak after Forty Years in Exile*. Preface by Jiří Nehnevajsa. Palm Springs, Palm Springs Publishing, 1988. 228 pp. (In Czech in Palm Springs in 1989.)

Ivan Gadourek, *The Political Control of Czechoslovakia. A Study in Social Control of a Soviet Satellite State*. Leiden, Kroese, 1953. 286 pp. Westport, Greenwood Press, 1974.

Galia Golan, *The Czechoslovak Reform Movement: Communism in Crisis, 1962–1968*. London, Cambridge University Press, 1971. 450 pp.

Galia Golan, *Reform Rule in Czechoslovakia: The Dubček Era, 1968–1969*. London, Cambridge University Press, 1973. 328 pp.

Zdeněk Hejzlar and Vladimir V. Kusin, *Czechoslovakia 1968: Chronology, Bibliography, Annotation*. London and New York, Garland, 1975. 316 pp.

A. Heneka [et al.] (eds.), *Besieged Culture: Czechoslovakia Ten Years after Helsinki*. Translated by Joyce Dahlberg et al. Introduction by Jan Vladislav. Collages by Jiří Kolář. Stockholm and Vienna, Charta 77 Foundation and International Helsinki Federation for Human Rights, 1985. 300 pp., 2nd edition 1986.

Ladislav Holý, *The Little Czech and the Great Czech Nation: National Identity and the Post-Communist Transformation of Society*. Cambridge, Cambridge University Press, 1996. 226 pp. (Published in Czech as *Malý český člověk a skvělý český národ: Národní identita a postkomunistická transformace společnosti*, Prague, 2001.)

Peter Hruby, *Fools and Heroes: The Changing Role of Communist Intellectuals in Czechoslovakia*. Oxford and New York, Pergamon, 1980. 266 pp.

Wilma Abeles Iggers, *Women of Prague: Ethnic Diversity and Social Change from the Eighteenth Century to the Present*. Providence and Oxford, Berghahn Books, 1995. 382 pp.

Hilary A. James and Jiří P. Musil, *Prague, My Love: An Unusual Guide Book to the Hidden Corners of Prague*. Prague, Crossroads of Prague, 1992. 398 pp.

Robert Rhodes James (ed.), *The Czechoslovak Crisis: 1968*. London, Weidenfeld & Nicolson, 1969. 204 pp.

Barbara Wolfe Jancar, *Czechoslovakia and the Absolute Monopoly of Power: A Study of Political Power in a Communist System*. New York et al., Praeger, 1971. 330 pp.

Frank L. Kaplan, *Winter into Spring: The Czechoslovak Press and the Reform Movement, 1963–1968*. Boulder, East European Quarterly, and New York, Columbia University Press, 1977. 208 pp.

Karel Kaplan, *The Short March: The Communist Take-Over in Czechoslovakia, 1945–1948*. London, Hurst, 1986. 208 pp. New York, St. Martin's Press, 1987.

Karel Kaplan, *The Communist Party in Power: A Profile of Party Politics in Czechoslovakia*. Edited and translated by Fred Eidlin. Boulder and London, Westview Press, 1987. 232 pp.

Jan Kavan and Zdena Tomin (eds.), *Voices from Prague: Czechoslovakia, Human Rights and the Peace Movement*. London, Palach Press, 1983. 76 pp.

Rosemary Kavan, *Freedom at a Price: An English Woman's Life in Czechoslovakia*. Introduction by William Shawcross, epilogue by Jan Kavan. London, Verso, 1985. 240 pp. Published as *Love and Freedom. My Unexpected Life in Prague*. Foreword by Arthur Miller, introduction by William Shawcross. New York, Hill & Wang, 1988. 278 pp. London, Grafton, 1989. (In Czech in Brno in 1997.)

Pavel Kohout, *From the Diary of a Counterrevolutionary*. Translated by George Theiner. New York, McGraw-Hill, 1972. 308 pp. (In Czech in Prague in 1997.)

Josef Korbel, *The Communist Subversion of Czechoslovakia, 1938–1948: The Failure of Coexistence*. Princeton, Princeton University Press, 1959. 258 pp.

Josef Korbel, *Twentieth-Century Czechoslovakia: The Meanings of Its History*. New York, Columbia University Press, 1977. 346 pp.

Karel Kornell, *I am a Czech*. Lewes, Book Guild, 1986. 190 pp.

Jaroslav Krejčí, *Social Change and Stratification in Postwar Czechoslovakia*. New York, Columbia University Press, and London, Macmillan, 1972. 208 pp.

Zdenek Krystufek, *The Soviet Regime in Czechoslovakia*. Boulder and New York, Columbia University Press, 1981. 340 pp.

Vladimír Victor Kusín, *The Intellectual Origins of the Prague Spring: The Development of Reformist Ideas in Czechoslovakia, 1956–1967*. London, Cambridge University Press, 1971. 154 pp. Cambridge, Cambridge University Press, 2002.

Vladimír Victor Kusín, *Political Grouping in the Czechoslovak Reform Movement*. London, Macmillan, 1972. 224 pp.

Vladimír Victor Kusín (ed.), *The Czechoslovak Reform Movement 1968*. London, International Research Documents and Santa Barbara, ABC-Clio Press, 1973. 358 pp.

Vladimír V. Kusín, *From Dubček to Charter 77: A Study of "Normalization" in Czechoslovakia 1968–1978*. Edinburgh, Q Press, and New York, St Martin's Press, 1978. 354 pp.

Karel Kyncl and Ivan Kyncl, *After the Spring Came Winter*. Translated by George Theiner. Photography by Ivan Kyncl. Stockholm, Askelin & Hägglund, 1985. 104 pp.

Alan Levy, *Rowboat to Prague*. New York, Grossman, 1972. 532 pp. Revised edition as *So Many Heroes*. Sagaponack, Second Chance Press, 1980. 390 pp. (In Czech in Toronto in 1975, in Prague in 1991.)

Robert Littell (ed.), *The Czech Black Book*. Prepared by the Institute of History of the

Czechoslovak Academy of Science. Translated by F. A. Prager. London, Pall Mall Press, and New York, Praeger, 1969. 304 pp. (Orig. published in Czech as *Sedm pražských dnů*, Prague, 1968.)

Eugen Loebl, *Sentenced and Tried: The Stalinist Purges in Czechoslovakia*. Translated from the German by Maurice Michael. Postscript by Dušan Pokorný. London, Elek Books, 1969. 272 pp. Published as *Stalinism in Prague: The Loebl Story*. Edited and introduction by Herman Starobin. New York, Grove Press, 1969. 328 pp. (Orig. in Slovak *Svedectvo o procese*, Bratislava, 1968.)

Eugen Loebl, *My Mind on Trial*. New York, Harcourt, 1976. 236 pp. (In Slovak *Trýzeň svedomia* in Toronto in 1978.)

Artur London, *On Trial*. Translated from the French by Alastair Hamilton. London, Macdonald, 1970. 454 pp. As *The Confession*, New York, Morrow, 1970. (In Czech in Prague in 1969.)

Radomír Luža, *The Transfer of the Sudeten Germans: A Study of Czech–German Relations, 1933–1962*. New York, New York University Press, and London, Routledge, 1964. 366 pp.

Victor Samuel Mamatey and Radomír Luža (eds.), *A History of the Czechoslovak Republic 1918–1948*. Princeton, Princeton University Press, 1973. 534 pp.

Heda Margolius, *I Do Not Want to Remember: Auschwitz 1941–Prague 1968*. Translated by Erazim Kohák. London, Weidenfeld & Nicolson, 1973. 174 pp.

Heda Margolius-Kovály, *Under a Cruel Star: A Life in Prague 1941–1968*. Translated by Francis Epstein and Helen Epstein with the author. Cambridge, Plunkett Lake Press, 1986. 192 pp. New York, Holmes & Meier, 1997. Published as *Prague Farewell*. London, Gollancz, 1988. 224 pp. London, Indigo, 1997. (Published in Czech as *Na vlastní kůži*. A study by Erazim Kohák. Toronto, 1973, Prague, 1992.)

Vojtech Mastny (ed.), *Czechoslovakia: Crisis in World Communism*. Introduction by Vojtech Mastny. New York, Facts on File, 1972. 392 pp.

Peter Meyer (= Josef Guttmann) [et al.], *The Jews in the Soviet Satellites*. Syracuse, Syracuse University Press, 1953. 638 pp. Westport, Greenwood Press, 1971.

Zdeněk Mlynář, *Night Frost in Prague: The End of Humane Socialism*. Translated by Paul Wilson. London, Hurst, and New York, Karz, 1980. 300 pp. (In Czech *Mráz přichází z Kremlu*, Cologne, 1979, Prague, 1990.)

Ladislav Mňačko, *The Seventh Night: A Personal Inside View of the First Week of the Occupation of Czechoslovakia*. Foreword and translated from Slovak by Harry Schwartz. London, Dent and Panther, 1969. New York, Dutton, 1969. 220 pp. (In Slovak in 1990.)

Martin Roy Myant, *The Rise and Fall of Czech Capitalism: Economic Development in the Czech Republic since 1989*. Cheltenham and Northampton, Edward Elgar, 2003. 288 pp.

Lubomír Nový [et al.] (eds.), *Czech Philosophy in the XXth Century*. Washington, Paideia, 1994. 234 pp. (In Czech *Kapitoly z dějin české filozofie 20. století*, Brno, 1992.)

Andrew Oxley [et. al.], *Czechoslovakia: The Party and the People*. London, Allen Lane, 1973. 304 pp.

Luděk Pachman, *Checkmate in Prague: The Memoirs of a Grandmaster*. Translated from the German by Rosemary Brown. London, Faber, and New York, Macmillan, 1975. 216 pp. (In Czech in 2001.)

Benjamin B. Page, *The Czechoslovak Reform Movement, 1963–1968: A Study in the Theory of Socialism*. Amsterdam, Grüner, 1973. 126 pp.

Michael Parrish, *The 1968 Czechoslovak Crisis: A Bibliography, 1968–1970*. Santa Barbara, Clio Press, 1971. 42 pp.

Cecil Parrott, *The Serpent and the Nightingale*. London, Faber & Faber, 1977. 224 pp.
David W. Paul, *The Cultural Limits of Revolutionary Politics: Change and Continuity in Socialist Czechoslovakia*. Boulder and New York, Columbia University Press, 1979. 362 pp.
Jiří Pelikán (ed.), *The Czechoslovak Political Trials, 1950–1954: The Suppressed Report of the Dubček Government's Commission of Inquiry, 1968*. Preface and postscript by Jiří Pelikán. London, Macdonald, and Stanford, Stanford University Press, 1971. 360 pp.
Jiří Pelikán (ed.), *The Secret Vysočany Kongress: Proceedings and Documents of the Extraordinary Fourteenth Congress of the Communist Party of Czechoslovakia, 22 August 1968*. Translated by George Theiner and Derek Viney. Preface by Jiří Pelikán. London, Penguin, and New York, St Martin's Press, 1971. 304 pp.
Jiří Pelikán, *Socialist Opposition in Eastern Europe: Czechoslovak Example*. Translated by Marian Sling and Vladimir and Ruth Tosek. London, Allison & Busby, and New York, St Martin's Press, 1976. 222 pp.
Miloslav Rechcigl Jr (ed.), *The Czechoslovak Contribution to World Culture*. Foreword by René Wellek, introduction by Miloslav Rechcigl. The Hague et al., Mouton, 1964. 682 pp. (For a chapter dealing with literature and literary criticism see pp. 17–90.)
Miloslav Rechcígl Jr (ed.), *Czechoslovakia Past and Present. I–II.* Vol.1: *Political, International, Social, and Economic Aspects*. Vol. 2: *Essays on the Arts and Sciences.* The Hague, Mouton, 1968. 1889 pp.
Robin Alison Remington (ed.), *Winter in Prague: Documents on Czechoslovak Communism in Crisis*. Introduction by William E. Griffith. Cambridge and London, MIT Press, 1969. 474 pp.
Hans-Peter Riese (ed.), *Since the Prague Spring: The Continuing Struggle for Human Rights in Czechoslovakia*. Translated from the German by Eugen Loebl. New York, Random House, 1979. 208 pp.
Hubert Ripka, *Czechoslovakia Enslaved: The Story of the Communist Coup d'Etat*. Translated from French. London, Gollancz, 1950. 340 pp. Westport, Hyperion Press, 1979. (In French *Le coup de Prague*, 1949; in Czech *Únorová tragédie*, 1995.)
Michel Salomon, *Prague Notebook: The Strangled Revolution*. Translated from French by H. Eustis. Boston, Little, Brown & Co., 1971. 362 pp. (In French *Prague*, 1968.)
Derek Sayer, *The Coasts of Bohemia. A Czech History*. Translated by Alena Sayer. Princeton, Princeton University Press, 1998. 442 pp.
Harry Schwartz, *Prague's 200 Days: The Struggle for Democracy in Czechoslovakia*. New York, Praeger, and London, Pall Mall, 1969. 274 pp.
Radoslav Selucký, *Czechoslovakia: The Plan that Failed.* Translated by Derek Viney. Introduction by Kamil Winter. London, Nelson, 1970. 150 pp.
William Shawcross, *Dubcek*. London, Weidenfeld & Nicolson, and New York, Simon & Schuster, 1970. 318 pp. Published as *Dubcek: Dubcek and Czechoslovakia 1968–1990.* London, Hogarth, 1990. 244 pp.
Ota Šik, *Czechoslovakia: The Bureaucratic Economy*. White Plains, International Arts and Sciences Press, 1972. 138 pp.
Milan Šimečka, *The Restoration of Order: The Normalization of Czechoslovakia, 1969–1976*. Translated by A. G. Brain (Alice and Gerald Turner). Preface by Zdeněk Mlynář. London, Verso, 1984. 168 pp.
Milan Šimečka, *Letters from Prison*. Edited and translated by Gerald Turner. Prague, Twisted Spoon Press, 2002. 154 pp.
Harold Gordon Skilling, *Czechoslovakia's Interrupted Revolution*. Princeton, Princeton University Press, 1976. 924 pp.

Harold Gordon Skilling, *Charter 77 and Human Rights in Czechoslovakia*. London, Allen & Unwin, 1981. 364 pp. (Introduction, pp. 3–195, and documents, pp. 199–327.)

Harold Gordon Skilling, *Samizdat and an Independent Society in Central and Eastern Europe*. Columbus, Ohio State University Press, and Basingstoke, Mcmillan Press, 1989. 294 pp.

Harold Gordon Skilling and Paul Wilson (eds.), *Civic Freedom in Central Europe: Voices from Czechoslovakia*. Introduction by Harold Gordon Skilling (pp. 3–32). New York, St Martin's Press, and Basingstoke and London, Macmillan, 1991. 152 pp. (Texts on"parallel polis" by Václav Benda, Jiří Dienstbier, Václav Havel, Ladislav Hejdánek, Martin Jirous, Eva Kantůrková, Jan Šimsa, Josef Zvěřina et al.)

Harold Gordon Skilling (ed.), *Czechoslovakia 1918–88: Seventy Years from Independence*. New York, St Martin's Press, and London and Basingstoke, Macmillan, 1991. 232 pp. (Texts by Harold Gordon Skilling, Jiří Kovtun, Jaroslav Opat, Radoslav Selucký, Igor Hájek, Václav Havel et al.)

Josefa Slánská, *Report on My Husband*. Translated and introduction by Edith Pargeter. Foreword Pavel Kohout. London and New York, Atheneum and Hutchinson, 1969. 208 pp. (In Czech in Prague in 1990.)

Norman Stone and Eduard Strouhal (eds.), *Czechoslovakia: Crossroads and Crises, 1918–88*. Basingstoke, Macmillan, 1989. 336 pp.

Jan Stránský, *East Wind over Prague*. London, Hollis & Carter, 1950. 244 pp. New York, Random House, 1951. Reprint, Westport, Greenwood, 1979.

Zdenek Suda, *The Czechoslovak Socialist Republic*. Baltimore, J. Hopkins, 1969. 180 pp.

Ivan Sviták, *The Czechoslovak Experiment, 1968–1969*. Translated by Eva Vanek et al. New York, Columbia University Press, 1971. 244 pp.

Ivan Sviták, *Film in the Manipulated World: Reviews from Prague, 1963–1967*. Translated by William Brzorad and Peter Beales. Chico, 1987. 80 pp.

Ivan Sviták, *The Unbearable Burden of History: The Sovietization of Czechoslovakia*. Vol. 2: *Prague Spring Revisited*. Vol. 3: *The Era of Abnormalization*. Prague, Academia, 1990. Vol. 2: 220 pp. Vol. 3: 280 pp.

Tad Szulc, *Czechoslovakia since World War II*. New York, Viking Press, 1971. 504 pp. New York, Grosset & Dunlap, 1972.

Edward Taborsky, *Communism in Czechoslovakia, 1948–1960*. Princeton, Princeton University Press, 1961. 628 pp.

Pavel Tigrid, *Why Dubček Fell*. Translated by the author and L. Lawrence. London, Macdonald 1971. 230 pp. (In Czech *Kvadratura kruhu*, Paris 1970.)

Aviezer Tucker, *The Philosophy and Politics of Czech Dissidence from Patočka to Havel*. Pittsburg, University of Pittsburg Press, 2000. 296 pp.

Otto Ulč, *The Judge in a Communist State: A View from Within*. Columbus, Ohio University Press, 1972. 308 pp.

Otto Ulč, *Politics in Czechoslovakia*. Foreword by Jan F. Triska. San Francisco, Freeman, 1974. 182 pp.

Anna Naninka Vanicek, *Passion Play: Underground Rock Music in Czechoslovakia, 1968–1989*. North York, York University, 1997.

Bernard Wheaton and Zdeněk Kavan, *The Velvet Revolution: Czechoslovakia, 1988–1991*. Boulder et al., Westview Press, 1992. 256 pp.

Joseph G. Whelan, *Aspects of Intellectual Ferment and Dissent in Czechoslovakia*. Washington, US Gov. Print. Off., 1969. 166 pp.

Tim D. Whipple (ed.), *After the Velvet Revolution: Václav Havel and the New Leaders of Czechoslovakia Speak Out*. New York, Freedom House, 1991. 328 pp.

Kieran Williams, *The Prague Spring and its Aftermath: Czechoslovak Politics, 1968–1970*. Cambridge, Cambridge University Press, 1997. 270 pp.

Philip Windsor and Adam Roberts, *Czechoslovakia: Reform, Repression and Resistance*. Foreword by A. Buchan. London, Chatto & Windus, 1969. 200 pp.

Ira William Zartman (ed.), *Czechoslovakia: Intervention and Impact*. New York, New York University Press, 1970. 128 pp.

Zbyněk Anthony Bohuslav Zeman, *Prague Spring: A Report on Czechoslovakia 1968*. Harmondsworth, Penguin, and New York, Hill & Wang, 1969. 170 pp.

Paul Ernest Zinner, *Communist Strategy and Tactics in Czechoslovakia, 1918–1948*. New York, Praeger, and London, Pall Mall, 1963. 264 pp. Westport, Greenwood Press, 1975.

INDEX

This index contains all the names and literary works mentioned in this volume, with the exception of the bibliography. The names of literary works are given in *italics*. For Czech writers, dates of birth and death are given. Substantial mentions are marked with **bold characters.**

www.ingramcontent.com/pod-product-compliance
Lightning Source LLC
Chambersburg PA
CBHW081401090726
47908CB00012B/2754

* 9 7 8 1 8 4 5 1 9 4 4 0 6 *